Python Testing Cookbook

Over 70 simple but incredibly effective recipes for taking control of automated testing using powerful Python testing tools

Greg L. Turnquist

PACKT PUBLISHING

BIRMINGHAM - MUMBAI

Python Testing Cookbook

Copyright © 2011 Packt Publishing

All rights reserved. No part of this book may be reproduced, stored in a retrieval system, or transmitted in any form or by any means, without the prior written permission of the publisher, except in the case of brief quotations embedded in critical articles or reviews.

Every effort has been made in the preparation of this book to ensure the accuracy of the information presented. However, the information contained in this book is sold without warranty, either express or implied. Neither the author, nor Packt Publishing, and its dealers and distributors will be held liable for any damages caused or alleged to be caused directly or indirectly by this book.

Packt Publishing has endeavored to provide trademark information about all of the companies and products mentioned in this book by the appropriate use of capitals. However, Packt Publishing cannot guarantee the accuracy of this information.

First published: May 2011

Production Reference: 1100511

Published by Packt Publishing Ltd.
32 Lincoln Road
Olton
Birmingham, B27 6PA, UK.

ISBN 978-1-849514-66-8

www.packtpub.com

Cover Image by Asher Wishkerman (a.wishkerman@mpic.de)

Credits

Author
Greg L. Turnquist

Reviewers
Matthew Closson
Chetan Giridhar
Sylvain Hellegouarch
Maurice HT Ling

Acquisition Editor
Tarun Singh

Development Editor
Hyacintha D'Souza

Technical Editors
Pallavi Kachare
Shreerang Deshpande

Copy Editor
Laxmi Subramanian

Project Coordinator
Srimoyee Ghoshal

Proofreader
Bernadette Watkins

Indexer
Hemangini Bari

Production Coordinator
Adline Swetha Jesuthas

Cover Work
Adline Swetha Jesuthas

About the Author

Greg L. Turnquist has worked in the software industry since 1997. He is an active participant in the open source community, and has contributed patches to several projects including MythTV, Spring Security, MediaWiki, and the TestNG Eclipse plugin. As a test-bitten script junky, he has always sought the right tool for the job. He is a firm believer in agile practices and automated testing. He has developed distributed systems, LAMP-based setups, and supported mission-critical systems hosted on various platforms.

After graduating from Auburn University with a Master's in Computer Engineering, Greg started working with Harris Corporation. He worked on many contracts utilizing many types of technology. In 2006, he created the Spring Python project and went on to write Spring Python 1.1 in 2010. He joined SpringSource, a division of VMware in 2010, as part of their international software development team.

> I would like to extend my thanks to Sylvain Hellegouarch, Matt Closson, as well as my editors, for taking the time to technically review this book and provide valuable feedback. I thank my one-year-old daughter for pulling me away when I needed a break and my one-month-old son for giving me MANY opportunities in the middle of the night to work on this book. I especially thank my precious wife Sara for the support, encouragement, patience, and most importantly for saying "I think we should strike while the iron is hot" when I was offered this writing opportunity.

About the Reviewers

Matthew Closson is a creative technologist and entrepreneur at heart. He is currently employed as a software engineer by Philips Healthcare. He is passionate about software testing, systems integration, and web technologies. When not obsessing over Ruby and C# code, this elusive developer is likely to be found reading at the local bookstore or relaxing on the beach.

Chetan Giridhar has more than five years experience of working in the software services industry, product companies, and research organizations. He has a string background of C/C++, Java (certified Java professional) and has a good command of Perl, Python scripting languages, using which he has developed useful tools and automation frameworks. His articles on Code Reviews, Software Automation, and Agile methodologies have been published in international magazines including TestingExperience and AgileRecord for which he has received appreciation from other industry experts on his website—TechnoBeans. Chetan has also co-authored a book on *Design Patterns in Python* that is listed at Python's Official Website. He has given lectures on **Python Programming** to software professionals and at educational institutes including the Indian Institute of Astrophysics, Bangalore. Chetan holds a B.E. in Electrical Engineering from the University of Mumbai and feels that the world is full of knowledge.

> I take this opportunity to thank Rahul Verma, who has guided and inspired me, Ashok Mallya and Rishi Ranjan, for their encouragement and for the confidence they have shown in me. Special thanks to my parents Jayant and Jyotsana Giridhar, and my wife Deepti, who have all been a constant support.

Sylvain Hellegouarch is a senior software engineer with several years experience in development and performance testing in various companies, both in France and in the United Kingdom. Passionate about open-source software, he has written several Python projects around communication protocols such as HTTP, XMPP, and the Atom Publishing Protocol. He has been part of the CherryPy team since 2004 and has also authored the *CherryPy Essentials* book, published by Packt Publishing in 2007. Sylvain also reviewed *Spring Python,* published by Packt Publishing in 2010. His current interests are set on the open-data movement and the wave of innovation it brings to public services. When away from his computer, Sylvain plays the guitar and the drums or spends his time with friends and family.

Maurice HT Ling completed his Ph.D. in Bioinformatics and B.Sc(Hons) in Molecular and Cell Biology from The University of Melbourne where he worked on microarray analysis and text mining for protein-protein interactions. He is currently a Senior Scientist (Bioinformatics) in Life Technologies and an Honorary Fellow in The University of Melbourne, Australia. Maurice holds several Chief Editorships including The Python Papers, Computational and Mathematical Biology, and Methods and Cases in Computational, Mathematical, and Statistical Biology. In Singapore, he co-founded the Python User Group (Singapore) and has been the co-chair of PyCon Asia-Pacific since 2010. In his free time, Maurice likes to train in the gym, read, and enjoy a good cup of coffee. He is also a Senior Fellow of the International Fitness Association, USA. His personal website is: `http://maurice.vodien.com`.

www.PacktPub.com

Support files, eBooks, discount offers and more

You might want to visit `www.PacktPub.com` for support files and downloads related to your book.

Did you know that Packt offers eBook versions of every book published, with PDF and ePub files available? You can upgrade to the eBook version at `www.PacktPub.com` and as a print book customer, you are entitled to a discount on the eBook copy. Get in touch with us at `service@packtpub.com` for more details.

At `www.PacktPub.com`, you can also read a collection of free technical articles, sign up for a range of free newsletters and receive exclusive discounts and offers on Packt books and eBooks.

PACKTLIB

`http://PacktLib.PacktPub.com`

Do you need instant solutions to your IT questions? PacktLib is Packt's online digital book library. Here, you can access, read and search across Packt's entire library of books.

Why Subscribe?

- Fully searchable across every book published by Packt
- Copy and paste, print and bookmark content
- On demand and accessible via web browser

Free Access for Packt account holders

If you have an account with Packt at `www.PacktPub.com`, you can use this to access PacktLib today and view nine entirely free books. Simply use your login credentials for immediate access.

Table of Contents

Preface	**1**
Chapter 1: Using Unittest To Develop Basic Tests	**5**
Introduction	5
Asserting the basics	7
Setting up and tearing down a test harness	11
Running test cases from the command line with increased verbosity	14
Running a subset of test case methods	16
Chaining together a suite of tests	18
Defining test suites inside the test module	21
Retooling old test code to run inside unittest	25
Breaking down obscure tests into simple ones	29
Testing the edges	35
Testing corner cases by iteration	39
Chapter 2: Running Automated Test Suites with Nose	**45**
Introduction	45
Getting nosy with testing	46
Embedding nose inside Python	49
Writing a nose extension to pick tests based on regular expressions	52
Writing a nose extension to generate a CSV report	59
Writing a project-level script that lets you run different test suites	66
Chapter 3: Creating Testable Documentation with doctest	**77**
Introduction	77
Documenting the basics	78
Catching stack traces	82
Running doctests from the command line	85
Coding a test harness for doctest	88
Filtering out test noise	92

Table of Contents

Printing out all your documentation including a status report	96
Testing the edges	101
Testing corner cases by iteration	104
Getting nosy with doctest	107
Updating the project-level script to run this chapter's doctests	110

Chapter 4: Testing Customer Stories with Behavior Driven Development — 117

Introduction	117
Naming tests that sound like sentences and stories	120
Testing separate doctest documents	126
Writing a testable story with doctest	130
Writing a testable novel with doctest	136
Writing a testable story with Voidspace	142
Mock and nose	142
Writing a testable story with mockito and nose	147
Writing a testable story with Lettuce	150
Using Should DSL to write succinct assertions with Lettuce	158
Updating the project-level script to run this chapter's BDD tests	163

Chapter 5: High Level Customer Scenarios with Acceptance Testing — 169

Introduction	170
Installing Pyccuracy	172
Testing the basics with Pyccuracy	176
Using Pyccuracy to verify web app security	179
Installing the Robot Framework	183
Creating a data-driven test suite with Robot	186
Writing a testable story with Robot	191
Tagging Robot tests and running a subset	197
Testing web basics with Robot	204
Using Robot to verify web app security	208
Creating a project-level script to verify this chapter's acceptance tests	212

Chapter 6: Integrating Automated Tests with Continuous Integration — 217

Introduction	217
Generating a continuous integration report for Jenkins using NoseXUnit	220
Configuring Jenkins to run Python tests upon commit	222
Configuring Jenkins to run Python tests when scheduled	227
Generating a CI report for TeamCity using teamcity-nose	231
Configuring TeamCity to run Python tests upon commit	234
Configuring TeamCity to run Python tests when scheduled	237

Chapter 7: Measuring your Success with Test Coverage — 241
- Introduction — 241
- Building a network management application — 243
- Installing and running coverage on your test suite — 251
- Generating an HTML report using coverage — 255
- Generating an XML report using coverage — 257
- Getting nosy with coverage — 259
- Filtering out test noise from coverage — 261
- Letting Jenkins get nosy with coverage — 264
- Updating the project-level script to provide coverage reports — 269

Chapter 8: Smoke/Load Testing—Testing Major Parts — 275
- Introduction — 275
- Defining a subset of test cases using import statements — 277
- Leaving out integration tests — 281
- Targeting end-to-end scenarios — 285
- Targeting the test server — 290
- Coding a data simulator — 298
- Recording and playing back live data in real time — 303
- Recording and playing back live data as fast as possible — 311
- Automating your management demo — 319

Chapter 9: Good Test Habits for New and Legacy Systems — 323
- Introduction — 324
- Something is better than nothing — 324
- Coverage isn't everything — 326
- Be willing to invest in test fixtures — 328
- If you aren't convinced on the value of testing, your team won't be either — 330
- Harvesting metrics — 331
- Capturing a bug in an automated test — 332
- Separating algorithms from concurrency — 333
- Pause to refactor when test suite takes too long to run — 334
- Cash in on your confidence — 336
- Be willing to throw away an entire day of changes — 337
- Instead of shooting for 100 percent coverage, try to have a steady growth — 339
- Randomly breaking your app can lead to better code — 340

Index — 343

Preface

Testing has always been a part of software development. For decades, comprehensive testing was defined by complex manual test procedures backed by big budgets; but something revolutionary happened in 1998. In his *Guide to Better Smalltalk*, Smalltalk guru Kent Beck introduced an automated test framework called SUnit. This triggered an avalanche of test frameworks including JUnit, PyUnit, and many others for different languages and various platforms, dubbed the xUnit movement. Automated testing was made a cornerstone of the agile movement when 17 top software experts signed the Agile Manifesto in 2001.

Testing includes many different styles including unit testing, integration testing, acceptance testing, smoke testing, load testing, and countless others. This book digs in and explores testing at all the important levels while using the nimble power of Python. It also shows many tools.

This book is meant to expand your knowledge of testing from something you either heard about or have practiced a little into something you can apply at any level to meet your needs in improving software quality. I hope to give you the tools to reap huge rewards in better software development and customer satisfaction.

What this book covers

Chapter 1, Using Unittest to Develop Basic Tests, gives you a quick introduction to the most commonly used test framework in the Python community.

Chapter 2, Running Automated Tests with Nose, introduces the most ubiquitous Python test tool and gets busy by showing how to write specialized plugins.

Chapter 3, Creating Testable Documentation with doctest, shows many different ways to use Python's docstrings to build runnable doctests as well as writing custom test runners.

Chapter 4, Testing Customer Stories with Behavior Driven Development, dives into writing easy-to-read testable customer stories using doctest, mocking, and Lettuce/Should DSL.

Chapter 5, High Level Customer Scenarios with Acceptance Testing, helps you get into the mindset of the customer and write tests from their perspective using Pyccuracy and the Robot Framework.

Chapter 6, Integrating Automated Tests with Continuous Integration, shows how to add continuous integration to your development process with Jenkins and TeamCity.

Chapter 7, Measuring your Success with Test Coverage, explores how to create coverage reports and interpret them correctly. It also digs in to see how to tie them in with your continuous integration system.

Chapter 8, Smoke/Load Testing—Testing Major Parts, shows how to create smoke test suites to get a pulse from the system. It also shows how to put the system under load to make sure it can handle the current load as well as finding the next breaking point for future loads.

Chapter 9, Good Test Habits for New and Legacy Systems, shows many different lessons learned from the author about what works when it comes to software testing.

What you need for this book

You will need Python 2.6 or above. The recipes in this book have NOT been tested against Python 3+. This book uses many other Python test tools, but includes detailed steps to show how to install and use them.

Who this book is for

This book is for Python developers who want to take testing to the next level. It covers different styles of testing, giving any developer an expanded set of testing skills to help write better systems. It also captures lessons learned from the author, explaining not only how to write better tests but why.

Conventions

In this book, you will find a number of styles of text that distinguish between different kinds of information. Here are some examples of these styles, and an explanation of their meaning.

Code words in text are shown as follows: "Create a new file called `recipe1.py` to store all of this recipe's code."

A block of code is set as follows:

```
def test_parsing_millenia(self):
    value = RomanNumeralConverter("M")
    self.assertEquals(1000, value.convert_to_decimal())
```

When we wish to draw your attention to a particular part of a code block, the relevant lines or items are set in bold:

```
if __name__ == "__main__":
    unittest.main()
```

New terms and **important words** are shown in bold. Words that you see on the screen, in menus or dialog boxes for example, appear in the text like this: "The **unittest** module provides a convenient way to find all the test methods in a TestClass".

> Warnings or important notes appear in a box like this.

> Tips and tricks appear like this.

Reader feedback

Feedback from our readers is always welcome. Let us know what you think about this book—what you liked or may have disliked. Reader feedback is important for us to develop titles that you really get the most out of.

To send us general feedback, simply send an e-mail to feedback@packtpub.com, and mention the book title via the subject of your message.

If there is a book that you need and would like to see us publish, please send us a note in the **SUGGEST A TITLE** form on www.packtpub.com or e-mail suggest@packtpub.com.

If there is a topic that you have expertise in and you are interested in either writing or contributing to a book, see our author guide on www.packtpub.com/authors.

Customer support

Now that you are the proud owner of a Packt book, we have a number of things to help you to get the most from your purchase.

Downloading the example code

You can download the example code files for all Packt books you have purchased from your account at http://www.PacktPub.com. If you purchased this book elsewhere, you can visit http://www.PacktPub.com/support and register to have the files e-mailed directly to you.

Errata

Although we have taken every care to ensure the accuracy of our content, mistakes do happen. If you find a mistake in one of our books—maybe a mistake in the text or the code—we would be grateful if you would report this to us. By doing so, you can save other readers from frustration and help us improve subsequent versions of this book. If you find any errata, please report them by visiting `http://www.packtpub.com/support`, selecting your book, clicking on the **errata submission form** link, and entering the details of your errata. Once your errata are verified, your submission will be accepted and the errata will be uploaded on our website, or added to any list of existing errata, under the Errata section of that title. Any existing errata can be viewed by selecting your title from `http://www.packtpub.com/support`.

Piracy

Piracy of copyright material on the Internet is an ongoing problem across all media. At Packt, we take the protection of our copyright and licenses very seriously. If you come across any illegal copies of our works, in any form, on the Internet, please provide us with the location address or website name immediately so that we can pursue a remedy.

Please contact us at `copyright@packtpub.com` with a link to the suspected pirated material.

We appreciate your help in protecting our authors, and our ability to bring you valuable content.

Questions

You can contact us at `questions@packtpub.com` if you are having a problem with any aspect of the book, and we will do our best to address it.

1
Using Unittest To Develop Basic Tests

In this chapter, we will cover:

- Asserting the basics
- Setting up and tearing down a test harness
- Running test cases from the command line
- Running a subset of test case methods
- Chaining together a suite of tests
- Defining test suites inside the test case
- Retooling old test code to run inside unittest
- Breaking down obscure tests into simple ones
- Testing the edges
- Testing corner cases by iteration

Introduction

Testing has always been a part of software development. However, the world was introduced to a new concept called **automated testing** when Kent Beck and Erich Gamma introduced JUnit for Java development (`http://junit.org`). It was based on Kent's earlier work with Smalltalk and automated testing (`http://www.xprogramming.com/testfram.htm`). In this day and age, automated testing has become a well-accepted concept in the software industry.

Using Unittest To Develop Basic Tests

A Python version, originally dubbed **PyUnit**, was created in 1999 and added to Python's standard set of libraries later in 2001 in Python 2.1 (http://docs.python.org/library/unittest.html). Since then, the Python community referred to it as **unittest**, the name of the library imported into the test code.

Unittest is the foundation of automated testing in the Python world. In this chapter, we will explore the basics of testing and asserting code functionality, building suites of tests, test situations to avoid, and finally testing edges, and corner cases.

For all the recipes in this chapter, we will use virtualenv (http://pypi.python.org/pypi/virtualenv) to create a controlled Python runtime environment. Unittest is part of the standard library, which requires no extra installation steps. But, in later chapters, using virtualenv will allow us to conveniently install other test tools without cluttering up our default Python installation.

1. To install virtualenv, either download it from the site mentioned previously, or if you have easy_install, just type: easy_install virtualenv.

   > For some systems, you may need to install it either as root or by using sudo

2. After installing virtualenv, use it to create a clean environment named ptc (an abbreviation used for Python Testing Cookbook) by using --no-site-packages.

3. Activate the virtual Python environment. This can vary, depending on which shell you are using.

```
(ptc)gturnquist-mbp:01 gturnquist$ python recipe1.py
........
----------------------------------------------------------------------
Ran 8 tests in 0.000s

OK
(ptc)gturnquist-mbp:01 gturnquist$
```

4. Finally, verify that the environment is active by checking the path of pip.

   > For more information on the usage and benefits of virtualenv, please read http://iamzed.com/2009/05/07/a-primer-on-virtualenv.

Asserting the basics

The basic concept of an automated unittest test case is to instantiate part of our code, subject it to operations, and verify certain results using assertions.

- If the results are as expected, unittest counts it as a test success
- If the results don't match, an exception is thrown and unittest counts it as a test failure

Getting ready

Unittest was added to Python's standard *batteries included* library suite and doesn't require any extra installation.

How to do it...

With these steps, we will code a simple program and then write some automated tests using unittest:

1. Create a new file called `recipe1.py` in which to put all of this recipe's code. Pick a class to test. This is known as the **class under test**. For this recipe, we'll pick a class that uses a simplistic Roman numeral converter:

   ```
   class RomanNumeralConverter(object):
     def __init__(self, roman_numeral):
       self.roman_numeral = roman_numeral
       self.digit_map = {"M":1000, "D":500,   "C":100, "L":50, "X":10,
   "V":5, "I":1}

     def convert_to_decimal(self):
       val = 0
       for char in self.roman_numeral:
         val += self.digit_map[char]
       return val
   ```

   > This Roman numeral converter applies the simple rules of addition, but it doesn't have the special subtraction patterns such as XL mapping to 40. The purpose is not to have the best Roman numeral converter, but to observe the various test assertions.

Using Unittest To Develop Basic Tests

2. Write a new class and give it the same name with `Test` appended to the end, subclassing `unittest.TestCase`. Appending a test class with `Test` is a common convention, but not a requirement. Extending `unittest.TestCase` is a requirement needed to hook into unittest's standard test runner.

    ```
    import unittest

    class RomanNumeralConverterTest(unittest.TestCase):
    ```

3. Create several methods whose names start with `test`, so they are automatically picked up by the test number of unittest.

    ```
    def test_parsing_millenia(self):
      value = RomanNumeralConverter("M")
      self.assertEquals(1000, value.convert_to_decimal())

    def test_parsing_century(self):
      value = RomanNumeralConverter("C")
      self.assertEquals(100, value.convert_to_decimal())

    def test_parsing_half_century(self):
      value = RomanNumeralConverter("L")
      self.assertEquals(50, value.convert_to_decimal())

    def test_parsing_decade(self):
      value = RomanNumeralConverter("X")
      self.assertEquals(10, value.convert_to_decimal())

    def test_parsing_half_decade(self):
      value = RomanNumeralConverter("V")
      self.assertEquals(5, value.convert_to_decimal())

    def test_parsing_one(self):
      value = RomanNumeralConverter("I")
      self.assertEquals(1, value.convert_to_decimal())

    def test_empty_roman_numeral(self):
      value = RomanNumeralConverter("")
      self.assertTrue(value.convert_to_decimal() == 0)
      self.assertFalse(value.convert_to_decimal() > 0)

    def test_no_roman_numeral(self):
      value = RomanNumeralConverter(None)
      self.assertRaises(TypeError, value.convert_to_decimal)
    ```

4. Make the entire script runnable and then use unittest's test runner.

    ```
    if __name__ == "__main__":
      unittest.main()
    ```

5. Run the file from the command line.

```
(ptc)gturnquist-mbp:01 gturnquist$ python recipe1.py
........
Ran 8 tests in 0.000s

OK
(ptc)gturnquist-mbp:01 gturnquist$
```

How it works...

In the first step, we picked a class to test. Next, we created a separate test class. By naming the test class [class under test]Test, it is easy to tell which class is under test. Each test method name must start with test, so that unittest will automatically pick it up and run it. To add more tests, just define more test methods. Each of these tests utilizes various assertions.

- assertEquals(first, second[, msg]): Compares first and second expressions; and fails, if they don't have the same value. We can optionally print a special message if there is a failure.
- assertTrue(expression[, msg]): Tests the expression and fails if it is false. We can optionally print a special message if there is a failure.
- assertFalse(expression[, msg]): Tests the expression and fails if it is true. We can optionally print a special message if there is a failure.
- assertRaises(exception, callable, ...): Runs the callable, with any arguments, for the callable listed afterwards, and fails if it doesn't raise the exception.

There's more...

Unittest provides many options for asserting, failing, and other convenient options. The following sections show some recommendations on how to pick and choose from these options.

assertEquals is preferred over assertTrue and assertFalse

When an assertEquals fails, the first and second values are printed in the error report, giving better feedback of what went wrong. assertTrue and assertFalse simply report failure. Not all testable results fit this but, if possible, use assertEquals.

Using Unittest To Develop Basic Tests

It's important to understand the concept of equality. When comparing integers, strings, and other scalars, it's very simple. It doesn't work as well with collections like dictionaries, lists, and sets. Complex, custom-defined objects may carry custom definitions of equality. These complex objects may require more fine-grained assertions. That is why it's probably a good idea to also include some test methods that directly target equality and inequality when working with custom objects.

self.fail([msg]) can usually be rewritten with assertions

Unittest has a `self.fail([msg])` operation that unconditionally causes the test to fail, along with an optional message. This was not shown earlier because it is not recommended for use.

The `fail` method is often used to detect certain situations like exceptions. A common idiom is as follows:

```
import unittest
class BadTest(unittest.TestCase):
  def test_no_roman_numeral(self):
    value = RomanNumeralConverter(None)
    try:
      value.convert_to_decimal()
      self.fail("Expected a TypeError")
    except TypeError, e:
      pass
```

This tests the same behavior as the earlier `test_no_roman_numeral`. The problem with this approach is that, when the code is working properly, the `fail` method is never executed. Code which is not executed regularly is at risk of becoming out of date and invalid. This will also interfere with coverage reports. Instead, it is better to use `assertRaises` as we used in the earlier examples. For other situations, look at rewriting the test using the other assertions.

Our version of Python can impact our options

Python's official documentation on unittest shows many other assertions, however, they depend on the version of Python we are using. Some have been deprecated; others are only available in later versions like Python 2.7.

If our code must support multiple versions of Python, then we must use the lowest common denominator. This recipe shows core assertions available in all versions since Python 2.1.

> A newer unittest2 (`http://pypi.python.org/pypi/unittest2/`) is under development that backports several of these newer unittest features into Python 2.4+. However, due to unittest2 being in the beta stage at the time of writing and limitations to the size of this book, I decided to focus on unittest.

Setting up and tearing down a test harness

Unittest provides an easy mechanism to configure the state of the system when a piece of code is put through a test. It also allows us to clean things up afterwards, if necessary. This is commonly needed when a particular test case has repetitive steps used in every test method.

Barring any references to external variables or resources that carry state from one test method to the next, each test method starts from the same state.

How to do it...

With the following steps, we will setup and teardown a test harness for each test method.

1. Create a new file called `recipe2.py` in which to put all our code for this recipe.
2. Pick a class to test. In this case, we will use a slightly altered version of our Roman numeral converter, where the function, not the constructor, provides the input value to convert.

    ```
    class RomanNumeralConverter(object):
      def __init__(self):
        self.digit_map = {"M":1000, "D":500, "C":100, "L":50, "X":10, "V":5, "I":1}
      def convert_to_decimal(self, roman_numeral):
        val = 0
        for char in roman_numeral:
          val += self.digit_map[char]
        return val
    ```

3. Create a test class using the same name as the class under test with `Test` appended to the end.

    ```
    import unittest
    class RomanNumeralConverterTest(unittest.TestCase):
    ```

4. Create a `setUp` method that creates an instance of the class under test.

    ```
    def setUp(self):
      print "Creating a new RomanNumeralConverter..."
      self.cvt = RomanNumeralConverter()
    ```

5. Create a `tearDown` method that destroys the instance of the class under test.

    ```
    def tearDown(self):
      print "Destroying the RomanNumeralConverter..."
      self.cvt = None
    ```

Using Unittest To Develop Basic Tests

6. Create all the test methods using `self.converter`.

   ```
   def test_parsing_millenia(self):
     self.assertEquals(1000, \
             self.cvt.convert_to_decimal("M"))
   def test_parsing_century(self):
     self.assertEquals(100, \
             self.cvt.convert_to_decimal("C"))
   def test_parsing_half_century(self):
     self.assertEquals(50, \
             self.cvt.convert_to_decimal("L"))
   def test_parsing_decade(self):
     self.assertEquals(10, \
             self.cvt.convert_to_decimal("X"))
   def test_parsing_half_decade(self):
     self.assertEquals(5, self.cvt.convert_to_decimal("V"))
   def test_parsing_one(self):
     self.assertEquals(1, self.cvt.convert_to_decimal("I"))
   def test_empty_roman_numeral(self):
     self.assertTrue(self.cvt.convert_to_decimal("") == 0)
     self.assertFalse(self.cvt.convert_to_decimal("") > 0)
   def test_no_roman_numeral(self):
     self.assertRaises(TypeError, \
             self.cvt.convert_to_decimal, None)
   ```

7. Make the entire script runnable and then use the test runner of unittest.

   ```
   if __name__ == "__main__":
     unittest.main()
   ```

8. Run the file from the command line.

Chapter 1

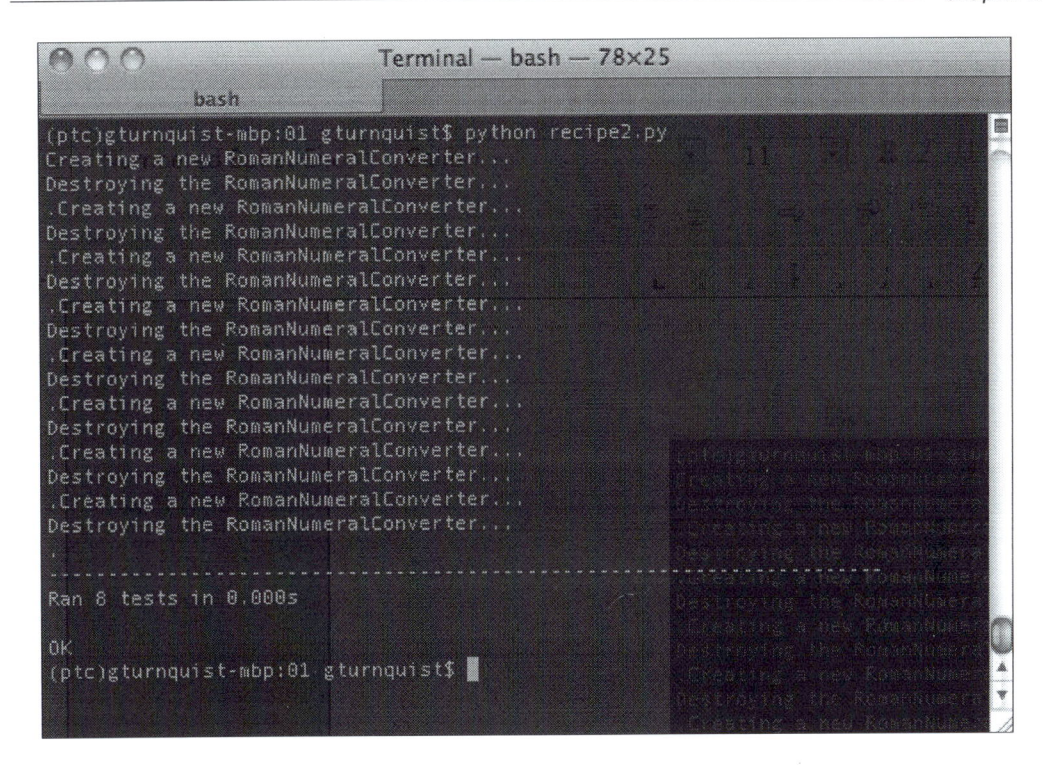

```
(ptc)gturnquist-mbp:01 gturnquist$ python recipe2.py
Creating a new RomanNumeralConverter...
Destroying the RomanNumeralConverter...
.Creating a new RomanNumeralConverter...
Destroying the RomanNumeralConverter...
.Creating a new RomanNumeralConverter...
Destroying the RomanNumeralConverter...
.Creating a new RomanNumeralConverter...
Destroying the RomanNumeralConverter...
.Creating a new RomanNumeralConverter...
Destroying the RomanNumeralConverter...
.Creating a new RomanNumeralConverter...
Destroying the RomanNumeralConverter...
.Creating a new RomanNumeralConverter...
Destroying the RomanNumeralConverter...
.Creating a new RomanNumeralConverter...
Destroying the RomanNumeralConverter...
.
----------------------------------------------------------------------
Ran 8 tests in 0.000s

OK
(ptc)gturnquist-mbp:01 gturnquist$
```

How it works...

In the first step, we picked a class to test. Next, we created a separate test class. By naming the test class [class under test]Test, it is easy to tell which class is under test.

Then, we defined a setUp method that unittest runs before every test method. Next, we created a tearDown method that unittest runs after every test method. In this case, we added a print statement in each of them to demonstrate unittest re-running these two methods for every test method. In reality, it would probably add too much noise to our testing.

One deficiency of unittest is the lack of setUpClass/tearDownClass and setUpModule/tearDownModule, providing the opportunity to run code in greater scopes than at the test method level. This has been added to unittest2, and has been described by some as handy, but won't be covered within the scope of this book.

Using Unittest To Develop Basic Tests

> **Each test case can have one setUp and one tearDown method**
>
> Our `RomanNumeralConverter` is pretty simple and fits easily into a single test class. But the test class allows only one `setUp` method and one `tearDown` method. If different combinations of `setUp`/`tearDown` methods are needed for various test scenarios, then this is a cue to code more test classes.
>
> Just because we write a `setUp` method doesn't mean we need a `tearDown` method. In our case, we could have skipped destroying the `RomanNumeralConverter`, because a new instance would be replacing it for every test method. It was really for demonstration purposes only. What are the other uses of those cases which need a `tearDown` method? Using a library that requires some sort of `close` operation is a prime candidate for writing a `tearDown` method.

Running test cases from the command line with increased verbosity

It is easy to adjust the test runner to print out every test method as it is run.

How to do it...

In the following steps, we will run test cases with more detailed output, giving us better insight to how things run:

1. Create a new file called `recipe3.py` in which to store this recipe's code.

2. Pick a class to test. In this case, we will use our Roman numeral converter:

   ```
   class RomanNumeralConverter(object):
     def __init__(self, roman_numeral):
       self.roman_numeral = roman_numeral
       self.digit_map = {"M":1000, "D":500, "C":100, "L":50, "X":10, "V":5, "I":1}

     def convert_to_decimal(self):
       val = 0
       for char in self.roman_numeral:
         val += self.digit_map[char]
       return val
   ```

3. Create a test class using the same name as the class under test with `Test` appended to the end.

   ```
   import unittest
   ```

```
class RomanNumeralConverterTest(unittest.TestCase):
```

4. Create several test methods. For this recipe, the tests have been deliberately coded to fail.

   ```
   def test_parsing_millenia(self):
       value = RomanNumeralConverter("M")
       self.assertEquals(1000, value.convert_to_decimal())

   def test_parsing_century(self):
       "This test method is coded to fail for demo."
       value = RomanNumeralConverter("C")
       self.assertEquals(10, value.convert_to_decimal())
   ```

5. Define a test suite that automatically loads all the test methods, and then runs them with a higher level of verbosity.

   ```
   if __name__ == "__main__":
       suite = unittest.TestLoader().loadTestsFromTestCase( \
                   RomanNumeralConverterTest)
       unittest.TextTestRunner(verbosity=2).run(suite)
   ```

6. Run the file from the command line. Notice how the test method that fails prints out its Python docstring:

```
(ptc)gturnquist-mbp:01 gturnquist$ python recipe3.py
This test method is coded to fail for demo. ... FAIL
test_parsing_millenia (__main__.RomanNumeralConverterTest) ... ok

======================================================================
FAIL: This test method is coded to fail for demo.
----------------------------------------------------------------------
Traceback (most recent call last):
  File "recipe3.py", line 23, in test_parsing_century
    self.assertEquals(10, value.convert_to_decimal())
AssertionError: 10 != 100

----------------------------------------------------------------------
Ran 2 tests in 0.000s

FAILED (failures=1)
(ptc)gturnquist-mbp:01 gturnquist$
```

How it works...

A key part of automated testing is organizing the tests. The base units are called **test cases**. These can be combined together into **test suites**. Python's `unittest` module provides `TestLoader().loadTestsFromTestCase` to fetch all the `test*` methods automatically into a test suite. This test suite is then run through unittest's `TextTestRunner` with an increased level of verbosity.

> `TextTestRunner` is unittest's only test runner. Later in this book, we will look at other test tools that have different runners, including one that plugs in a different unittest test runner.

The previous screenshot shows each method along with its module and class name, as well as success/failure.

There's more...

This recipe not only demonstrates how to turn up the verbosity of running tests, but also shows what happens when a test case fails. It renames the `test` method with the **document** string embedded in the `test` method, and prints the details later after all the test methods have been reported.

Running a subset of test case methods

Sometimes it's convenient to run only a subset of test methods in a given test case. This recipe will show how to run either the whole test case, or pick a subset from the command line.

How to do it...

The following steps show how to code a command-line script to run subsets of tests:

1. Create a new file named `recipe4.py` in which to put all the code for this recipe.

2. Pick a class to test. In this case, we will use our Roman numeral converter.

   ```
   class RomanNumeralConverter(object):
      def __init__(self, roman_numeral):
         self.roman_numeral = roman_numeral
         self.digit_map = {"M":1000, "D":500, "C":100, "L":50, "X":10, "V":5, "I":1}

      def convert_to_decimal(self):
         val = 0
         for char in self.roman_numeral:
   ```

```
        val += self.digit_map[char]
    return val
```

3. Create a test class using the same name as the class under test with `Test` appended to the end.

   ```
   import unittest
   class RomanNumeralConverterTest(unittest.TestCase):
   ```

4. Create several test methods.

   ```
       def test_parsing_millenia(self):
           value = RomanNumeralConverter("M")
           self.assertEquals(1000, value.convert_to_decimal())

       def test_parsing_century(self):
           value = RomanNumeralConverter("C")
           self.assertEquals(100, value.convert_to_decimal())
   ```

5. Write a main runner that either runs the entire test case or accepts a variable number of test methods.

   ```
   if __name__ == "__main__":
     import sys
     suite = unittest.TestSuite()
     if len(sys.argv) == 1:
         suite = unittest.TestLoader().loadTestsFromTestCase(\
                     RomanNumeralConverterTest)
     else:
       for test_name in sys.argv[1:]:
         suite.addTest(\
             RomanNumeralConverterTest(test_name))

     unittest.TextTestRunner(verbosity=2).run(suite)
   ```

Using Unittest To Develop Basic Tests

6. Run the recipe with no extra command-line arguments, and see it run all the tests. Also run it with a test method name, and see it run only the specified test method.

```
(ptc)gturnquist-mbp:01 gturnquist$ python recipe4.py
test_parsing_century (__main__.RomanNumeralConverterTest) ... ok
test_parsing_millenia (__main__.RomanNumeralConverterTest) ... ok
----------------------------------------------------------------------
Ran 2 tests in 0.000s

OK
(ptc)gturnquist-mbp:01 gturnquist$ python recipe4.py test_parsing_century
test_parsing_century (__main__.RomanNumeralConverterTest) ... ok
----------------------------------------------------------------------
Ran 1 test in 0.000s

OK
(ptc)gturnquist-mbp:01 gturnquist$
```

How it works...

For this test case, we coded a couple of test methods. But instead of simply running all the tests, or defining a fixed list, we used Python's `sys` library to parse the command-line arguments. If there are no extra arguments, it runs the entire test case. If there are extra arguments, then they are assumed to be test method names. It uses unittest's inbuilt ability to specify test method names when instantiating `RomanNumeralConverterTest`.

> **Python 2.7 has this built in; Python 2.6 and earlier versions don't**
>
> Python 2.6 doesn't have this feature, which makes this recipe useful. If we are using Python 2.7, there is a command-line version we can use. If we need to support multiple versions of Python, this recipe can be quite handy.

Chaining together a suite of tests

Unittest makes it easy to chain together test cases into a TestSuite. A TestSuite can be run just like a TestCase, but it also provides additional functionality to add a single test, multiple tests, and count them.

Chapter 1

Why do we need this? Chaining together tests into a suite gives us the ability to pull together more than one module of test cases for a test run, as well as picking and choosing a subset of test cases. Up until now, we have generally run all the test methods from a single class. TestSuite gives us an alternative means to define a block of testing.

How to do it...

In the following steps, we will code multiple test case classes, and then load their test methods into suites so we can run them.

1. Create a new file named `recipe5.py` in which to put our sample application and test cases.

2. Pick a class to test. In this case, we will use our Roman numeral converter.

   ```
   class RomanNumeralConverter(object):
     def __init__(self):
       self.digit_map = {"M":1000, "D":500, "C":100, "L":50, "X":10, "V":5, "I":1}
     def convert_to_decimal(self, roman_numeral):
       val = 0
       for char in roman_numeral:
         val += self.digit_map[char]
       return val
   ```

3. Create two test classes with various test methods spread between them.

   ```
   import unittest

   class RomanNumeralConverterTest(unittest.TestCase):
     def setUp(self):
       self.cvt = RomanNumeralConverter()

     def test_parsing_millenia(self):
       self.assertEquals(1000, \
             self.cvt.convert_to_decimal("M"))

     def test_parsing_century(self):
       self.assertEquals(100, \
             self.cvt.convert_to_decimal("C"))

   class RomanNumeralComboTest(unittest.TestCase):
     def setUp(self):
       self.cvt = RomanNumeralConverter()

     def test_multi_millenia(self):
       self.assertEquals(4000, \
             self.cvt.convert_to_decimal("MMMM"))

     def test_multi_add_up(self):
   ```

Using Unittest To Develop Basic Tests

```
        self.assertEquals(2010, \
                self.cvt.convert_to_decimal("MMX"))
```

4. Create a test runner in a separate file named `recipe5_runner.py` that pulls in both test cases.

```
if __name__ == "__main__":
    import unittest
    from recipe5 import *

    suite1 = unittest.TestLoader().loadTestsFromTestCase( \
                    RomanNumeralConverterTest)
    suite2 = unittest.TestLoader().loadTestsFromTestCase( \
                    RomanNumeralComboTest)
    suite = unittest.TestSuite([suite1, suite2])
    unittest.TextTestRunner(verbosity=2).run(suite)
```

5. Execute the test runner, and observe how tests are pulled in from both test cases.

```
(ptc)gturnquist-mbp:01 gturnquist$ python recipe5_runner.py
test_parsing_century (recipe5.RomanNumeralConverterTest) ... ok
test_parsing_millenia (recipe5.RomanNumeralConverterTest) ... ok
test_multi_add_up (recipe5.RomanNumeralComboTest) ... ok
test_multi_millenia (recipe5.RomanNumeralComboTest) ... ok

----------------------------------------------------------------------
Ran 4 tests in 0.000s

OK
(ptc)gturnquist-mbp:01 gturnquist$
```

How it works...

The `unittest` module provides a convenient way to find all the test methods in a `TestClass` and bundle them together as a suite using its `loadTestsFromTestCase`. To further the usage of test suites, we are able to combine these two suites together as a single suite using `unittest.TestSuite([list...])`. The `TestSuite` class is designed to act like a `TestCase` class, even though it doesn't subclass `TestClass`, allowing us to run it using `TextTestRunner`. This recipe shows the verbosity turned up, allowing us to see exactly which test methods were run, and which test case they came from.

There's more...

In this recipe, we ran the tests from a different file from where the test cases are defined. This is different from the previous recipes where the runnable code and the test case were contained in the same file. Since the runner is defining the tests we run, we can easily create more runners that combine different suites of tests.

Name of the test case should be significant

In the previous recipes, it has been advised to name the test case as `[class under test] Test`. This is to make it apparent to the reader that the class under test and the related test share an important relationship. Now that we are introducing another test case, we need to pick a different name. The name should explain clearly why these particular test methods are split out into a separate class. For this recipe, the methods are split out to show more complex combinations of Roman numerals.

Defining test suites inside the test module

Each test module can provide one or more methods that define a different test suite. One method can exercise all the tests in a given module; another method can define a particular subset.

How to do it...

With the following steps, we will create some methods that define test suites using different means:

1. Create a new file called `recipe6.py` in which to put our code for this recipe.

2. Pick a class to test. In this case, we will use our Roman numeral converter.

   ```
   class RomanNumeralConverter(object):
       def __init__(self):
           self.digit_map = {"M":1000, "D":500, "C":100, "L":50, "X":10, "V":5, "I":1}

       def convert_to_decimal(self, roman_numeral):
           val = 0
           for char in roman_numeral:
               val += self.digit_map[char]
           return val
   ```

3. Create a test class using the same name as the class under test with `Test` appended to the end.

   ```
   import unittest
   ```

Using Unittest To Develop Basic Tests

```
class RomanNumeralConverterTest(unittest.TestCase):
```

4. Write a series of test methods, including a setUp method that creates a new instance of the RomanNumeralConverter for each test method.

```
import unittest
class RomanNumeralConverterTest(unittest.TestCase):
  def setUp(self):
    self.cvt = RomanNumeralConverter()
  def test_parsing_millenia(self):
    self.assertEquals(1000, \
        self.cvt.convert_to_decimal("M"))
  def test_parsing_century(self):
    self.assertEquals(100, \
        self.cvt.convert_to_decimal("C"))
  def test_parsing_half_century(self):
    self.assertEquals(50, \
        self.cvt.convert_to_decimal("L"))
  def test_parsing_decade(self):
    self.assertEquals(10, \
        self.cvt.convert_to_decimal("X"))
  def test_parsing_half_decade(self):
    self.assertEquals(5, self.cvt.convert_to_decimal("V"))
  def test_parsing_one(self):
    self.assertEquals(1, self.cvt.convert_to_decimal("I"))
  def test_empty_roman_numeral(self):
    self.assertTrue(self.cvt.convert_to_decimal("") == 0)
    self.assertFalse(self.cvt.convert_to_decimal("") > 0)
  def test_no_roman_numeral(self):
    self.assertRaises(TypeError, \
        self.cvt.convert_to_decimal, None)
  def test_combo1(self):
    self.assertEquals(4000, \
        self.cvt.convert_to_decimal("MMMM"))
  def test_combo2(self):
    self.assertEquals(2010, \
        self.cvt.convert_to_decimal("MMX"))
  def test_combo3(self):
    self.assertEquals(4668, \
        self.cvt.convert_to_decimal("MMMMDCLXVIII"))
```

5. Create some methods in the recipe's module (but not in the test case) that define different test suites.

```
def high_and_low():
  suite = unittest.TestSuite()
  suite.addTest(\
    RomanNumeralConverterTest("test_parsing_millenia"))
```

```
    suite.addTest(\
      RomanNumeralConverterTest("test_parsing_one"))
    return suite
def combos():
    return unittest.TestSuite(map(RomanNumeralConverterTest,\
        ["test_combo1", "test_combo2", "test_combo3"]))
def all():
    return unittest.TestLoader().loadTestsFromTestCase(\
              RomanNumeralConverterTest)
```

6. Create a runner that will iterate over each of these test suites and run them through unittest's `TextTestRunner`.

```
if __name__ == "__main__":
  for suite_func in [high_and_low, combos, all]:
    print "Running test suite '%s'" % suite_func.func_name
    suite = suite_func()
    unittest.TextTestRunner(verbosity=2).run(suite)
```

7. Run the combination of test suites, and see the results.

How it works...

We pick a class to test and define a number of test methods that check things out. Then we define a few module-level methods such as, high_and_low, combos, and all, to define test suites. Two of them contain fixed subsets of methods while all dynamically loads the test* methods from the class. Finally, the main part of our module iterates over a listing of all these functions that generate suites in order to smoothly create and run them.

There's more...

All of our test suites were run from the recipe's main runner. But this probably wouldn't be the case for a real project. Instead, the idea is to define different suites, and code a mechanism to pick which suite to run. Each suite is geared towards a different purpose, and it is necessary to allow the developer to pick which suite to run. This can be done by coding a command-line script using Python's optparse module to define command-line flags to pick one of these suites.

Test suite methods must be outside of the test class

If we make these suite-defining methods members of the test class, we would have to instantiate the test class. Classes that extend unittest.TestCase have a specialized init method that doesn't work well with an instance that is created just to call a non-test method. That is why the methods are outside the test class. While these methods can be in other modules, it is very convenient to define them inside the module containing the test code, to keep things in proximity.

Why have different suites?

What if we started our project off by running all tests? Sounds like a good idea, right? But what if the time to run the entire test suite grew to over an hour? There is a certain threshold after which developers tend to stop running tests, and *nothing is worse than an un-run test suite*. By defining subsets of tests, it is easy to run alternate suites during the day, and then perhaps run the comprehensive test suite once a day.

- all is the comprehensive suite
- high_and_low is an example of testing the edges
- combos is a random sampling of values used to show that things are generally working

Defining our test suites is a judgment call. It's also worth it to re-evaluate each test suite every so often. If one test suite is getting too costly to run, consider moving some of its more expensive tests to another suite.

optparse is being phased out and replaced by argparse

While `optparse` is a convenient way to add command-line flags to Python scripts, it won't be available forever. Python 2.7 has deprecated this module and is continuing this development in `argparse`.

Retooling old test code to run inside unittest

Sometimes, we may have developed demo code to exercise our system. We don't have to rewrite it to run it inside unittest. Instead, it is easy to hook it up to the test framework and run it with some small changes.

How to do it...

With these steps, we will dive into capturing the test code that was written without using unittest, and repurposing it with minimal effort to run inside unittest.

1. Create a file named `recipe7.py` in which to put our application code that we will be testing.

2. Pick a class to test. In this case, we will use our Roman numeral converter.

   ```python
   class RomanNumeralConverter(object):
       def __init__(self):
           self.digit_map = {"M":1000, "D":500, "C":100, "L":50, "X":10, "V":5, "I":1}
       def convert_to_decimal(self, roman_numeral):
           val = 0
           for char in roman_numeral:
               val += self.digit_map[char]
           return val
   ```

3. Create a new file named `recipe7_legacy.py` to contain test code that doesn't use the `unittest` module.

4. Create a set of legacy tests that are coded, based on Python's `assert` function, not with unittest, along with a runner.

   ```python
   from recipe7 import *

   class RomanNumeralTester(object):
       def __init__(self):
           self.cvt = RomanNumeralConverter()

       def simple_test(self):
           print "+++ Converting M to 1000"
           assert self.cvt.convert_to_decimal("M") == 1000

       def combo_test1(self):
           print "+++ Converting MMX to 2010"
   ```

Using Unittest To Develop Basic Tests

```python
        assert self.cvt.convert_to_decimal("MMXX") == 2010
    def combo_test2(self):
      print "+++ Converting MMMMDCLXVIII to 4668"
      val = self.cvt.convert_to_decimal("MMMMDCLXVII")
      self.check(val, 4668)
    def other_test(self):
      print "+++ Converting MMMM to 4000"
      val = self.cvt.convert_to_decimal("MMMM")
      self.check(val, 4000)
    def check(self, actual, expected):
      if (actual != expected):
        raise AssertionError("%s doesn't equal %s" % \
            (actual, expected))
    def test_the_system(self):
      self.simple_test()
      self.combo_test1()
      self.combo_test2()
      self.other_test()
if __name__ == "__main__":
  tester = RomanNumeralTester()
  tester.test_the_system()
```

[📝 This set of legacy tests is meant to represent legacy test code that our team has developed to exercise things before unittest was an option.]

5. Run the legacy tests. What is wrong with this situation? Did all the test methods run? Have we caught all the bugs?

```
(ptc)gturnquist-mbp:01 gturnquist$ python recipe7_legacy.py
+++ Converting M to 1000
+++ Converting MMX to 2010
Traceback (most recent call last):
  File "recipe7_legacy.py", line 38, in <module>
    tester.test_the_system()
  File "recipe7_legacy.py", line 32, in test_the_system
    self.combo_test1()
  File "recipe7_legacy.py", line 13, in combo_test1
    assert self.cvt.convert_to_decimal("MMXX") == 2010
AssertionError
(ptc)gturnquist-mbp:01 gturnquist$
```

6. Create a new file called `recipe7_pyunit.py`.

7. Create a unittest set of tests, wrapping each legacy test method inside unittest's `FunctionTestCase`.

```
from recipe7 import *
from recipe7_legacy import *
import unittest
if __name__ == "__main__":
  tester = RomanNumeralTester()
  suite = unittest.TestSuite()
  for test in [tester.simple_test, tester.combo_test1, \
        tester.combo_test2, tester.other_test]:
    testcase = unittest.FunctionTestCase(test)
    suite.addTest(testcase)
  unittest.TextTestRunner(verbosity=2).run(suite)
```

8. Run the unittest test. Did all the tests run this time? Which test failed? Where is the bug?

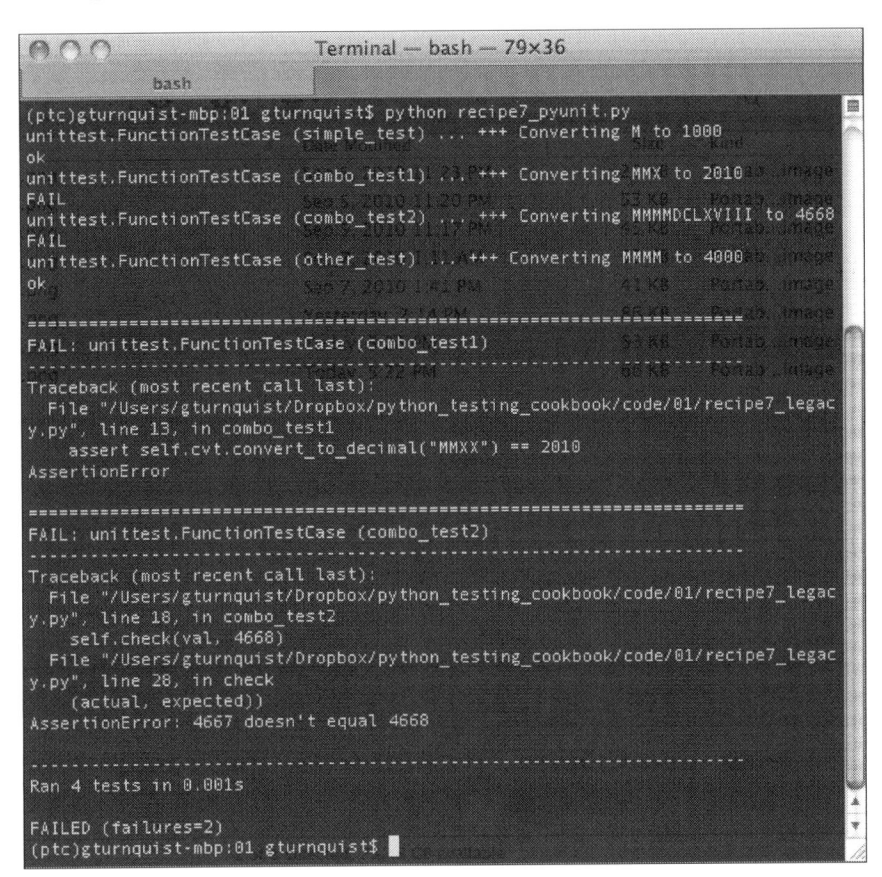

```
(ptc)gturnquist-mbp:01 gturnquist$ python recipe7_pyunit.py
unittest.FunctionTestCase (simple_test) ... +++ Converting M to 1000
ok
unittest.FunctionTestCase (combo_test1) ... +++ Converting MMX to 2010
FAIL
unittest.FunctionTestCase (combo_test2) ... +++ Converting MMMMDCLXVIII to 4668
FAIL
unittest.FunctionTestCase (other_test) ...A+++ Converting MMMM to 4000
ok

======================================================================
FAIL: unittest.FunctionTestCase (combo_test1)
----------------------------------------------------------------------
Traceback (most recent call last):
  File "/Users/gturnquist/Dropbox/python_testing_cookbook/code/01/recipe7_legac
y.py", line 13, in combo_test1
    assert self.cvt.convert_to_decimal("MMXX") == 2010
AssertionError

======================================================================
FAIL: unittest.FunctionTestCase (combo_test2)
----------------------------------------------------------------------
Traceback (most recent call last):
  File "/Users/gturnquist/Dropbox/python_testing_cookbook/code/01/recipe7_legac
y.py", line 18, in combo_test2
    self.check(val, 4668)
  File "/Users/gturnquist/Dropbox/python_testing_cookbook/code/01/recipe7_legac
y.py", line 28, in check
    (actual, expected))
AssertionError: 4667 doesn't equal 4668

----------------------------------------------------------------------
Ran 4 tests in 0.001s

FAILED (failures=2)
(ptc)gturnquist-mbp:01 gturnquist$
```

Using Unittest To Develop Basic Tests

How it works...

Python provides a convenient `assert` statement that tests a condition. When true, the code continues. When false, it raises an `AssertionError`. In the first test runner, we have several tests that check results using a mixture of `assert` statements or raising an `AssertionError`.

unittest provides a convenient class, `unittest.FunctionTestCase`, that wraps a bound function as a unittest test case. If an `AssertionError` is thrown, `FunctionTestCase` catches it, flags it as a test *failure*, and proceeds to the next test case. If any other type of exception is thrown, it will be flagged as a test error. In the second test runner, we wrap each of these legacy test methods with `FunctionTestCase`, and chain them together in a suite for unittest to run.

As seen by running the second test run, there is a bug lurking in the third test method. We were not aware of it, because the test suite was prematurely interrupted.

Another deficiency of Python's `assert` statement is shown by the first failure, as seen in the previous screenshot. When an assert fails, there is little to no information about the values that were compared. All we have is the line of code where it failed. The second assert in that screenshot was more useful, because we coded a custom checker that threw a custom `AssertionError`.

There's more...

Unittest does more than just run tests. It has a built-in mechanism to trap errors and failures, and then it continues running as much of our test suite as possible. This helps, because we can shake out more errors and fix more things within a given test run. This is especially important when a test suite grows to the point of taking minutes or hours to run.

Where are the bugs?

They exist in the test methods, and fundamentally were made by making slight alterations in the Roman numeral being converted.

```
def combo_test1(self):
    print "+++ Converting MMX to 2010"
    assert self.cvt.convert_to_decimal("MMXX") == 2010
def combo_test2(self):
    print "+++ Converting MMMMDCLXVIII to 4668"
    val = self.cvt.convert_to_decimal("MMMMDCLXVII")
    self.check(val, 4668)
```

The `combo_test1` test method prints out that it is converting MMX, but actually tries to convert MMXX. The `combo_test2` test method prints out that it is converting MMMMDCLXVIII, but actually tries to convert MMMMDCLXVII.

This is a contrived example, but have you ever run into bugs just as small that drove you mad trying to track them down? The point is, showing how easy or hard it can be to track them down is based on how the values are checked. Python's `assert` statement isn't very effective at telling us what values are compared where. The customized `check` method is much better at pinpointing the problem with `combo_test2`.

> This highlights the problem with having comments or print statements trying to reflect what the asserts do. They can easily get out of sync and the developer may face some problems trying to track down bugs. Avoiding this situation is known as the DRY principle (Don't Repeat Yourself).

FunctionTestCase is a temporary measure

The `FunctionTestCase` is a test case that provides an easy way to quickly migrate tests based on Python's `assert` statement, so they can be run with unittest. But things shouldn't stop there. If we take the time to convert `RomanNumeralTester` into a unittest `TestCase`, then we gain access to other useful features like the various `assert*` methods that come with `TestCase`. It's a good investment. The `FunctionTestCase` just lowers the bar to migrate to unittest.

Breaking down obscure tests into simple ones

Unittest provides the means to test the code through a series of assertions. I have often felt the temptation to exercise many aspects of a particular piece of code within a single test method. If any part fails, it becomes obscured as to which part failed. It is preferable to split things up into several smaller test methods, so that when some part of the code under test fails, it is obvious.

How to do it...

With these steps, we will investigate what happens when we put too much into a single test method.

1. Create a new file named `recipe8.py` in which to put our application code for this recipe.
2. Pick a class to test. In this case, we will use an alternative version of the Roman numeral converter, which converts both ways.
   ```
   class RomanNumeralConverter(object):
     def __init__(self):
       self.digit_map = {"M":1000, "D":500, "C":100, "L":50, "X":10, "V":5, "I":1}
   ```

```
def convert_to_decimal(self, roman_numeral):
    val = 0
    for char in roman_numeral:
        val += self.digit_map[char]
    return val
def convert_to_roman(self, decimal):
    val = ""
    while decimal > 1000:
        val += "M"
        decimal -= 1000
    while decimal > 500:
        val += "D"
        decimal -= 500
    while decimal > 100:
        val += "C"
        decimal -= 100
    while decimal > 50:
        val += "L"
        decimal -= 50
    while decimal > 10:
        val += "X"
        decimal -= 10
    while decimal > 5:
        val += "V"
        decimal -= 5
    while decimal > 1:
        val += "I"
        decimal -= 1
    return val
```

3. Create a new file called `recipe8_obscure.py` in which to put some longer test methods.

4. Create some test methods that combine several test assertions.

```
import unittest
from recipe8 import *

class RomanNumeralTest(unittest.TestCase):
    def setUp(self):
        self.cvt = RomanNumeralConverter()

    def test_convert_to_decimal(self):
        self.assertEquals(0, self.cvt.convert_to_decimal(""))
        self.assertEquals(1, self.cvt.convert_to_decimal("I"))
        self.assertEquals(2010, \
                self.cvt.convert_to_decimal("MMX"))
        self.assertEquals(4000, \
                self.cvt.convert_to_decimal("MMMM"))
```

```python
    def test_convert_to_roman(self):
        self.assertEquals("", self.cvt.convert_to_roman(0))
        self.assertEquals("II", self.cvt.convert_to_roman(2))
        self.assertEquals("V", self.cvt.convert_to_roman(5))
        self.assertEquals("XII", \
                self.cvt.convert_to_roman(12))
        self.assertEquals("MMX", \
                self.cvt.convert_to_roman(2010))
        self.assertEquals("MMMM", \
                self.cvt.convert_to_roman(4000))

if __name__ == "__main__":
    unittest.main()
```

5. Run the obscure tests. Why did it fail? Where is the bug? It reports that `II` is not equal to `I`, so something appears to be off. If this the only bug?

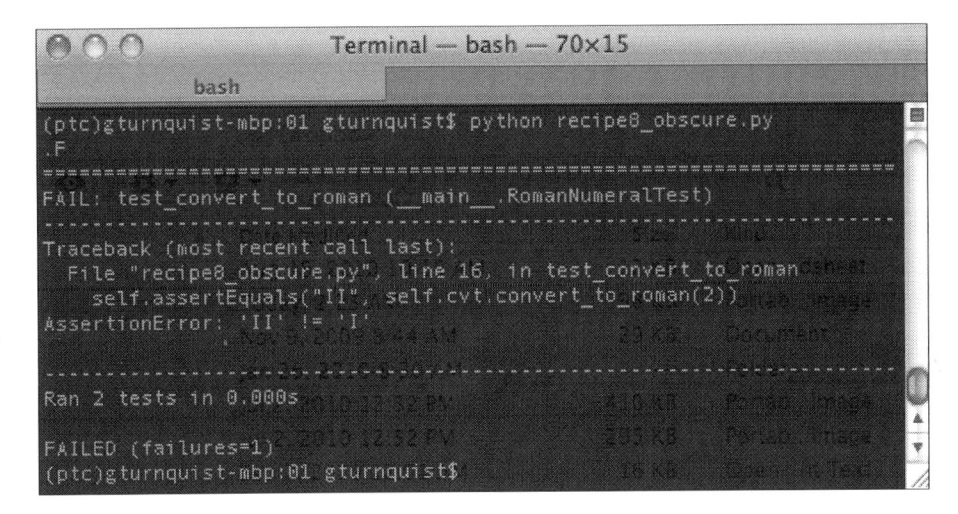

```
(ptc)gturnquist-mbp:01 gturnquist$ python recipe8_obscure.py
.F
======================================================================
FAIL: test_convert_to_roman (__main__.RomanNumeralTest)
----------------------------------------------------------------------
Traceback (most recent call last):
  File "recipe8_obscure.py", line 16, in test_convert_to_roman
    self.assertEquals("II", self.cvt.convert_to_roman(2))
AssertionError: 'II' != 'I'

----------------------------------------------------------------------
Ran 2 tests in 0.000s

FAILED (failures=1)
(ptc)gturnquist-mbp:01 gturnquist$
```

6. Create another file called `recipe8_clear.py` to create a more fine-grained set of test methods.
7. Split up the assertions into separate test methods to give a higher fidelity of output.

```python
import unittest
from recipe8 import *

class RomanNumeralTest(unittest.TestCase):
    def setUp(self):
        self.cvt = RomanNumeralConverter()

    def test_to_decimal1(self):
        self.assertEquals(0, self.cvt.convert_to_decimal(""))
```

```python
    def test_to_decimal2(self):
        self.assertEquals(1, self.cvt.convert_to_decimal("I"))
    def test_to_decimal3(self):
        self.assertEquals(2010, \
                self.cvt.convert_to_decimal("MMX"))
    def test_to_decimal4(self):
        self.assertEquals(4000, \
                self.cvt.convert_to_decimal("MMMM"))
    def test_convert_to_roman1(self):
        self.assertEquals("", self.cvt.convert_to_roman(0))
    def test_convert_to_roman2(self):
        self.assertEquals("II", self.cvt.convert_to_roman(2))
    def test_convert_to_roman3(self):
        self.assertEquals("V", self.cvt.convert_to_roman(5))
    def test_convert_to_roman4(self):
        self.assertEquals("XII", \
                self.cvt.convert_to_roman(12))
    def test_convert_to_roman5(self):
        self.assertEquals("MMX", \
                self.cvt.convert_to_roman(2010))
    def test_convert_to_roman6(self):
        self.assertEquals("MMMM", \
                self.cvt.convert_to_roman(4000))
if __name__ == "__main__":
    unittest.main()
```

8. Run the clearer test suite. Is it a bit clearer where the bug is? What did we trade in to get this higher degree of test failure? Was it worth the effort?

```
(ptc)gturnquist-mbp:01 gturnquist$ python recipe8_clear.py
.FFFFF,...
======================================================================
FAIL: test_convert_to_roman2 (__main__.RomanNumeralTest)
----------------------------------------------------------------------
Traceback (most recent call last):
  File "recipe8_clear.py", line 24, in test_convert_to_roman2
    self.assertEquals("II", self.cvt.convert_to_roman(2))
AssertionError: 'II' != 'I'

======================================================================
FAIL: test_convert_to_roman3 (__main__.RomanNumeralTest)
----------------------------------------------------------------------
Traceback (most recent call last):
  File "recipe8_clear.py", line 27, in test_convert_to_roman3
    self.assertEquals("V", self.cvt.convert_to_roman(5))
AssertionError: 'V' != 'IIII'

======================================================================
FAIL: test_convert_to_roman4 (__main__.RomanNumeralTest)
----------------------------------------------------------------------
Traceback (most recent call last):
  File "recipe8_clear.py", line 30, in test_convert_to_roman4
    self.assertEquals("XII", self.cvt.convert_to_roman(12))
AssertionError: 'XII' != 'XI'

======================================================================
FAIL: test_convert_to_roman5 (__main__.RomanNumeralTest)
----------------------------------------------------------------------
Traceback (most recent call last):
  File "recipe8_clear.py", line 33, in test_convert_to_roman5
    self.assertEquals("MMX", self.cvt.convert_to_roman(2010))
AssertionError: 'MMX' != 'MMVIIII'

======================================================================
FAIL: test_convert_to_roman6 (__main__.RomanNumeralTest)
----------------------------------------------------------------------
Traceback (most recent call last):
  File "recipe8_clear.py", line 36, in test_convert_to_roman6
    self.assertEquals("MMMM", self.cvt.convert_to_roman(4000))
AssertionError: 'MMMM' != 'MMMDCCCCLXXXXVIIII'

----------------------------------------------------------------------
Ran 10 tests in 0.001s

FAILED (failures=5)
```

How it works...

In this case, we created a modified Roman numeral converter that converts both ways. We then started creating test methods to exercise things. Since each of these tests were a simple, one-line assertion, it was convenient to put them all in the same test method.

Using Unittest To Develop Basic Tests

In the second test case, we put each assertion into a separate test method. Running it exposes the fact that there are multiple bugs in this Roman numeral converter.

There's more...

When we started off writing tests, it was very convenient to bundle all these assertions into a single test method. After all, if everything is working, there is no harm, right? But what if everything does *not* work, what do we have to deal with? An obscure error report!

Where is the bug?

The obscured test runner may not be clear. All we have to go on is II != I. Not much. The clue is that it is only off by one. The clear test runner gives more clues. We see that V != IIII, XII != XI, and some more. Each of these failures shows things being off by one.

The bug involves the various Boolean conditions in the while checks:

```
while decimal > 1000:
while decimal > 500:
while decimal > 100:
while decimal > 50:
while decimal > 10:
while decimal > 5:
while decimal > 1:
```

Instead of testing *greater than*, it should test for *greater than or equal to*. This causes it to skip out of each Roman numeral before counting the last one.

What is the right size for a test method?

In this recipe, we broke things down to a single assertion per test. But I wouldn't advise thinking along these lines.

If we look a little closer, each test method also involves a single usage of the Roman numeral API. For the converter, there is only one result to examine when exercising the code. For other systems, the output may be more complex. It is completely warranted to use several assertions in the same test method to check the outcome by making that single call.

When we proceed to make more calls to the Roman numeral API, it should signal us to consider splitting it off into a new test method.

This opens up the question: *what is a unit of code?* There has been much debate over what defines a unit of code, and what makes a good unit test. There are many opinions. Hopefully, reading this chapter and weighing it against the other test tactics covered throughout this book will help you enhance your own opinion and ultimately improve your own testing talent.

Unittests versus integration tests

Unittest can easily help us write both unit tests as well as integration tests. Unit tests exercise smaller blocks of code. When writing unit tests, it is best to keep the testing as small and fine grained as possible.

When we move up to a higher level (such as integration testing), it makes sense to test multiple steps in a single test method. But this is only recommended if there are adequate low-level unit tests. This will shed some light on whether it is broken at the unit level, or whether there is a sequence of steps that causes the error.

Integration tests often extend to things like external systems. For example, many argue that unit testing should never connect to a database, talk to an LDAP server, or interact with other systems.

> Just because we are using unittest, it doesn't mean the tests we are writing are unit tests. Later in this book, we will visit the concept that unittest can be used to write many types of tests including integration tests, smoke tests, and other types of tests as well.

Testing the edges

When we write automated tests, we pick the inputs and assert the expected outputs. It is important to test the limits of the inputs to make sure our code can handle good and bad inputs. This is also known as **testing corner cases**.

How to do it...

As we dig into this recipe, we will look for good boundaries to test against.

1. Create a new file named `recipe9.py` in which to put all our code for this recipe.

2. Pick a class to test. In this recipe, we'll use another variation of our Roman numeral converter. This one doesn't process values greater than 4000.

   ```
   class RomanNumeralConverter(object):
     def __init__(self):
       self.digit_map = {"M":1000, "D":500, "C":100, "L":50, "X":10, "V":5, "I":1}
     
     def convert_to_decimal(self, roman_numeral):
       val = 0
       for char in roman_numeral:
         val += self.digit_map[char]
       if val > 4000:
   ```

```
            raise Exception("We don't handle values over 4000")
        return val

    def convert_to_roman(self, decimal):
        if decimal > 4000:
            raise Exception("We don't handle values over 4000")
        val = ""
        mappers = [(1000,"M"), (500,"D"), (100,"C"), (50,"L"), (10,"X"), (5,"V"), (1,"I")]
        for (mapper_dec, mapper_rom) in mappers:
            while decimal >= mapper_dec:
                val += mapper_rom
                decimal -= mapper_dec
        return val
```

3. Create a test case that sets up an instance of the Roman numeral converter.

```
import unittest
class RomanNumeralTest(unittest.TestCase):
    def setUp(self):
        self.cvt = RomanNumeralConverter()
```

4. Add several test methods that exercise the edges of converting to Roman numeral notation.

```
    def test_to_roman_bottom(self):
        self.assertEquals("I", self.cvt.convert_to_roman(1))
    def test_to_roman_below_bottom(self):
        self.assertEquals("", self.cvt.convert_to_roman(0))
    def test_to_roman_negative_value(self):
        self.assertEquals("", self.cvt.convert_to_roman(-1))
    def test_to_roman_top(self):
        self.assertEquals("MMMM", \
                self.cvt.convert_to_roman(4000))
    def test_to_roman_above_top(self):
        self.assertRaises(Exception, \
                self.cvt.convert_to_roman, 4001)
```

5. Add several test methods that exercise the edges of converting to decimal notation.

```
    def test_to_decimal_bottom(self):
        self.assertEquals(1, self.cvt.convert_to_decimal("I"))
    def test_to_decimal_below_bottom(self):
        self.assertEquals(0, self.cvt.convert_to_decimal(""))
    def test_to_decimal_top(self):
```

```
        self.assertEquals(4000, \
            self.cvt.convert_to_decimal("MMMM"))
    def test_to_decimal_above_top(self):
        self.assertRaises(Exception, \
            self.cvt.convert_to_decimal, "MMMMI")
```

6. Add some tests that exercise the tiers of converting decimals to Roman numerals.

```
    def test_to_roman_tier1(self):
        self.assertEquals("V", self.cvt.convert_to_roman(5))
    def test_to_roman_tier2(self):
        self.assertEquals("X", self.cvt.convert_to_roman(10))
    def test_to_roman_tier3(self):
        self.assertEquals("L", self.cvt.convert_to_roman(50))
    def test_to_roman_tier4(self):
        self.assertEquals("C", self.cvt.convert_to_roman(100))
    def test_to_roman_tier5(self):
        self.assertEquals("D", self.cvt.convert_to_roman(500))
    def test_to_roman_tier6(self):
        self.assertEquals("M", \
            self.cvt.convert_to_roman(1000))
```

7. Add some tests that input unexpected values to the Roman numeral converter.

```
    def test_to_roman_bad_inputs(self):
        self.assertEquals("", self.cvt.convert_to_roman(None))
        self.assertEquals("I", self.cvt.convert_to_roman(1.2))
    def test_to_decimal_bad_inputs(self):
        self.assertRaises(TypeError, \
            self.cvt.convert_to_decimal, None)
        self.assertRaises(TypeError, \
            self.cvt.convert_to_decimal, 1.2)
```

8. Add a unit test runner.

```
if __name__ == "__main__":
    unittest.main()
```

9. Run the test case.

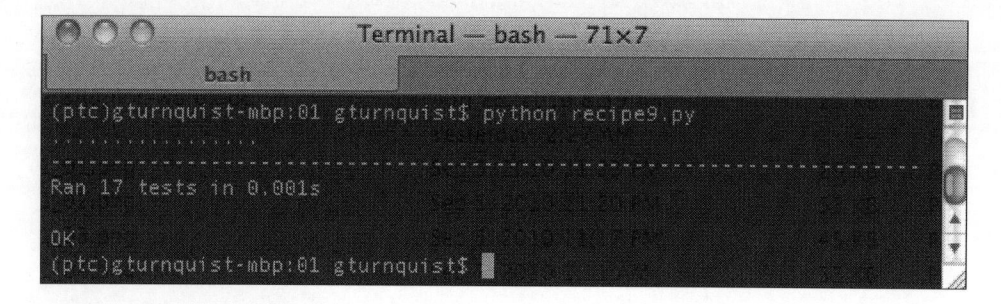

```
(ptc)gturnquist-mbp:01 gturnquist$ python recipe9.py
.................
-----------------
Ran 17 tests in 0.001s

OK
(ptc)gturnquist-mbp:01 gturnquist$
```

How it works...

We have a specialized Roman numeral converter that only converts values up to MMMM or 4000. We have written several test methods to exercise it. The immediate edges we write tests for are 1 and 4000. We also write some tests for one step past that: 0 and 4001. To make things complete, we also test against -1.

There's more...

A key part of the algorithm involves handling the various tiers of Roman numerals (5, 10, 50, 100, 500, and 1000). These could be considered *mini-edges*, so we wrote tests to check that the code handled those as well. Do you think we should test one past the mini-edges?

It's recommended that we should. Many bugs erupt due to coding *greater than*, when it should be *greater than or equal* (or vice versa), and so on. Testing one past the boundary, in both directions, is the perfect way to make sure that things are working exactly as expected. We also need to check bad inputs, so we tried converting None and a float.

That previous statement raises an important question: *how many invalid types should we test against*? Because Python is dynamic, we can expect a lot of input types. So what is reasonable? If our code hinges on a dictionary lookup, like certain parts of our Roman numeral API does, then confirming that we correctly handle a KeyError would probably be adequate. We don't need to input lots of different types if they all result in a KeyError.

Identifying the edges is important

It's important to identify the edges of our system, because we need to know our software can handle these boundaries. We also need to know it can handle both sides of these boundaries that are good values and bad values. That is why we need to check 4000 and 4001, as well as 0 and 1. This is a common place where software breaks.

Chapter 1

Testing for unexpected conditions

Does this sound a little awkward? Expect the unexpected? Our code involves converting integers and strings back and forth. By 'unexpected', we mean types of inputs passed in when someone uses our library that doesn't understand the edges, or wires it to receive inputs that are wider ranging types than we expected to receive.

A common occurrence of misuse is when a user of our API is working against a collection such as a list and accidentally passes the entire list instead of a single value by iteration. Another often seen situation is when a user of our API passes in None due to some other bug in their code. It's good to know that our API is resilient enough to handle this.

Testing corner cases by iteration

While developing code, new corner case inputs are often discovered. Being able to capture these inputs in an iterable array makes it easy to add related test methods.

How to do it...

In this recipe, we will look at a different way to test corner cases.

1. Create a new file called `recipe10.py` in which to put all our code for this recipe.

2. Pick a class to test. In this recipe, we'll use another variation of our Roman numeral converter. This one doesn't process values greater than 4000.

   ```
   class RomanNumeralConverter(object):
     def __init__(self):
       self.digit_map = {"M":1000, "D":500, "C":100, "L":50, "X":10, "V":5, "I":1}

     def convert_to_decimal(self, roman_numeral):
       val = 0
       for char in roman_numeral:
         val += self.digit_map[char]
       if val > 4000:
         raise Exception(\
           "We don't handle values over 4000")
       return val

     def convert_to_roman(self, decimal):
       if decimal > 4000:
         raise Exception(\
           "We don't handle values over 4000")
       val = ""
       mappers = [(1000,"M"), (500,"D"), (100,"C"), (50,"L"),
   (10,"X"), (5,"V"), (1,"I")]
   ```

39

Using Unittest To Develop Basic Tests

```
        for (mapper_dec, mapper_rom) in mappers:
          while decimal >= mapper_dec:
            val += mapper_rom
            decimal -= mapper_dec
        return val
```

3. Create a test class to exercise the Roman numeral converter.

```
    import unittest

    class RomanNumeralTest(unittest.TestCase):
      def setUp(self):
        self.cvt = RomanNumeralConverter()
```

4. Write a test method that exercises the edges of the Roman numeral converter.

```
      def test_edges(self):
        r = self.cvt.convert_to_roman
        d = self.cvt.convert_to_decimal
        edges = [("equals", r, "I", 1),\
              ("equals", r, "", 0),\
              ("equals", r, "", -1),\
              ("equals", r, "MMMM", 4000),\
              ("raises", r, Exception, 4001),\
              ("equals", d, 1, "I"),\
              ("equals", d, 0, ""),\
              ("equals", d, 4000, "MMMM"),\
              ("raises", d, Exception, "MMMMI")
              ]

        [self.checkout_edge(edge) for edge in edges]
```

5. Create a test method that exercises the tiers converting from decimal to Roman numerals.

```
      def test_tiers(self):
        r = self.cvt.convert_to_roman
        edges = [("equals", r, "V", 5),\
              ("equals", r, "VIIII", 9),\
              ("equals", r, "X", 10),\
              ("equals", r, "XI", 11),\
              ("equals", r, "XXXXVIIII", 49),\
              ("equals", r, "L", 50),\
              ("equals", r, "LI", 51),\
              ("equals", r, "LXXXXVIIII", 99),\
              ("equals", r, "C", 100),\
              ("equals", r, "CI", 101),\
              ("equals", r, "CCCCLXXXXVIIII", 499),\
```

```
            ("equals", r, "D", 500),\
            ("equals", r, "DI", 501),\
            ("equals", r, "M", 1000)\
        ]
        [self.checkout_edge(edge) for edge in edges]
```

6. Create a test method that exercises a set of invalid inputs.

```
    def test_bad_inputs(self):
        r = self.cvt.convert_to_roman
        d = self.cvt.convert_to_decimal
        edges = [("equals", r, "", None),\
            ("equals", r, "I", 1.2),\
            ("raises", d, TypeError, None),\
            ("raises", d, TypeError, 1.2)\
        ]
        [self.checkout_edge(edge) for edge in edges]
```

7. Code a utility method that iterates over the edge cases and runs different assertions based on each edge.

```
    def checkout_edge(self, edge):
        if edge[0] == "equals":
            f, output, input = edge[1], edge[2], edge[3]
            print("Converting %s to %s..." % (input, output))
            self.assertEquals(output, f(input))
        elif edge[0] == "raises":
            f, exception, args = edge[1], edge[2], edge[3:]
            print("Converting %s, expecting %s" % \
                        (args, exception))
            self.assertRaises(exception, f, *args)
```

8. Make the script runnable by loading the test case into `TextTestRunner`.

```
if __name__ == "__main__":
    suite = unittest.TestLoader().loadTestsFromTestCase( \
                RomanNumeralTest)
    unittest.TextTestRunner(verbosity=2).run(suite)
```

9. Run the test case.

```
(ptc)gturnquist-mbp:01 gturnquist$ python recipe10.py
test_bad_inputs (__main__.RomanNumeralTest) ... Converting None to ...
Converting 1.2 to I...
Converting (None,), expecting <type 'exceptions.TypeError'>
Converting (1.2,), expecting <type 'exceptions.TypeError'>
ok
test_edges (__main__.RomanNumeralTest) ... Converting 1 to I...
Converting 0 to ...
Converting -1 to ...
Converting 4000 to MMMM...
Converting (4001,), expecting <type 'exceptions.Exception'>
Converting I to 1...
Converting  to 0...
Converting MMMM to 4000...
Converting ('MMMMI',), expecting <type 'exceptions.Exception'>
ok
test_tiers (__main__.RomanNumeralTest) ... Converting 5 to V...
Converting 9 to VIIII...
Converting 10 to X...
Converting 11 to XI...
Converting 49 to XXXXVIIII...
Converting 50 to L...
Converting 51 to LI...
Converting 99 to LXXXXVIIII...
Converting 100 to C...
Converting 101 to CI...
Converting 499 to CCCCLXXXXVIIII...
Converting 500 to D...
Converting 501 to DI...
Converting 1000 to M...
ok

----------------------------------------------------------------------
Ran 3 tests in 0.002s

OK
(ptc)gturnquist-mbp:01 gturnquist$
```

How it works...

We have a specialized Roman numeral converter that only converts values up to MMMM or 4000. The immediate edges which we write tests for are 1 and 4000. We also write some tests for one step past that: 0 and 4001. To make things complete, we also test against -1.

But we've written the tests a little differently. Instead of writing each test input/output combination as a separate test method, we capture the input and output values in a tuple that is embedded in a list. We then feed it to our test iterator, `checkout_edge`. Because we need both `assertEquals` and `assertRaises` calls, the tuple also includes either `equals` or `raises` to flag which assertion to use.

Finally, to make it flexibly handle the convertion of both Roman numerals and decimals, the handles on the `convert_to_roman` and `convert_to_decimal` functions of our Roman numeral API is embedded in each tuple as well.

As shown in the following highlighted parts, we grab a handle on `convert_to_roman`, and store it in `r`. Then we embed it in the third element of the highlighted tuple, allowing the `checkout_edge` function to call it when needed.

```
def test_bad_inputs(self):
    r = self.cvt.convert_to_roman
    d = self.cvt.convert_to_decimal
    edges = [("equals", r, "", None),\
        ("equals", r, "I", 1.2),\
        ("raises", d, TypeError, None),\
        ("raises", d, TypeError, 1.2)\
    ]
    
    [self.checkout_edge(edge) for edge in edges]
```

There's more...

A key part of the algorithm involves handling the various tiers of Roman numerals (5, 10, 50, 100, 500, and 1000). These could be considered *mini-edges*, so we wrote a separate test method that has a list of input/output values to check those out as well. In the recipe *Testing the edges*, we didn't include testing before and after these mini-edges, for example 4 and 6 for 5. Now that it only takes one line of data to capture this test, we have it in this recipe. The same was done for all the others (except 1000).

Finally, we need to check bad inputs, so we created one more test method where we try to convert `None` and a `float` to and from Roman numeral.

Does this defy the recipe—Breaking down obscure tests into simple ones?

In a way, it does. If something goes wrong in one of the test data entries, then that entire test method will have failed. That is one reason why the other recipe split things up into three test methods instead of one big test method to cover them all. This is a judgment call about when it makes sense to view inputs and outputs as more data than test method. If you find the same sequence of test steps occurring repeatedly, consider whether it makes sense to capture the values in some sort of table structure, like the list used in this recipe.

How does this compare with the recipe—Testing the edges?

In case it wasn't obvious, these are the exact same tests used in the recipe *Testing the edges*. The question is, *which version do you find more readable*? Both are perfectly acceptable. Breaking things up into separate methods makes it more fine-grained and easier to spot if something goes wrong. Collecting things together into a data structure, the way we did in this recipe makes it more succinct, and could spur us on to write more test combinations as we did for the conversion tiers.

In my opinion, when testing algorithmic functions that have simple inputs and outputs, it's more suitable to use this recipe's mechanism to code an entire battery of test inputs in this concise format, for example, a mathematical function, a sorting algorithm, or perhaps a transform function.

When testing functions that are more logical and imperative, the other recipe may be more useful. For example, functions that interact with a database, cause changes in the state of the system, or other types of side effects that aren't encapsulated in the return value, would be hard to capture using this recipe.

See also

- Breaking down obscure tests into simple ones
- Testing the edges

2
Running Automated Test Suites with Nose

In this chapter, we will cover:

- Getting nosy with testing
- Embedding nose inside Python
- Writing a nose extension to pick tests based on regular expressions
- Writing a nose extension to generate a CSV report
- Writing a project-level script that lets you run different test suites

Introduction

In the previous chapter, we looked at several ways to utilize unittest in creating automated tests. Now, we will look at different ways to gather the tests together and run them. Nose is a useful utility built to discover tests and run them. It is flexible, can be run from either command-line or embedded inside scripts, and is extensible through plugin. Due to its embeddable nature, higher level tools, such as project scripts, it can be built with testing as an option.

What does nose offer that unittest does not? Key things include automatic test discovery and a useful plugin API. There are many nose plugins that provide everything from specially formatted test reports to integration with other tools. We will explore this in more detail in this chapter and in the latter parts of this book.

Running Automated Test Suites with Nose

> For more information about nose refer to
> `http://somethingaboutorange.com/mrl/projects/nose`.

We need to activate our virtual environment and then install nose for these various recipes.

Create a virtual environment, activate it, and verify that the tools are working:

```
gturnquist-mbp:tmp gturnquist$ virtualenv --no-site-packages ptc
New python executable in ptc/bin/python
Installing setuptools............done.
gturnquist-mbp:tmp gturnquist$ . ptc/bin/activate
(ptc)gturnquist-mbp:tmp gturnquist$ which python
/Users/gturnquist/tmp/ptc/bin/python
(ptc)gturnquist-mbp:tmp gturnquist$ which easy_install
/Users/gturnquist/tmp/ptc/bin/easy_install
(ptc)gturnquist-mbp:tmp gturnquist$
```

Next, using `pip`, install nose, as shown in the following screenshot:

```
(ptc)gturnquist-mbp:~ gturnquist$ pip install nose
Downloading/unpacking nose
  Downloading nose-1.0.0.tar.gz (718Kb): 718Kb downloaded
  Running setup.py egg_info for package nose
    no previously-included directories found matching 'doc/.build'
Installing collected packages: nose
  Running setup.py install for nose
    no previously-included directories found matching 'doc/.build'
    Installing nosetests-2.6 script to /Users/gturnquist/ptc/bin
    Installing nosetests script to /Users/gturnquist/ptc/bin
Successfully installed nose
```

Getting nosy with testing

Nose automatically discovers tests when fed with a package, a module, or a file.

How to do it...

With the following steps, we will explore how nose automatically finds test cases and runs them:

1. Create a new file called `recipe11.py` in which to put all our code for this recipe.

2. Create a class to test. For this recipe, we will use a shopping cart application that lets us load items and then calculate the bill.

```
class ShoppingCart(object):
    def __init__(self):
        self.items = []
    def add(self, item, price):
        self.items.append(Item(item, price))
        return self
    def item(self, index):
        return self.items[index-1].item
    def price(self, index):
        return self.items[index-1].price
    def total(self, sales_tax):
        sum_price = sum([item.price for item in self.items])
        return sum_price*(1.0 + sales_tax/100.0)
    def __len__(self):
        return len(self.items)
class Item(object):
    def __init__(self, item, price):
        self.item = item
        self.price = price
```

3. Create a test case that exercises the various parts of the shopping cart application.

```
import unittest
class ShoppingCartTest(unittest.TestCase):
    def setUp(self):
        self.cart = ShoppingCart().add("tuna sandwich", 15.00)
    def test_length(self):
        self.assertEquals(1, len(self.cart))
    def test_item(self):
        self.assertEquals("tuna sandwich", self.cart.item(1))
    def test_price(self):
        self.assertEquals(15.00, self.cart.price(1))
    def test_total_with_sales_tax(self):
        self.assertAlmostEquals(16.39, \
                                self.cart.total(9.25), 2)
```

Running Automated Test Suites with Nose

4. Use the command-line `nosetests` tool to run this recipe by filename and also by module.

```
(ptc)gturnquist-mbp:02 gturnquist$ nosetests recipe11.py
....
Ran 4 tests in 0.004s

OK
(ptc)gturnquist-mbp:02 gturnquist$ nosetests recipe11
....
Ran 4 tests in 0.003s

OK
(ptc)gturnquist-mbp:02 gturnquist$
```

How it works...

We started off by creating a simple application that lets us load up a `ShoppingCart` with `Items`. This application lets us look up each item and its price. Finally, we can calculate the total billing amount including the sales tax.

Next, we coded some test methods to exercise all these features using unittest.

Finally, we used the command-line `nosetests` tool that discovers test cases and automatically runs them. This saved us from handcoding any test runner to load test suites.

There's more...

What's so important about not writing the test runner? What do we gain by using `nosetests`? After all, unittest gives us the ability to embed an auto-discovering test runner like this:

```
if __name__ == "__main__":
    unittest.main()
```

Would the same block of code work, if the tests spread across several modules? No, because `unittest.main()` only looks in the current module. To grow into multiple modules, we need to start loading tests using unittest's `loadTestsFromTestCase` method or other customized suites. It doesn't matter how we assemble suites. When we are at risk of missing test cases, `nosetests` conveniently lets us search for all tests, or a subset, as needed.

A common situation on projects is to spread out test cases between lots of modules. Instead of writing one big test case, we typically break things up into smaller test cases based on various setups, scenarios, and other logical groupings. It's a common practice to split up test cases based on which module is being tested. The point is that manually loading all the test cases for a real world test suite can become labor intensive.

Nose is extensible

Auto-discovery of tests isn't the only reason to use nose. Later in this chapter, we will explore how we can write a plugin to customize what it discovers and also the output of a test run.

Nose is embeddable

All the functionality which nose provides can be utilized either by command line, or from inside a Python script. We will also explore this further in this chapter.

See also

Asserting the basics section mentioned in *Chapter 1*

Embedding nose inside Python

It's very convenient to embed nose inside a Python script. This lets us create higher level test tools besides letting the developer add testing to an existing tool.

How to do it...

With these steps, we will explore using nose's API inside a Python script to run some tests:

1. Create a new file called `recipe12.py` to contain the code from this recipe.
2. Create a class to test. For this recipe, we will use a shopping cart application that lets us load items and then calculate the bill.

   ```
   class ShoppingCart(object):
       def __init__(self):
           self.items = []
       def add(self, item, price):
           self.items.append(Item(item, price))
           return self
       def item(self, index):
           return self.items[index-1].item
       def price(self, index):
           return self.items[index-1].price
   ```

```
        def total(self, sales_tax):
            sum_price = sum([item.price for item in self.items])
            return sum_price*(1.0 + sales_tax/100.0)
        def __len__(self):
            return len(self.items)
    class Item(object):
        def __init__(self, item, price):
            self.item = item
            self.price = price
```

3. Create a test case with several test methods.

```
import unittest
class ShoppingCartTest(unittest.TestCase):
    def setUp(self):
        self.cart = ShoppingCart().add("tuna sandwich", 15.00)
    def test_length(self):
        self.assertEquals(1, len(self.cart))
    def test_item(self):
        self.assertEquals("tuna sandwich", self.cart.item(1))
    def test_price(self):
        self.assertEquals(15.00, self.cart.price(1))
    def test_total_with_sales_tax(self):
        self.assertAlmostEquals(16.39, \
                        self.cart.total(9.25), 2)
```

4. Create a script named `recipe12_nose.py` to use nose's API to run tests.

5. Make the script runnable and use nose's `run()` method to run selected arguments.

```
if __name__ == "__main__":
    import nose
    nose.run(argv=["", "recipe12", "--verbosity=2"])
```

6. Run the test script from the command line and see the verbose output.

```
test_item (recipe12.ShoppingCartTest) ... ok
test_length (recipe12.ShoppingCartTest) ... ok
test_price (recipe12.ShoppingCartTest) ... ok
test_total_with_sales_tax (recipe12.ShoppingCartTest) ... ok

----------------------------------------------------------------------
Ran 4 tests in 0.001s

OK
(ptc)gturnquist-mbp:02 gturnquist$
```

How it works...

In the test-running code, we are using `nose.run()`. With no arguments, it simply picks up on `sys.argv` and acts like the command-line `nosetests`. But in this recipe, we are plugging in the name of the current module along with an increased verbosity.

There's more

Unittest has `unittest.main()`, which discovers and runs test cases as well. How is this different? `unittest.main()` is geared to discover the test cases in the same module where it is run. `nose.run()` is geared to let us pass in command-line arguments or load them programmatically.

For example, look at the following steps which we must complete to turn up verbosity with unittest:

```
if __name__ == "__main__":
    import unittest
    from recipe12 import *
    suite = unittest.TestLoader().loadTestsFromTestCase(\
                                        ShoppingCartTest)
    unittest.TextTestRunner(verbosity=2).run(suite)
```

We had to import the test cases, use a test loader to create a test suite, and then run it through the `TextTestRunner`.

To do the same thing with nose, this is all we need:

```
if __name__ == "__main__":
    import nose
    nose.run(argv=["", "recipe12", "--verbosity=2"])
```

Running Automated Test Suites with Nose

This is much more succinct. Any command-line options we could use with `nosetests` are able to be used here. This comes in handy when we use nose plugin, which we will explore in more detail in this chapter and through the rest of the book.

Writing a nose extension to pick tests based on regular expressions

Out-of-the-box test tools like nose are very useful. But, eventually, we reach a point where the options don't match our needs. Nose has the powerful ability to code custom plugins, that gives us the ability to fine tune nose to meet our needs. This recipe will help us write a plugin that allows us to selectively choose test methods by matching their method names using a regular expression when we run `nosetests`.

Getting ready

We need to have `easy_install` loaded in order to install the nose plugins which we are about to create. If you don't already have it, please visit http://pypi.python.org/pypi/setuptools to download and install the package as indicated at the site.

If you just installed it now, then you will have to:

- Rebuild your `virtualenv` used for running code samples in this book
- Reinstall `nose` using `pip`

How to do it...

With the following steps, we will code a nose plugin that picks test methods to run by using a regular expression.

1. Create a new file called `recipe13.py` to contain the code for this recipe.

2. Create a shopping cart application where we can build some tests around it.

    ```python
    class ShoppingCart(object):
        def __init__(self):
            self.items = []
        def add(self, item, price):
            self.items.append(Item(item, price))
            return self
        def item(self, index):
            return self.items[index-1].item
        def price(self, index):
            return self.items[index-1].price
    ```

```python
    def total(self, sales_tax):
        sum_price = sum([item.price for item in self.items])
        return sum_price*(1.0 + sales_tax/100.0)
    def __len__(self):
        return len(self.items)
class Item(object):
    def __init__(self, item, price):
        self.item = item
        self.price = price
```

3. Create a test case that contains several test methods, including one that does *not* start with the word `test`.

```python
import unittest
class ShoppingCartTest(unittest.TestCase):
    def setUp(self):
        self.cart = ShoppingCart().add("tuna sandwich", 15.00)
    def length(self):
        self.assertEquals(1, len(self.cart))
    def test_item(self):
        self.assertEquals("tuna sandwich", self.cart.item(1))
    def test_price(self):
        self.assertEquals(15.00, self.cart.price(1))
    def test_total_with_sales_tax(self):
        self.assertAlmostEquals(16.39, \
                        self.cart.total(9.25), 2)
```

4. Run the module using `nosetests` from the command line, with `verbosity` turned on. How many test methods get run? How many test methods did we define?

```
(ptc)gturnquist-mbp:02 gturnquist$ nosetests recipe13.py --verbosity=2
test_item (recipe13.ShoppingCartTest) ... ok
test_price (recipe13.ShoppingCartTest) ... ok
test_total_with_sales_tax (recipe13.ShoppingCartTest) ... ok

Ran 3 tests in 0.003s

OK
(ptc)gturnquist-mbp:02 gturnquist$
```

5. Create a new file called `recipe15_plugin.py` to write a nose plugin for this recipe.

6. Capture a handle to `sys.stderr` to support debugging and verbose output.

   ```
   import sys
   err = sys.stderr
   ```

7. Create a nose plugin named `RegexPicker` by subclassing `nose.plugins.Plugin`.

   ```
   import nose
   import re
   from nose.plugins import Plugin
   class RegexPicker(Plugin):
       name = "regexpicker"
       def __init__(self):
           Plugin.__init__(self)
           self.verbose = False
   ```

   Nose plugin requires a class level name. This is used to define the— `with-<name>` command-line option.

8. Override `Plugin.options` and add an option to provide the pattern on the command line.

   ```
   def options(self, parser, env):
       Plugin.options(self, parser, env)
       parser.add_option("--re-pattern",
           dest="pattern", action="store",
           default=env.get("NOSE_REGEX_PATTERN", "test.*"),
           help=("Run test methods that have a method name matching this regular expression"))
   ```

9. Override `Plugin.configuration` by having it fetch the pattern and verbosity level from the options.

   ```
   def configure(self, options, conf):
       Plugin.configure(self, options, conf)
       self.pattern = options.pattern
       if options.verbosity >= 2:
           self.verbose = True
           if self.enabled:
               err.write("Pattern for matching test methods is %s\n" % self.pattern)
   ```

   When we extend `Plugin`, we inherit some other features, like `self.enabled`, which is switched on when `-with--<name>` is used with nose.

10. Override `Plugin.wantedMethod`, so that it accepts test methods that match our regular expression.

    ```
    def wantMethod(self, method):
        wanted = \
            re.match(self.pattern, method.func_name) is not None
        if self.verbose and wanted:
            err.write("nose will run %s\n" % method.func_name)
        return wanted
    ```

    Write a test runner that programmatically tests our plugin by running the same test case that we ran earlier.

    ```
    if __name__ == "__main__":
        args = ["", "recipe13", "--with-regexpicker", \
                "--re-pattern=test.*|length", "--verbosity=2"]
        print "With verbosity..."
        print "===================="
        nose.run(argv=args, plugin=[RegexPicker()])
        print "Without verbosity..."
        print "===================="
        args = args[:-1]
        nose.run(argv=args, plugin=[RegexPicker()])
    ```

11. Execute the test runner. Looking at the results in the following screenshot, how many test methods run this time?

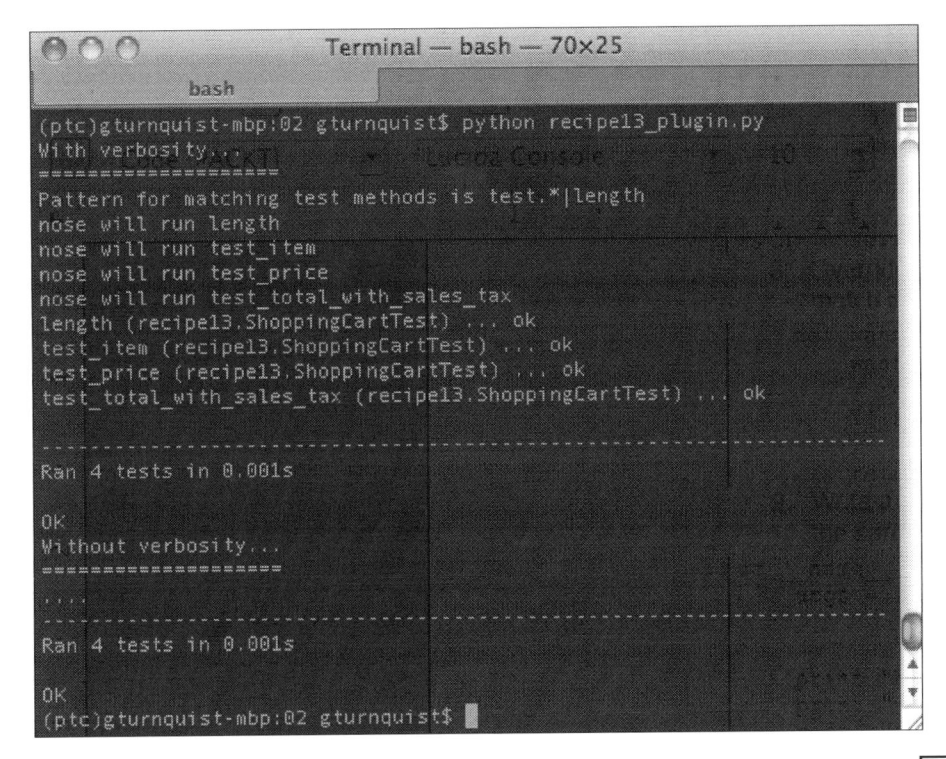

Running Automated Test Suites with Nose

12. Create a `setup.py` script that allows us to install and register our plugin with nosetests.

    ```
    import sys
    try:
        import ez_setup
        ez_setup.use_setuptools()
    except ImportError:
        pass

    from setuptools import setup

    setup(
        name="RegexPicker plugin",
        version="0.1",
        author="Greg L. Turnquist",
        author_email="Greg.L.Turnquist@gmail.com",
        description="Pick test methods based on a regular expression",
        license="Apache Server License 2.0",
        py_modules=["recipe13_plugin"],
        entry_points = {
            'nose.plugins': [
                'recipe13_plugin = recipe13_plugin:RegexPicker'
                ]
            }
        )
    ```

13. Install our new plugin.

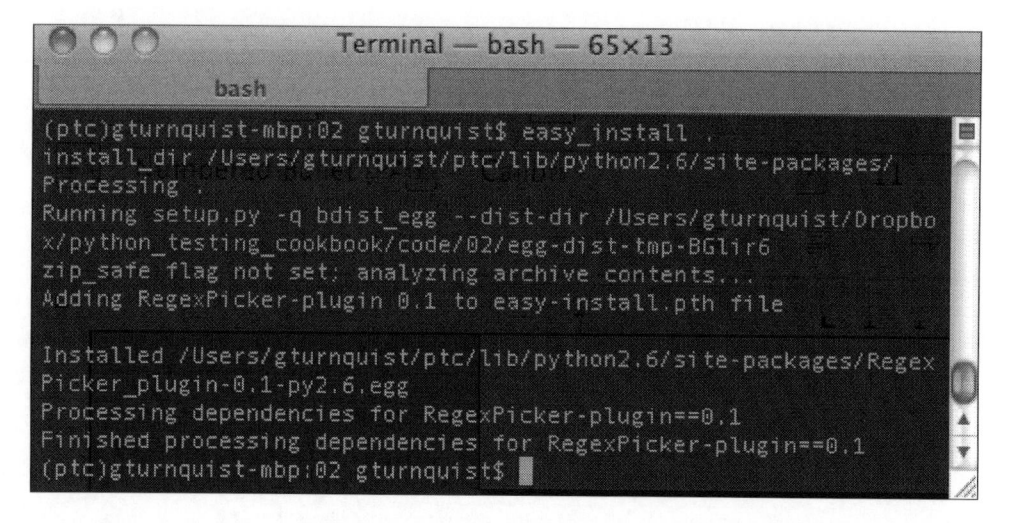

    ```
    (ptc)gturnquist-mbp:02 gturnquist$ easy_install .
    install_dir /Users/gturnquist/ptc/lib/python2.6/site-packages/
    Processing .
    Running setup.py -q bdist_egg --dist-dir /Users/gturnquist/Dropbo
    x/python_testing_cookbook/code/02/egg-dist-tmp-BGli r6
    zip_safe flag not set; analyzing archive contents...
    Adding RegexPicker-plugin 0.1 to easy-install.pth file

    Installed /Users/gturnquist/ptc/lib/python2.6/site-packages/Regex
    Picker_plugin-0.1-py2.6.egg
    Processing dependencies for RegexPicker-plugin==0.1
    Finished processing dependencies for RegexPicker-plugin==0.1
    (ptc)gturnquist-mbp:02 gturnquist$
    ```

14. Run `nosetests` using `--with-regexpicker` from the command line.

Chapter 2

```
(ptc)gturnquist-mbp:02 gturnquist$ nosetests --with-regexpicker --re-pattern="test.*|length"
 recipe13 --verbosity=2
Pattern for matching test methods is test.*|length
nose will run length
nose will run test_item
nose will run test_price
nose will run test_total_with_sales_tax
length (recipe13.ShoppingCartTest) ... ok
test_item (recipe13.ShoppingCartTest) ... ok
test_price (recipe13.ShoppingCartTest) ... ok
test_total_with_sales_tax (recipe13.ShoppingCartTest) ... ok

----------------------------------------------------------------------
Ran 4 tests in 0.004s

OK
(ptc)gturnquist-mbp:02 gturnquist$
```

How it works...

Writing a nose plugin has some requirements. First of all, we need the class level `name` attribute. It is used in several places that also includes defining the command-line switch to invoke our plugin, `--with-<name>`.

Next, we write `options`. There is no requirement to override `Plugin.options` but, in this case, we need a way to supply our plugin with the regular expression. To avoid destroying the useful machinery of `Plugin.options`, we call it first, and then add a line for our extra parameter using `parser.add_option`.

- The first, unnamed arguments are string versions of the parameter, and we can specify multiple ones. We could have had `-rp` and `--re-pattern` if we wanted to.
- `Dest`: This is the name of the attribute that stores the results (see configure).
- `Action`: This is specifies what to do with the value of the parameter (store, append, and so on.).
- `Default`: This is specifies what value to store when none is provided (notice we use `test.*` to match standard unittest behavior).
- `Help`: Provides help information to print out on the command line.

Nose uses Python's `optparse.OptionParser` library to define options.

> To find out more about Python's optparse.OptionParser please refer to: http://docs.python.org/library/optparse.html.

57

Then, we write `configure`. There is also no requirement to override `Plugin.configure`. Because we had an extra option, `--pattern`, we need to harvest it. We also want to turn on a flag driven by `verbosity`, a standard nose option.

There are many things we can do when writing a nose plugin. In our case, we wanted to zero in on **test selection**. There are several ways to load tests, including by module, and filename. After loading, they are then run through a method where they are voted in or out. These voters are called the `want*` methods and they include `wantModule`, `wantName`, `wantFunction`, and `wantMethod`, as well as some others. We implemented `wantMethod` where we tested if `method.func_name` matches our pattern using Python's `re` module. `want*` methods. These methods have three return value types:

- `True`: This test is wanted
- `False`: This test is *not* wanted (and will not be considered by another plugin)
- `None`: The plugin does not care. Another plugin (or nose) gets to choose. This can succinctly be achieved by not returning anything from the want* method.

> `wantMethod` only looks at functions defined inside classes. `nosetests` is geared to find tests by many different methods and is not confined to just searching subclasses of `unittest.TestCase`. If tests are found in the module, but not as class methods, then this pattern matching is not utilized. For this plugin to be more robust, we would need a lot of different tests and we would probably need to override the other `want*` test selectors.

There's more...

This recipe just scratches the surface on plugin functionality. It focuses on the test selection process.

Later in this chapter, we will explore generating a specialized report. This involves using other plugin hooks that gather information after each test is run, as well as generating the report after the test suite is exhausted. Nose provides a robust set of hooks allowing detailed customization to meet our changing needs.

> **Plugins should subclass nose.plugins.Plugin**
> There is a lot of valuable machinery built into `Plugin`. Subclassing is the recommended means of developing a plugin. If you don't, you may have to add on methods and attributes, which – you didn't realize – were needed by nose and that come for free when you subclass.

It's a good rule of thumb to subclass the parts of the nose API that we are plugging into instead of overriding.

Online documentation of the nose API is a little incomplete. It tends to assume too much knowledge of the reader. If we override and our plugin doesn't work correctly, it may be difficult to debug what is happening.

> **Do not subclass nose.plugins.IPluginInterface**
> This class is used for documentation purposes only. It provides information about each of the hooks our plugin can access. But it is not designed for subclassing real plugins.

Writing a nose extension to generate a CSV report

This recipe will help us write a plugin that generates a custom report listing successes and failures in a CSV file. It is used to demonstrate how to gather information after each test method completes.

Getting ready

We need to have `easy_install` loaded in order to install the nose plugin we are about to create. If you don't already have it, please visit `http://pypi.python.org/pypi/setuptools` to download and install the package as indicated on the site.

If you just installed it now, then you will have to:

- Rebuild your `virtualenv` used for running code samples in this book
- Reinstall nose using `easy_install`

Running Automated Test Suites with Nose

How to do it...

1. Create a new file named `recipe14.py` to contain the code for this recipe.

2. Create a shopping cart application that we can build some tests around.

   ```
   class ShoppingCart(object):
       def __init__(self):
           self.items = []
       def add(self, item, price):
           self.items.append(Item(item, price))
           return self
       def item(self, index):
           return self.items[index-1].item
       def price(self, index):
           return self.items[index-1].price
       def total(self, sales_tax):
           sum_price = sum([item.price for item in self.items])
           return sum_price*(1.0 + sales_tax/100.0)
       def __len__(self):
           return len(self.items)
   class Item(object):
       def __init__(self, item, price):
           self.item = item
           self.price = price
   ```

3. Create a test case that contains several test methods, including the one deliberately set to fail.

   ```
   import unittest
   class ShoppingCartTest(unittest.TestCase):
       def setUp(self):
           self.cart = ShoppingCart().add("tuna sandwich", 15.00)
       def test_length(self):
           self.assertEquals(1, len(self.cart))
       def test_item(self):
           self.assertEquals("tuna sandwich", self.cart.item(1))
       def test_price(self):
           self.assertEquals(15.00, self.cart.price(1))
       def test_total_with_sales_tax(self):
           self.assertAlmostEquals(16.39, \
                                   self.cart.total(9.25), 2)
   ```

```
        def test_assert_failure(self):
            self.fail("You should see this failure message in the
report.")
```

4. Run the module using `nosetests` from the command line. Looking at the output in the following screenshot, does it appear that a CSV report exists?

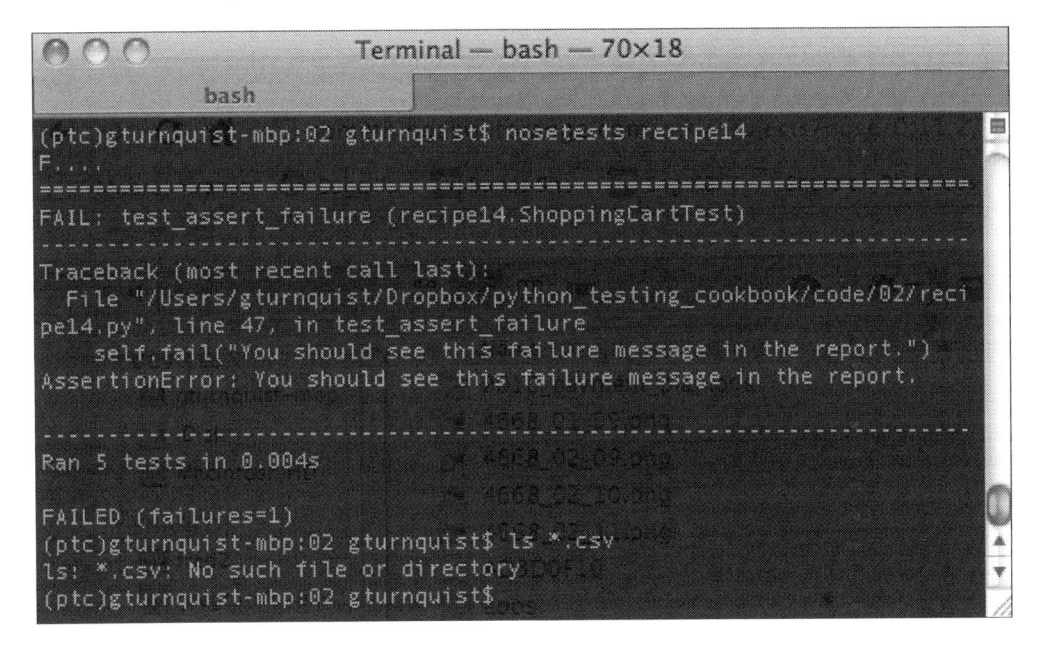

```
(ptc)gturnquist-mbp:02 gturnquist$ nosetests recipe14
F....
======================================================================
FAIL: test_assert_failure (recipe14.ShoppingCartTest)
----------------------------------------------------------------------
Traceback (most recent call last):
  File "/Users/gturnquist/Dropbox/python_testing_cookbook/code/02/reci
pe14.py", line 47, in test_assert_failure
    self.fail("You should see this failure message in the report.")
AssertionError: You should see this failure message in the report.

----------------------------------------------------------------------
Ran 5 tests in 0.004s

FAILED (failures=1)
(ptc)gturnquist-mbp:02 gturnquist$ ls *.csv
ls: *.csv: No such file or directory
(ptc)gturnquist-mbp:02 gturnquist$
```

5. Create a new file called `recipe14_plugin.py` to contain our new nose plugin.

6. Create a nose plugin named `CsvReport` by subclassing `nose.plugins.Plugin`.

```
import nose
import re
from nose.plugins import Plugin

class CsvReport(Plugin):
    name = "csv-report"

    def __init__(self):
        Plugin.__init__(self)
        self.results = []
```

Nose plugin requires a class level `name`. This is used to define the `-with--<name>` command-line option.

7. Override `Plugin.options` and add an option to provide the report's filename on the command line.

```
        def options(self, parser, env):
```

```
            Plugin.options(self, parser, env)
            parser.add_option("--csv-file",
                dest="filename", action="store",
                default=env.get("NOSE_CSV_FILE", "log.csv"),
                help=("Name of the report"))
```

8. Override `Plugin.configuration` by having it fetch the filename from the options.

```
        def configure(self, options, conf):
            Plugin.configure(self, options, conf)
            self.filename = options.filename
```

When we extend `Plugin`, we inherit some other features, like `self.enabled`, which is switched on when `--with-<name>` is used with nose.

9. Override `addSuccess`, `addFailure`, and `addError` to collect results in an internal list.

```
        def addSuccess(self, *args, **kwargs):
            test = args[0]
            self.results.append((test, "Success"))

        def addError(self, *args, **kwargs):
            test, error = args[0], args[1]
            self.results.append((test, "Error", error))

        def addFailure(self, *args, **kwargs):
            test, error = args[0], args[1]
            self.results.append((test, "Failure", error))
```

10. Override `finalize` to generate the CSV report.

```
        def finalize(self, result):
            report = open(self.filename, "w")
            report.write("Test,Success/Failure,Details\n")
            for item in self.results:
                if item[1] == "Success":
                    report.write("%s,%s\n" % (item[0], item[1]))
                else:
                    report.write("%s,%s,%s\n" % (item[0],item[1],\
                                                  item[2][1]))
            report.close()
```

11. Write a test runner that programmatically tests our plugin by running the same test case that we ran earlier.

```
    if __name__ == "__main__":
        args = ["", "recipe14", "--with-csv-report", \
```

Chapter 2

```
                    "--csv-file=recipe14.csv"]
nose.run(argv=args, plugin=[CsvReport()])
```

12. Execute the test runner. Looking at the output in the next screenshot, is there a test report now?

```
(ptc)gturnquist-mbp:02 gturnquist$ python recipe14_plugin.py
F....
======================================================================
FAIL: test_assert_failure (recipe14.ShoppingCartTest)
----------------------------------------------------------------------
Traceback (most recent call last):
  File "/Users/gturnquist/Dropbox/python_testing_cookbook/code/02/reci
pe14.py", line 47, in test_assert_failure
    self.fail("You should see this failure message in the report.")
AssertionError: You should see this failure message in the report.

----------------------------------------------------------------------
Ran 5 tests in 0.001s

FAILED (failures=1)
(ptc)gturnquist-mbp:02 gturnquist$ ls *.csv
recipe14.csv
(ptc)gturnquist-mbp:02 gturnquist$
```

13. Open up and view the report using your favorite spreadsheet.

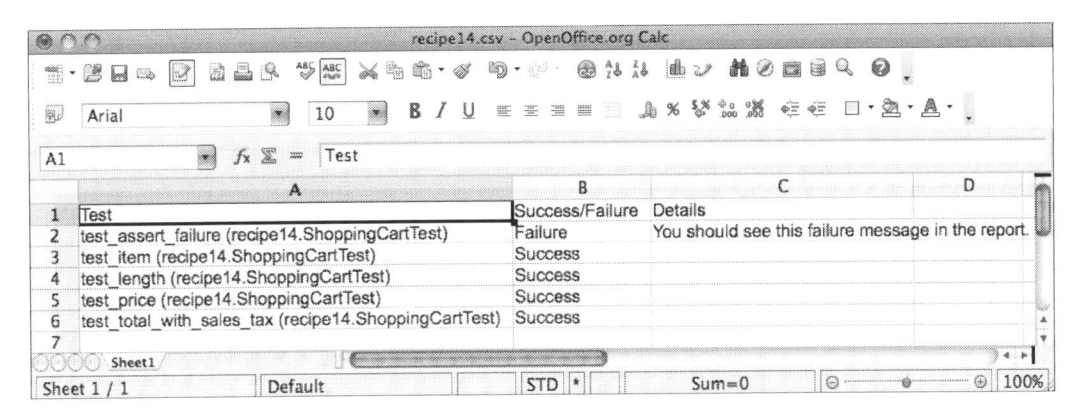

	A	B	C
1	Test	Success/Failure	Details
2	test_assert_failure (recipe14.ShoppingCartTest)	Failure	You should see this failure message in the report.
3	test_item (recipe14.ShoppingCartTest)	Success	
4	test_length (recipe14.ShoppingCartTest)	Success	
5	test_price (recipe14.ShoppingCartTest)	Success	
6	test_total_with_sales_tax (recipe14.ShoppingCartTest)	Success	

14. Create a `setup.py` script that allows us to install and register our plugin with `nosetests`.

```
import sys
try:
```

```python
        import ez_setup
        ez_setup.use_setuptools()
except ImportError:
    pass

from setuptools import setup
setup(
    name="CSV report plugin",
    version="0.1",
    author="Greg L. Turnquist",
    author_email="Greg.L.Turnquist@gmail.com",
    description="Generate CSV report",
    license="Apache Server License 2.0",
    py_modules=["recipe14_plugin"],
    entry_points = {
        'nose.plugins': [
            'recipe14_plugin = recipe14_plugin:CsvReport'
            ]
        }
    )
```

15. Install our new plugin.

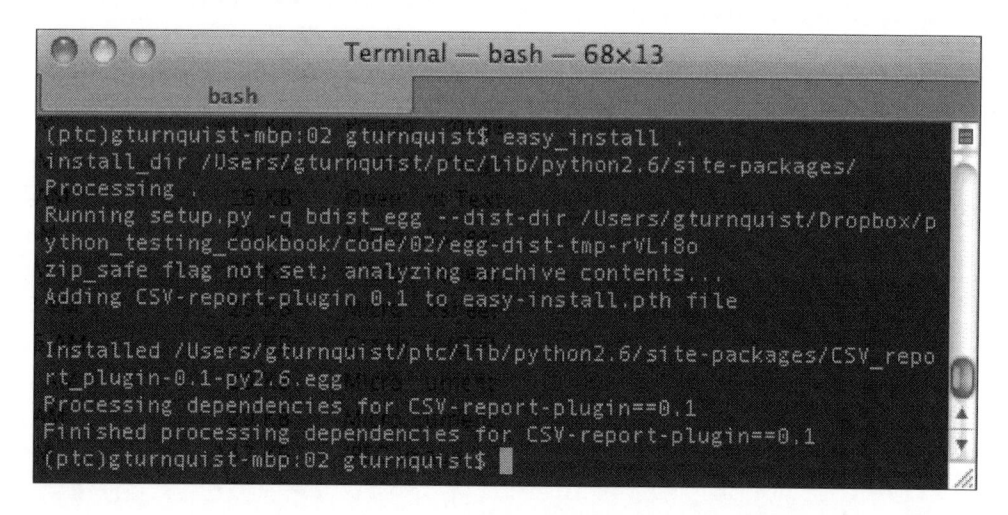

```
(ptc)gturnquist-mbp:02 gturnquist$ easy_install .
install_dir /Users/gturnquist/ptc/lib/python2.6/site-packages/
Processing .
Running setup.py -q bdist_egg --dist-dir /Users/gturnquist/Dropbox/p
ython_testing_cookbook/code/02/egg-dist-tmp-rVLi8o
zip_safe flag not set; analyzing archive contents...
Adding CSV-report-plugin 0.1 to easy-install.pth file

Installed /Users/gturnquist/ptc/lib/python2.6/site-packages/CSV_repo
rt_plugin-0.1-py2.6.egg
Processing dependencies for CSV-report-plugin==0.1
Finished processing dependencies for CSV-report-plugin==0.1
(ptc)gturnquist-mbp:02 gturnquist$
```

16. Run `nosetests` using `--with-csv-report` from the command line.

```
(ptc)gturnquist-mbp:02 gturnquist$ nosetests --with-csv-report --csv-file=log.csv
 recipe14.py
F....
======================================================================
FAIL: test_assert_failure (recipe14.ShoppingCartTest)
----------------------------------------------------------------------
Traceback (most recent call last):
  File "/Users/gturnquist/Dropbox/python_testing_cookbook/code/02/recipe14.py", l
ine 47, in test_assert_failure
    self.fail("You should see this failure message in the report.")
AssertionError: You should see this failure message in the report.

----------------------------------------------------------------------
Ran 5 tests in 0.004s

FAILED (failures=1)
(ptc)gturnquist-mbp:02 gturnquist$ ls *.csv
log.csv         recipe14.csv
(ptc)gturnquist-mbp:02 gturnquist$
```

In the previous screenshot, notice how we have the previous log file, `recipe14.csv` and the new one, `log.csv`.

How it works...

Writing a nose plugin has some requirements. First of all, we need the class level `name` attribute. It is used in several places including defining the command-line switch to invoke our plugin, `--with-<name>`.

Next, we write `options`. There is no requirement to override `Plugin.options`. But, in this case, we need a way to supply our plugin with the name of the CSV report it will write. To avoid destroying the useful machinery of `Plugin.options`, we call it first, and then add a line for our extra parameter using `parser.add_option`.

- The first, unnamed arguments are string versions of the parameter
- `dest`: This is the name of the attribute to store the results (see configure)
- `action`: This tells what to do with the value of the parameter (store, append, etc.)
- `default`: This tells what value to store when none is provided
- `help`: This provides help information to print out on the command line

Nose uses Python's `optparse.OptionParser` library to define options.

> To find out more about `optparse.OptionParser` visit http://docs.python.org/optparse.html.

Then, we write `configure`. There is also no requirement to override `Plugin.configure`. Because we had an extra option, `--csv-file`, we need to harvest it.

In this recipe, we want to capture the test case as well as the error report whenever a test method completes. To do this, we implement `addSuccess`, `addFailure`, and `addError`. Because nose varies in what arguments are sent to these methods when called either programmatically or by command-line, we must use Python's `*args`.

- The first slot of this tuple contains the `test`, an instance of `nose.case.Test`. Simply printing it is sufficient for our needs.
- The second slot of this tuple contains the `error`, an instance of the 3-tuple for `sys.exc_info()`. It is only included for `addFailure` and `addError`.
- No other slots of this tuple are documented on nose's website. We generally ignore them.

There's more...

This recipe digs a little deeper into the plugin functionality. It focuses on processing done after a test method succeeds, fails, or causes an error. In our case, we just gather the results to put into a report. We could do other things, like capture stack traces, e-mail failures to the development team, or send a page to the QA team letting them know a test suite is complete.

For more details about writing a nose plugin, read the recipe *Writing a nose extension* to pick tests based on regular expressions.

Writing a project-level script that lets you run different test suites

Python, with its multi-paradigm nature, makes it easy to build applications as well as provide scripting support to things.

This recipe will help us explore building a project-level script that allows us to run different test suites. We will also show some extra command-line options to create hooks for packaging, publishing, registering, and writing automated documentation.

How to do it...

1. Create a script called `recipe15.py` that parses a set of options using Python's `getopt` library.

   ```
   import getopt
   import glob
   import logging
   ```

```
import nose
import os
import os.path
import pydoc
import re
import sys
```

```
def usage():
    print
    print "Usage: python recipe15.py [command]"
    print
    print "\t--help"
    print "\t--test"
    print "\t--suite [suite]"
    print "\t--debug-level [info|debug]"
    print "\t--package"
    print "\t--publish"
    print "\t--register"
    print "\t--pydoc"
    print
```

```
try:
    optlist, args = getopt.getopt(sys.argv[1:],
            "ht",
            ["help", "test", "suite=", \
             "debug-level=", "package", \
             "publish", "register", "pydoc"])
except getopt.GetoptError:
    # print help information and exit:
    print "Invalid command found in %s" % sys.argv
    usage()
    sys.exit(2)
```

2. Create a function that maps to –test.

```
def test(test_suite, debug_level):
    logger = logging.getLogger("recipe15")
    loggingLevel = debug_level
    logger.setLevel(loggingLevel)
    ch = logging.StreamHandler()
    ch.setLevel(loggingLevel)
    formatter = logging.Formatter("%(asctime)s - %(name)s - %(levelname)s - %(message)s")
    ch.setFormatter(formatter)
    logger.addHandler(ch)

    nose.run(argv=["", test_suite, "--verbosity=2"])
```

3. Create stub functions that support `package`, `publish`, and `register`.

   ```python
   def package():
       print "This is where we can plug in code to run " + \
           "setup.py to generate a bundle."
   def publish():
       print "This is where we can plug in code to upload " + \
           "our tarball to S3 or some other download site."
   def register():
       print "setup.py has a built in function to " + \
           "'register' a release to PyPI. It's " + \
           "convenient to put a hook in here."
       # os.system("%s setup.py register" % sys.executable)
   ```

4. Create a function to auto-generate docs using Python's `pydoc` module.

   ```python
   def create_pydocs():
       print "It's useful to use pydoc to generate docs."
       pydoc_dir = "pydoc"
       module = "recipe15_all"
       __import__(module)

       if not os.path.exists(pydoc_dir):
           os.mkdir(pydoc_dir)

       cur = os.getcwd()
       os.chdir(pydoc_dir)
       pydoc.writedoc("recipe15_all")
       os.chdir(cur)
   ```

5. Add some code that defines debug levels and then parses options to allow users to override.

   ```python
   debug_levels = {"info":logging.INFO, "debug":logging.DEBUG}
   # Default debug level is INFO
   debug_level = debug_levels["info"]

   for option in optlist:
       if option[0] in ("--debug-level"):
           # Override with a user-supplied debug level
           debug_level = debug_levels[option[1]]
   ```

6. Add some code that scans the command-line options for `-help`, and if found, exits the script.

   ```python
   # Check for help requests, which cause all other
   # options to be ignored.
   for option in optlist:
   ```

```
        if option[0] in ("--help", "-h"):
            usage()
            sys.exit(1)
```

7. Finish it by iterating through each of the command-line options, and invoking the other functions based on which options are picked.

```
# Parse the arguments, in order
for option in optlist:
    if option[0] in ("--test"):
        print "Running recipe15_checkin tests..."
        test("recipe15_checkin", debug_level)

    if option[0] in ("--suite"):
        print "Running test suite %s..." % option[1]
        test(option[1], debug_level)

    if option[0] in ("--package"):
        package()

    if option[0] in ("--publish"):
        publish()

    if option[0] in ("--register"):
        register()

    if option[0] in ("--pydoc"):
        create_pydocs()
```

8. Run the `recipe15.py` script with `-help`.

```
(ptc)gturnquist-mbp:02 gturnquist$ python recipe15.py --help
Usage: python recipe15.py [command]

        --help
        --test
        --suite [suite]
        --debug-level [info|debug]
        --package
        --publish
        --register
        --pydoc

(ptc)gturnquist-mbp:02 gturnquist$
```

Running Automated Test Suites with Nose

9. Create a new file called `recipe15_checkin.py` to create a new test suite.

10. Reuse the test cases from the recipe *Getting nosy with testing* to define a check in test suite.

    ```
    import recipe11

    class Recipe11Test(recipe11.ShoppingCartTest):
        pass
    ```

11. Run the `recipe15.py` script, using -test -package -publish -register -pydoc. In the following screenshot, do you notice how it exercises each option in the same sequence as it was supplied on the command line?

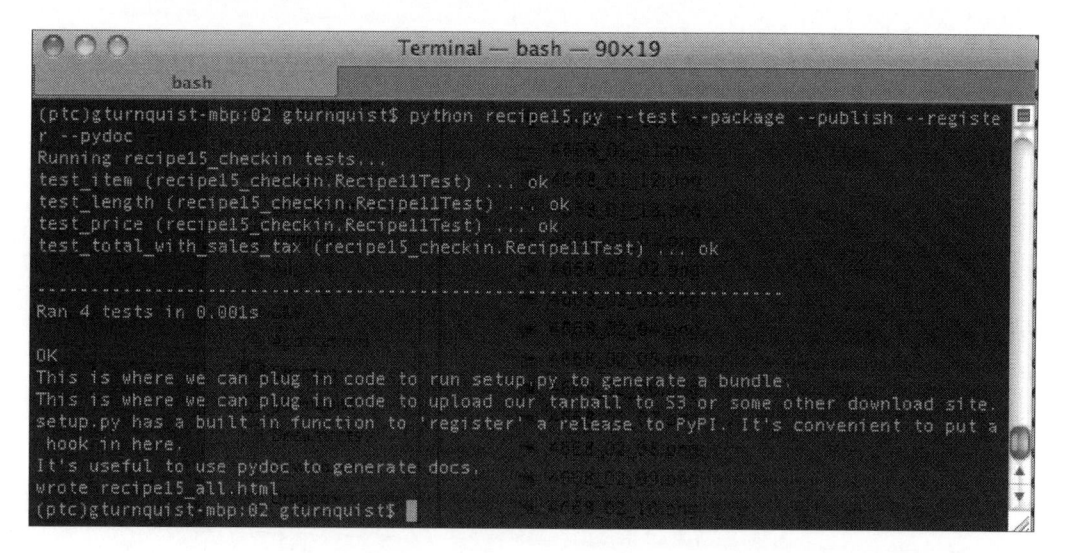

```
(ptc)gturnquist-mbp:02 gturnquist$ python recipe15.py --test --package --publish --register --pydoc
Running recipe15_checkin tests...
test_item (recipe15_checkin.Recipe11Test) ... ok
test_length (recipe15_checkin.Recipe11Test) ... ok
test_price (recipe15_checkin.Recipe11Test) ... ok
test_total_with_sales_tax (recipe15_checkin.Recipe11Test) ... ok
----------------------------------------------------------------------
Ran 4 tests in 0.001s

OK
This is where we can plug in code to run setup.py to generate a bundle.
This is where we can plug in code to upload our tarball to S3 or some other download site.
setup.py has a built in function to 'register' a release to PyPI. It's convenient to put a hook in here.
It's useful to use pydoc to generate docs.
wrote recipe15_all.html
(ptc)gturnquist-mbp:02 gturnquist$
```

12. Inspect the report generated in the `pydoc` directory.

Chapter 2

```
recipe15_all  /Users/gturnquist/Dropbox/python_testing_cookboo

Modules
    recipe11        recipe12        recipe13        recipe14

Classes
    recipe11.ShoppingCartTest(unittest.TestCase)
        Recipe11Test
    recipe12.ShoppingCartTest(unittest.TestCase)
        Recipe12Test
    recipe13.ShoppingCartTest(unittest.TestCase)
```

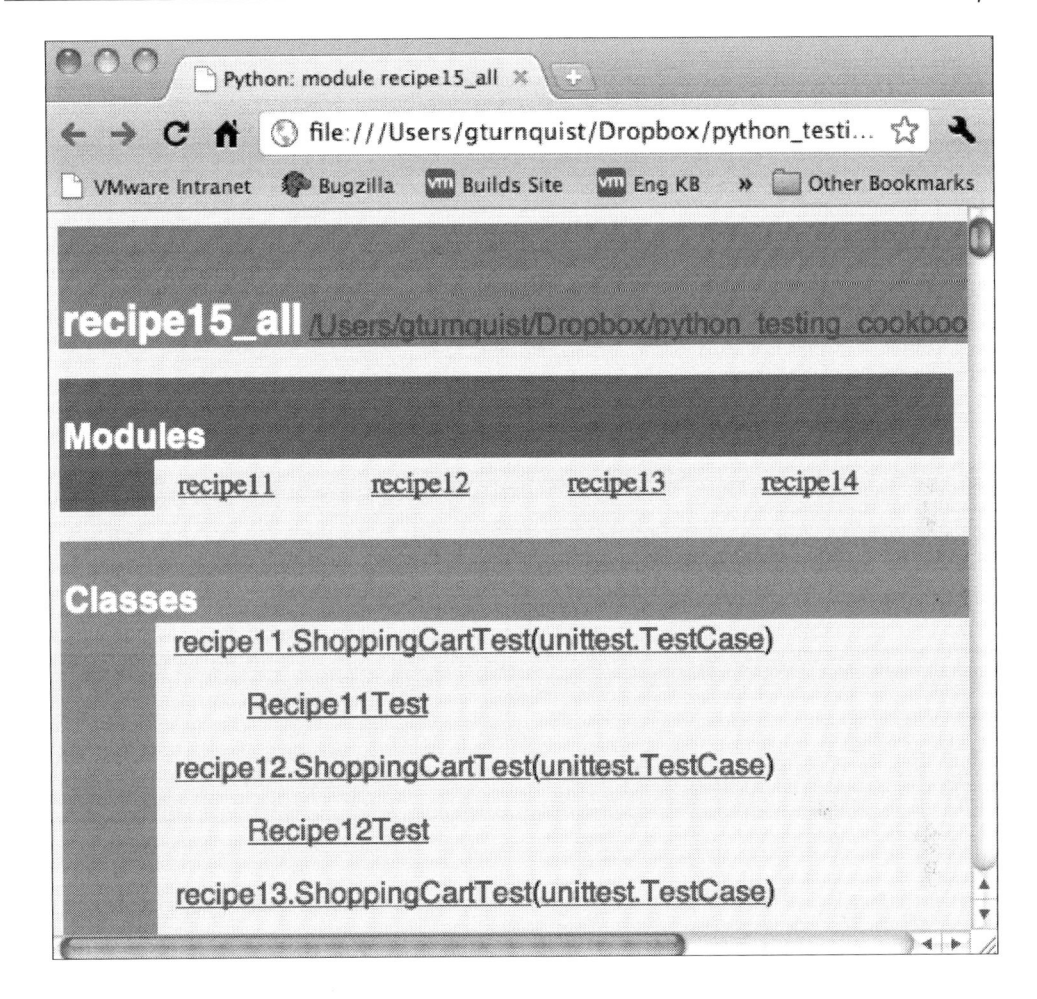

13. Create a new file named `recipe15_all.py` to define another new test suite.

14. Reuse the test code from the earlier recipes of this chapter to define an `all` test suite.

    ```
    import recipe11
    import recipe12
    import recipe13
    import recipe14
    class Recipe11Test(recipe11.ShoppingCartTest):
        pass
    class Recipe12Test(recipe12.ShoppingCartTest):
        pass
    class Recipe13Test(recipe13.ShoppingCartTest):
    ```

71

```
        pass
    class Recipe14Test(recipe14.ShoppingCartTest):
        pass
```

15. Run the `recipe15.py` script with `-suite=recipe15_all`.

```
(ptc)gturnquist-mbp:02 gturnquist$ python recipe15.py --suite=recipe15_all
Running test suite recipe15_all...
test_item (recipe15_all.Recipe11Test) ... ok
test_length (recipe15_all.Recipe11Test) ... ok
test_price (recipe15_all.Recipe11Test) ... ok
test_total_with_sales_tax (recipe15_all.Recipe11Test) ... ok
test_item (recipe15_all.Recipe12Test) ... ok
test_length (recipe15_all.Recipe12Test) ... ok
test_price (recipe15_all.Recipe12Test) ... ok
test_total_with_sales_tax (recipe15_all.Recipe12Test) ... ok
test_item (recipe15_all.Recipe13Test) ... ok
test_price (recipe15_all.Recipe13Test) ... ok
test_total_with_sales_tax (recipe15_all.Recipe13Test) ... ok
test_assert_failure (recipe15_all.Recipe14Test) ... FAIL
test_item (recipe15_all.Recipe14Test) ... ok
test_length (recipe15_all.Recipe14Test) ... ok
test_price (recipe15_all.Recipe14Test) ... ok
test_total_with_sales_tax (recipe15_all.Recipe14Test) ... ok

======================================================================
FAIL: test_assert_failure (recipe15_all.Recipe14Test)
----------------------------------------------------------------------
Traceback (most recent call last):
  File "/Users/gturnquist/Dropbox/python_testing_cookbook/code/02/recipe14
.py", line 47, in test_assert_failure
    self.fail("You should see this failure message in the report.")
AssertionError: You should see this failure message in the report.

----------------------------------------------------------------------
Ran 16 tests in 0.004s

FAILED (failures=1)
(ptc)gturnquist-mbp:02 gturnquist$
```

How it works...

This script uses Python's `getopt` library, which is modeled after the C programming language's `getopt()` function. This means we use the API to define a set of commands, and then we iterate over the options, calling corresponding functions.

> Visit `http://docs.python.org/library/getopt.html` for more details on the `getopt` library.

- `usage`: This is a function to provide help to the user.
- `key`: The option definitions are included in the following block:

    ```
    optlist, args = getopt.getopt(sys.argv[1:],
            "ht",
            ["help", "test", "suite=", \
            "debug-level=", "package", \
            "publish", "register", "pydoc"])
    ```

    - We parse everything in the arguments except the first, being the executable itself.
    - `"ht"` defined the short options: `-h` and `-t`.
    - The list defines long options. Those with `"="` accept an argument. Those without are flags.
    - If an option is received that isn't in the list, an exception is thrown, we print out `usage()`, and then exit.

- `test`: This activates loggers, which can be very useful if our app uses Python's `logging` library.
- `package`: This generates tarballs. We created a stub, but it can be handy to provide a shortcut by running `setup.py sdist|bdist`.
- `publish`: Its function is to push tarballs to the deployment site. We created a stub, but deploying it to an S3 site or somewhere else is useful.
- `register`: This registers the module with PyPI. We created a stub, but it would be handy to provide a shortcut to running `setup.py register`.
- `create_pydocs`: They are the auto-generated docs. Generating HTML files based on code is very convenient.

With each of these functions defined, we can iterate over the options that were parsed. For this script, there is a sequence as follows:

1. Check if there is a debugging override. We default to `logging.INFO`, but provide the ability to switch to `logging.DEBUG`.
2. Check if `-h` or `-help` was called. If so, print out the `usage()` information and then exit with no more parsing.
3. Finally, iterate over the options, and call their corresponding functions.

To exercise things, we first called this script with the `-help` option. That printed out the command choices we had.

Then we called it with all the options to demonstrate the features. The script is coded to exercise a `check in` suite when we use `-test`. This is a short test suite, which simulates running a quicker test meant to tell if things look alright.

Finally, we called the script with `-suite=recipe15_all`. This test suite simulates running a more complete test suite that typically takes longer.

There's more

The features which this script provides could easily be handled by commands that are already built. We looked at `nosetests` earlier in this chapter and saw how it can flexibly take arguments to pick tests.

Using `setup.py` to generate tarballs and register releases is also a commonly used feature in the Python community.

So why write this script? Because we can tap into all of these features with a single command script, as `setup.py` contains a prebuilt set of commands that involve bundling and uploading to the Python Project Index. Doing other tasks like generating **pydocs**, deploying to another location like an Amazon S3 bucket, or any other system level task is not included. This script demonstrates how easy it is to wire in other command-line options and link them with the project management functions.

We can also conveniently embed the usage of `pydoc`. Basically, any Python library that serves project management needs can be embedded as well.

> On an existing project, I developed a script to provide a unified way to embed version info into a templated `setup.py` as well as documentation generated by `pydoc`, `sphinx`, and `DocBook`. The script saved me from having to remember all the commands needed to manage the project.
>
> Why didn't I extend `distutils` to create my own commands? It was personally a matter of taste. I preferred using `getopt` and working outside the framework of `distutils` instead of creating and registering new subcommands.

Why use getopt instead of optparse?

Python has several options to handle command-line option parsing. `getopt` is possibly the simplest. It is meant to quickly allow defining short and long options, but it has limits. It requires custom coding help output, as we did with the usage function.

It also requires custom handling of the arguments. `optparse` provides more sophisticated options, such as better handling of arguments and auto-built help. But it also requires more code to get functional. `optparse` is also targeted to be replaced by `argparse` in the future.

It is left as an exercise for you to write an alternative version of this script using `optparse` to assess which one is a better solution.

3
Creating Testable Documentation with doctest

In this chapter, we will cover:

- Documenting the basics
- Catching stack traces
- Running doctests from the command line
- Coding a test harness for doctest
- Filtering out test noise
- Printing out all your documentation including a status report
- Testing the edges
- Testing corner cases by iteration
- Getting nosy with doctest
- Updating the project-level script to run this chapter's doctests

Introduction

Python provides the useful ability to embed comments inside functions that are accessible from a Python shell. These are known as **docstrings**.

A docstring provides the ability to embed not only information, but also code samples that are runnable.

Creating Testable Documentation with doctest

There is an old adage that *comments aren't code*. Comments don't undergo syntax checks and are often not maintained, thus the information they carry can lose its value over time. `doctest` counters this by turning comments into code which can serve many useful purposes.

In this chapter, we will explore different ways to use `doctest` to develop testing, documentation, and project support. No special setup is required, as `doctest` is part of Python's standard libraries.

Documenting the basics

Python provides out-of-the-box capability to put comments in code known as docstrings. Docstrings can be read when looking at the source and also when inspecting the code interactively from a Python shell. In this recipe, we will demonstrate how these interactive docstrings can be used as runnable tests.

What does this provide? It offers easy-to-read code samples for the users. Not only are the code samples readable, they are also runnable, meaning we can ensure the documentation stays up to date.

How to do it...

With the following steps, we will create an application combined with runnable docstring comments, and see how to execute these tests:

1. Create a new file named `recipe16.py` to contain all the code we write for this recipe.

2. Create a function that converts base-10 numbers to any other base using recursion.

```python
def convert_to_basen(value, base):
    import math
    def _convert(remaining_value, base, exp):
        def stringify(value):
            if value > 9:
                return chr(value + ord('a')-10)
            else:
                return str(value)
        if remaining_value >= 0 and exp >= 0:
            factor = int(math.pow(base, exp))
            if factor <= remaining_value:
                multiple = remaining_value / factor
                return stringify(multiple) + \
                    _convert(remaining_value-multiple*factor, \
                             base, exp-1)
```

```
            else:
                return "0" + \
                    _convert(remaining_value, base, exp-1)
        else:
            return ""
    return "%s/%s" % (_convert(value, base, \
                        int(math.log(value, base))), base)
```

3. Add a docstring just below the external function, as shown in the highlighted section of the following code. This docstring declaration includes several examples of using the function.

```
def convert_to_basen(value, base):
    """Convert a base10 number to basen.edur
    >>> convert_to_basen(1, 2)
    '1/2'
    >>> convert_to_basen(2, 2)
    '10/2'
    >>> convert_to_basen(3, 2)
    '11/2'
    >>> convert_to_basen(4, 2)
    '100/2'
    >>> convert_to_basen(5, 2)
    '101/2'
    >>> convert_to_basen(6, 2)
    '110/2'
    >>> convert_to_basen(7, 2)
    '111/2'
    >>> convert_to_basen(1, 16)
    '1/16'
    >>> convert_to_basen(10, 16)
    'a/16'
    >>> convert_to_basen(15, 16)
    'f/16'
    >>> convert_to_basen(16, 16)
    '10/16'
    >>> convert_to_basen(31, 16)
    '1f/16'
    >>> convert_to_basen(32, 16)
    '20/16'
    """
    import math
```

Creating Testable Documentation with doctest

4. Add a test runner block that invokes Python's `doctest` module.

   ```
   if __name__ == "__main__":
       import doctest
       doctest.testmod()
   ```

5. From an interactive Python shell, import the recipe and view its documentation.

   ```
   (ptc)gturnquist-mbp:03 gturnquist$ python
   Python 2.6.1 (r261:67515, Feb 11 2010, 00:51:29)
   [GCC 4.2.1 (Apple Inc. build 5646)] on darwin
   Type "help", "copyright", "credits" or "license" for more information.
   >>> import recipe16
   >>> print recipe16.convert_to_basen.__doc__
   Convert a base10 number to basen.

       >>> convert_to_basen(1, 2)
       '1/2'
       >>> convert_to_basen(2, 2)
       '10/2'
       >>> convert_to_basen(3, 2)
       '11/2'
       >>> convert_to_basen(4, 2)
       '100/2'
       >>> convert_to_basen(5, 2)
       '101/2'
       >>> convert_to_basen(6, 2)
       '110/2'
       >>> convert_to_basen(7, 2)
       '111/2'
       >>> convert_to_basen(1, 16)
       '1/16'
       >>> convert_to_basen(10, 16)
       'a/16'
       >>> convert_to_basen(15, 16)
       'f/16'
       >>> convert_to_basen(16, 16)
       '10/16'
       >>> convert_to_basen(31, 16)
       '1f/16'
       >>> convert_to_basen(32, 16)
       '20/16'
   >>>
   ```

6. Run the code from the command line. In the next screenshot, notice how nothing is printed. This is what happens when all the tests pass.

Chapter 3

[Terminal screenshot showing:
```
(ptc)gturnquist-mbp:03 gturnquist$ python recipe16.py
(ptc)gturnquist-mbp:03 gturnquist$
```
]

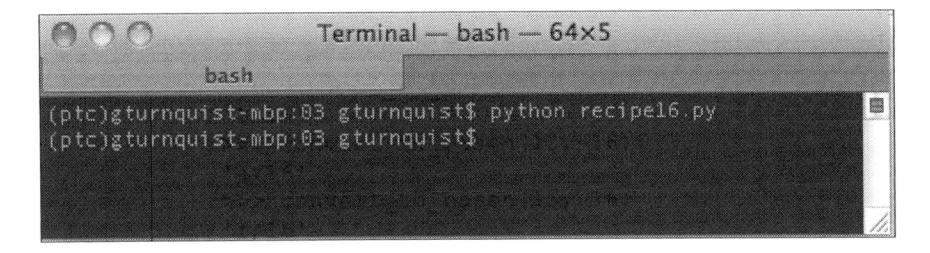

7. Run the code from the command line with `-v` to increase verbosity. In the following screenshot, we see a piece of the output, showing what was run and what was expected. This can be useful when debugging `doctest`.

[Terminal screenshot showing:
```
        convert_to_basen(31, 16)
Expecting:
    '1f/16'
ok
Trying:
    convert_to_basen(32, 16)
Expecting:
    '20/16'
ok
1 items had no tests:
    __main__
1 items passed all tests:
   13 tests in __main__.convert_to_basen
13 tests in 2 items.
13 passed and 0 failed.
Test passed.
(ptc)gturnquist-mbp:03 gturnquist$
```
]

How it works...

The `doctest` module looks for blocks of Python inside `docstrings` and runs it like real code. `>>>` is the same prompt we see when we use the interactive Python shell. The following line shows the expected output. `doctest` runs the statements it sees and then compares the actual with the expected output.

Later in this chapter, we will see how to catch things like stack traces, errors, and also add extra code that equates to a test fixture.

Creating Testable Documentation with doctest

There's more...

`doctest` is very picky when matching expected output with actual results.

- An extraneous space or tab can cause things to break.
- Structures like dictionaries are tricky to test, because Python doesn't guarantee the order of items. On each test run, the items could be stored in a different order. Simply printing out a dictionary is bound to break it.
- It is strongly advised not to include object references in expected outputs. These values also vary every time the test is run.

Catching stack traces

It's a common fallacy to write tests only for successful code paths. We also need to code against error conditions including the ones that generate stack traces. With this recipe, we will explore how stack traces are pattern-matched in doc testing that allows us to confirm expected errors.

How to do it...

With the following steps, we will see how to use `doctest` to verify error conditions:

1. Create a new file called `recipe17.py` to write all our code for this recipe.

2. Create a function that converts base 10 numbers to any other base using recursion.

   ```
   def convert_to_basen(value, base):
       import math
       def _convert(remaining_value, base, exp):
           def stringify(value):
               if value > 9:
                   return chr(value + ord('a')-10)
               else:
                   return str(value)
           if remaining_value >= 0 and exp >= 0:
               factor = int(math.pow(base, exp))
               if factor <= remaining_value:
                   multiple = remaining_value / factor
                   return stringify(multiple) + \
                       _convert(remaining_value-multiple*factor, \
                                base, exp-1)
               else:
                   return "0" + \
   ```

```
                        _convert(remaining_value, base, exp-1)
        else:
            return ""
    return "%s/%s" % (_convert(value, base, \
                    int(math.log(value, base))), base)
```

3. Add a `docstring` just below the external function declaration that includes two examples that are expected to generate stack traces.

    ```
    def convert_to_basen(value, base):
        """Convert a base10 number to basen.
        >>> convert_to_basen(0, 2)
        Traceback (most recent call last):
            ...
        ValueError: math domain error
        >>> convert_to_basen(-1, 2)
        Traceback (most recent call last):
            ...
        ValueError: math domain error
        """
        import math
    ```

4. Add a test runner block that invokes Python's `doctest` module.

    ```
    if __name__ == "__main__":
        import doctest
        doctest.testmod()
    ```

5. Run the code from the command line. In the following screenshot, notice how nothing is printed. This is what happens when all the tests pass.

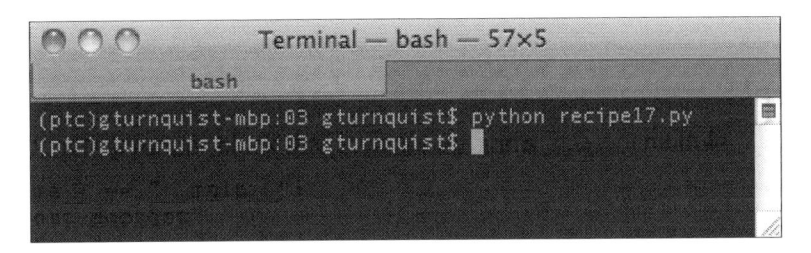

Creating Testable Documentation with doctest

6. Run the code from the command line with `-v` to increase verbosity. In the next screenshot, we can see that 0 and -1 generate math domain errors. This is due to using `math.log` to find the starting exponent.

```
(ptc)gturnquist-mbp:03 gturnquist$ python recipe17.py -v
Trying:
    convert_to_basen(0, 2)
Expecting:
    Traceback (most recent call last):
    ...
    ValueError: math domain error
ok
Trying:
    convert_to_basen(-1, 2)
Expecting:
    Traceback (most recent call last):
    ...
    ValueError: math domain error
ok
1 items had no tests:
    __main__
1 items passed all tests:
    2 tests in __main__.convert_to_basen
2 tests in 2 items.
2 passed and 0 failed.
Test passed.
(ptc)gturnquist-mbp:03 gturnquist$
```

How it works...

The `doctest` module looks for blocks of Python inside `docstrings` and runs it like real code. `>>>` is the same prompt we see when we use the interactive Python shell. The following line shows the expected output. `doctest` runs the statements it sees and then compares the actual output with the expected output.

With regard to stack traces, there is a lot of detailed information provided in the stack trace. Pattern matching the entire trace is ineffective. By using the ellipsis, we are able to skip the intermediate parts of the stack trace and just match on the distinguishing part: `ValueError: math domain error`.

This is valuable, because our users can see not only the way it handles good values, but will also observe what errors to expect when bad values are provided.

Chapter 3

Running doctests from the command line

We have seen how to develop tests by embedding runnable fragments of code in `docstrings`. But for each of these tests we had to make the module runnable. What if we wanted to run something other than our doctests from the command line? We would have to get rid of the `doctest.testmod()` statements!

> The good news is that starting with Python 2.6, there is a command-line option to run a specific module using `doctest` without coding a runner.
>
> Typing: `python -m doctest -v example.py` will import `example.py` and run it through `doctest.testmod()`. According to documentation, this may fail if the module is part of a package and imports other submodules.

How to do it...

In the following steps, we will create a simple application. We will add some doctests and then run them from the command line without writing a special test runner.

1. Create a new file called `recipe18.py` to store the code written for this recipe.

2. Create a function that converts base 10 numbers to any other base using recursion.

```python
def convert_to_basen(value, base):
    import math
    def _convert(remaining_value, base, exp):
        def stringify(value):
            if value > 9:
                return chr(value + ord('a')-10)
            else:
                return str(value)
        if remaining_value >= 0 and exp >= 0:
            factor = int(math.pow(base, exp))
            if factor <= remaining_value:
                multiple = remaining_value / factor
                return stringify(multiple) + \
                   _convert(remaining_value-multiple*factor, \
                            base, exp-1)
            else:
                return "0" + \
                    _convert(remaining_value, base, exp-1)
        else:
            return ""
```

Creating Testable Documentation with doctest

```
        return "%s/%s" % (_convert(value, base, \
                       int(math.log(value, base))), base)
```

3. Add a `docstring` just below the external function declaration that includes some of the tests.

```
def convert_to_basen(value, base):
    """Convert a base10 number to basen.
    >>> convert_to_basen(10, 2)
    '1010/2'
    >>> convert_to_basen(15, 16)
    'f/16'
    >>> convert_to_basen(0, 2)
    Traceback (most recent call last):
        ...
    ValueError: math domain error
    >>> convert_to_basen(-1, 2)
    Traceback (most recent call last):
        ...
    ValueError: math domain error
    """
    import math
```

4. Run the code from the command line using `-m doctest`. As shown in the following screenshot, no output indicates that all the tests have passed.

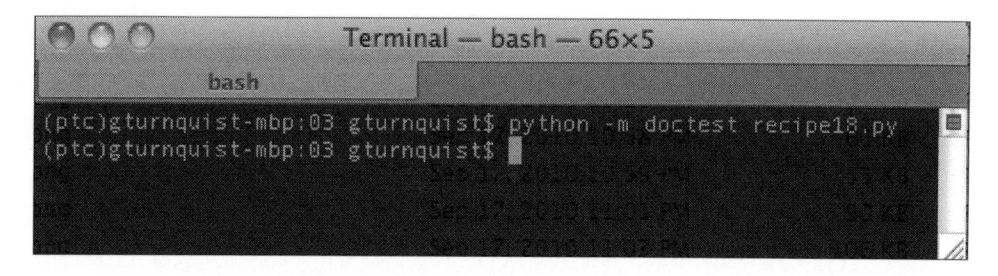

```
(ptc)gturnquist-mbp:03 gturnquist$ python -m doctest recipe18.py
(ptc)gturnquist-mbp:03 gturnquist$
```

5. Run the code from the command line with `-v` to increase verbosity. What happens if we forget to include `-m doctest`? Using the `-v` option helps us to avoid this by giving us a warm fuzzy that our tests are working.

Chapter 3

```
(ptc)gturnquist-mbp:03 gturnquist$ python -m doctest recipe18.py -v
Trying:
    convert_to_basen(10, 2)
Expecting:
    '1010/2'
ok
Trying:
    convert_to_basen(15, 16)
Expecting:
    'f/16'
ok
Trying:
    convert_to_basen(0, 2)
Expecting:
    Traceback (most recent call last):
    ...
    ValueError: math domain error
ok
Trying:
    convert_to_basen(-1, 2)
Expecting:
    Traceback (most recent call last):
    ...
    ValueError: math domain error
ok
1 items had no tests:
    recipe18
1 items passed all tests:
    4 tests in recipe18.convert_to_basen
4 tests in 2 items.
4 passed and 0 failed.
Test passed.
(ptc)gturnquist-mbp:03 gturnquist$
```

How it works...

In the previous chapters, we were using the __main__ block of a module to run other test suites. What if we wanted to do the same here? We would have to pick whether __main__ would be for unittest tests, doctests, or both! What if we didn't even want to run testing through __main__, but instead run our application?

That is why Python added the option of invoking testing right from the command line using `-m doctest`.

Creating Testable Documentation with doctest

> Don't you want to *know* for sure if your tests are running or, whether they are working? Is the test suite really doing what it promised? With other tools, we usually have to embed print statements, or deliberate failures, just to know things are being trapped properly. Doesn't doctest's -v option provide a convenient quick glance at what's happening?

Coding a test harness for doctest

The tests we have written so far are very simple, because the function we are testing is simple. There are two inputs and one output with no side effects. No objects have to be created. This isn't the most common use case for us. Often, we have objects that interact with other objects.

The doctest module supports creating objects, invoking methods, and checking results. With this recipe, we will explore this in more detail.

An important aspect of doctest is that it finds individual instances of docstrings, and runs them in a local context. Variables declared in one docstring cannot be used in another docstring.

How to do it...

1. Create a new file called recipe19.py to contain the code from this recipe.

2. Write a simple shopping cart application.

```python
class ShoppingCart(object):
    def __init__(self):
        self.items = []
    def add(self, item, price):
        self.items.append(Item(item, price))
        return self
    def item(self, index):
        return self.items[index-1].item
    def price(self, index):
        return self.items[index-1].price
    def total(self, sales_tax):
        sum_price = sum([item.price for item in self.items])
        return sum_price*(1.0 + sales_tax/100.0)
    def __len__(self):
        return len(self.items)
```

```
class Item(object):
    def __init__(self, item, price):
        self.item = item
        self.price = price
```

3. Insert a docstring at the top of the module, before the `ShoppingCart` class declaration.

```
"""
This is documentation for the this entire recipe.
With it, we can demonstrate usage of the code.

>>> cart = ShoppingCart().add("tuna sandwich", 15.0)
>>> len(cart)
1
>>> cart.item(1)
'tuna sandwich'
>>> cart.price(1)
15.0
>>> print round(cart.total(9.25), 2)
16.39
"""
class ShoppingCart(object):
    ...
```

Creating Testable Documentation with doctest

4. Run the recipe using `-m doctest` and `-v` for verbosity.

```
(ptc)gturnquist-mbp:03 gturnquist$ python -m doctest recipe19.py -v
Trying:
    cart = ShoppingCart().add("tuna sandwich", 15.0)
Expecting nothing
ok
Trying:
    len(cart)
Expecting:
    1
ok
Trying:
    cart.item(1)
Expecting:
    'tuna sandwich'
ok
Trying:
    cart.price(1)
Expecting:
    15.0
ok
Trying:
    print round(cart.total(9.25), 2)
Expecting:
    16.39
ok
9 items had no tests:
    recipe19.Item
    recipe19.Item.__init__
    recipe19.ShoppingCart
    recipe19.ShoppingCart.__init__
    recipe19.ShoppingCart.__len__
    recipe19.ShoppingCart.add
    recipe19.ShoppingCart.item
    recipe19.ShoppingCart.price
    recipe19.ShoppingCart.total
1 items passed all tests:
   5 tests in recipe19
5 tests in 10 items.
5 passed and 0 failed.
Test passed.
(ptc)gturnquist-mbp:03 gturnquist$
```

5. Copy all the code we just wrote from `recipe19.py` into a new file called `recipe19b.py`.

6. Inside `recipe19b.py` add another docstring to `item`, which attempts to re-use the `cart` variable defined at the top of the module.

```
def item(self, index):
    """
    >>> cart.item(1)
    'tuna sandwich'
```

```
    """
    return self.items[index-1].item
```

7. Run this variant of the recipe. Why does it fail? Wasn't `cart` declared in the earlier docstring?

```
(ptc)gturnquist-mbp:03 gturnquist$ python -m doctest recipe19b.py
**********************************************************************
File "recipe19b.py", line 26, in recipe19b.ShoppingCart.item
Failed example:
    cart.item(1)
Exception raised:
    Traceback (most recent call last):
      File "/System/Library/Frameworks/Python.framework/Versions/2.6/lib/python2.6/doctest.py", line 1231, in __run
        compileflags, 1) in test.globs
      File "<doctest recipe19b.ShoppingCart.item[0]>", line 1, in <module>
        cart.item(1)
    NameError: name 'cart' is not defined
**********************************************************************
1 items had failures:
   1 of   1 in recipe19b.ShoppingCart.item
***Test Failed*** 1 failures.
(ptc)gturnquist-mbp:03 gturnquist$
```

How it works...

The `doctest` module looks for every `docstring`. For each `docstring` it finds, it creates a shallow copy of the module's global variables and then runs the code and checks results. Apart from that, every variable created is locally scoped and then cleaned up when the test is complete. This means that our second `docstring` that was added later cannot see the `cart` that was created in our first `docstring`. That is why the second run failed.

There is no equivalent to a `setUp` method as we used with some of the unittest recipes. If there is no `setUp` option with `doctest`, then what value is this recipe? It highlights a key limitation of doctest that all developers must understand before using it.

There's more...

The `doctest` module provides an incredibly convenient way to add testability to our documentation. But this is not a substitute for a full-fledged testing framework, like unittest. As noted earlier, there is no equivalent to a `setUp`. There is also no syntax checking of the Python code embedded in the `docstrings`.

Creating Testable Documentation with doctest

Mixing the right level of `doctests` with unittest (or other testing framework we pick) is a matter of judgment.

Filtering out test noise

Various options help `doctest` ignore noise, such as whitespace, in test cases. This can be useful, because it allows us to structure the expected outcome in a better way, to ease reading for the users.

We can also flag some tests that can be skipped. This can be used where we want to document known issues, but haven't yet patched the system.

Both of these situations can easily be construed as noise, when we are trying to run comprehensive testing, but are focused on other parts of the system. In this recipe, we will dig in to ease the strict checking done by `doctest`. We will also look at how to ignore entire tests, whether it's on a temporary or permanent basis.

How to do it...

With the following steps, we will experiment with filtering out test results and easing certain restrictions of `doctest`.

1. Create a new file called `recipe20.py` to contain the code from this recipe.

2. Create a recursive function that converts base10 numbers into other bases.

```
def convert_to_basen(value, base):
    import math

    def _convert(remaining_value, base, exp):
        def stringify(value):
            if value > 9:
                return chr(value + ord('a')-10)
            else:
                return str(value)

        if remaining_value >= 0 and exp >= 0:
            factor = int(math.pow(base, exp))
            if factor <= remaining_value:
                multiple = remaining_value / factor
                return stringify(multiple) + \
                    _convert(remaining_value-multiple*factor, \
                             base, exp-1)
            else:
                return "0" + \
                    _convert(remaining_value, base, exp-1)
```

```
        else:
            return ""
    return "%s/%s" % (_convert(value, base, \
                    int(math.log(value, base))), base)
```

3. Add a docstring that includes a test to exercise a range of values as well as documenting a future feature that is not yet implemented.

```
def convert_to_basen(value, base):
    """Convert a base10 number to basen.

    >>> [convert_to_basen(i, 16) for i in range(1,16)] #doctest: +NORMALIZE_WHITESPACE
    ['1/16', '2/16', '3/16', '4/16', '5/16', '6/16', '7/16', '8/16',
    '9/16', 'a/16', 'b/16', 'c/16', 'd/16', 'e/16', 'f/16']

    FUTURE: Binary may support 2's complement in the future, but not now.
    >>> convert_to_basen(-10, 2) #doctest: +SKIP
    '0110/2'
    """
    import math
```

4. Add a test runner.

```
if __name__ == "__main__":
    import doctest
    doctest.testmod()
```

5. Run the test case in verbose mode.

6. Copy the code from `recipe20.py` into a new file called `recipe20b.py`.

7. Edit `recipe20b.py` by updating the docstring to include another test exposing that our function doesn't convert 0.

```
def convert_to_basen(value, base):
    """Convert a base10 number to basen.

    >>> [convert_to_basen(i, 16) for i in range(1,16)] #doctest: +NORMALIZE_WHITESPACE
    ['1/16', '2/16', '3/16', '4/16', '5/16', '6/16', '7/16', '8/16',
     '9/16', 'a/16', 'b/16', 'c/16', 'd/16', 'e/16', 'f/16']

    FUTURE: Binary may support 2's complement in the future, but not now.
    >>> convert_to_basen(-10, 2) #doctest: +SKIP
    '0110/2'

    BUG: Discovered that this algorithm doesn't handle 0. Need to patch it.
    TODO: Renable this when patched.
    >>> convert_to_basen(0, 2)
    '0/2'
    """
    import math
```

8. Run the test case. Notice what is different about this version of the recipe; and why does it fail?

```
(ptc)gturnquist-mbp:03 gturnquist$ python recipe20b.py
**********************************************************************
File "recipe20b.py", line 14, in __main__.convert_to_basen
Failed example:
    convert_to_basen(0, 2)
Exception raised:
    Traceback (most recent call last):
      File "/System/Library/Frameworks/Python.framework/Versions/2.6/lib/python2.6/doctest.py", line 1231, in __run
        compileflags, 1) in test.globs
      File "<doctest __main__.convert_to_basen[2]>", line 1, in <module>
        convert_to_basen(0, 2)
      File "recipe20b.py", line 41, in convert_to_basen
        int(math.log(value, base))), base)
    ValueError: math domain error
**********************************************************************
1 items had failures:
   1 of   2 in __main__.convert_to_basen
***Test Failed*** 1 failures.
(ptc)gturnquist-mbp:03 gturnquist$
```

9. Copy the code from `recipe20b.py` into a new file called `recipe20c.py`.

10. Edit `recipe20c.py` and update the docstring indicating that we will skip the test for now.

    ```
    def convert_to_basen(value, base):
        """Convert a base10 number to basen.

        >>> [convert_to_basen(i, 16) for i in range(1,16)] #doctest: +NORMALIZE_WHITESPACE
        ['1/16', '2/16', '3/16', '4/16', '5/16', '6/16', '7/16', '8/16',
         '9/16',  'a/16', 'b/16', 'c/16', 'd/16', 'e/16', 'f/16']

        FUTURE: Binary may support 2's complement in the future, but not now.
        >>> convert_to_basen(-10, 2) #doctest: +SKIP
        '0110/2'

        BUG: Discovered that this algorithm doesn't handle 0. Need to patch it.
        TODO: Renable this when patched.
        >>> convert_to_basen(0, 2) #doctest: +SKIP
        '0/2'
        """
        import math
    ```

11. Run the test case.

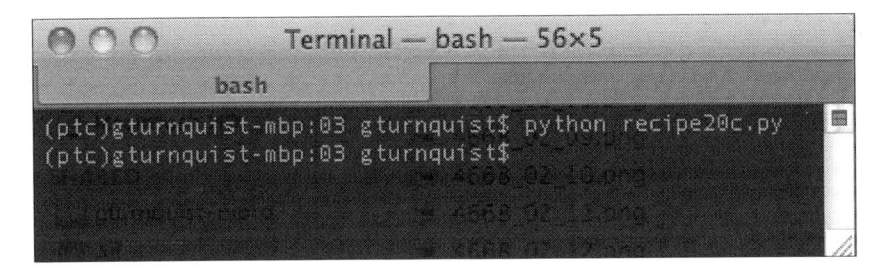

How it works...

In this recipe, we revisit the function for converting from base-10 to any base numbers. The first test shows it being run over a range. Normally, Python would fit this array of results on one line. To make it more readable, we spread the output across two lines. We also put some arbitrary spaces between the values to make the columns line up better.

Creating Testable Documentation with doctest

This is something that `doctest` definitely would *not* support, due to its strict pattern matching nature. By using `#doctest: +NORMALIZE_WHITESPACE`, we are able to ask `doctest` to ease this restriction. There are still constraints. For example, the first value in the expected array cannot have any whitespace in front of it. (*Believe me, I tried for maximum readability!*) But wrapping the array to the next line no longer breaks the test.

We also have a test case that is really meant as documentation only. It indicates a future requirement that shows how our function would handle negative binary values. By adding `#doctest: +SKIP`, we are able to command `doctest` to skip this particular instance.

Finally, we see the scenario where we discover that our code doesn't handle 0. As the algorithm gets the highest exponent by taking a logarithm, there is a math problem. We capture this edge case with a test. We then confirm that the code fails in classic **test driven design** (**TDD**) fashion. The final step would be to fix the code to handle this edge case. But we decide, in a somewhat contrived fashion, that we don't have enough time in the current sprint to fix the code. To avoid breaking our **continuous integration** (**CI**) server, we mark the test with a `TO-DO` statement and add `#doctest: +SKIP`.

There's more...

Both the situations that we have marked up with `#doctest: +SKIP`, are cases where eventually we will want to remove the `SKIP` tag and have them run. There may be other situations where we will never remove `SKIP`. Demonstrations of code that have big fluctuations may not be readily testable without making them unreadable. For example, functions that return dictionaries are harder to test, because the order of results varies. We can bend it to pass a test, but we may lose the value of documentation to make it presentable to the reader.

Printing out all your documentation including a status report

Since this chapter has been about both documentation and testing, let's build a script that takes a set of modules and prints out a complete report, showing all documentation as well as running any given tests.

This is a valuable recipe, because it shows us how to use Python's APIs to harvest a code-driven runnable report. This means the documentation is accurate and up to date, reflecting the current state of our code.

How to do it...

In the following steps, we will write an application and some doctests. Then we will build a script to harvest a useful report.

Chapter 3

1. Create a new file called `recipe21_report.py` to contain the script that harvests our report.

2. Start creating a script by importing Python's `inspect` library as the basis for drilling down into a module `from inspect import*`

3. Add a function that focuses on either printing out an item's __doc__ string or prints out **no documentation found**.

   ```
   def print_doc(name, item):
       if item.__doc__:
           print "Documentation for %s" % name
           print "-------------------------------"
           print item.__doc__
           print "-------------------------------"
       else:
           print "Documentation for %s - None" % name
   ```

4. Add a function that prints out the documentation based on a given module. Make sure this function looks for classes, methods, and functions, and prints out their docs.

   ```
   def print_docstrings(m, prefix=""):
       print_doc(prefix + "module %s" % m.__name__, m)
       for (name, value) in getmembers(m, isclass):
           if name == '__class__': continue
           print_docstrings(value, prefix=name + ".")
       for (name, value) in getmembers(m, ismethod):
           print_doc("%s%s()" % (prefix, name), value)
       for (name, value) in getmembers(m, isfunction):
           print_doc("%s%s()" % (prefix, name), value)
   ```

5. Add a runner that parses the command-line string, and iterates over each provided module.

   ```
   if __name__ == "__main__":
       import sys
       import doctest

       for arg in sys.argv[1:]:
           if arg.startswith("-"): continue
           print "================================"
           print "== Processing module %s" % arg
           print "================================"
           m = __import__(arg)
           print_docstrings(m)
           print "Running doctests for %s" % arg
   ```

Creating Testable Documentation with doctest

```
        print "----------------------------------"
        doctest.testmod(m)
```

5. Create a new file called `recipe21.py` to contain an application with tests that we will run the earlier script against.

6. In `recipe21.py`, create a shopping cart app and fill it with `docstrings` and doctests.

```
""" This is documentation for the entire recipe.
With it, we can demonstrate usage of the code.
>>> cart = ShoppingCart().add("tuna sandwich", 15.0)
>>> len(cart)
1
>>> cart.item(1)
'tuna sandwich'
>>> cart.price(1)
15.0
>>> print round(cart.total(9.25), 2)
16.39
"""

class ShoppingCart(object):
    """
    This object is used to store the goods.
    It conveniently calculates total cost including
    tax.
    """
    def __init__(self):
        self.items = []

    def add(self, item, price):
        "Add an item to the internal list."
        self.items.append(Item(item, price))
        return self

    def item(self, index):
        "Look up the item. The cart is a 1-based index."
        return self.items[index-1].item

    def price(self, index):
        "Look up the price. The cart is a 1-based index."
        return self.items[index-1].price

    def total(self, sales_tax):
        "Add up all costs, and then apply a sales tax."
        sum_price = sum([item.price for item in self.items])
        return sum_price*(1.0 + sales_tax/100.0)
```

```
        def __len__(self):
            "Support len(cart) operation."
            return len(self.items)
    class Item(object):
        def __init__(self, item, price):
            self.item = item
            self.price = price
```

7. Run the report script against this module using -v, and look at the screen's output.

```
================================
== Processing module recipe21
================================
Documentation for module recipe21
--------------------------------

This is documentation for the this entire recipe.
With it, we can demonstrate usage of the code.

>>> cart = ShoppingCart().add("tuna sandwich", 15.0)
>>> len(cart)
1
>>> cart.item(1)
'tuna sandwich'
>>> cart.price(1)
15.0
>>> print round(cart.total(9.25), 2)
16.39

--------------------------------
Documentation for Item.module Item - None
Documentation for Item.__init__() - None
Documentation for ShoppingCart.module ShoppingCart
--------------------------------

    This object is used to store the goods.
    It conveniently calculates total cost including
    tax.
...
Running doctests for recipe21
```

Creating Testable Documentation with doctest

```
----------------------------------
Trying:
    cart = ShoppingCart().add("tuna sandwich", 15.0)
Expecting nothing
ok
Trying:
    len(cart)
Expecting:
    1
ok
5 tests in 10 items.
5 passed and 0 failed.
Test passed.
```

How it works...

This script is tiny, yet harvests a lot of useful information.

By using Python's standard `inspect` module, we are able to drill down starting at the module level. The reflective way to look up a docstring is by accessing the `__doc__` property of an object. This is contained in modules, classes, methods, and functions. They exist in other places, but we limited our focus for this recipe.

We ran it in verbose mode, to show that the tests were actually executed. We hand parsed the command-line options, but `doctest` automatically looks for `-v` to decide whether or not to turn on verbose output. To prevent our module processor from catching this and trying to process it as another module, we added a line to skip any `-xyz` style flags.

```
if arg.startswith("-"): continue
```

There's more...

We could spend more time enhancing this script. For example, we could dump this out with an HTML markup, making it viewable in a web browser. We could also find third party libraries to export it in other ways.

We could also work on refining where it looks for `docstrings` and how it handles them. In our case, we just printed them to the screen. A more reusable approach would be to return some type of structure containing all the information. Then the caller can decide whether to print to screen, encode it in HTML, or generate a PDF document.

This isn't necessary, however, because this recipe's focus is on seeing how to mix these powerful out-of-the-box options which Python provides into a quick and useful tool.

Testing the edges

Tests need to exercise the boundaries of our code up to and beyond the range limits. In this recipe, we will dig into defining and testing edges with doctest.

How to do it...

With the following steps, we will see how to write code that tests the edges of our software.

1. Create a new file named `recipe22.py` and use it to store all of our code for this recipe.

2. Create a function that converts base 10 numbers to anything between base 2 and base 36.

```
def convert_to_basen(value, base):
    if base < 2 or base > 36:
        raise Exception("Only support bases 2-36")
    import math
    def _convert(remaining_value, base, exp):
        def stringify(value):
            if value > 9:
                return chr(value + ord('a')-10)
            else:
                return str(value)
        if remaining_value >= 0 and exp >= 0:
            factor = int(math.pow(base, exp))
            if factor <= remaining_value:
                multiple = remaining_value / factor
                return stringify(multiple) + \
                   _convert(remaining_value-multiple*factor, \
                            base, exp-1)
            else:
                return "0" + \
                    _convert(remaining_value, base, exp-1)
        else:
            return ""
    return "%s/%s" % (_convert(value, base, \
                      int(math.log(value, base))), base)
```

Creating Testable Documentation with doctest

3. Add a docstring just below our function declaration that includes tests showing base 2 edges, base 36 edges, and the invalid base 37.

```
def convert_to_basen(value, base):
    """Convert a base10 number to basen.

    These show the edges for base 2.
    >>> convert_to_basen(1, 2)
    '1/2'
    >>> convert_to_basen(2, 2)
    '10/2'
    >>> convert_to_basen(0, 2)
    Traceback (most recent call last):
        ...
    ValueError: math domain error

    These show the edges for base 36.
    >>> convert_to_basen(1, 36)
    '1/36'
    >>> convert_to_basen(35, 36)
    'z/36'
    >>> convert_to_basen(36, 36)
    '10/36'
    >>> convert_to_basen(0, 36)
    Traceback (most recent call last):
        ...
    ValueError: math domain error

    These show the edges for base 37.
    >>> convert_to_basen(1, 37)
    Traceback (most recent call last):
        ...
    Exception: Only support bases 2-36
    >>> convert_to_basen(36, 37)
    Traceback (most recent call last):
        ...
    Exception: Only support bases 2-36
    >>> convert_to_basen(37, 37)
    Traceback (most recent call last):
        ...
    Exception: Only support bases 2-36
    >>> convert_to_basen(0, 37)
    Traceback (most recent call last):
        ...
```

```
            Exception: Only support bases 2-36
            """
            if base < 2 or base > 36:
```

4. Add a test runner.

   ```
   if __name__ == "__main__":
       import doctest
       doctest.testmod()
   ```

5. Run the recipe.

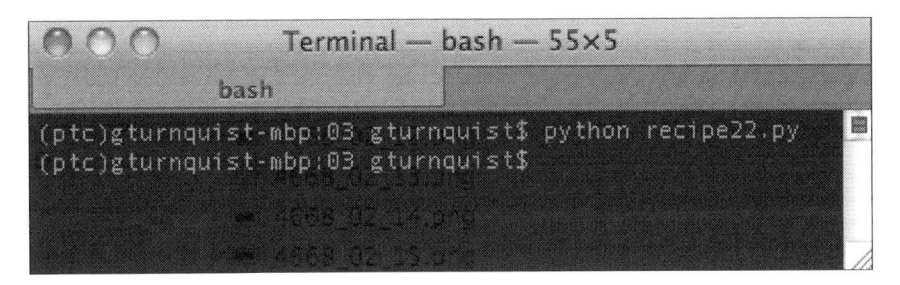

How it works...

This version has a limit of handling base 2 through base 36.

> For base 36, it uses a through z. This compared to base 16 using a through f. 35 in base 10 is represented as z in base 36.

We include several tests, including one for base 2 and base 36. We also test the maximum value before rolling over, and the next value, to show the rollover. For base 2, this is 1 and 2. For base 36, this is 35 and 36.

We have also included tests for 0 to show that our function doesn't handle this for any base. We also test base 37, which is invalid as well.

There's more...

It's important that our software works for valid inputs. It's just as important that our software works as expected for invalid inputs. We have documentation that can be viewed by our users when using our software that documents these edges. And thanks to Python's `doctest` module, we can test it and make sure that our software performs correctly.

See also

Testing the edges section mentioned in *Chapter 1*

Testing corner cases by iteration

Corner cases will appear as we continue to develop our code. By capturing corner cases in an iterable list, there is less code to write and capture another test scenario. This can increase our efficiency at testing new scenarios.

How to do it...

1. Create a new file called `recipe23.py` and use it to store all our code for this recipe.

2. Create a function that converts base 10 to any other base.

```python
def convert_to_basen(value, base):
    import math

    def _convert(remaining_value, base, exp):
        def stringify(value):
            if value > 9:
                return chr(value + ord('a')-10)
            else:
                return str(value)
        if remaining_value >= 0 and exp >= 0:
            factor = int(math.pow(base, exp))
            if factor <= remaining_value:
                multiple = remaining_value / factor
                return stringify(multiple) + \
                    _convert(remaining_value-multiple*factor, \
                            base, exp-1)
            else:
                return "0" + \
                    _convert(remaining_value, base, exp-1)
        else:
            return ""
    return "%s/%s" % (_convert(value, base, \
                    int(math.log(value, base))), base)
```

Chapter 3

3. Add some doc tests that include an array of input values to generate an array of expected outputs. Include one failure.

```
def convert_to_basen(value, base):
    """Convert a base10 number to basen.
    Base 2
    >>> inputs = [(1,2,'1/2'), (2,2,'11/2')]
    >>> for value,base,expected in inputs:
    ...     actual = convert_to_basen(value,base)
    ...     assert actual == expected, 'expected: %s actual: %s' % (expected, actual)
    >>> convert_to_basen(0, 2)
    Traceback (most recent call last):
        ...
    ValueError: math domain error
    Base 36.
    >>> inputs = [(1,36,'1/36'), (35,36,'z/36'), (36,36,'10/36')]
    >>> for value,base,expected in inputs:
    ...     actual = convert_to_basen(value,base)
    ...     assert actual == expected, 'expected: %s actual: %s' % (expected, value)
    >>> convert_to_basen(0, 36)
    Traceback (most recent call last):
        ...
    ValueError: math domain error
    """
    import math
```

4. Add a test runner.

```
if __name__ == "__main__":
    import doctest
    doctest.testmod()
```

5. Run the recipe.

```
(ptc)gturnquist-mbp:03 gturnquist$ python recipe23.py
**********************************************************************
File "recipe23.py", line 6, in __main__.convert_to_basen
Failed example:
    for value,base,expected in inputs:
        actual = convert_to_basen(value,base)
        assert actual == expected, 'expected: %s actual: %s' % (expect
ed, actual)
Exception raised:
    Traceback (most recent call last):
      File "/System/Library/Frameworks/Python.framework/Versions/2.6/l
ib/python2.6/doctest.py", line 1231, in __run
        compileflags, 1) in test.globs
      File "<doctest __main__.convert_to_basen[1]>", line 3, in <modul
e>
        assert actual == expected, 'expected: %s actual: %s' % (expect
ed, actual)
    AssertionError: expected: 11/2 actual: 10/2
**********************************************************************
1 items had failures:
   1 of   6 in __main__.convert_to_basen
***Test Failed*** 1 failures.
(ptc)gturnquist-mbp:03 gturnquist$
```

> In the previous screenshot, the key information is on this line: **AssertionError: expected: 11/2 actual: 10/2**. Is this test failure a bit contrived? Sure it is. But seeing a test case shows useful output is not. It's important to verify that our tests give us enough information to fix either the tests or the code.

How it works...

We created an array with each entry containing both the input data as well as the expected output. This provides us with an easy way to glance at a set of test cases.

Then, we iterate over each test case, calculate the actual value, and run it through a Python `assert`. An important part that is needed is the custom message `'expected: %s actual: %s'`. Without it, we would never get the information to tell us which test case failed.

> **What if one test case fails?**
> If one of the tests in the array fails, then that code block exits and skips over the rest of the tests. This is the trade off for having a more succinct set of tests.

Does this type of test fit better into doctest or unittest?

Here are some criteria that are worth considering when deciding whether to put these tests in `doctest`:

- Is the code easy to comprehend at a glance?
- Is this clear, succinct, useful information when users view the docstrings?

If there is little value in having this in the documentation, and if it clutters the code, then that is a strong hint that this test block belongs to a separate test module.

See also

Testing corner cases by iteration section of *Chapter 1*

Getting nosy with doctest

Up to this point, we have been either appending modules with a test runner, or we have typed `python -m doctest <module>` on the command line to exercise our tests.

In the previous chapter, we introduced the powerful library `nose` (refer to `http://somethingaboutorange.com/mrl/projects/nose` for more details).

For a quick recap, nose:

- Provides us with the convenient test discovering tool `nosetests`
- Is pluggable, with a huge ecosystem of available plugins
- Includes a built-in plugin targeted at finding `doctests` and running them

Creating Testable Documentation with doctest

Getting ready

We need to activate our virtual environment (virtualenv) and then install nose for this recipe.

1. Create a virtual environment, activate it, and verify the tools are working.

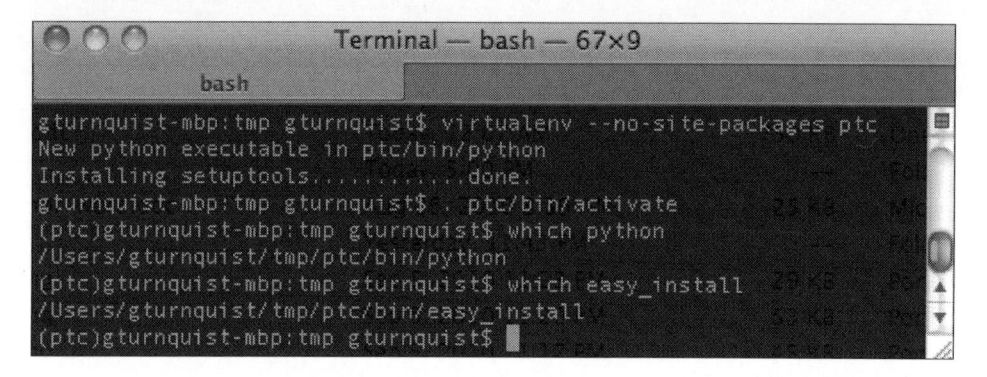

2. Using `pip`, install nose.

> This recipe assumes you have built all of the previous recipes in this chapter. If you have built only some of them, your results may appear different.

How to do it...

1. Run `nosetests -with-doctest` against all the modules in this folder. If you notice, it prints a very short . . . . . F.F . . . F, indicating that three tests have failed.

2. Run `nosetests -with-doctest -v` to get a more verbose output. In the following screenshot, notice how the tests that failed are the same ones that failed for the previous recipes in this chapter. It is also valuable to see the `<module>.<method>` format with either `ok` or `FAIL`.

Chapter 3

```
(ptc)gturnquist-mbp:03 gturnquist$ nosetests --with-doctest -v
Doctest: recipe16.convert_to_basen ... ok
Doctest: recipe17.convert_to_basen ... ok
Doctest: recipe18.convert_to_basen ... ok
Doctest: recipe19 ... ok
Doctest: recipe19b ... ok
Doctest: recipe19b.ShoppingCart.item ... FAIL
Doctest: recipe20.convert_to_basen ... ok
Doctest: recipe20b.convert_to_basen ... FAIL
Doctest: recipe20c.convert_to_basen ... ok
Doctest: recipe21 ... ok
Doctest: recipe22.convert_to_basen ... ok
Doctest: recipe23.convert_to_basen ... FAIL
```

3. Run `nosetests --with-doctest` against both the `recipe19.py` file as well as the `recipe19` module, in different combinations.

```
(ptc)gturnquist-mbp:03 gturnquist$ nosetests --with-doctest recipe19
.
----------------------------------------------------------------------
Ran 1 test in 0.007s

OK
(ptc)gturnquist-mbp:03 gturnquist$ nosetests --with-doctest recipe19.py
.
----------------------------------------------------------------------
Ran 1 test in 0.007s

OK
(ptc)gturnquist-mbp:03 gturnquist$ nosetests --with-doctest recipe19 recipe19.py
..
----------------------------------------------------------------------
Ran 2 tests in 0.006s

OK
(ptc)gturnquist-mbp:03 gturnquist$
```

How it works...

`nosetests` is targeted at discovering test cases and then running them. With this plugin, when it finds a docstring, it uses the `doctest` library to programmatically test it.

The `doctest` plugin is built around the assumption that doctests are not in the same package as other tests, like unittest. This means it will only run doctests found from non-test packages.

Creating Testable Documentation with doctest

There isn't a whole lot of complexity in the nosetests tool, and...that's the idea!. In this recipe, we have seen how to use `nosetests` to get a hold of all the doctests we have built so far in this chapter.

See also

Getting nosy with testing section mentioned in *Chapter 2*

Updating the project-level script to run this chapter's doctests

This recipe will help us explore building a project-level script that allows us to run different test suites. We will also focus on how to run it in our `doctests`.

How to do it...

With the following steps, we will craft a command-line script to allow us to manage a project including running `doctests`.

1. Create a new file called `recipe25.py` to contain all the code for this recipe.

2. Add code that parses a set of options using Python's `getopt` library.

```python
import getopt
import glob
import logging
import nose
import os
import os.path
import re
import sys

def usage():
    print
    print "Usage: python recipe25.py [command]"
    print
    print "\t--help"
    print "\t--doctest"
    print "\t--suite [suite]"
    print "\t--debug-level [info|debug]"
    print "\t--package"
    print "\t--publish"
    print "\t--register"
    print
```

```
try:
    optlist, args = getopt.getopt(sys.argv[1:],
            "h",
            ["help", "doctest", "suite=", \
             "debug-level=", "package", \
             "publish", "register"])
except getopt.GetoptError:
    # print help information and exit:
    print "Invalid command found in %s" % sys.argv
    usage()
    sys.exit(2)
```

3. Create a function that maps to –test.

```
def test(test_suite, debug_level):
    logger = logging.getLogger("recipe25")
    loggingLevel = debug_level
    logger.setLevel(loggingLevel)
    ch = logging.StreamHandler()
    ch.setLevel(loggingLevel)
    formatter = logging.Formatter("%(asctime)s - %(name)s - %(levelname)s - %(message)s")
    ch.setFormatter(formatter)
    logger.addHandler(ch)

    nose.run(argv=["", test_suite, "--verbosity=2"])
```

4. Create a function that maps to –doctest.

```
def doctest(test_suite=None):
    args = ["", "--with-doctest"]
    if test_suite is not None:
        print "Running doctest suite %s" % test_suite
        args.extend(test_suite.split(','))
        nose.run(argv=args)
    else:
        nose.run(argv=args)
```

5. Create stub functions that support package, publish, and register.

```
def package():
    print "This is where we can plug in code to run " + \
          "setup.py to generate a bundle."
def publish():
    print "This is where we can plug in code to upload " + \
          "our tarball to S3 or some other download site."
```

Creating Testable Documentation with doctest

```
def register():
    print "setup.py has a built in function to " + \
        "'register' a release to PyPI. It's " + \
        "convenient to put a hook in here."
    # os.system("%s setup.py register" % sys.executable)
```

6. Add some code that detects if the option list is empty. If so, have it print out the help menu and exit the script.

```
if len(optlist) == 0:
    usage()
    sys.exit(1)
```

7. Add some code that defines debug levels and then parses options to allow the user to override.

```
debug_levels = {"info":logging.INFO, "debug":logging.DEBUG}
# Default debug level is INFO
debug_level = debug_levels["info"]
```

```
for option in optlist:
    if option[0] in ("--debug-level"):
        # Override with a user-supplied debug level
        debug_level = debug_levels[option[1]]
```

8. Add some code that scans the command-line options for –help, and, if found, exits the script.

```
# Check for help requests, which cause all other
# options to be ignored.
for option in optlist:
    if option[0] in ("--help", "-h"):
        usage()
        sys.exit(1)
```

9. Add code that checks if –doctest has been picked. If so, have it specially scan –suite and run it through method `doctest()`. Otherwise, run –suite through method `test()`.

```
ran_doctests = False
for option in optlist:
    # If --doctest is picked, then --suite is a
    # suboption.
    if option[0] in ("--doctest"):
        suite = None
        for suboption in optlist:
            if suboption[0] in ("--suite"):
```

```
                suite = suboption[1]
            print "Running doctests..."
            doctest(suite)
            ran_doctests = True

if not ran_doctests:
    for option in optlist:
        if option[0] in ("--suite"):
            print "Running test suite %s..." % option[1]
            test(option[1], debug_level)
```

10. Finish it by iterating through each of the command-line options, and invoking the other functions based on the options that are picked.

```
# Parse the arguments, in order
for option in optlist:
    if option[0] in ("--package"):
        package()

    if option[0] in ("--publish"):
        publish()

    if option[0] in ("--register"):
        register()
```

11. Run the script with –help.

```
(ptc)gturnquist-mbp:03 gturnquist$ python recipe25.py --help

Usage: python recipe25.py [command]

        --help
        --doctest
        --suite [suite]
        --debug-level [info|debug]
        --package
        --publish
        --register
(ptc)gturnquist-mbp:03 gturnquist$
```

Creating Testable Documentation with doctest

12. Run the script with `-doctest`. Notice the first few lines of output in the following screenshot. It shows how the tests have passed and failed along with detailed output.

```
(ptc)gturnquist-mbp:03 gturnquist$ python recipe25.py --doctest
Running doctests...
....F.F...F....F.F...F
======================================================================
FAIL: Doctest: recipe19b.ShoppingCart.item
----------------------------------------------------------------------
Traceback (most recent call last):
  File "/System/Library/Frameworks/Python.framework/Versions/2.6/lib/python
2.6/doctest.py", line 2131, in runTest
    raise self.failureException(self.format_failure(new.getvalue()))
AssertionError: Failed doctest test for recipe19b.ShoppingCart.item
  File "/Users/gturnquist/Dropbox/python_testing_cookbook/code/03/recipe19b
.py", line 24, in item

----------------------------------------------------------------------
File "/Users/gturnquist/Dropbox/python_testing_cookbook/code/03/recipe19b.p
y", line 26, in recipe19b.ShoppingCart.item
Failed example:
    cart.item(1)
Exception raised:
    Traceback (most recent call last):
      File "/System/Library/Frameworks/Python.framework/Versions/2.6/lib/py
thon2.6/doctest.py", line 1231, in __run
        compileflags, 1) in test.globs
```

> The output is much longer. It has been trimmed for the sake of brevity.

13. Run the script with `-doctest -suite=recipe16,recipe17.py`.

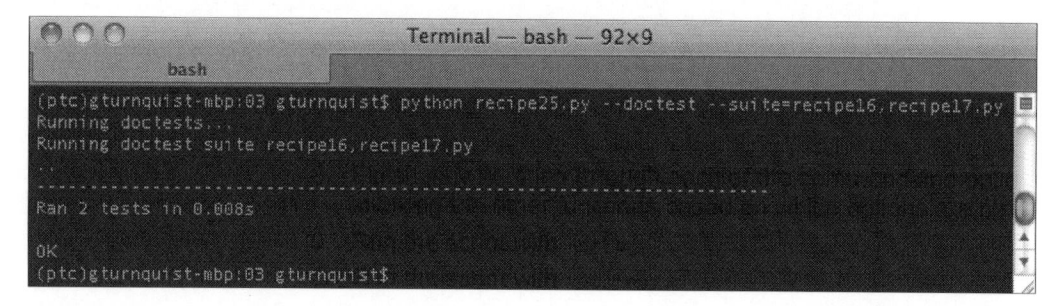

```
(ptc)gturnquist-mbp:03 gturnquist$ python recipe25.py --doctest --suite=recipe16,recipe17.py
Running doctests...
Running doctest suite recipe16,recipe17.py
..
----------------------------------------------------------------------
Ran 2 tests in 0.008s

OK
(ptc)gturnquist-mbp:03 gturnquist$
```

> We deliberately used `recipe16.py` and `recipe17.py` to demonstrate that it works with both module names and filenames.

How it works...

Just like the recipe in *Writing a project-level script* mentioned in *Chapter 2*, which lets you run different test suites, this script uses Python's `getopt` library, which is modeled after the C `getopt()` function (refer to `http://docs.python.org/library/getopt.html` for more details).

We have wired the following functions:

- `Usage`: This is a function to provide help to the user
- The key option definitions are included in the following block:

    ```
    optlist, args = getopt.getopt(sys.argv[1:],
        "h",
        ["help", "doctest", "suite=", \
        "debug-level=", "package", \
        "publish", "register"])
    ```

    - We parse everything in the arguments except the first, being the executable itself.
    - `"h"` defined the short option: `-h`.
    - The list defines long options. Those with `"="` accept an argument. Those without are flags.
    - If an option is received that isn't in the list, an exception is thrown, we print out `usage()`, and then exit.

- `doctest`: This runs modules through nose using `-with-doctest`
- `package`, `publish`, and `register`: These are just like the functions described in the previous chapter's project-level script recipe

With each of these functions defined, we can now iterate over the options that were parsed. For this script, there is a sequence:

1. Check if there is a debugging override. We default to `logging.INFO`, but provide the ability to switch to `logging.DEBUG`.
2. Check if `-h` or `-help` was called. If so, print out the `usage()` information and then exit with no more parsing.
3. Because `-suite` can be used either by itself to run unittest tests, or as a suboption for -doctest, we have to parse through things and figure out whether or not `-doctest` was used.
4. Finally, iterate over the options, and call their corresponding functions.

To exercise things, we first called this script with the `-help` option that printed out the command choices we had.

Creating Testable Documentation with doctest

Then we called it with `-doctest` to see how it handled finding all the doctests in this folder. In our case, we found all the recipes for this chapter including three test failures.

Finally, we called the script with `-doctest -suite=recipe16,recipe17.py`. This shows how we can pick a subset of tests delineated by the comma. With this example, we see that nose can process either by module name (`recipe16`) or by filename (`recipe17`).

There's more

The features this script provides could easily be handled by already built commands. We looked at `nosetests` with `doctest` earlier in this chapter and saw how it can flexibly take arguments to pick tests.

Using `setup.py` to generate tarballs and register releases is also a commonly used feature in the Python community.

So why write this script? Because, we can exploit all these features with a single command.

There are more details that can be found in the previous chapter about *project-level script* recipe, such as reasons for using `getopt`.

See also

There are more details that can be found in the previous chapter such as reasons for *using getopt*.

4
Testing Customer Stories with Behavior Driven Development

In this chapter, we will cover:

- Naming tests that sound like sentences and stories
- Testing separate `doctest` documents
- Writing a testable story with `doctest`
- Writing a testable novel with `doctest`
- Writing a testable story with Voidspace Mock and nose
- Writing a testable story with mockito and nose
- Writing a testable story with Lettuce
- Using Should DSL to write succinct assertions with Lettuce
- Updating the project-level script to run this chapter's BDD tests

Introduction

Behavior Driven Development (BDD) was created as a response to **Test Driven Development (TDD)** by Dan North. It focuses on writing automated tests in a natural language that non-programmers can read.

> Programmers wanted to know where to start, what to test and what not to test, how much to test in one go, what to call their tests, and how to understand why a test fails.

Testing Customer Stories with Behavior Driven Development

> *The deeper I got into TDD, the more I felt that my own journey had been less of a wax-on, wax-off process of gradual mastery than a series of blind alleys. I remember thinking, 'If only someone had told me that!' far more often than I thought, 'Wow, a door has opened.' I decided it must be possible to present TDD in a way that gets straight to the good stuff and avoids all the pitfalls—Dan North.*

> To discover more about Dan North please visit: `http://blog.dannorth.net/introducing-bdd`.

The tests that we have written in prior unittest recipes had a style of `testThis` and `testThat`. BDD takes the approach of getting out of speaking programmer-ese and instead shifting to a more customer-oriented perspective.

Dan North goes on to point out how Chris Stevenson wrote a specialized test runner for Java's JUnit that printed test results in a different way. Let's take a look at the following test code:

```
public class FooTest extends TestCase {
    public void testIsASingleton() {}
    public void testAReallyLongNameIsAGoodThing() {}
}
```

This code when run through AgileDox (`http://agiledox.sourceforge.net/`) will print out in the following format:

```
Foo
- is a singleton
- a really long name is a good thing
```

AgileDox does several things:

- Prints out the test name with the suffix `Test` dropped
- Strips out the `test` prefix from each test method
- Converts the remainder into a sentence

AgileDox is a Java tool, so we won't be exploring it in this chapter. But there are many Python tools available, and we will look at some including doctest, voidspace mock, mockito, and Lettuce. All of these tools give us the means to write tests in a more natural language and empower customers, QA, and test teams to develop story-based tests.

> All the tools and styles of BDD could easily fill up an entire book. This chapter intends to introduce the philosophy of BDD along with some strong, stable tools used to effectively test our system's behavior.

For this chapter, let's use the same shopping cart application for each recipe. Create a file called `cart.py` and add the following code.

```python
class ShoppingCart(object):
    def __init__(self):
        self.items = []
    def add(self, item, price):
        for cart_item in self.items:
            # Since we found the item, we increment
            # instead of append
            if cart_item.item == item:
                cart_item.q += 1
                return self
        # If we didn't find, then we append
        self.items.append(Item(item, price))
        return self
    def item(self, index):
        return self.items[index-1].item
    def price(self, index):
        return self.items[index-1].price * self.items[index-1].q
    def total(self, sales_tax):
        sum_price = sum([item.price*item.q for item in self.items])
        return sum_price*(1.0 + sales_tax/100.0)
    def __len__(self):
        return sum([item.q for item in self.items])
class Item(object):
    def __init__(self, item, price, q=1):
        self.item = item
        self.price = price
        self.q = q
```

This shopping cart:

- Is one-based, meaning the first item and price are at [1] not [0]
- Includes the ability to have multiples of the same item
- Will calculate total price and then add taxes

This application isn't complex. Instead, it provides us opportunities throughout this chapter to test various customer stories and scenarios that aren't necessarily confined to simple unit testing.

Naming tests that sound like sentences and stories

Test methods should read like sentences and test cases should read like titles of chapters. This is part of BDD's philosophy of making tests easy-to-read for non-programmers.

Getting ready

For this recipe, we will be using the shopping cart application shown at the beginning of this chapter.

How to do it...

With the following steps, we will explore how to write a custom nose plugin that formats results as a BDD-style report.

1. Create a file called `recipe26.py` to contain our test cases.
2. Create a unittest test where the test case represents a cart with one item, and the test methods read like sentences.

   ```
   import unittest
   from cart import *

   class CartWithOneItem(unittest.TestCase):
       def setUp(self):
           self.cart = ShoppingCart().add("tuna sandwich", 15.00)
       def test_when_checking_the_size_should_be_one_based(self):
           self.assertEquals(1, len(self.cart))
       def test_when_looking_into_cart_should_be_one_based(self):
           self.assertEquals("tuna sandwich", self.cart.item(1))
           self.assertEquals(15.00, self.cart.price(1))
       def test_total_should_have_in_sales_tax(self):
           self.assertAlmostEquals(15.0*1.0925, \
                               self.cart.total(9.25), 2)
   ```

3. Add a unittest test where the test case represents a cart with two items, and the test methods read like sentences.

   ```
   class CartWithTwoItems(unittest.TestCase):
       def setUp(self):
           self.cart = ShoppingCart() \
                           .add("tuna sandwich", 15.00) \
                           .add("rootbeer", 3.75)
   ```

```python
    def test_when_checking_size_should_be_two(self):
        self.assertEquals(2, len(self.cart))
    def test_items_should_be_in_same_order_as_entered(self):
        self.assertEquals("tuna sandwich", self.cart.item(1))
        self.assertAlmostEquals(15.00, self.cart.price(1), 2)
        self.assertEquals("rootbeer", self.cart.item(2))
        self.assertAlmostEquals(3.75, self.cart.price(2), 2)
    def test_total_price_should_have_in_sales_tax(self):
        self.assertAlmostEquals((15.0+3.75)*1.0925, \
                                self.cart.total(9.25), 2)
```

4. Add a unittest test where the test case represents a cart with no items, and the test methods read like sentences.

```python
class CartWithNoItems(unittest.TestCase):
    def setUp(self):
        self.cart = ShoppingCart()
    def test_when_checking_size_should_be_empty(self):
        self.assertEquals(0, len(self.cart))
    def test_finding_item_out_of_range_should_raise_error(self):
        self.assertRaises(IndexError, self.cart.item, 2)
    def test_finding_price_out_of_range_should_raise_error(self):
        self.assertRaises(IndexError, self.cart.price, 2)
    def test_when_looking_at_total_price_should_be_zero(self):
        self.assertAlmostEquals(0.0, self.cart.total(9.25), 2)
    def test_adding_items_returns_back_same_cart(self):
        empty_cart = self.cart
        cart_with_one_item = self.cart.add("tuna sandwich", \
                                            15.00)
        self.assertEquals(empty_cart, cart_with_one_item)
        cart_with_two_items = self.cart.add("rootbeer", 3.75)
        self.assertEquals(empty_cart, cart_with_one_item)
        self.assertEquals(cart_with_one_item, \
                          cart_with_two_items)
```

> BDD encourages using very descriptive sentences for method names. Several of these method names were shortened to fit the format of this book.

5. Create another file called `recipe26_plugin.py` to contain our customized BDD runner.

6. Create a nose plugin that can be used as `--with-bdd` to print out results.

```
import sys
err = sys.stderr

import nose
import re
from nose.plugins import Plugin

class BddPrinter(Plugin):
    name = "bdd"

    def __init__(self):
        Plugin.__init__(self)
        self.current_module = None
```

7. Create a handler that prints out either the module or the test method, with extraneous information stripped out.

```
def beforeTest(self, test):
    test_name = test.address()[-1]
    module, test_method = test_name.split(".")
    if self.current_module != module:
        self.current_module = module
        fmt_mod = re.sub(r"([A-Z])([a-z]+)", \
                         r"\1\2 ", module)
        err.write("\nGiven %s" % fmt_mod[:-1].lower())
    message = test_method[len("test"):]
    message = " ".join(message.split("_"))
    err.write("\n- %s" % message)
```

8. Create a handler for success, failure, and error messages.

```
def addSuccess(self, *args, **kwargs):
    test = args[0]
    err.write(" : Ok")

def addError(self, *args, **kwargs):
    test, error = args[0], args[1]
    err.write(" : ERROR!\n")

def addFailure(self, *args, **kwargs):
    test, error = args[0], args[1]
    err.write(" : Failure!\n")
```

9. Create a new file called `recipe26_runner.py` to contain a test runner for exercising this recipe.

10. Create a test runner that pulls in the test cases and runs them through nose, printing out results in an easy-to-read fashion.

    ```
    if __name__ == "__main__":
        import nose
        from recipe26_plugin import *

        nose.run(argv=["", "recipe26", "--with-bdd"], \
                            plugins=[BddPrinter()])
    ```

11. Run the test runner.

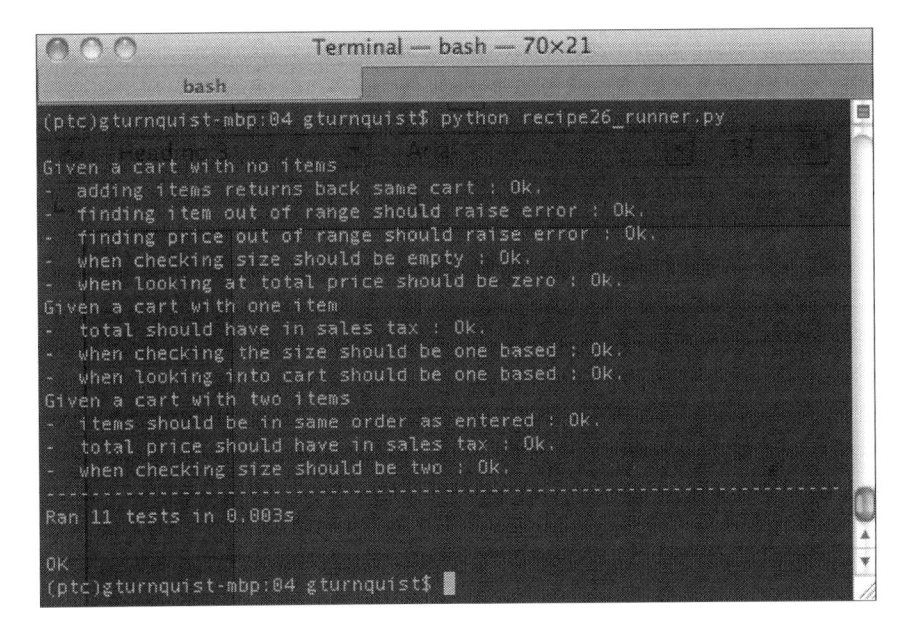

    ```
    (ptc)gturnquist-mbp:04 gturnquist$ python recipe26_runner.py
    Given a cart with no items
    -   adding items returns back same cart : Ok.
    -   finding item out of range should raise error : Ok.
    -   finding price out of range should raise error : Ok.
    -   when checking size should be empty : Ok.
    -   when looking at total price should be zero : Ok.
    Given a cart with one item
    -   total should have in sales tax : Ok.
    -   when checking the size should be one based : Ok.
    -   when looking into cart should be one based : Ok.
    Given a cart with two items
    -   items should be in same order as entered : Ok.
    -   total price should have in sales tax : Ok.
    -   when checking size should be two : Ok.
    ----------------------------------------------------------------------
    Ran 11 tests in 0.003s

    OK
    (ptc)gturnquist-mbp:04 gturnquist$
    ```

12. Introduce a couple of bugs in the test cases, and re-run the test runner to see how this alters the output.

    ```
            def test_when_checking_the_size_should_be_one_based(self):
                self.assertEquals(2, len(self.cart))
    ...
            def test_items_should_be_in_same_order_as_entered(self):
                self.assertEquals("tuna sandwich", self.cart.item(1))
                self.assertAlmostEquals(14.00, self.cart.price(1), 2)
                self.assertEquals("rootbeer", self.cart.item(2))
                self.assertAlmostEquals(3.75, self.cart.price(2), 2)
    ```

13. Run the tests again.

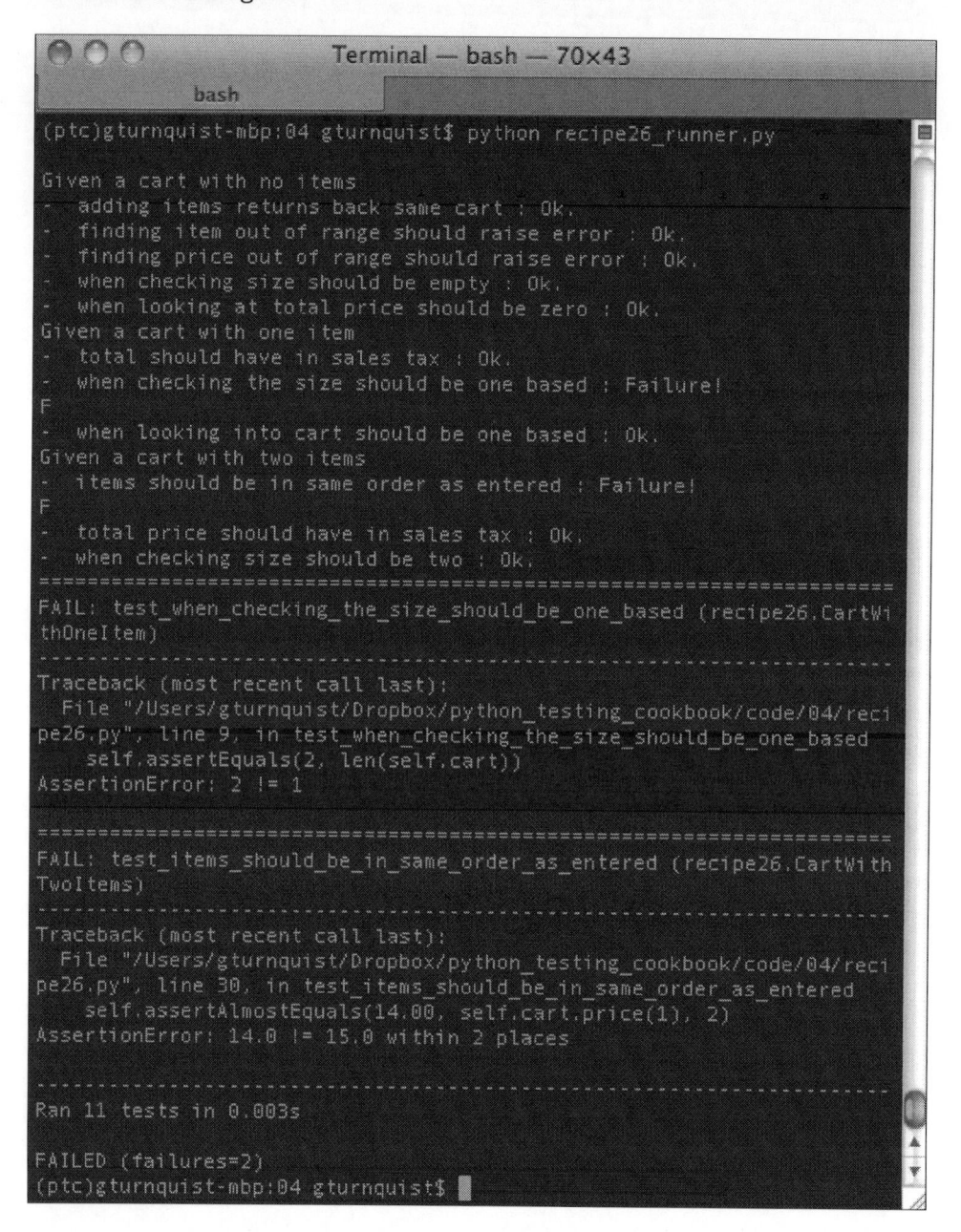

```
(ptc)gturnquist-mbp:04 gturnquist$ python recipe26_runner.py
Given a cart with no items
 - adding items returns back same cart : Ok.
 - finding item out of range should raise error : Ok.
 - finding price out of range should raise error : Ok.
 - when checking size should be empty : Ok.
 - when looking at total price should be zero : Ok.
Given a cart with one item
 - total should have in sales tax : Ok.
 - when checking the size should be one based : Failure!
F
 - when looking into cart should be one based : Ok.
Given a cart with two items
 - items should be in same order as entered : Failure!
F
 - total price should have in sales tax : Ok.
 - when checking size should be two : Ok.
======================================================================
FAIL: test_when_checking_the_size_should_be_one_based (recipe26.CartWi
thOneItem)
----------------------------------------------------------------------
Traceback (most recent call last):
  File "/Users/gturnquist/Dropbox/python_testing_cookbook/code/04/reci
pe26.py", line 9, in test_when_checking_the_size_should_be_one_based
    self.assertEquals(2, len(self.cart))
AssertionError: 2 != 1

======================================================================
FAIL: test_items_should_be_in_same_order_as_entered (recipe26.CartWith
TwoItems)
----------------------------------------------------------------------
Traceback (most recent call last):
  File "/Users/gturnquist/Dropbox/python_testing_cookbook/code/04/reci
pe26.py", line 30, in test_items_should_be_in_same_order_as_entered
    self.assertAlmostEquals(14.00, self.cart.price(1), 2)
AssertionError: 14.0 != 15.0 within 2 places

----------------------------------------------------------------------
Ran 11 tests in 0.003s

FAILED (failures=2)
(ptc)gturnquist-mbp:04 gturnquist$
```

How it works...

The test cases are written as nouns, describing the object being tested. `CartWithTwoItems` describes a series of test methods centered on a shopping cart that is pre-populated with two items.

The test methods are written like sentences strung together with underscores instead of spaces. They have to be prefixed with `test_`, so that unittest will pick them up. `test_items_should_be_in_same_order_as_entered` should represent "items should be in same order as entered"

The idea is we should be able to quickly understand what is being tested by putting these two together: Given a cart with two items, the items should be in the same order as entered.

While we could read through the test code with this thought process, mentally subtracting out the cruft of underscores and the `test` prefix, this can become a real cognitive load for us. To make it easier, we coded a quick nose plugin that split up the camel case tests and replaced the underscores with spaces. This led to the useful report format.

Using this type of quick tool encourages us to write detailed test methods that will be easy to read on output. The feedback not just to us but to our test team and customers can be very effective at fostering communications, confidence in software, and help with generating new test stories.

There's more

The example test methods shown here were deliberately shortened to fit the format of the book. Don't try to make them as short as possible. Instead, try to descriptively describe the expected output.

The plugin isn't installable

This plugin was coded to quickly generate a report. To make it reusable especially with `nosetests` you may want to read *Running automated test suites with nose* mentioned in Chapter 2 to get more details on creating a `setup.py` script to support the installation.

See also

Writing a nose extension to pick tests based on regular expressions; and *Writing a nose extension to generate a CSV report* as discussed in *Chapter 2*

Testing separate doctest documents

BDD doesn't require that we use any particular tool. Instead, it's more focused on the approach to testing. That is why it's possible to using Python `doctests` to write BDD test scenarios. `Doctests` aren't restricted to the module's code. With this recipe, we will explore creating independent text files to run through Python's doctest library.

If this is `doctest`, why wasn't it included in the previous chapter's recipes? Because the context of writing up a set of tests in separate test document fits more naturally into the philosophy of BDD than with testable `docstrings` that are available for introspection when working with a library.

Getting ready

For this recipe, we will be using the shopping cart application shown at the beginning of this chapter.

How to do it...

With the following steps, we will explore capturing various test scenarios in `doctest` files and then running them.

1. Create a file called `recipe27_scenario1.doctest` that contains doctest-style type tests to exercise the shopping cart.

   ```
   This is a way to exercise the shopping cart
   from a pure text file containing tests.
   First, we need to import the modules
   >>> from cart import *
   Now, we can create an instance of a cart
   >>> cart = ShoppingCart()
   Here we use the API to add an object. Because
   it returns back the cart, we have to deal with
   the output
   >>> cart.add("tuna sandwich", 15.00) #doctest:+ELLIPSIS
   <cart.ShoppingCart object at ...>
   Now we can check some other outputs
   >>> cart.item(1)
   'tuna sandwich'
   >>> cart.price(1)
   15.0
   >>> cart.total(0.0)
   15.0
   ```

> [Notice that there are no quotes surrounding the text.]

2. Create another scenario in the file `recipe27_scenario2.doctest` that tests the boundaries of the shopping cart.

   ```
   This is a way to exercise the shopping cart
   from a pure text file containing tests.

   First, we need to import the modules
   >>> from cart import *

   Now, we can create an instance of a cart
   >>> cart = ShoppingCart()

   Now we try to access an item out of range,
   expecting an exception.
   >>> cart.item(5)
   Traceback (most recent call last):
   ...
   IndexError: list index out of range

   We also expect the price method to fail
   in a similar way.
   >>> cart.price(-2)
   Traceback (most recent call last):
   ...
   IndexError: list index out of range
   ```

3. Create a file called `recipe27.py` and put in the test runner code that finds files ending in `.doctest` and runs them through doctest's `testfile` method.

   ```python
   if __name__ == "__main__":
       import doctest
       from glob import glob
       for file in glob("recipe27*.doctest"):
           print "Running tests found in %s" % file
           doctest.testfile(file)
   ```

4. Run the test suite.

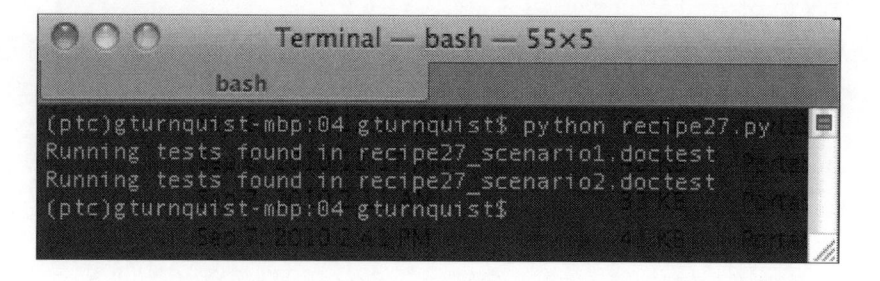

```
(ptc)gturnquist-mbp:04 gturnquist$ python recipe27.py
Running tests found in recipe27_scenario1.doctest
Running tests found in recipe27_scenario2.doctest
(ptc)gturnquist-mbp:04 gturnquist$
```

5. Run the test suite with -v.

```
(ptc)gturnquist-mbp:04 gturnquist$ python recipe27.py -v
Running tests found in recipe27_scenario1.doctest
Trying:
    from cart import *
Expecting nothing
ok
Trying:
    cart = ShoppingCart()
Expecting nothing
ok
Trying:
    cart.add("tuna sandwich", 15.00) #doctest:+ELLIPSIS
Expecting:
    <cart.ShoppingCart object at ...>
ok
Trying:
    cart.item(1)
Expecting:
    'tuna sandwich'
ok
Trying:
    cart.price(1)
Expecting:
    15.0
ok
Trying:
    cart.total(0.0)
Expecting:
    15.0
ok
1 items passed all tests:
    6 tests in recipe27_scenario1.doctest
6 tests in 1 items.
6 passed and 0 failed.
Test passed.
Running tests found in recipe27_scenario2.doctest
Trying:
    from cart import *
Expecting nothing
ok
```

How it works...

`Doctest` provides the convenient `testfile` function that will exercise a block of pure text as if it were contained inside a docstring. This is why no quotations are needed compared to when we had doctests inside docstrings. The text files aren't docstrings.

In fact, if we include triple quotes around the text, the tests won't work correctly. Let's take the first scenario—put `"""` at the top and bottom of the file, and save it as `recipe27_bad_scenario.txt`. Then let's create a file called `recipe27_bad.py` and create an alternate test runner that runs our bad scenario.

```
if __name__ == "__main__":
    import doctest
    doctest.testfile("recipe27_bad_scenario.txt")
```

We get the following error message:

```
(ptc)gturnquist-mbp:04 gturnquist$ python recipe27_bad.py
**********************************************************************
File "recipe27_bad_scenario.txt", line 24, in recipe27_bad_scenario.txt
Failed example:
    cart.total(0.0)
Expected:
    15.0
    """
Got:
    15.0
**********************************************************************
1 items had failures:
   1 of   6 in recipe27_bad_scenario.txt
***Test Failed*** 1 failures.
(ptc)gturnquist-mbp:04 gturnquist$
```

It has confused the tail end triple quotes as part of the expected output. It's best to just leave them out.

There's more...

What is so great about moving `docstrings` into separate files? Isn't this the same thing that we were doing in *Creating testable documentation with doctest* recipe discussed in *Chapter 3*? Yes and no. Yes, it's technically the same thing: `doctest` exercising blocks of code embedded in test.

Testing Customer Stories with Behavior Driven Development

But BDD is more than simply a technical solution. It is driven by the philosophy of *customer-readable scenarios*. BDD aims to test the behavior of the system. The behavior is often defined by customer-oriented scenarios. Getting a hold of these scenarios is strongly encouraged when our customer can easily understand the scenarios that we have captured. It is further enhanced when the customer can see what passes and fails and, in turn, sees a realistic status of what has been accomplished.

By decoupling our test scenarios from the code and putting them into separate files, we have the key ingredient to making readable tests for our customers using `doctest`.

Doesn't this defy the usability of docstrings?

In *Chapter 3* there are several recipes that show how convenient it is to embed examples of code usage in `docstrings`. They are convenient, because we can read the `docstrings` from an interactive Python shell. What do you think is different about pulling some of this out of the code into separate scenario files? Do you think there are some `doctests` that would be useful in `docstrings` and others that may serve us better in separate scenario files?

Writing a testable story with doctest

Capturing a succinct story in a `doctest` file is the key to BDD. Another aspect of BDD is providing a readable report including the results.

Getting ready

For this recipe, we will be using the shopping cart application shown at the beginning of this chapter.

How to do it...

With the following steps, we will see how to write a custom `doctest` runner to make our own report.

1. Create a new file called `recipe28_cart_with_no_items.doctest` to contain our `doctest` scenario.
2. Create a `doctest` scenario that exercises the shopping cart.

    ```
    This scenario demonstrates a testable story.

    First, we need to import the modules
    >>> from cart import *

    >>> cart = ShoppingCart()

    #when we add an item
    >>> cart.add("carton of milk", 2.50) #doctest:+ELLIPSIS
    <cart.ShoppingCart object at ...>
    ```

```
#the first item is a carton of milk
>>> cart.item(1)
'carton of milk'
#the first price is $2.50
>>> cart.price(1)
2.5
#there is only one item
>>> len(cart)
1
This shopping cart lets us grab more than one
of a particular item.
#when we add a second carton of milk
>>> cart.add("carton of milk", 2.50) #doctest:+ELLIPSIS
<cart.ShoppingCart object at ...>
#the first item is still a carton of milk
>>> cart.item(1)
'carton of milk'
#but the price is now $5.00
>>> cart.price(1)
5.0
#and the cart now has 2 items
>>> len(cart)
2
#for a total (with 10% taxes) of $5.50
>>> cart.total(10.0)
5.5
```

3. Create a new file called `recipe28.py` to contain our custom `doctest` runner.

4. Create a customer `doctest` runner by subclassing `DocTestRunner`.

    ```
    import doctest.

    class BddDocTestRunner(doctest.DocTestRunner):
        """
        This is a customized test runner. It is meant
        to run code examples like DocTestRunner,
        but if a line preceeds the code example
        starting with '#', then it prints that
        comment.

        If the line starts with '#when', it is printed
        out like a sentence, but with no outcome.

        If the line starts with '#', but not '#when'
    ```

Testing Customer Stories with Behavior Driven Development

```
        it is printed out indented, and with the
        outcome.
        """
```

5. Add a `report_start` function that looks for comments starting with # before an example.

```
def report_start(self, out, test, example):
    prior_line = example.lineno-1
    line_before = test.docstring.splitlines()[prior_line]
    if line_before.startswith("#"):
        message = line_before[1:]
        if line_before.startswith("#when"):
            out("* %s\n" % message)
            example.silent = True
            example.indent = False
        else:
            out("   - %s: " % message)
            example.silent = False
            example.indent = True
    else:
        example.silent = True
        example.indent = False
    doctest.DocTestRunner(out, test, example)
```

6. Add a `report_success` function that conditionally prints out `ok`.

```
def report_success(self, out, test, example, got):
    if not example.silent:
        out("ok\n")
    if self._verbose:
        if example.indent: out("     ")
        out(">>> %s\n" % example.source[:-1])
```

7. Add a `report_failure` function that conditionally prints out `FAIL`.

```
def report_failure(self, out, test, example, got):
    if not example.silent:
        out("FAIL\n")
    if self._verbose:
        if example.indent: out("     ")
        out(">>> %s\n" % example.source[:-1])
```

8. Add a runner that replaces `doctest.DocTestRunner` with our customer runner, and then looks for doctest files to run.

```
if __name__ == "__main__":
    from glob import glob
```

```
doctest.DocTestRunner = BddDocTestRunner

for file in glob("recipe28*.doctest"):
    given = file[len("recipe28_"):]
    given = given[:-len(".doctest")]
    given = " ".join(given.split("_"))
    print "==================================="
    print "Given a %s..." % given
    print "==================================="
    doctest.testfile(file)
```

9. Use the runner to exercise our scenario.

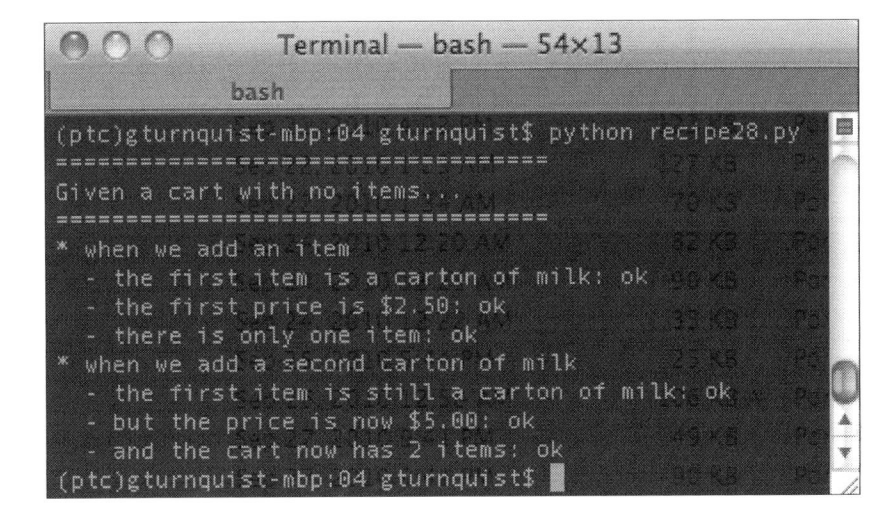

```
(ptc)gturnquist-mbp:04 gturnquist$ python recipe28.py
===================================
Given a cart with no items...
===================================
* when we add an item
    - the first item is a carton of milk: ok
    - the first price is $2.50: ok
    - there is only one item: ok
* when we add a second carton of milk
    - the first item is still a carton of milk: ok
    - but the price is now $5.00: ok
    - and the cart now has 2 items: ok
(ptc)gturnquist-mbp:04 gturnquist$
```

Testing Customer Stories with Behavior Driven Development

10. Use the runner to exercise our scenario with `-v`.

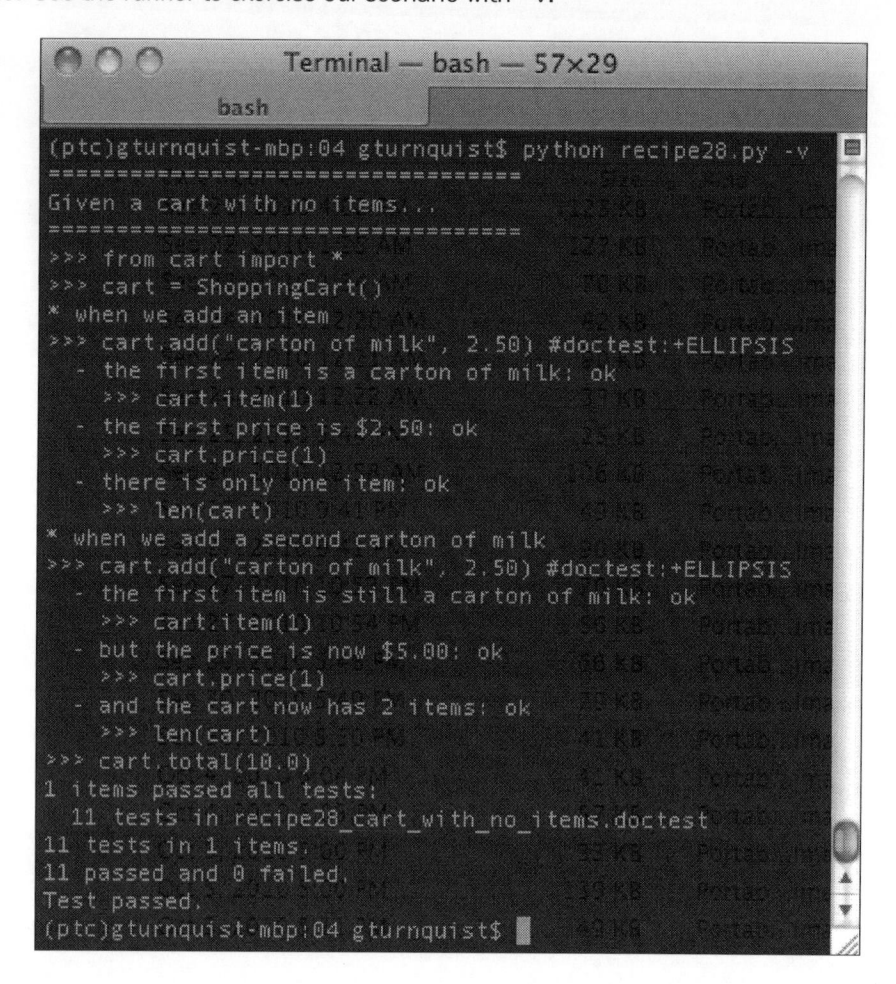

```
(ptc)gturnquist-mbp:04 gturnquist$ python recipe28.py -v
=========================================
Given a cart with no items...
=========================================
>>> from cart import *
>>> cart = ShoppingCart()
* when we add an item
>>> cart.add("carton of milk", 2.50) #doctest:+ELLIPSIS
    - the first item is a carton of milk: ok
    >>> cart.item(1)
    - the first price is $2.50: ok
    >>> cart.price(1)
    - there is only one item: ok
    >>> len(cart)
* when we add a second carton of milk
>>> cart.add("carton of milk", 2.50) #doctest:+ELLIPSIS
    - the first item is still a carton of milk: ok
    >>> cart.item(1)
    - but the price is now $5.00: ok
    >>> cart.price(1)
    - and the cart now has 2 items: ok
    >>> len(cart)
>>> cart.total(10.0)
1 items passed all tests:
   11 tests in recipe28_cart_with_no_items.doctest
11 tests in 1 items.
11 passed and 0 failed.
Test passed.
(ptc)gturnquist-mbp:04 gturnquist$
```

11. Alter the test scenario so that one of the expected outcomes fails.

    ```
    #there is only one item
    >>> len(cart)
    4668
    ```

    > Notice we have changed the expected outcome from `1` to `4668`, to guarantee a failure.

12. Use the runner with `-v` again, and see the results.

134

```
(ptc)gturnquist-mbp:04 gturnquist$ python recipe28.py -v
======================================
Given a cart with no items...
======================================
>>> from cart import *
>>> cart = ShoppingCart()
* when we add an item
>>> cart.add("carton of milk", 2.50) #doctest:+ELLIPSIS
    - the first item is a carton of milk: ok
    >>> cart.item(1)
    - the first price is $2.50: ok
    >>> cart.price(1)
    - there is only one item: FAIL
    >>> len(cart)
* when we add a second carton of milk
>>> cart.add("carton of milk", 2.50) #doctest:+ELLIPSIS
    - the first item is still a carton of milk: ok
    >>> cart.item(1)
    - but the price is now $5.00: ok
    >>> cart.price(1)
    - and the cart now has 2 items: ok
    >>> len(cart)
    - for a total (with 10% taxes) of $5.50: ok
    >>> cart.total(10.0)
**********************************************************************
1 items had failures:
   1 of  11 in recipe28_cart_with_no_items.doctest
11 tests in 1 items.
10 passed and 1 failed.
***Test Failed*** 1 failures.
(ptc)gturnquist-mbp:04 gturnquist$
```

How it works...

`Doctest` provides a convenient means to write a testable scenario. For starters, we wrote up a series of behaviors we wanted the shopping cart application to prove. To polish things up, we added lot of detailed comments, so that anyone reading this document can clearly understand things.

This provides us with a testable scenario. However, it leaves us short of one key thing: *a succinct report*.

Unfortunately, `doctest` won't print out all these detailed comments for us.

To make this usable from a BDD perspective, we need the ability to embed selective comments that get printed out when the test sequence runs. To do that we will subclass `doctest.DocTestRunner` and insert our version of handling of the `docstring`.

There's more...

`DocTestRunner` conveniently gives us a handle on the `docstring` as well as the exact line number where the code example starts. We coded our `BddDocTestRunner` to look at the line preceding it, and check to see if it started with #, our custom marker for a piece of text to print out during a test run.

A `#when` comment is considered a cause. In other words, a *when* causes one or more *effects*. While `doctest` will still verify the code involved with a *when*; for BDD purposes, we don't really care about the outcome, so we silently ignore it.

Any other # comments are considered *effects*. For each of these, we strip out the # then print the sentence indented, so we can easily see which *when* it is tied to. Finally, we print out either `ok` or `FAIL` to indicate the results.

This means we can add all the detail we want to the documentation. But for blocks of tests, we can add statements that will be printed as either *causes* (`#when`) or *effects* (`#anything else`).

Writing a testable novel with doctest

Running a series of story tests showcases your code's expected behavior. We have previously seen in the *Writing a testable story with doctest* recipe how to build a testable story and have it generate a useful report.

With this recipe, we will see how to use this tactic to string together multiple testable stories to form a testable novel.

Getting ready

For this recipe, we will be using the shopping cart application shown at the beginning of this chapter.

We will also re-use the `BddDocTestRunner` defined in this chapter's *Writing a testable story with doctest* recipe. But we will slightly alter it in the following steps.

How to do it...

With the following steps, we will look at how to write a testable novel:

1. Create a new file called `recipe29.py`.
2. Copy the code containing the `BddDocTestRunner` from the *Writing a testable story with doctest* recipe into `recipe29.py`.
3. Alter the `__main__` runnable to only search for this recipe's `doctest` scenarios.

    ```
    if __name__ == "__main__":
        from glob import glob

        doctest.DocTestRunner = BddDocTestRunner

        for file in glob("recipe29*.doctest"):
            given = file[len("recipe29_"):]
            given = given[:-len(".doctest")]
            given = " ".join(given.split("_"))
            print "===================================="
            print "Given a %s..." % given
            print "===================================="
            doctest.testfile(file)
    ```

4. Create a new file called `recipe29_cart_we_will_load_with_identical_items.doctest`.
5. Add a scenario to it that tests the cart by adding two instances of the same object.

    ```
    >>> from cart import *
    >>> cart = ShoppingCart()

    #when we add an item
    >>> cart.add("carton of milk", 2.50) #doctest:+ELLIPSIS
    <cart.ShoppingCart object at ...>

    #the first item is a carton of milk
    >>> cart.item(1)
    'carton of milk'

    #the first price is $2.50
    >>> cart.price(1)
    2.5

    #there is only one item
    >>> len(cart)
    1

    This shopping cart let's us grab more than one
    of a particular item.
    #when we add a second carton of milk
    ```

Testing Customer Stories with Behavior Driven Development

```
>>> cart.add("carton of milk", 2.50) #doctest:+ELLIPSIS
<cart.ShoppingCart object at ...>
#the first item is still a carton of milk
>>> cart.item(1)
'carton of milk'
#but the price is now $5.00
>>> cart.price(1)
5.0
#and the cart now has 2 items
>>> len(cart)
2
#for a total (with 10% taxes) of $5.50
>>> cart.total(10.0)
5.5
```

6. Create another file called recipe29_cart_we_will_load_with_two_different_items.docstest.

7. In that file, create another scenario that tests the cart by adding two different instances.

```
>>> from cart import *
>>> cart = ShoppingCart()
#when we add a carton of milk...
>>> cart.add("carton of milk", 2.50) #doctest:+ELLIPSIS
<cart.ShoppingCart object at ...>
#when we add a frozen pizza...
>>> cart.add("frozen pizza", 3.00) #doctest:+ELLIPSIS
<cart.ShoppingCart object at ...>
#the first item is the carton of milk
>>> cart.item(1)
'carton of milk'
#the second item is the frozen pizza
>>> cart.item(2)
'frozen pizza'
#the first price is $2.50
>>> cart.price(1)
2.5
#the second price is $3.00
>>> cart.price(2)
3.0
#the total with no tax is $5.50
```

```
>>> cart.total(0.0)
5.5
#the total with 10% tax is $6.05
>>> print round(cart.total(10.0), 2)
6.05
```

8. Create a new file called `recipe29_cart_that_we_intend_to_keep_empty.doctest`.

9. In that file, create a third scenario that tests the cart by adding nothing and yet tries to access values outside the range.

```
>>> from cart import *
```
```
#when we create an empty shopping cart
>>> cart = ShoppingCart()
```
```
#accessing an item out of range generates an exception
>>> cart.item(5)
Traceback (most recent call last):
...
IndexError: list index out of range
```
```
#accessing a price with a negative index causes an exception
>>> cart.price(-2)
Traceback (most recent call last):
...
IndexError: list index out of range
```
```
#calculating a price with no tax results in $0.00
>>> cart.total(0.0)
0.0
```
```
#calculating a price with a tax results in $0.00
>>> cart.total(10.0)
0.0
```

Testing Customer Stories with Behavior Driven Development

10. Use the runner to execute our scenarios.

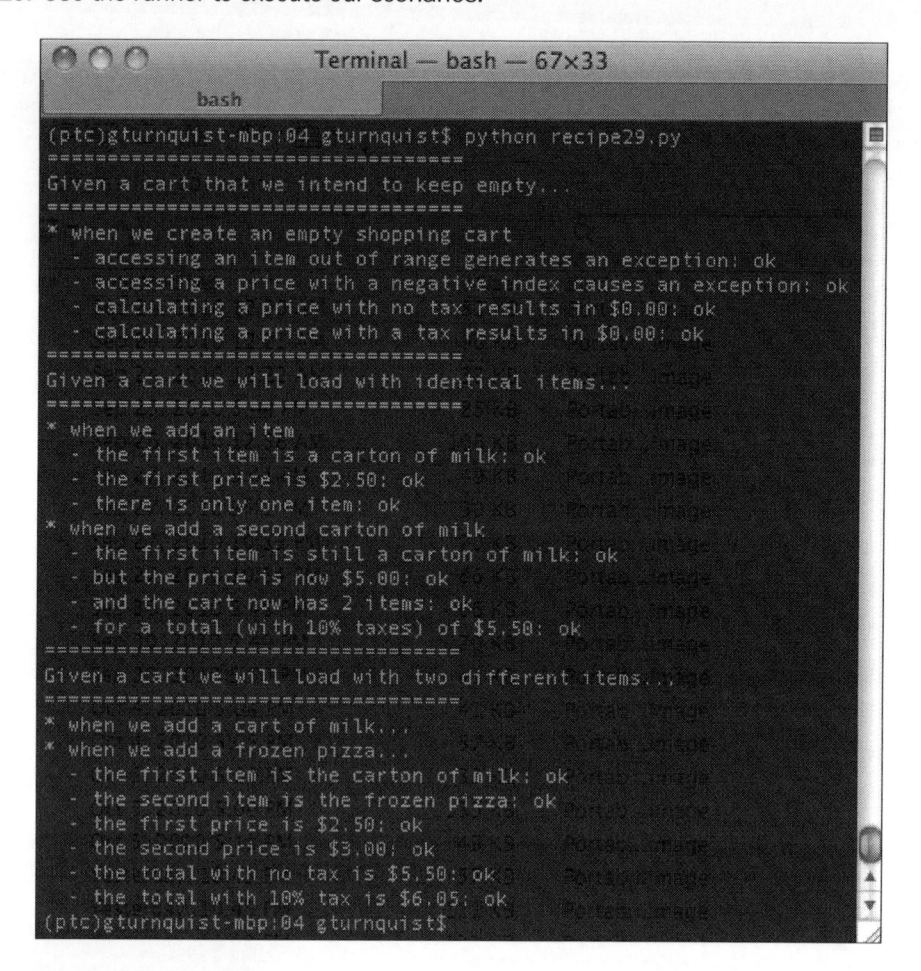

```
(ptc)gturnquist-mbp:04 gturnquist$ python recipe29.py
===================================
Given a cart that we intend to keep empty...
===================================
* when we create an empty shopping cart
    - accessing an item out of range generates an exception: ok
    - accessing a price with a negative index causes an exception: ok
    - calculating a price with no tax results in $0.00: ok
    - calculating a price with a tax results in $0.00: ok
===================================
Given a cart we will load with identical items...
===================================
* when we add an item
    - the first item is a carton of milk: ok
    - the first price is $2.50: ok
    - there is only one item: ok
* when we add a second carton of milk
    - the first item is still a carton of milk: ok
    - but the price is now $5.00: ok
    - and the cart now has 2 items: ok
    - for a total (with 10% taxes) of $5.50: ok
===================================
Given a cart we will load with two different items...
===================================
* when we add a cart of milk...
* when we add a frozen pizza...
    - the first item is the carton of milk: ok
    - the second item is the frozen pizza: ok
    - the first price is $2.50: ok
    - the second price is $3.00: ok
    - the total with no tax is $5.50: ok
    - the total with 10% tax is $6.05: ok
(ptc)gturnquist-mbp:04 gturnquist$
```

How it works...

We reuse the test runner developed in the previous recipe. The key is extending the scenarios to ensure that we have complete coverage of the expected scenarios.

We need to be sure that we can handle:

- A cart with two identical items
- A cart with two different items
- The degenerate situation of an empty shopping cart

There's more...

A valuable part of writing tests is picking useful names. In our situation, each testable story started with an empty cart. However, if we named each scenario 'given an empty cart' would cause an overlap and not result in a very effective report.

So instead, we named them based on our story's intention:

```
recipe29_cart_we_will_load_with_identical_items.doctest
recipe29_cart_we_will_load_with_two_different_items.doctest
recipe29_cart_that_we_intend_to_keep_empty.doctest
```

This leads to:

- Given a cart we will load with identical items
- Given a cart we will load with two different items
- Given a cart that we intend to keep empty

The purpose of these scenarios is much clearer.

Naming scenarios are much like certain aspects of software development that are more a craft than a science. Tuning the performance tends to be more scientific, because it involves an iterative process of measurement and adjustment. But naming scenarios along with their causes and effects tends to be more of a craft. It involves communicating with all the stakeholders including QA and customers, so everyone can read and understand the stories.

> **Don't be intimidated. Be ready to embrace change**
>
> Start writing your stories. Make them work. Then share them with your stakeholders. Feedback is important, and that is the purpose of using story-based testing.
>
> Be ready for criticism and suggested changes. Be ready for more story requests. In fact, don't be surprised if some of your customers or QA want to write their own stories. That is a positive sign.
>
> If you are new to this type of customer interaction, don't worry. You will develop valuable communication skills and build a solid professional relationship with your stakeholders. And at the same time, your code quality will certainly improve.

Writing a testable story with Voidspace Mock and nose

When our code interacts with other classes through methods and attributes, these are referred to as collaborators. Mocking out collaborators using **Voidspace Mock** (http://www.voidspace.org.uk/python/mock, created by Michael Foord) provides a key tool for BDD. Mocks provide a way for provided canned behavior compared to stubs, which provide canned state. While mocks by themselves don't define BDD, their usage keenly overlaps the ideas of BDD.

To further demonstrate the behavioral nature of the tests, we will also use the **spec** nose plugin found in the **Pinocchio** project (http://darcs.idyll.org/~t/projects/pinocchio/doc).

> As stated on the project's website, Voidspace Mock is experimental. This book was written using version 0.7.0 beta 3. There is the risk that more API changes will occur before reaching a stable 1.0 version. Given this project's high quality, excellent documentation, and many articles in the blogosphere, I strongly feel it deserves a place in this book.

Getting ready

For this recipe, we will be using the shopping cart application shown at the beginning of this chapter with some slight modifications.

1. Create a new file called `recipe30_cart.py` and copy all the code from `cart.py` created in the introduction of this chapter.

2. Alter `__init__` to add an extra `storer` attribute used for persistence.
   ```
   class ShoppingCart(object):
       def __init__(self, storer=None):
           self.items = []
           self.storer = storer
   ```

3. Add a `store` method that uses the `storer` to save the cart.
   ```
   def store(self):
       return self.storer.store_cart(self)
   ```

4. Add a `retrieve` method that updates the internal `items` by using the `storer`.
   ```
   def restore(self, id):
       self.items = self.storer.retrieve_cart(id).items
       return self
   ```

> The specifics of the API of the `storer` will be given further down in this recipe.

We need to activate our virtual environment and then install Voidspace Mock for this recipe.

1. Create a virtual environment, activate it, and verify the tools are working.

```
gturnquist-mbp:tmp gturnquist$ virtualenv --no-site-packages ptc
New python executable in ptc/bin/python
Installing setuptools............done.
gturnquist-mbp:tmp gturnquist$ . ptc/bin/activate
(ptc)gturnquist-mbp:tmp gturnquist$ which python
/Users/gturnquist/tmp/ptc/bin/python
(ptc)gturnquist-mbp:tmp gturnquist$ which easy_install
/Users/gturnquist/tmp/ptc/bin/easy_install
(ptc)gturnquist-mbp:tmp gturnquist$
```

2. Install `voidspace mock` by typing `pip install mock`.
3. Install the latest version of `pinocchio` by typing `pip install http://darcs.idyll.org/~t/projects/pinocchio-latest.tar.gz`.
4. This version of `pinocchio` raises some warnings. To prevent them, we also need to install `figleaf` by typing `pip install figleaf`.

How to do it...

With the following steps, we will explore how to use mock to write a testable story:

1. In `recipe30_cart.py`, create a `DataAccess` class with empty methods for storing and retrieving shopping carts.

    ```
    class DataAccess(object):
        def store_cart(self, cart):
            pass
        def retrieve_cart(self, id):
            pass
    ```

2. Create a new file called `recipe30.py` to write test code.

3. Create an automated unittest that exercises the cart by mocking out the methods of `DataAccess`.

```
import unittest
from copy import deepcopy
from recipe30_cart import *
from mock import Mock

class CartThatWeWillSaveAndRestoreUsingVoidspaceMock(unittest.TestCase):
    def test_fill_up_a_cart_then_save_it_and_restore_it(self):
        # Create an empty shopping cart
        cart = ShoppingCart(DataAccess())

        # Add a couple of items
        cart.add("carton of milk", 2.50)
        cart.add("frozen pizza", 3.00)

        self.assertEquals(2, len(cart))

        # Create a clone of the cart for mocking
        # purposes.
        original_cart = deepcopy(cart)

        # Save the cart at this point in time into a database
        # using a mock
        cart.storer.store_cart = Mock()
        cart.storer.store_cart.return_value = 1
        cart.storer.retrieve_cart = Mock()
        cart.storer.retrieve_cart.return_value = original_cart

        id = cart.store()

        self.assertEquals(1, id)

        # Add more items to cart
        cart.add("cookie dough", 1.75)
        cart.add("ginger ale", 3.25)

        self.assertEquals(4, len(cart))

        # Restore the cart to the last point in time
        cart.restore(id)

        self.assertEquals(2, len(cart))

        cart.storer.store_cart.assert_called_with(cart)
        cart.storer.retrieve_cart.assert_called_with(1)
```

4. Run the test using `nosetests` with the `spec` plugin.

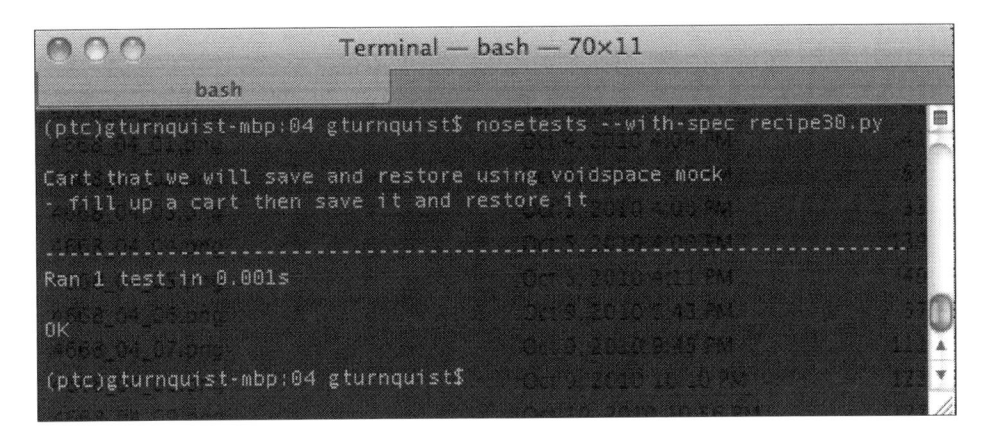

How it works...

Mocks are test doubles that confirm method calls, which is the 'behavior'. This is different from stubs, which provide canned data, allowing us to confirm state.

Many mocking libraries are based on the *record/replay* pattern. They first require the test case to *record* every behavior the mock will be subjected to when used. Then we plug the mock into our code, allowing our code to invoke calls against it. Finally, we execute *replay*, and the Mock library compares the method calls we expected with the ones that actually happened.

A common issue with record/replay mocking is that, if we miss a single method call, our test fails. Capturing all the method calls can become very challenging when trying to mock out third-party systems, or dealing with variable calls that may be tied to complex system states.

The Voidspace Mock library differs by using the *action/assert* pattern. We first generate a mock and define how we want it to react to certain *actions*. Then, we plug it into our code, allowing our code to operate against it. Finally, we *assert* what happened to the mock, only picking the operations we care about. There is no requirement to assert every behavior experienced by the mock.

Why is this important? Record/replay requires that we record the method calls that are made by our code, third-party system, and all the other layers in the call chain. Frankly, we may not need this level of confirmation of behavior. Often, we are primarily interested in the top layer of interaction. Action/assert lets us cut back on the behavior calls we care about. We can set up our mock to generate the necessary top level actions and essentially ignore the lower level calls, which a record/replay mock would force us to record.

In this recipe, we mocked the `DataAccess` operations `store_cart` and `retrieve_cart`. We defined their `return_value` and at the end of the test, we asserted that they were called.

```
cart.storer.store_cart.assert_called_with(cart)
cart.storer.retrieve_cart.assert_called_with(1)
```

`cart.storer` was the internal attribute that we injected with our mock.

> **Mocking a method**: This means replacing a call to a real method with one to a mock object.
>
> **Stubbing a method**: This means replacing a call to a real method with one to a stub.

There's more...

Because this test case focuses on storing and retrieving from the cart's perspective, we didn't have to define the real `DataAccess` calls. That is why we simply put `pass` in their method definitions.

This conveniently lets us work on the behavior of persistence without forcing us to choose whether the cart would be stored in a relational database, a `NoSQL` database, a flat file, or any other file format. This shows that our shopping cart and data persistence are nicely decoupled.

Tell me more about the spec nose plugin!

We quickly skimmed over the useful `spec` plugin for nose. It provides the same essential functionality that we coded by hand in the *Naming tests so they sound like sentences and stories* section. It converts test case names and test method names into readable results. It gives us a runnable `spec`. This plugin works with unittest and doesn't care whether or not we were using Voidspace Mock.

Why didn't we reuse the plugin from the recipe 'Naming tests so they sound like sentences and stories'?

Another way to phrase this question is, 'Why did we write that recipe's plugin in the first place? An important point of using test tools is to understand how they work, and how to write our own extensions. The *Naming tests so they sound like sentences and stories* section not only discussed the philosophy of naming tests, but also explored ways to write nose plugins to support this need. In this recipe, our focus was on using Voidspace Mock to verify certain behaviors, and not on coding nose plugins. Producing a nice BDD report was easily served by the existing `spec` plugin.

See also

Writing a testable story with mockito and nose

Writing a testable story with mockito and nose

When our code interacts with other classes through methods and attributes, these are referred to as collaborators. Mocking out collaborators using **mockito** (http://code.google.com/p/mockito and http://code.google.com/p/mockito-python) provides a key tool for BDD. Mocks provide a way for providing canned behavior compared to stubs, which provide canned state. While mocks by themselves don't define BDD, their usage keenly overlaps the ideas of BDD.

To further demonstrate the behavioral nature of the tests, we will also use the spec nose plugin found in the pinocchio project (http://darcs.idyll.org/~t/projects/pinocchio/doc).

Getting ready

For this recipe, we will be using the shopping cart application shown at the beginning of this chapter with some slight modifications.

1. Create a new file called recipe31_cart.py and copy all the code from cart.py created in the introduction of this chapter.

2. Alter __init__ to add an extra storer attribute used for persistence.

   ```
   class ShoppingCart(object):
       def __init__(self, storer=None):
           self.items = []
           self.storer = storer
   ```

3. Add a store method that uses the storer to save the cart.

   ```
   def store(self):
       return self.storer.store_cart(self)
   ```

4. Add a retrieve method that updates the internal items by using the storer.

   ```
   def restore(self, id):
       self.items = self.storer.retrieve_cart(id).items
       return self
   ```

Testing Customer Stories with Behavior Driven Development

The specifics of the API of the `storer` will be given further down in this recipe.

We need to activate our virtual environment and then install `mockito` for this recipe.

1. Create a virtual environment, activate it, and verify the tools are working:

   ```
   gturnquist-mbp:tmp gturnquist$ virtualenv --no-site-packages ptc
   New python executable in ptc/bin/python
   Installing setuptools.............done.
   gturnquist-mbp:tmp gturnquist$ . ptc/bin/activate
   (ptc)gturnquist-mbp:tmp gturnquist$ which python
   /Users/gturnquist/tmp/ptc/bin/python
   (ptc)gturnquist-mbp:tmp gturnquist$ which easy_install
   /Users/gturnquist/tmp/ptc/bin/easy_install
   (ptc)gturnquist-mbp:tmp gturnquist$
   ```

2. Install `mockito` by typing `pip install mockito`.

Install `pinocchio` and `figleaf` using the same steps from the *Writing a testable story with Voidspace Mock and nose* recipe.

How to do it...

With the following steps, we will explore how to use mocking to write a testable story:

1. In `recipe31_cart.py`, create a `DataAccess` class with empty methods for storing and retrieving shopping carts.

   ```
   class DataAccess(object):
       def store_cart(self, cart):
           pass
       def retrieve_cart(self, id):
           pass
   ```

2. Create a new file called `recipe31.py` for writing test code.

3. Create an automated unit test that exercises the cart by mocking out the methods of `DataAccess`.

   ```
   import unittest
   from copy import deepcopy
   from recipe31_cart import *
   from mockito import *

   class CartThatWeWillSaveAndRestoreUsingMockito(unittest.TestCase):
       def test_fill_up_a_cart_then_save_it_and_restore_it(self):
           # Create an empty shopping cart
   ```

```python
cart = ShoppingCart(DataAccess())
# Add a couple of items
cart.add("carton of milk", 2.50)
cart.add("frozen pizza", 3.00)
self.assertEquals(2, len(cart))
# Create a clone of the cart for mocking
# purposes.
original_cart = deepcopy(cart)
# Save the cart at this point in time into a database
# using a mock
cart.storer = mock()
when(cart.storer).store_cart(cart).thenReturn(1)
when(cart.storer).retrieve_cart(1). \
                    thenReturn(original_cart)
id = cart.store()
self.assertEquals(1, id)
# Add more items to cart
cart.add("cookie dough", 1.75)
cart.add("ginger ale", 3.25)
self.assertEquals(4, len(cart))
# Restore the cart to the last point in time
cart.restore(id)
self.assertEquals(2, len(cart))
verify(cart.storer).store_cart(cart)
verify(cart.storer).retrieve_cart(1)
```

4. Run the test using `nosetests` with the `spec` plugin.

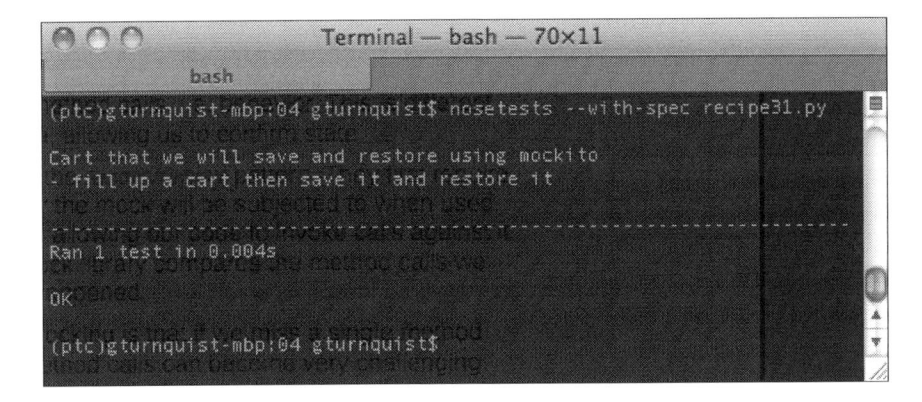

```
(ptc)gturnquist-mbp:04 gturnquist$ nosetests --with-spec recipe31.py
Cart that we will save and restore using mockito
- fill up a cart then save it and restore it
----------------------------------------------------------------------
Ran 1 test in 0.004s

OK
(ptc)gturnquist-mbp:04 gturnquist$
```

How it works...

This recipe is very similar to the earlier recipe *Writing a testable story with voidspace mock and nose*. For details about mocking and the benefits with regards to BDD, it is very useful to read that recipe.

Let's compare the syntax of Voidspace Mock with mockito to get a feel for the differences. Look at the following voidspace mock block of code.

```
cart.storer.store_cart = Mock()
cart.storer.store_cart.return_value = 1
cart.storer.retrieve_cart = Mock()
cart.storer.retrieve_cart.return_value = original_cart
```

It shows the function `store_cart` being mocked.

```
cart.storer = mock()
when(cart.storer).store_cart(cart).thenReturn(1)
when(cart.storer).retrieve_cart(1). \
                 thenReturn(original_cart)
```

Mockito approaches this by mocking out the entire `storer` object. Mockito originated as a Java mocking tool, which explains its Java-ish APIs like `thenReturn` compared with voidspace mock's Pythonic style of `return_value`.

Some find this influence from Java on Python's implementation of mockito distasteful. Frankly, I believe that is insufficient reason to discard a library. In the previous example, mockito records the desired behavior in a more succinct fashion, something that would definitely offset the Java-like API.

See also

Writing a testable story with voidspace mock and nose

Writing a testable story with Lettuce

Lettuce (http://lettuce.it) is a Cucumber-like BDD tool built for Python.

Cucumber (http://cukes.info) was developed by the Ruby community and provides a way to write scenarios in a textual style. By letting our stakeholders read the stories, they can easily discern what the software is expected to do.

This recipe shows how to install Lettuce, write a test story, and then wire it into our shopping cart application to exercise our code.

Getting ready

For this recipe, we will be using the shopping cart application shown at the beginning of this chapter. We also need to install Lettuce and its dependencies.

Install lettuce by typing `pip install lettuce`.

How to do it...

In the following steps, we will explore creating some testable stories with Lettuce, and wiring it to runnable Python code:

1. Create a new folder called `recipe32` to contain all the files in this recipe.

2. Create a file named `recipe32.feature` to capture our story. Write the top-level description of our new feature, based on our shopping cart.

   ```
   Feature: Shopping cart
     As a shopper
     I want to load up items in my cart
     So that I can check out and pay for them
   ```

3. Let's first create a scenario that captures the behavior of the cart when it's empty.

   ```
   Scenario: Empty cart
     Given an empty cart
     Then looking up the fifth item causes an error
     And looking up a negative price causes an error
     And the price with no taxes is $0.00
     And the price with taxes is $0.00
   ```

4. Add another scenario that shows what happens when we add cartons of milk.

   ```
   Scenario: Cart getting loaded with multiple of the same
     Given an empty cart
     When I add a carton of milk for $2.50
     And I add another carton of milk for $2.50
     Then the first item is a carton of milk
     And the price is $5.00
     And the cart has 2 items
     And the total cost with 10% taxes is $5.50
   ```

5. Add a third scenario that shows what happens when we combine a carton of milk and a frozen pizza.

   ```
   Scenario: Cart getting loaded with different items
     Given an empty cart
     When I add a carton of milk
     And I add a frozen pizza
   ```

```
            Then the first item is a carton of milk
            And the second item is a frozen pizza
            And the first price is $2.50
            And the second price is $3.00
            And the total cost with no taxes is $5.50
            And the total cost with 10% taes is $6.05
```

6. Let's run the story through Lettuce to see what the outcome is, considering we haven't linked this story to any Python code. In the following screenshot, it's impossible to discern the color of the outputs. The feature and scenario declarations are white. **Given**, **When**, and **Then** are undefined and colored yellow. This shows that we haven't tied the steps to any code yet.

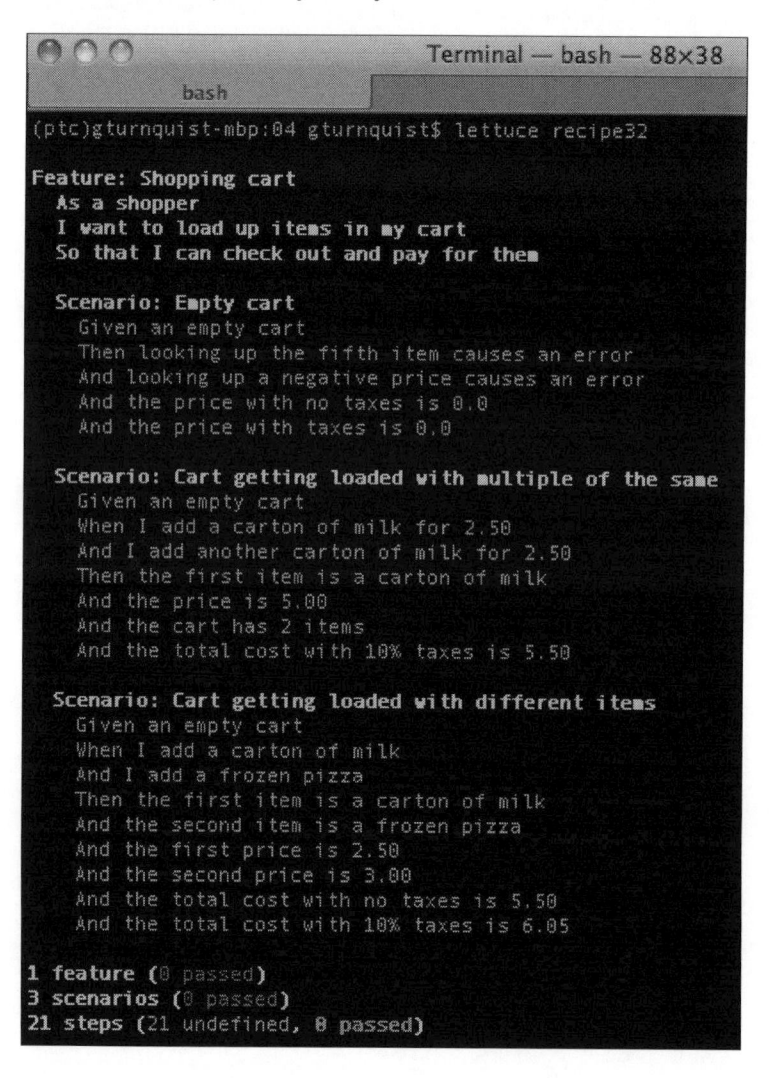

```
(ptc)gturnquist-mbp:04 gturnquist$ lettuce recipe32

Feature: Shopping cart
  As a shopper
  I want to load up items in my cart
  So that I can check out and pay for them

  Scenario: Empty cart
    Given an empty cart
    Then looking up the fifth item causes an error
    And looking up a negative price causes an error
    And the price with no taxes is 0.0
    And the price with taxes is 0.0

  Scenario: Cart getting loaded with multiple of the same
    Given an empty cart
    When I add a carton of milk for 2.50
    And I add another carton of milk for 2.50
    Then the first item is a carton of milk
    And the price is 5.00
    And the cart has 2 items
    And the total cost with 10% taxes is 5.50

  Scenario: Cart getting loaded with different items
    Given an empty cart
    When I add a carton of milk
    And I add a frozen pizza
    Then the first item is a carton of milk
    And the second item is a frozen pizza
    And the first price is 2.50
    And the second price is 3.00
    And the total cost with no taxes is 5.50
    And the total cost with 10% taxes is 6.05

1 feature (0 passed)
3 scenarios (0 passed)
21 steps (21 undefined, 0 passed)
```

7. Create a new file in `recipe32` called `steps.py` to implement the steps needed to support the Givens.

8. Add some code to `steps.py` to implement the first Given.

   ```
   from lettuce import *
   from cart import *

   @step("an empty cart")
   def an_empty_cart(step):
       world.cart = ShoppingCart()
   ```

9. To run the steps, we need to make sure the current path that contains the `cart.py` module is part of our *PYTHONPATH*.

   > For Linux and Mac OSX systems, type `export PYTHONPATH=/path/to/cart.py`.
   >
   > For Windows, go to **Control Panel | System | Advanced**, click **Environment Variables**, and either edit the existing `PYTHONPATH` variable or add a new one, pointing to the folder that contains `cart.py`.

10. Run the stories again. It's hard to see in the following screenshot, but **Given an empty cart** is now green.

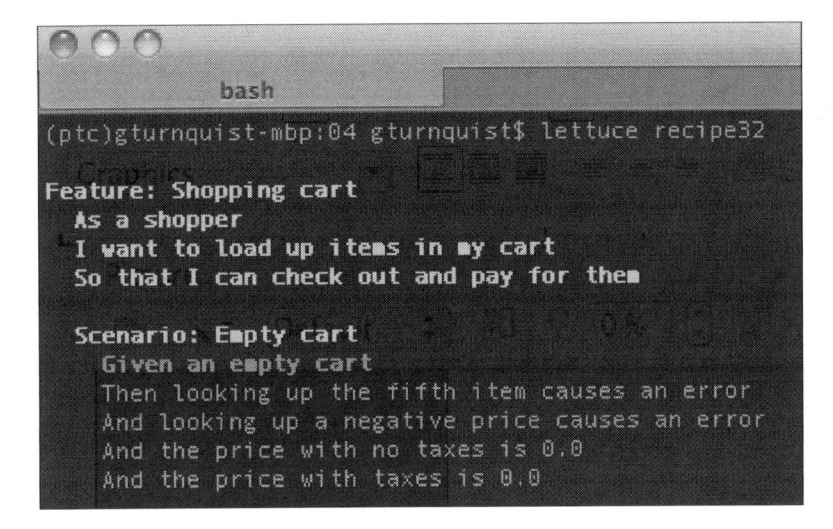

    ```
    (ptc)gturnquist-mbp:04 gturnquist$ lettuce recipe32
    Feature: Shopping cart
      As a shopper
      I want to load up items in my cart
      So that I can check out and pay for them

      Scenario: Empty cart
        Given an empty cart
        Then looking up the fifth item causes an error
        And looking up a negative price causes an error
        And the price with no taxes is 0.0
        And the price with taxes is 0.0
    ```

    > While this screenshot only focuses on the first scenario, all three scenarios have the same Givens. The code we wrote satisfied all three Givens.

11. Add code to `steps.py` that implements support for the first scenario's *Thens*.

    ```
    @step("looking up the fifth item causes an error")
    def looking_up_fifth_item(step):
        try:
            world.cart.item(5)
            raise AssertionError("Expected IndexError")
        except IndexError, e:
            pass

    @step("looking up a negative price causes an error")
    def looking_up_negative_price(step):
        try:
            world.cart.price(-2)
            raise AssertionError("Expected IndexError")
        except IndexError, e:
            pass

    @step("the price with no taxes is (.*)")
    def price_with_no_taxes(step, total):
        assert world.cart.total(0.0) == float(total)

    @step("the price with taxes is (.*)")
    def price_with_taxes(step, total):
        assert world.cart.total(10.0) == float(total)
    ```

12. Run the stories again and notice how the first scenario is completely passing.

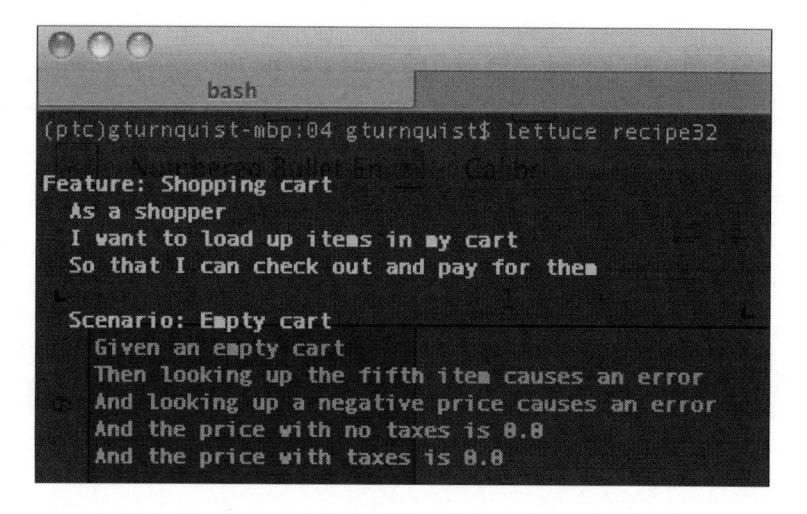

    ```
    (ptc)gturnquist-mbp:04 gturnquist$ lettuce recipe32

    Feature: Shopping cart
      As a shopper
      I want to load up items in my cart
      So that I can check out and pay for them

      Scenario: Empty cart
        Given an empty cart
        Then looking up the fifth item causes an error
        And looking up a negative price causes an error
        And the price with no taxes is 0.0
        And the price with taxes is 0.0
    ```

13. Now add code to `steps.py` to implement the steps needed for the second scenario.

    ```
    @step("I add a carton of milk for (.*)")
    def add_a_carton_of_milk(step, price):
        world.cart.add("carton of milk", float(price))
    ```

```
@step("I add another carton of milk for (.*)")
def add_another_carton_of_milk(step, price):
    world.cart.add("carton of milk", float(price))

@step("the first item is a carton of milk")
def check_first_item(step):
    assert world.cart.item(1) == "carton of milk"

@step("the price is (.*)")
def check_first_price(step, price):
    assert world.cart.price(1) == float(price)

@step("the cart has (.*) items")
def check_size_of_cart(step, num_items):
    assert len(world.cart) == float(num_items)

@step("the total cost with (.*)% taxes is (.*)")
def check_total_cost(step, tax_rate, total):
    assert world.cart.total(float(tax_rate)) == float(total)
```

14. Finally, add code to `steps.py` to implement the steps needed for the last scenario.

```
@step("I add a carton of milk")
def add_a_carton_of_milk(step):
    world.cart.add("carton of milk", 2.50)

@step("I add a frozen pizza")
def add_a_frozen_pizza(step):
    world.cart.add("frozen pizza", 3.00)

@step("the second item is a frozen pizza")
def check_the_second_item(step):
    assert world.cart.item(2) == "frozen pizza"

@step("the first price is (.*)")
def check_the_first_price(step, price):
    assert world.cart.price(1) == float(price)

@step("the second price is (.*)")
def check_the_second_price(step, price):
    assert world.cart.price(2) == float(price)

@step("the total cost with no taxes is (.*)")
def check_total_cost_with_no_taxes(step, total):
    assert world.cart.total(0.0) == float(total)

@step("the total cost with (.*)% taxes is (.*)")
def check_total_cost_with_taxes(step, tax_rate, total):
    assert round(world.cart.total(float(tax_rate)),2) == \
                                           float(total)
```

Testing Customer Stories with Behavior Driven Development

15. Run the story by typing `lettuce recipe32` and see how they are all now passing. In the next screenshot, we have all the tests passing and everything is green.

```
(ptc)gturnquist-mbp:04 gturnquist$ lettuce recipe32

Feature: Shopping cart
  As a shopper
  I want to load up items in my cart
  So that I can check out and pay for them

  Scenario: Empty cart
    Given an empty cart
    Then looking up the fifth item causes an error
    And looking up a negative price causes an error
    And the price with no taxes is 0.0
    And the price with taxes is 0.0

  Scenario: Cart getting loaded with multiple of the same
    Given an empty cart
    When I add a carton of milk for 2.50
    And I add another carton of milk for 2.50
    Then the first item is a carton of milk
    And the price is 5.00
    And the cart has 2 items
    And the total cost with 10% taxes is 5.50

  Scenario: Cart getting loaded with different items
    Given an empty cart
    When I add a carton of milk
    And I add a frozen pizza
    Then the first item is a carton of milk
    And the second item is a frozen pizza
    And the first price is 2.50
    And the second price is 3.00
    And the total cost with no taxes is 5.50
    And the total cost with 10% taxes is 6.05

1 feature (1 passed)
3 scenarios (3 passed)
21 steps (21 passed)
```

How it works...

Lettuce uses the popular **Given/When/Then** style of BDD story telling.

> **Givens**: It involves setting up a scenario. This often includes creating objects. For each of our scenarios, we created an instance of the ShoppingCart. This is very similar to unittest's setup method.

- **Thens**: It acts on the Givens. These are the operations we want to exercise in a scenario. We can exercise more than one Then.
- **Whens**: It involves testing the final results of the Thens. In our code, we mostly used Python asserts. In a couple of cases, where we needed to detect an exception, we wrapped the call with a `try-catch` block with a `throw` if the expected exception didn't occur.

It doesn't matter in what order we put the **Given/Then/When**. Lettuce will record everything so that all the Givens are listed first, followed by all the Whens, and then all the Thens. Lettuce puts on the final polish by translating successive Given/When/Then into And for better readability.

There's more...

If you look closely at some of the steps, you will notice some wildcards.

```
@step("the total cost with (.*)% taxes is (.*)")
def check_total_cost(step, tax_rate, total):
    assert world.cart.total(float(tax_rate)) == float(total)
```

The `@step` string lets us dynamically grab parts of the string as variables by using pattern matchers.

- The first (.*) is a pattern to capture the `tax_rate`
- The second (.*) is a pattern to capture the `total`

The method definition shows these two extra variables added in. We can name them anything we want. This gives us the ability to actually drive the tests, data and all, from `recipe32.feature` and only use `steps.py` to link things together in a generalized way.

> It's important to point out that actual values stored in `tax_rate` and `total` are Unicode strings. Because the test involves floating point numbers, we have to convert the variables or the `assert` fails.

How complex should a story be?

In this recipe, we fit everything into a single story. Our story involved all the various shopping cart operations. As we write more scenarios, we may expand this into multiple stories. This goes back to the concept discussed in the *Breaking down obscure tests into simple ones* section of *Chapter 1*. If we overload a single scenario with too many steps, it may get too complex. It is better if we can visualize a single thread of execution that is easy to verify at the end.

Don't mix wiring code with application code

The project's website shows a sample building a factorial function. It has both the factorial function as well as the wiring in a single file. For demo purposes this is alright. But for actual production use, it is best to decouple the application from the Lettuce wiring. This encourages a clean interface and demonstrates usability.

Lettuce works great using folders

Lettuce, by default, will look for a `features` folder wherever we run it, and discover any files ending in `.feature`. That way it can automatically find all of our stories and run them.

It is possible to override the features directory with `-s` or `--scenarios`.

See also

Breaking down obscure tests into simple ones section from *Chapter 1*

Using Should DSL to write succinct assertions with Lettuce

Lettuce (`http://lettuce.it`) is a BDD tool built for Python.

The **Should DSL** (`http://www.should-dsl.info`) provides a simpler way to write assertions for Thens.

This recipe shows how to install Lettuce and Should DSL. Then, we will write a test story. Finally, we will wire it into our shopping cart application using the Should DSL to exercise our code.

Getting ready

For this recipe, we will be using the shopping cart application shown at the beginning of this chapter. We also need to install Lettuce and its dependencies:

- Install lettuce by typing `pip install lettuce`
- Install Should DSL by typing `pip install should_dsl`

How to do it...

With the following steps, we will use the Should DSL to write more succinct assertions in our test stories:

1. Create a new directory called `recipe33` to contain all the files for this recipe.

2. Create a new file in `recipe33` called `recipe33.feature` to contain our test scenarios.
3. Create a story in `recipe33.feature` with several scenarios to exercise our shopping cart.

```
Feature: Shopping cart
  As a shopper
  I want to load up items in my cart
  So that I can check out and pay for them

    Scenario: Empty cart
      Given an empty cart
      Then looking up the fifth item causes an error
      And looking up a negative price causes an error
      And the price with no taxes is 0.0
      And the price with taxes is 0.0
    Scenario: Cart getting loaded with multiple of the same
      Given an empty cart
      When I add a carton of milk for 2.50
      And I add another carton of milk for 2.50
      Then the first item is a carton of milk
      And the price is 5.00
      And the cart has 2 items
      And the total cost with 10% taxes is 5.50
    Scenario: Cart getting loaded with different items
      Given an empty cart
      When I add a carton of milk
      And I add a frozen pizza
      Then the first item is a carton of milk
      And the second item is a frozen pizza
      And the first price is 2.50
      And the second price is 3.00
      And the total cost with no taxes is 5.50
      And the total cost with 10% taxes is 6.05
```

4. Write a set of assertions using Should DSL.

```
from lettuce import *
from should_dsl import should, should_not
from cart import *

@step("an empty cart")
def an_empty_cart(step):
    world.cart = ShoppingCart()

@step("looking up the fifth item causes an error")
def looking_up_fifth_item(step):
    (world.cart.item, 5) |should| throw(IndexError)
```

```python
@step("looking up a negative price causes an error")
def looking_up_negative_price(step):
    (world.cart.price, -2) |should| throw(IndexError)

@step("the price with no taxes is (.*)")
def price_with_no_taxes(step, total):
    world.cart.total(0.0) |should| equal_to(float(total))

@step("the price with taxes is (.*)")
def price_with_taxes(step, total):
    world.cart.total(10.0) |should| equal_to(float(total))

@step("I add a carton of milk for 2.50")
def add_a_carton_of_milk(step):
    world.cart.add("carton of milk", 2.50)

@step("I add another carton of milk for 2.50")
def add_another_carton_of_milk(step):
    world.cart.add("carton of milk", 2.50)

@step("the first item is a carton of milk")
def check_first_item(step):
    world.cart.item(1) |should| equal_to("carton of milk")

@step("the price is 5.00")
def check_first_price(step):
    world.cart.price(1) |should| equal_to(5.0)

@step("the cart has 2 items")
def check_size_of_cart(step):
    len(world.cart) |should| equal_to(2)

@step("the total cost with 10% taxes is 5.50")
def check_total_cost(step):
    world.cart.total(10.0) |should| equal_to(5.5)

@step("I add a carton of milk")
def add_a_carton_of_milk(step):
    world.cart.add("carton of milk", 2.50)

@step("I add a frozen pizza")
def add_a_frozen_pizza(step):
    world.cart.add("frozen pizza", 3.00)

@step("the second item is a frozen pizza")
def check_the_second_item(step):
    world.cart.item(2) |should| equal_to("frozen pizza")

@step("the first price is 2.50")
def check_the_first_price(step):
    world.cart.price(1) |should| equal_to(2.5)

@step("the second price is 3.00")
```

```python
def check_the_second_price(step):
    world.cart.price(2) |should| equal_to(3.0)

@step("the total cost with no taxes is 5.50")
def check_total_cost_with_no_taxes(step):
    world.cart.total(0.0) |should| equal_to(5.5)

@step("the total cost with 10% taxes is (.*)")
def check_total_cost_with_taxes(step, total):
    world.cart.total(10.0) |should| close_to(float(total), \
                                            delta=0.1)
```

5. Run the story.

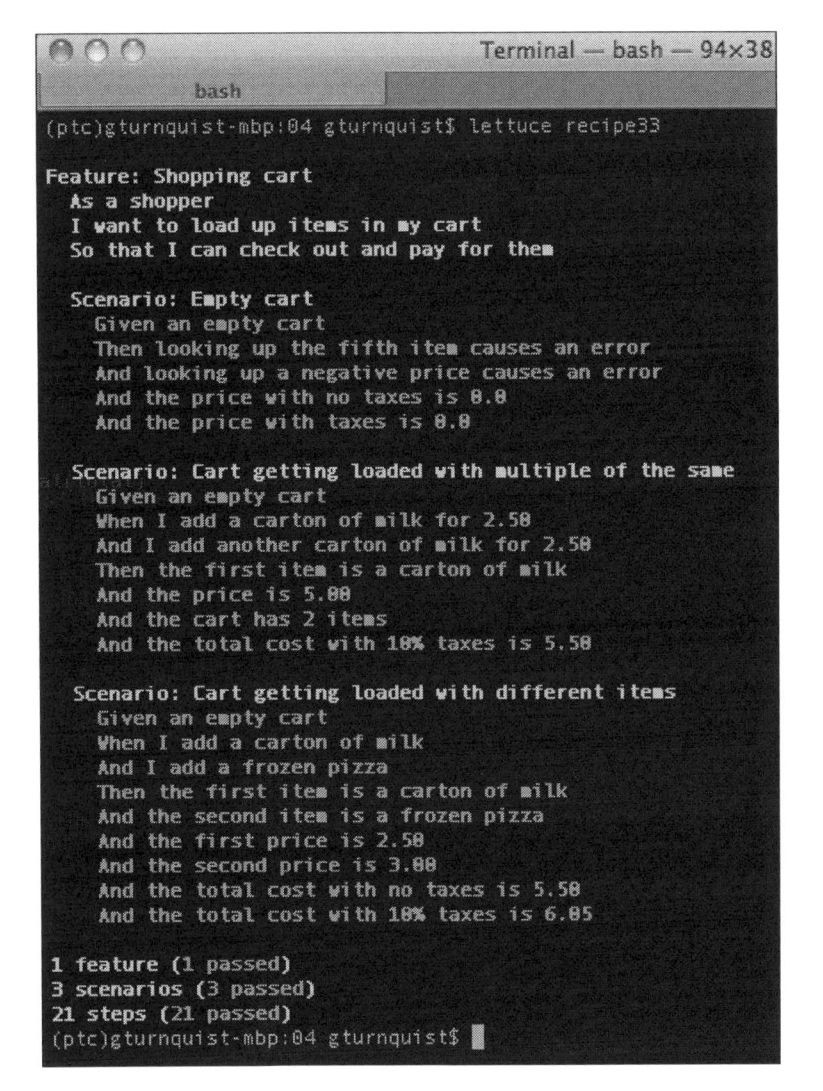

```
(ptc)gturnquist-mbp:04 gturnquist$ lettuce recipe33
Feature: Shopping cart
  As a shopper
  I want to load up items in my cart
  So that I can check out and pay for them

  Scenario: Empty cart
    Given an empty cart
    Then looking up the fifth item causes an error
    And looking up a negative price causes an error
    And the price with no taxes is 0.0
    And the price with taxes is 0.0

  Scenario: Cart getting loaded with multiple of the same
    Given an empty cart
    When I add a carton of milk for 2.50
    And I add another carton of milk for 2.50
    Then the first item is a carton of milk
    And the price is 5.00
    And the cart has 2 items
    And the total cost with 10% taxes is 5.50

  Scenario: Cart getting loaded with different items
    Given an empty cart
    When I add a carton of milk
    And I add a frozen pizza
    Then the first item is a carton of milk
    And the second item is a frozen pizza
    And the first price is 2.50
    And the second price is 3.00
    And the total cost with no taxes is 5.50
    And the total cost with 10% taxes is 6.05

1 feature (1 passed)
3 scenarios (3 passed)
21 steps (21 passed)
(ptc)gturnquist-mbp:04 gturnquist$
```

Testing Customer Stories with Behavior Driven Development

How it works...

The previous recipe (*Writing a testable story with Lettuce*), shows more details on how Lettuce works. This recipe demonstrates how to use the Should DSL to make useful assertions.

Why do we need Should DSL? The simplest checks we write involve testing values to confirm the behavior of the shopping cart application. In the previous recipe, we mostly used Python assertions.

```
assert len(context.cart) == 2
```

This is pretty easy to understand. Should DSL offers a simple alternative.

```
len(context.cart) |should| equal_to(2)
```

Does this look like much of a difference? Some say yes, others say no. It is wordier, and for some this is easier to read. For others, it isn't.

So why are we visiting this? Because, Should DSL has more than just `equal_to`. There are many more:

- `be`: check identity
- `contain, include, be_into`: verify if an object is contained or contains another
- `be_kind_of`: check types
- `be_like`: checks using a regular expression
- `be_thrown_by, throws`: check that an exception is thrown
- `close_to`: check if value is close, given a delta
- `end_with`: check if a string ends with a given suffix
- `equal_to`: check value equality
- `respond_to`: check if an object has a given attribute or method
- `start_with`: check if a string starts with a given prefix

There are other alternatives as well, but this provides a diverse set of comparisons. If we imagine the code needed to write assertions that check the same things, then things get more complex.

For example, let's think about confirming expected exceptions. In the previous recipe, we needed to confirm that an `IndexError` is thrown when accessing an item outside the boundaries of our cart. A simple Python `assert` didn't work, so instead we coded this pattern.

```
try:
    world.cart.price(-2)
    raise AssertionError("Expected an IndexError")
except IndexError, e:
    pass
```

This is clunky and ugly. Now, imagine a more complex, more realistic system, and the idea of having to use this pattern for lots of test situations where we want to verify that proper exception is thrown. This can quickly become an expensive coding task.

Thankfully, Should DSL turns this pattern of exception assertion into a one-liner.

```
(world.cart.price, -2) |should| throw(IndexError)
```

This is clear and concise. We can instantly understand that invoking this method with these arguments should throw a certain exception. If no exception is raised, or a different one is raised, it will fail and give us clear feedback.

> If you notice, Should DSL requires the method call to be split up into a tuple, with the first element of the tuple being the method handle, and the rest being the arguments for the method.

There's more...

In the sample code listed in this chapter, we used |should|. But Should DSL also comes with |should_not|. Sometimes, the condition we want to express is best captured with a |should_not|. Combined with all the matchers listed earlier, we have a plethora of opportunities to test things, positive or negative.

But don't forget, we can still use Python's plain old `assert` if it is easier to read. The idea is to have plenty of ways to express the same verification of behavior.

See also

Writing a testable story with Lettuce

Updating the project-level script to run this chapter's BDD tests

In this chapter, we have developed several tactics to write and exercise BDD tests. This should help us in developing new projects. An invaluable tool for any project is having a top-level script used to manage things like packaging, bundling, and testing.

This recipe shows how to create a command-line project script that will run all the tests we created in this chapter using the various runners.

Testing Customer Stories with Behavior Driven Development

Getting ready

For this recipe, we need to have coded all the recipes from this chapter.

How to do it...

With the following steps, we will create a project-level script that will run all the test recipes from this chapter.

1. Create a new file called `recipe34.py`.
2. Add code that uses the `getopt` library for parsing command-line arguments.

```
import getopt
import logging
import nose
import os
import os.path
import re
import sys
import lettuce
import doctest
from glob import glob

def usage():
    print
    print "Usage: python recipe34.py [command]"
    print
    print "\t--help"
    print "\t--test"
    print "\t--package"
    print "\t--publish"
    print "\t--register"
    print

try:
    optlist, args = getopt.getopt(sys.argv[1:],
            "h",
            ["help", "test", "package", "publish", "register"])
except getopt.GetoptError:
    # print help information and exit:
    print "Invalid command found in %s" % sys.argv
    usage()
    sys.exit(2)
```

3. Add a test function that uses our custom nose plugin `BddPrinter`.

   ```
   def test_with_bdd():
       from recipe26_plugin import BddPrinter
       suite = ["recipe26", "recipe30", "recipe31"]
       print("Running suite %s" % suite)
       args = [""]
       args.extend(suite)
       args.extend(["--with-bdd"])
       nose.run(argv=args, plugins=[BddPrinter()])
   ```

4. Add a test function that exercises file-based doctests.

   ```
   def test_plain_old_doctest():
       for extension in ["doctest", "txt"]:
           for doc in glob("recipe27*.%s" % extension):
               print("Testing %s" % doc)
               doctest.testfile(doc)
   ```

5. Add a test function that exercises doctests using a customized `doctest` runner.

   ```
   def test_customized_doctests():
       from recipe28 import BddDocTestRunner

       old_doctest_runner = doctest.DocTestRunner
       doctest.DocTestRunner = BddDocTestRunner

       for recipe in ["recipe28", "recipe29"]:
           for file in glob("%s*.doctest" % recipe):
               given = file[len("%s_" % recipe):]
               given = given[:-len(".doctest")]
               given = " ".join(given.split("_"))
               print("===================================")
               print("%s: Given a %s..." % (recipe, given))
               print( "===================================")
               doctest.testfile(file)
               print
       doctest.DocTestRunner = old_doctest_runner
   ```

6. Add a test function that exercises `lettuce` tests.

   ```
   def test_lettuce_scenarios():
       print("Running suite recipe32")
       lettuce.Runner(os.path.abspath("recipe32"), verbosity=3).run()
       print

       print("Running suite recipe33")
       lettuce.Runner(os.path.abspath("recipe33"), verbosity=3).run()
       print
   ```

7. Add a top-level test function that runs all of our test functions and can be wired to the command-line option.

   ```
   def test():
       test_with_bdd()
       test_plain_old_doctest()
       test_customized_doctests()
       test_lettuce_scenarios()
   ```

8. Add some extra stub functions that represent packaging, publishing, and registration options.

   ```
   def package():
       print "This is where we can plug in code to run " + \
             "setup.py to generate a bundle."
   def publish():
       print "This is where we can plug in code to upload " + \
             "our tarball to S3 or some other download site."
   def register():
       print "setup.py has a built in function to " + \
             "'register' a release to PyPI. It's " + \
             "convenient to put a hook in here."
       # os.system("%s setup.py register" % sys.executable)
   ```

9. Add code to parse the command-line options.

   ```
   if len(optlist) == 0:
       usage()
       sys.exit(1)
   # Check for help requests, which cause all other
   # options to be ignored.
   for option in optlist:
       if option[0] in ("--help", "-h"):
           usage()
           sys.exit(1)

   # Parse the arguments, in order
   for option in optlist:
       if option[0] in ("--test"):
           test()
       if option[0] in ("--package"):
           package()
       if option[0] in ("--publish"):
           publish()
       if option[0] in ("--register"):
           register()
   ```

10. Run the script with no options.

```
Running suite recipe33
Feature: Shopping cart                                          # recipe33/recipe33.feat
  As a shopper                                                  # recipe33/recipe33.feat
  I want to load up items in my cart                            # recipe33/recipe33.feat
  So that I can check out and pay for them                      # recipe33/recipe33.feat

  Scenario: Empty cart                                          # recipe33/recipe33.feat
    Given an empty cart                                         # recipe33/steps.py:6
    Then looking up the fifth item causes an error              # recipe33/steps.py:10
    And looking up a negative price causes an error             # recipe33/steps.py:14
    And the price with no taxes is 0.0                          # recipe33/steps.py:18
    And the price with taxes is 0.0                             # recipe33/steps.py:22

  Scenario: Cart getting loaded with multiple of the same       # recipe33/recipe33.feat
    Given an empty cart                                         # recipe33/steps.py:6
    When I add a carton of milk for 2.50                        # recipe33/steps.py:50
    And I add another carton of milk for 2.50                   # recipe33/steps.py:30
    Then the first item is a carton of milk                     # recipe33/steps.py:34
    And the price is 5.00                                       # recipe33/steps.py:38
    And the cart has 2 items                                    # recipe32/steps.py:49
    And the total cost with 10% taxes is 5.50                   # recipe33/steps.py:46

  Scenario: Cart getting loaded with different items            # recipe33/recipe33.feat
    Given an empty cart                                         # recipe33/steps.py:6
    When I add a carton of milk                                 # recipe33/steps.py:50
    And I add a frozen pizza                                    # recipe33/steps.py:54
    Then the first item is a carton of milk                     # recipe33/steps.py:34
    And the second item is a frozen pizza                       # recipe33/steps.py:58
    And the first price is 2.50                                 # recipe32/steps.py:69
    And the second price is 3.00                                # recipe33/steps.py:66
    And the total cost with no taxes is 5.50                    # recipe33/steps.py:70
    And the total cost with 10% taxes is 6.05                   # recipe33/steps.py:74

1 feature (1 passed)
3 scenarios (3 passed)
21 steps (21 passed)
```

11. Run the script with `-test`.

    ```
    (ptc)gturnquist-mbp:04 gturnquist$ python recipe34.py --test
    Running suite ['recipe26', 'recipe30', 'recipe31']
    ...
      Scenario: Cart getting loaded with different items        # recipe33/recipe33.feature:22
        Given an empty cart                                     # recipe33/steps.py:6
        When I add a carton of milk                             # recipe33/steps.py:50
        And I add a frozen pizza                                # recipe33/steps.py:54
        Then the first item is a carton of milk                 # recipe33/steps.py:34
        And the second item is a frozen pizza                   # recipe33/steps.py:58
    ```

```
        And the first price is 2.50                            #
recipe32/steps.py:69
        And the second price is 3.00                           #
recipe33/steps.py:66
        And the total cost with no taxes is 5.50               #
recipe33/steps.py:70
        And the total cost with 10% taxes is 6.05              #
recipe33/steps.py:74

1 feature (1 passed)
3 scenarios (3 passed)
21 steps (21 passed)
```

12. Run the script using -package -publish -register.

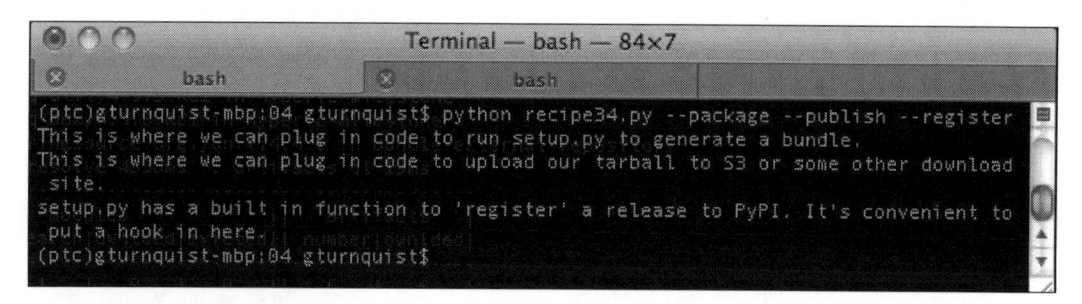

```
(ptc)gturnquist-mbp:04 gturnquist$ python recipe34.py --package --publish --register
This is where we can plug in code to run setup.py to generate a bundle.
This is where we can plug in code to upload our tarball to S3 or some other download
 site.
setup.py has a built in function to 'register' a release to PyPI. It's convenient to
 put a hook in here.
(ptc)gturnquist-mbp:04 gturnquist$
```

How it works...

This script uses Python's `getopt` library.

See also

For more details about how and why to use `getopt`, reasons to write a project-level script, and why we are using `getopt` instead of `optparse`, see the *Writing a project-level script that lets you run different test suites* section from *Chapter 2*.

5
High Level Customer Scenarios with Acceptance Testing

In this chapter, we will cover:

- Installing Pyccuracy
- Testing the basics with Pyccuracy
- Using Pyccuracy to verify web app security
- Installing the Robot Framework
- Creating a data-driven test suite with Robot
- Writing a testable story using Robot
- Tagging Robot tests and running a subset
- Testing web basics with Robot
- Using Robot to verify web app security
- Creating a project-level script to run this chapter's acceptance tests

Introduction

Acceptance testing involves writing tests to prove our code is, well, acceptable! But what does this mean? The context implies acceptable from a customer's perspective. Customers are usually more interested in what the software does, not how it does it. This means that tests are aimed at inputs and outputs and tend to be at a higher level than unit testing. This has sometimes been called black box testing, and is usually more system oriented. At the end of the day, it is often associated with testing that asserts whether or not the customer will accept the software.

There is an assumption amongst some developers that acceptance testing involves verifying the front end of web applications. In fact, several testing tools, including Pyccuracy, are built on the sole premise of testing web applications. When viewed from the perspective of whether or not a customer will accept the software, this would quite literally fit into *acceptable from a customer's perspective*.

But web testing isn't the only form of acceptance testing. Not all systems are web-based. If a subsystem is to be built by one team, and handed off to another team that plans to build another layer on top of it, an acceptance test may be required before the second team will accept it.

In this chapter, we will dig into some recipes that involve both web and non-web application acceptance testing.

To create an e-store web application for testing, follow these steps.

1. Make sure you have `mercurial` installed on your system.
    - For Mac, use either `mac ports` or `home brew`.
    - For Ubuntu/Debian, use `sudo apt-get install mercurial`
    - For other systems, you will need to do extra research in installing `mercurial`.

2. This also requires having compilable tools installed, like `gcc`.
    - For Ubuntu, use `sudo apt-get install build-essential`
    - For other systems, you will need to do extra research in installing `gcc`.

3. Install `satchmo`, an e-commerce website builder, by typing the following commands:
   ```
   pip install -r http://bitbucket.org/gturnquist/satchmo/raw/tip/scripts/requirements.txt
   ```

Chapter 5

```
pip install -e hg+http://bitbucket.org/gturnquist/
satchmo/#egg=satchmo
```

4. Install Python's `PIL` library for image processing: `pip install PIL`.
5. Edit `<virtualenv root>/lib/python2.6/site-packages/django/contrib/admin/templates/admin/login.html` to add `id="login"` to the `Log in <input>` tag. This allows Pyccuracy to grab the Log in button and 'click' it.
6. Run the `satchmo` script to create a store application: `clonesatchmo.py`.
7. When prompted about creating a super-user, say `yes`.
8. When prompted, enter a `username`.
9. When prompted, enter an `e-mail` address.
10. When prompted, enter a `password`.
11. Go into the store directory: `cd store`.
12. Startup store app: `python manage.py runserver`.

> If you have issues installing `satchmo` with these steps, visit the project site at `http://www.satchmoproject.com` and possibly their support group at `http://groups.google.com/group/satchmo-users`.

To create a non-web shopping cart application for testing, create `cart.py` with the following code:

```python
class ShoppingCart(object):
    def __init__(self):
        self.items = []
    def add(self, item, price):
        for cart_item in self.items:
            # Since we found the item, we increment
            # instead of append
            if cart_item.item == item:
                cart_item.q += 1
                return self
        # If we didn't find, then we append
        self.items.append(Item(item, price))
        return self
    def item(self, index):
        return self.items[index-1].item
    def price(self, index):
        return self.items[index-1].price * self.items[index-1].q
```

High Level Customer Scenarios with Acceptance Testing

```
        def total(self, sales_tax):
            sum_price = sum([item.price*item.q for item in self.items])
            return sum_price*(1.0 + sales_tax/100.0)
        def __len__(self):
            return sum([item.q for item in self.items])
    class Item(object):
        def __init__(self, item, price, q=1):
            self.item = item
            self.price = price
            self.q = q
```

This shopping cart:

- Is 1-based, meaning the first item and price are at [1] not [0]
- Includes the ability to have multiples of the same item
- Will calculate total price and then add taxes

This application isn't complex. Maybe it doesn't look exactly at a system level, but it does provide an easy application to write acceptance tests against.

Installing Pyccuracy

Pyccuracy is a useful tool for writing web acceptance tests using a BDD style language. This recipe shows all the steps needed to install and set it up for later recipes.

How to do it...

With these steps, we will install Pyccuracy and all the tools needed to run the scenarios later in this chapter.

1. Install `Pyccuracy` by typing `pip install pyccuracy`.
2. Download `selenium-server.jar` from `http://github.com/heynemann/pyccuracy/raw/master/lib/selenium-server.jar`.
3. Start it up by typing `java -jar selenium-server.jar`. Note that if you don't have Java installed, you definitely need to download and install it as well.
4. Install `lxml` by typing `pip install lxml`.
5. Create a simple test file called `recipe35.acc` and enter the following code:

   ```
   As a Yahoo User
   I want to search Yahoo
   So that I can test my installation of Pyccuracy

   Scenario 1 - Searching for Python Testing Cookbook
   ```

```
Given
    I go to "http://yahoo.com"
When
    I fill "p" textbox with "Python Testing Cookbook"
    And I click "search-submit" button and wait
Then
    I see "Python Testing Cookbook - Yahoo! Search Results" title
```

6. Run it by typing `pyccuracy_console -p test.acc`. The following screenshot shows it being run with Firefox (default for this system).

```
Scenario 1 of 1 <0.00%> - Searching for Python Testing Cookbook
    Given
        I go to "http://yahoo.com"
    When
        I fill "p" textbox with "Python Testing Cookbook"
        And I click "search-submit" button and wait
    Then
        I see "Python Testing Cookbook - Yahoo! Search Results" title

================
Test Run Summary
================
Status: SUCCESSFUL

Test Data Stats
---------------
Successful Stories.......1 of 1 (100.00%)
Successful Scenarios.....1 of 1 (100.00%)

Failed Stories...........0 of 1 (0.00%)
Failed Scenarios.........0 of 1 (0.00%)

Total timing: 11.02 secs
Scenarios/Minute: 5.45 scenarios per minute
```

7. Run it again, using a different web browser like Safari by typing `pyccuracy_console -p test.acc -b safari`.

High Level Customer Scenarios with Acceptance Testing

> At the time of writing, `Selenium` supported Firefox, Safari, Opera, and IE 7+, but not Chrome.

```
Scenario 1 of 1 (0.00%) - Searching for Python Testing Cookbook
    Given
        I go to "http://yahoo.com"
    When
        I fill "p" textbox with "Python Testing Cookbook"
        And I click "search-submit" button and wait
    Then
        I see "Python Testing Cookbook - Yahoo! Search Results" title

================
Test Run Summary
================
Status: SUCCESSFUL
Test Data Stats
---------------
Successful Stories......1 of 1 (100.00%)
Successful Scenarios....1 of 1 (100.00%)
Failed Stories..........0 of 1 (0.00%)
Failed Scenarios........0 of 1 (0.00%)

Total timing: 14.12 secs
Scenarios/Minute: 4.25 scenarios per minute
```

8. In the folder where we ran the test, there should now be a `report.html` file. Open it up using a browser to view the results. Then click on **Expand All**.

Chapter 5

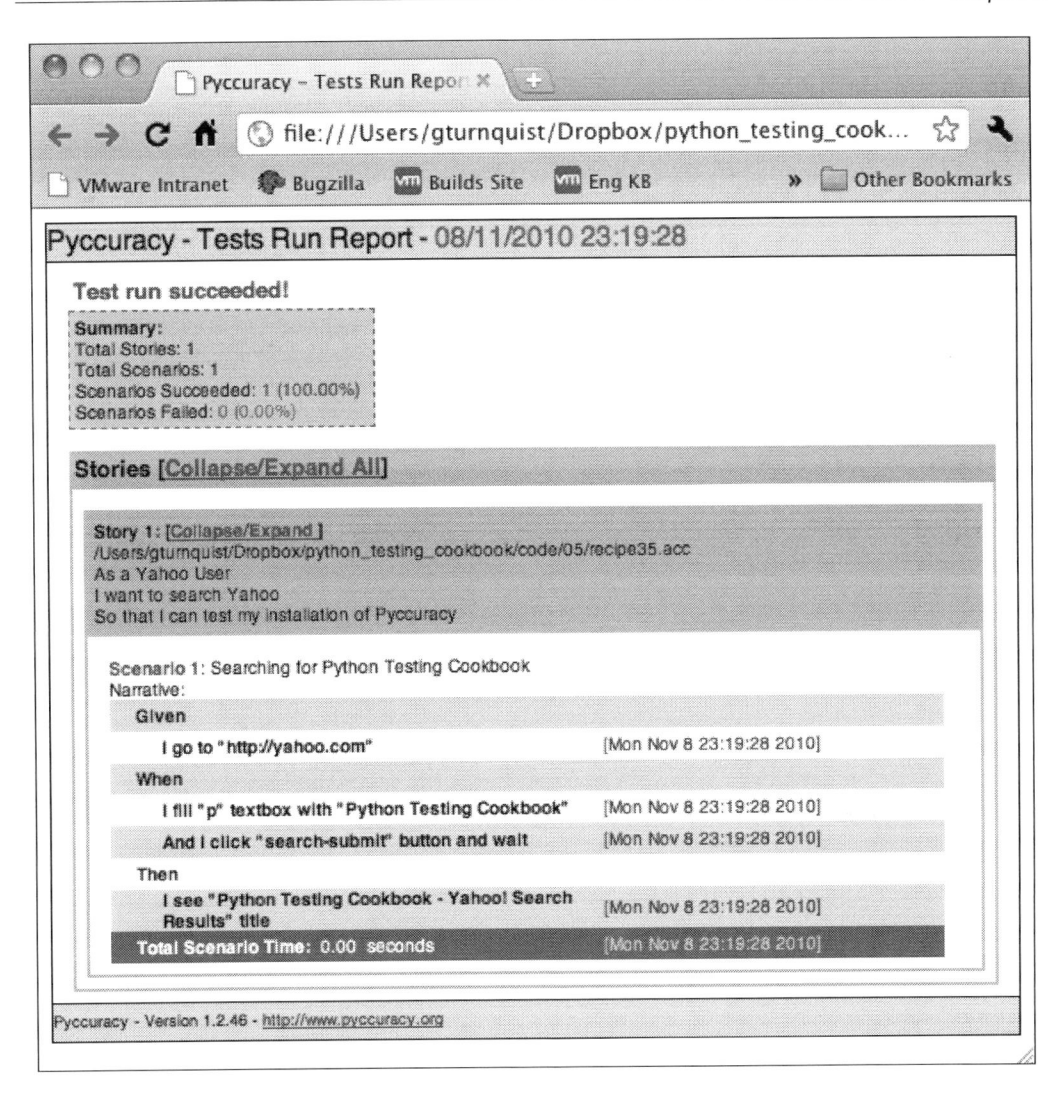

> **Pyccuracy - Tests Run Report - 08/11/2010 23:19:28**
>
> **Test run succeeded!**
>
> Summary:
> Total Stories: 1
> Total Scenarios: 1
> Scenarios Succeeded: 1 (100.00%)
> Scenarios Failed: 0 (0.00%)
>
> **Stories [Collapse/Expand All]**
>
> Story 1: [Collapse/Expand]
> /Users/gturnquist/Dropbox/python_testing_cookbook/code/05/recipe35.acc
> As a Yahoo User
> I want to search Yahoo
> So that I can test my installation of Pyccuracy
>
> Scenario 1: Searching for Python Testing Cookbook
> Narrative:
>
> | Given | |
> |---|---|
> | I go to "http://yahoo.com" | [Mon Nov 8 23:19:28 2010] |
> | **When** | |
> | I fill "p" textbox with "Python Testing Cookbook" | [Mon Nov 8 23:19:28 2010] |
> | And I click "search-submit" button and wait | [Mon Nov 8 23:19:28 2010] |
> | **Then** | |
> | I see "Python Testing Cookbook - Yahoo! Search Results" title | [Mon Nov 8 23:19:28 2010] |
> | **Total Scenario Time: 0.00 seconds** | [Mon Nov 8 23:19:28 2010] |
>
> Pyccuracy - Version 1.2.46 - http://www.pyccuracy.org

How it works...

Pyccuracy uses `Selenium`, a popular browser-driving application tester to run its scenarios. Pyccuracy provides an out-of-the-box Domain Specific Language (DSL) to write tests. The DSL provides the means to send commands to a test browser and also check the results, verifying web application behavior.

Later on in this chapter, there are several recipes which show more details of Pyccuracy.

High Level Customer Scenarios with Acceptance Testing

See also

- Testing the basics with Pyccuracy
- Using Pyccuracy to verify web app security

Testing the basics with Pyccuracy

Pyccuracy provides an easy-to-read set of operations to drive the front end of a web application. This recipe shows how to use it to drive a shopping cart application and verify application functionality.

Getting ready

1. If it isn't already running, start up the selenium server in another shell or window by typing: `java -jar selenium-server.jar`.

```
gturnquist-mbp:~ gturnquist$ java -jar selenium-server.jar
21:44:21.197 INFO - Java: Apple Inc. 17.1-b03-307
21:44:21.200 INFO - OS: Mac OS X 10.6.4 x86_64
21:44:21.317 INFO - v2.0 [a5], with Core v2.0 [a5]
21:44:21.981 INFO - RemoteWebDriver instances should connect to: http://192.168.183.1:4444/wd/hub
21:44:21.983 INFO - Version Jetty/5.1.x
21:44:21.984 INFO - Started HttpContext[/selenium-server/driver,/selenium-server/driver]
21:44:22.022 INFO - Started HttpContext[/selenium-server,/selenium-server]
21:44:22.022 INFO - Started HttpContext[/,/]
21:44:22.550 INFO - Started org.openqa.jetty.jetty.servlet.ServletHandler@76497934
21:44:22.550 INFO - Started HttpContext[/wd,/wd]
21:44:22.557 INFO - Started SocketListener on 0.0.0.0:4444
21:44:22.557 INFO - Started org.openqa.jetty.jetty.Server@43b09468
```

2. If the `satchmo` store application isn't already running, start it up in another shell or window by typing: `python manage.py runserver`.

> NOTE: This must run inside the `virtualenv` environment.

How to do it...

With these steps, we will explore the basics of writing a Pyccuracy test.

1. Create a new file called `recipe36.acc`.

2. Create a story for loading items into the shopping cart.

   ```
   As a store customer
   I want to put things into my cart
   So that I can verify the store's functionality.
   ```

3. Add a scenario where the empty cart is looked at in detail, with a confirmed balance of $0.00.

   ```
   Scenario 1 - Inspect empty cart in detail
   Given
        I go to "http://localhost:8000"
   When
        I click "Cart" link and wait
   Then
        I see that current page contains "Your cart is empty"
        And I see that current page contains "0 - $0.00"
   ```

4. Add another scenario where a book is selected, and two of them are added to the cart.

   ```
   Scenario 2 - Load up a cart with 2 of the same
   Given
        I go to "http://localhost:8000"
   When
        I click "Science Fiction" link
        And I click "Robots Attack!" link and wait
        And I fill "quantity" textbox with "2"
        And I click "addcart" button and wait
        And I click "Cart" link and wait
   Then
        I see that current page contains "Robots Attack!"
        And I see "quantity" textbox contains "2"
        And I see that current page contains "<td align="center">$7.99</td>"
        And I see that current page contains "<td align="center">$15.98</td>"
        And I see that current page contains "<td>$15.98</td>"
   ```

High Level Customer Scenarios with Acceptance Testing

5. Run the story by typing `pyccuracy_console -p recipe36.acc`.

```
(ptc)gturnquist-mbp:05 gturnquist$ pyccuracy_console -p recipe36.acc
Scenario 1 of 2 <0.00%> - Inspect empty cart in detail
    Given
        I go to "http://localhost:8000"
    When
        I click "Cart" link and wait
    Then
        I see that current page contains "Your cart is empty"
        And I see that current page contains "0 - $0.00"
Scenario 2 of 2 <50.00%> - Load up a cart with 2 of the same
    Given
        I go to "http://localhost:8000"
    When
        I click "Science Fiction" link
        And I click "Robots Attack!" link and wait
        And I fill "quantity" textbox with "2"
        And I click "addcart" button
        And I click "Cart" link and wait
    Then
        I see that current page contains "Robots Attack! (Hard cover)"
        And I see "quantity" textbox contains "2"
        And I see that current page contains "<td align="center">$7.99</td>"
        And I see that current page contains "<td align="center">$15.98</td>"
        And I see that current page contains "<td>$15.98</td>"

==================
Test Run Summary
==================
Status: SUCCESSFUL

Test Data Stats
---------------
Successful Stories......1 of 1 (100.00%)
Successful Scenarios....2 of 2 (100.00%)

Failed Stories..........0 of 1 (0.00%)
Failed Scenarios........0 of 2 (0.00%)

Total timing: 9.53 secs
Scenarios/Minute: 12.59 scenarios per minute
```

How it works...

Pyccuracy has a lot of built-in actions based on driving the browser or reading the page. These actions are patterns used to parse the story file, and generate commands sent to the selenium server, which in turn drives the browser, and then reads the results of the page.

The key is picking the right text to identify the element being actioned or read.

[💡 Web apps that are missing ID tags are much harder to look at.]

There's more...

The key is picking the right identifier and element type. With good identifiers, it is easy to do things like: *I click on Cart link*. Did you notice the issue we had with drilling into the shopping cart table? The HTML `<table>` tag had no identifier, which made it impossible for us to pick. Instead, we had to look at the whole page, and do a global search for some markup.

This makes it harder to read the test. A good solution is to alter the web app to include an ID in the `<table>` tag. Then we narrow down our acceptance criteria to just the table. With this application it was okay, but with complex web applications it will surely be much harder to find the exact bit of text we are looking for without good IDs.

This raises an interesting question: *should an application be amended to support a test?* Simply put, yes. It isn't a major upheaval to add some good identifiers to key HTML elements to support testing. It didn't involve major design changes to the application. The net result was easier to read test cases and better automated testing.

This begs another question: *what if making the application more testable DID involve major design changes?* This could be viewed as a major interruption in work. Or maybe it's a strong hint that our design has components that are too tightly coupled or not cohesive enough.

In software development, **coupling** and **cohesiveness** are subjective terms that aren't very measurable. What can be said is that applications that don't lend themselves to testing are often monolithic, hard to maintain, and probably have circular dependencies, which implies that it will be much harder for us to make changes (as developers) to meet needs without impacting the entire system.

Of course, all of this would be a big leap from our recipe's situation, where we simply lack an identifier for an HTML table. However, it's important to think *what if we need more changes than something so small*.

See also

Installing Pyccuracy

Using Pyccuracy to verify web app security

Applications often have login screens. Testing a secured web application requires us to capture the login process as a custom action. That way, we can re-use it repeatedly for as many scenarios as we need.

Getting ready

1. If it isn't already running, start up the selenium server in another shell or window by typing: `java -jar selenium-server.jar`.
2. If the `satchmo` store application isn't already running, start it up in another shell or window by typing: `python manage.py runserver`.

> NOTE: This must run inside the `virtualenv` environment.

How to do it...

With the following steps, we will exercise a web application's security and then see how to extend Pyccuracy by creating a custom action that does the same:

1. Create a new file called `recipe37.acc` to contain this recipe's scenario.
2. Create a story for exercising Django's admin application.

   ```
   As a system administrator
   I want to login to Django's admin page
   So that I can check the product catalog.
   ```

3. Add a scenario that logs in to the admin application.

   ```
   Scenario 1 - Logging in to the admin page
   Given
       I go to "http://localhost:8000/admin"
   When
       I fill "username" textbox with "gturnquist"
       And I fill "password" textbox with "password"
       And I click "login" button and wait
   Then
       I see that current page contains "<a href="product/product/">Products</a>"
   ```

4. Add a scenario that inspects the product catalog, using the custom login action.

   ```
   Scenario 2 - Check product catalog
   Given
       I am logged in with username "gturnquist" and password "password"
   When
       I click "Products" link and wait
   Then
       I see that current page contains "robot-attack"
   ```

5. Create a matching file called `recipe37.py` containing a custom defined action.
6. Code the custom action of logging in to admin action.

```
from pyccuracy.actions import ActionBase
from pyccuracy.errors import *

class LoggedInAction(ActionBase):
    regex = r'(And )?I am logged in with username [\"](?P<username>.+)[\"] and password [\"](?P<password>.+)[\"]$'

    def execute(self, context, username, password):
        self.execute_action(u'I go to "http://localhost:8000/admin"', context)
        logged_in = False
        try:
            self.execute_action(\
                u'And I see that current page contains "id_username"', context)
        except ActionFailedError:
            logged_in = True

        if not logged_in:
            self.execute_action(u'And I fill "username" textbox with "%s"' % username, context)
            self.execute_action(u'And I fill "password" textbox with "%s"' % password, context)
            self.execute_action(u'And I click "login" button', context)
```

7. Run the story by typing `pyccuracy_console -p recipe37.acc`.

```
(ptc)gturnquist-mbp:05 gturnquist$ pyccuracy_console -p recipe37.acc
Scenario 1 of 2 <0.00%> - Logging in to the admin page
    Given
        I go to "http://localhost:8000/admin"
    When
        I fill "username" textbox with "gturnquist"
        And I fill "password" textbox with "password"
        And I click "login" button and wait
    Then
        I see that current page contains "<a href="product/product/">Products</a>"
Scenario 2 of 2 <50.00%> - Check product catalog
    Given
        I am logged in with username "gturnquist" and password "password"
    When
        I click "Products" link and wait
    Then
        I see that current page contains "robot-attack"
================
Test Run Summary
================
Status: SUCCESSFUL

Test Data Stats
---------------
Successful Stories......1 of 1 (100.00%)
Successful Scenarios....2 of 2 (100.00%)

Failed Stories..........0 of 1 (0.00%)
Failed Scenarios........0 of 2 (0.00%)

Total timing: 9.86 secs
Scenarios/Minute: 12.18 scenarios per minute
```

How it works...

The first scenario shows the simple steps needed to exercise the login screen. After having proven the login screen works, it becomes cumbersome to repeat this procedure for more scenarios.

To handle this, we create a custom action in Python by extending `ActionBase`. Custom actions require a regular expression to define the DSL text. Next, we define an `execute` method to include a combination of application logic and Pyccuracy steps to execute. Essentially, we can define a set of steps to automatically execute actions and dynamically handle different situations.

In our situation, we coded it to handle whether or not the user was already logged in. With this custom action, we built the second scenario, and handled logging in with a single statement, allowing us to move on and test the core part of our scenario.

See also

Installing Pyccuracy

Installing the Robot Framework

The Robot Framework is a useful framework for writing acceptance tests using the **keyword** approach. Keywords are short-hand commands that are provided by various libraries and can also be user defined. This easily supports BDD-style `Given-When-Then` keywords. It also opens the door to third-party libraries defining custom keywords to integrate with other test tools, such as Selenium. It also means acceptance tests written using Robot Framework aren't confined to web applications.

This recipe shows all the steps needed to install the Robot Framework as well as the third party Robot Framework Selenium Library for use by later recipes.

How to do it...

1. Be sure to activate your `virtualenv` sandbox.
2. Install by typing: `easy_install robotframework`.

   > At the time of writing, Robot Framework was not able to be installed using `pip`.

3. Using any type of window navigator, go to `<virtualenv root>/build/robotframework/doc/quickstart` and open `quickstart.html` with your favorite browser. This is not only a guide but also a runnable test suite.
4. Switch to your virtualenv's build directory for Robot Framework: `cd <virtualenv root>/build/robotframework/doc/quickstart`.

5. Run the Quick Start manual through `pybot` to verify installation: `pybot quickstart.html`.

```
(ptc)gturnquist-mbp:quickstart gturnquist$ pybot quickstart.html
==============================================================================
Quickstart
==============================================================================
User can create an account and log in                                 | PASS |
------------------------------------------------------------------------------
User cannot log in with bad password                                  | PASS |
------------------------------------------------------------------------------
User can change password                                              | PASS |
------------------------------------------------------------------------------
Too short password                                                    | PASS |
------------------------------------------------------------------------------
Too long password                                                     | PASS |
------------------------------------------------------------------------------
Password without lowercase letters                                    | PASS |
------------------------------------------------------------------------------
Password without capital letters                                      | PASS |
------------------------------------------------------------------------------
Password without numbers                                              | PASS |
------------------------------------------------------------------------------
Password with special characters                                      | PASS |
------------------------------------------------------------------------------
User status is stored in database                                     | PASS |
------------------------------------------------------------------------------
Quickstart                                                            | PASS |
10 critical tests, 10 passed, 0 failed
10 tests total, 10 passed, 0 failed
==============================================================================
Output:  /users/gturnquist/ptc/build/robotframework/doc/quickstart/output.xml
Report:  /users/gturnquist/ptc/build/robotframework/doc/quickstart/report.html
Log:     /users/gturnquist/ptc/build/robotframework/doc/quickstart/log.html
(ptc)gturnquist-mbp:quickstart gturnquist$
```

6. Inspect the generated `report.html`, `log.html`, and `output.xml` files generated by the test run.
7. Install the Robot Framework Selenium library to allow integration with Selenium by first downloading: `http://robotframework-seleniumlibrary.googlecode.com/files/robotframework-seleniumlibrary-2.5.tar.gz`.
8. Unpack the tarball.
9. Switch to the directory: `cd robotframework-seleniumlibrary-2.5`.
10. Install the package: `python setup.py install`.
11. Switch to the demo directory: `cd demo`.
12. Start up the demo web app: `python rundemo.py demoapp start`.
13. Start up the Selenium server: `python rundemo.py selenium start`.

14. Run the demo tests: `pybot login_tests`.

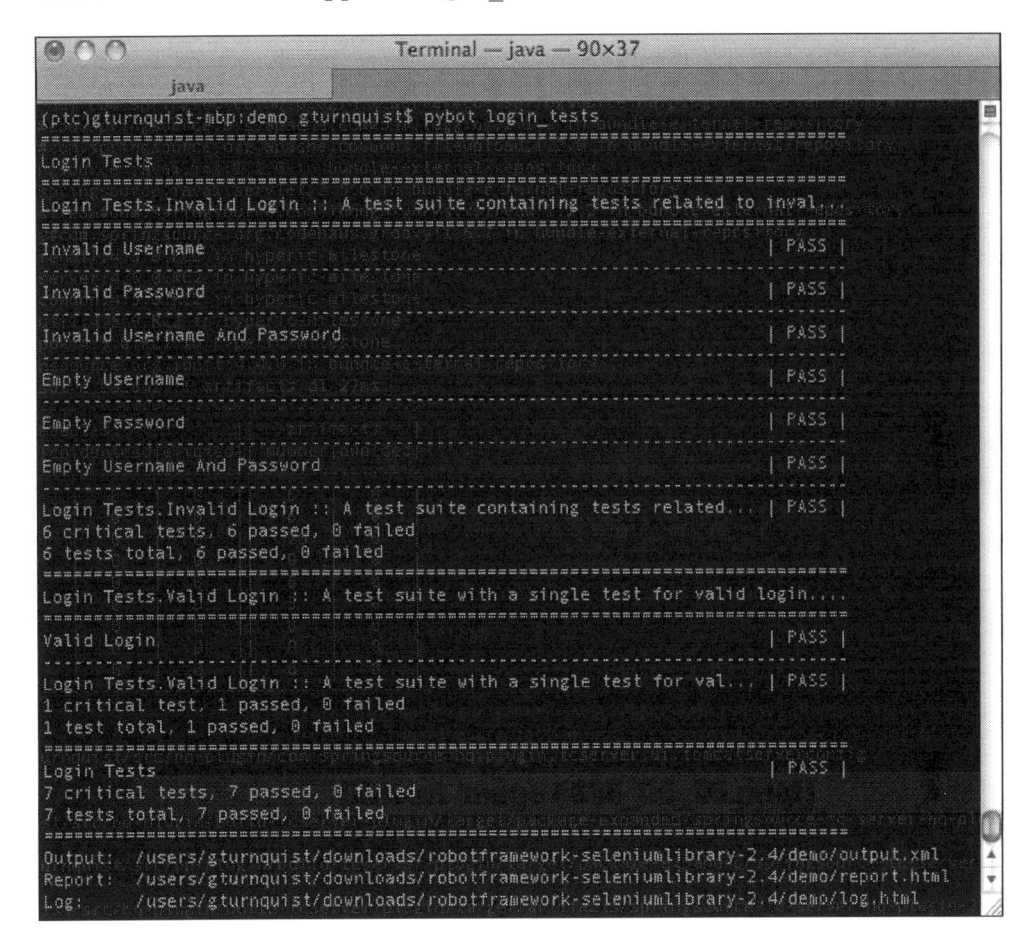

```
(ptc)gturnquist-mbp:demo_gturnquist$ pybot login_tests
==============================================================================
Login Tests
==============================================================================
Login Tests.Invalid Login :: A test suite containing tests related to inval...
==============================================================================
Invalid Username                                                      | PASS |
------------------------------------------------------------------------------
Invalid Password                                                      | PASS |
------------------------------------------------------------------------------
Invalid Username And Password                                         | PASS |
------------------------------------------------------------------------------
Empty Username                                                        | PASS |
------------------------------------------------------------------------------
Empty Password                                                        | PASS |
------------------------------------------------------------------------------
Empty Username And Password                                           | PASS |
------------------------------------------------------------------------------
Login Tests.Invalid Login :: A test suite containing tests related... | PASS |
6 critical tests, 6 passed, 0 failed
6 tests total, 6 passed, 0 failed
==============================================================================
Login Tests.Valid Login :: A test suite with a single test for valid login....
==============================================================================
Valid Login                                                           | PASS |
------------------------------------------------------------------------------
Login Tests.Valid Login :: A test suite with a single test for val... | PASS |
1 critical test, 1 passed, 0 failed
1 test total, 1 passed, 0 failed
==============================================================================
Login Tests                                                           | PASS |
7 critical tests, 7 passed, 0 failed
7 tests total, 7 passed, 0 failed
==============================================================================
Output:  /users/gturnquist/downloads/robotframework-seleniumlibrary-2.4/demo/output.xml
Report:  /users/gturnquist/downloads/robotframework-seleniumlibrary-2.4/demo/report.html
Log:     /users/gturnquist/downloads/robotframework-seleniumlibrary-2.4/demo/log.html
```

15. Shutdown the demo web app: `python rundemo.py demoapp stop`.
16. Shutdown the Selenium server: `python rundemo.py selenium stop`.
17. Inspect the generated `report.html`, `log.html`, `output.xml`, and `selenium_log.txt` files generated by the test run.

There's more...

With this recipe, we have installed the Robot Framework and one third-party library that integrates Robot with Selenium.

High Level Customer Scenarios with Acceptance Testing

There are many more third-party libraries that provide enhanced functionality to the Robot Framework. The options have enough potential to fill an entire book. So we must narrow our focus to some of the core features provided by Robot Framework, including both web and non-web testing.

Creating a data-driven test suite with Robot

Robot Framework uses **keywords** to define tests, test steps, variables, and other testing components. Keywords are short-hand commands that are provided by various libraries and can also be custom defined. This allows many different ways of writing and organizing tests.

In this recipe, we'll explore how to run the same test procedure with varying inputs and outputs. These can be described as data-driven tests.

Getting ready

1. We first need to activate our `virtualenv` setup.
2. For this recipe, we will use the shopping cart application.
3. Next, we need to install Robot Framework, as shown in the previous recipe.

How to do it...

The following steps will show us how to write a simple acceptance test using HTML tables.

1. Create a new file called `recipe39.html` to capture the tests and configurations.
2. Add an HTML paragraph and table that contains a set of data-driven test cases, as shown in the following browser screenshot.

This file shows a set of test cases based on varying parameters.

Test Case		Item 1	Price 1	Item 2	Price 2	Tax Rate	Total
Adding two items of the same kind with no sales tax	Adding items to cart	frozen pizza	2.50	frozen pizza	2.50	0.0	5.00
Adding two items of the same kind with sales tax	Adding items to cart	frozen pizza	2.50	frozen pizza	2.50	10.0	5.50
Adding two different items with no sales tax	Adding items to cart	frozen pizza	2.50	carton of milk	3.50	0.0	6.00
Adding two different items with sales tax	Adding items to cart	frozen pizza	2.50	carton of milk	3.50	10.0	6.60

3. Add another HTML paragraph and table defining the custom keywords **Adding items to cart** and **Add item**.

This table requires some custom keywords to implement these tests.

Keyword	Action	Argument	Argument	Argument	Argument	Argument	Argument
Adding items to cart	[Arguments]	${item1}	${price1}	${item2}	${price2}	${tax}	${total}
	Add item	${item1}	${price1}				
	Add item	${item2}	${price2}				
	${calculated total}=	Get total	${tax}				
	Should Be Equal	${calculated total}	${total}				
Add item	[Arguments]	${description}	${price}				
	Add item to cart	${description}	${price}				

4. Create a new file called `recipe39.py` to contain Python code that is wired into our custom keywords.

5. Create an old style Python class that implements the custom keywords needed for the scenarios.

```
from cart import *

class recipe39:
    def __init__(self):
        self.cart = ShoppingCart()

    def add_item_to_cart(self, description, price):
        self.cart.add(description, float(price))

    def get_total(self, tax):
        return format(self.cart.total(float(tax)), ".2f")
```

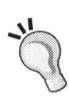

> It's important to define the class *old style*. If we define it as *new style* by subclassing `object`, Robot Framework's runner, `pybot`, won't find the methods and associate them with our HTML keywords.

6. Add a third HTML paragraph and table that loads our Python code to implement **Add item to cart** and **Get total**.

Now let's link in some Python code that wires in the cart.

Setting	Value
Library	recipe39.py

7. View the HTML file in your favorite browser.

This file shows a set of test cases based on varying parameters.

Test Case		Item 1	Price 1	Item 2	Price 2	Tax Rate	Total
Adding two items of the same kind with no sales tax	Adding items to cart	frozen pizza	2.50	frozen pizza	2.50	0.0	5.00
Adding two items of the same kind with sales tax	Adding items to cart	frozen pizza	2.50	frozen pizza	2.50	10.0	5.50
Adding two different items with no sales tax	Adding items to cart	frozen pizza	2.50	carton of milk	3.50	0.0	6.00
Adding two different items with sales tax	Adding items to cart	frozen pizza	2.50	carton of milk	3.50	10.0	6.60

This table requires some custom key words to implement these tests.

Keyword	Action	Argument	Argument	Argument	Argument	Argument	Argument
Adding items to cart	[Arguments]	${item1}	${price1}	${item2}	${price2}	${tax}	${total}
	Add item	${item1}	${price1}				
	Add item	${item2}	${price2}				
	${calculated total}=	Get total	${tax}				
	Should Be Equal	${calculated total}	${total}				
Add item	[Arguments]	${description}	${price}				
	Add item to cart	${description}	${price}				

Now let's link in some Python code that wires in the cart.

Setting	Value
Library	recipe39.py

8. Run the HTML file through `pybot` to exercise the tests by typing `pybot recipe39.html`.

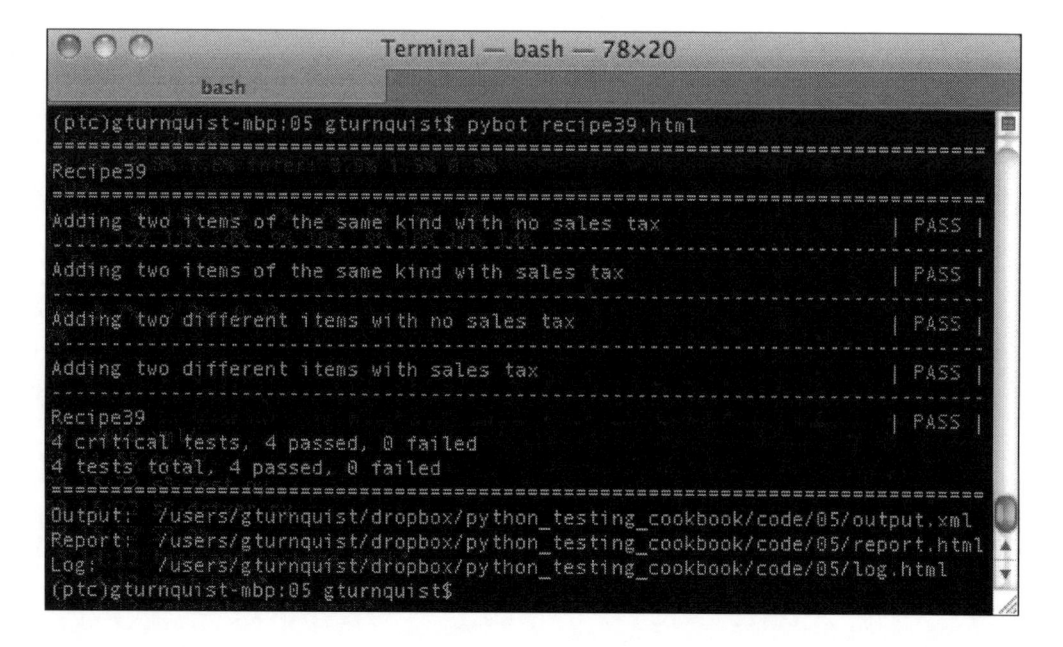

```
(ptc)gturnquist-mbp:05 gturnquist$ pybot recipe39.html
==============================================================================
Recipe39
==============================================================================
Adding two items of the same kind with no sales tax            | PASS |
------------------------------------------------------------------------------
Adding two items of the same kind with sales tax               | PASS |
------------------------------------------------------------------------------
Adding two different items with no sales tax                   | PASS |
------------------------------------------------------------------------------
Adding two different items with sales tax                      | PASS |
------------------------------------------------------------------------------
Recipe39                                                       | PASS |
4 critical tests, 4 passed, 0 failed
4 tests total, 4 passed, 0 failed
==============================================================================
Output:  /users/gturnquist/dropbox/python_testing_cookbook/code/05/output.xml
Report:  /users/gturnquist/dropbox/python_testing_cookbook/code/05/report.html
Log:     /users/gturnquist/dropbox/python_testing_cookbook/code/05/log.html
(ptc)gturnquist-mbp:05 gturnquist$
```

9. You can inspect `report.html` and `log.html` using your favorite browser for more details about the results.

How it works...

Robot Framework uses HTML tables to define test components. The header row of the table identifies what type of component the table defines.

The first table we created was a set of test cases. Robot Framework spots this by seeing `Test Case` in the first cell of the header row. The rest of the header cells aren't parsed, which leaves us free to put in descriptive text. In this recipe, each of our test cases is defined with one-line. The second column has `Adding items to cart` on every row, which is a custom keyword defined in the second table. The rest of the columns are arguments for this custom keyword.

The second table we wrote is used to define custom keywords. Robot Framework figures this out by seeing `Keyword` in the first cell of the header row. Our table defines two keywords.

- `Adding items to cart`:
    - The first line defines the arguments by starting with `[Arguments]` and six input variables: `${item1}`, `${price1}`, `${item2}`, `${price2}`, `${tax}`, and `${total}`.
    - The next set of lines are actions.
    - Lines two and three use another custom keyword: `Add item` with two arguments.
    - Line four defines a new variable, `${calculated total}`, which is assigned the results of another keyword, `Get total` with one argument, `${tax}` that is defined in our Python module.
    - The last line uses a built-in keyword, `Should Be Equal`, to confirm the output of `Get total` matches the original `${total}`.
- `Add item`:
    - The first line defines arguments by starting with `[Arguments]` and two input variables: `${description}` and `${price}`.
    - The second line uses another keyword, `Add item to cart`, that is defined in our Python module, with two named arguments, `${description}` and `${price}`.

The third table we made contains settings. This is identified by seeing `Setting` in the first cell of the header row. This table is used to import Python code that contains the final keywords by using the built-in keyword `Library`.

There's more...

Robot Framework maps our keywords to our Python code by a very simple convention:

- `Get total ${tax}` maps to `get_total(self, tax)`.
- `Add item to cart ${description} ${price}` maps to `add_item_to_cart(self, description, price)`.

> The reason we need `add_item_to_cart`, and couldn't have just written `add_item` to tie in to keyword `Add item` is because Robot Framework uses named arguments when connecting to Python code. Since each usage of `Add item` in our tables had a different variable name, we needed a separate keyword with distinct arguments.

Do I have to write HTML tables?

Robot Framework is driven by HTML tables, but it doesn't matter how the tables are generated. Many projects use tools like **reStructuredText** (http://docutils.sourceforge.net/rst.html) to write tables in a less verbose way, and then have a parser that converts it into HTML. A useful tool for converting .rst to HTML is **docutils** (http://docutils.sourceforge.net/). It provides a convenient rst2html.py script that will convert all the .rst tables into HTML.

Unfortunately, the format of this book makes it hard to present .rst as either code or with a screenshot. To see a good example, visit http://robotframework.googlecode.com/svn/tags/robotframework-2.5.4/doc/quickstart/quickstart.rst, the source for the online Quick Start HTML guide.

What are the best ways to write the code that implements our custom keywords?

We wrote a chunk of Python code to tie in our custom keywords with the `ShoppingCart` application. It is important to make this as light as possible. *Why?* Because when we deploy the actual application, this bridge shouldn't be a part of it. It may be tempting to use this bridge as an opportunity to bundle things up, or to transform things, but this should be avoided.

Instead, it is better to include these functions in the software application itself. Then this extra functionality becomes a part of the tested, deployed software functionality.

If we don't invest too heavily in the bridging code, it helps us to avoid making the software dependent on the test framework. For some reason, if we ever decided to switch to something other than Robot Framework, we wouldn't be tied into that particular tool due to having too much invested in the bridging code.

Robot Framework variables are unicode

Another critical factor in making our Python code work is recognizing that the input values are Unicode strings. Since the `ShoppingCart` is based on floating point values, we had to use Python's `float(input)` function to convert inputs, and `format(output, ".2f")` to convert outputs.

Does this contradict the previous section where we discussed keeping this bridge as light as possible? It doesn't. By using pure, built-in Python functions that have no side effects, we aren't getting in deep and instead are only messaging the formats to line things up. If we started manipulating containers, or converting strings to lists, and vice versa, or even defining new classes, then that would definitely be getting too heavy for this bridge.

See also

Installing the Robot Framework

Writing a testable story with Robot

As discussed earlier in this chapter, Robot Framework lets us use defined custom keywords.

This gives us the ability to structure keywords in any style. In this recipe, we will define custom keywords that implement the BDD Given-When-Then style of specification.

Getting ready

1. We first need to activate our `virtualenv` setup.
2. For this recipe, we will use the shopping cart application.
3. Next, we need to install Robot Framework, as shown in the previous sections of this chapter.

How to do it...

The following steps will explore how to write a BDD Given-When-Then style acceptance test.

1. Create a new file called `recipe40.html` to contain our HTML tables.

2. Create a story file in HTML with an opening statement.

> Feature: Shopping cart
>
> As a shopper
> I want to load up items in my cart
> So that I can check out and pay for them

3. Add a table with several scenarios used to exercise the Shopping Cart application with a series of Given-When-Then keywords.

Test Case	Steps				
Scenario: Seeing that an empty cart behaves correctly	Given an empty cart				
	Then item	5	is a		ERROR
	And price	-2	is		ERROR
	And the cart has	0	items		
	And the total cost with	0	% taxes is	0.00	
	And the total cost with	10	% taxes is	0.00	
Scenario: Seeing a cart getting loaded with multiple of the same	Given an empty cart				
	When I add a	carton of milk	for	2.50	
	And I add a	carton of milk	for	2.50	
	Then item	1	is a	carton of milk	
	And price	1	is	5.00	
	And the cart has	2	items		
	And the total cost with	10	% taxes is	5.50	
Scenario: Seeing a cart getting loaded with different items	Given an empty cart				
	When I add a	carton of milk	for	2.50	
	And I add a	frozen pizza	for	3.00	
	Then item	1	is a	carton of milk	
	And item	2	is a	frozen pizza	
	And price	1	is	2.50	
	And price	2	is	3.00	
	And the total cost with	0	% taxes is	5.50	
	And the total cost with	10	% taxes is	6.05	

4. Add a second table that defines all of our custom Given-When-Then keywords.

Here is where we define the actions in the Given-When-Then test cases.

Keyword	Action	Argument	Argument	Argument
Given an empty cart	create empty cart			
Then item	[Arguments]	${index}	${noop}	${description}
	${fetched item}=	Lookup item	${index}	
	Should Be Equal	${description}	${fetched item}	
And item	[Arguments]	${index}	${noop}	${description}
	Then item	${index}	${noop}	${description}
And price	[Arguments]	${index}	${noop}	${price}
	${calc price}=	Lookup price	${index}	
	Should Be Equal	${calc price}	${price}	
When I add a	[Arguments]	${description}	${noop}	${price}
	add item	${description}	${price}	
And I add a	[Arguments]	${description}	${noop}	${price}
	add item	${description}	${price}	
And the cart has	[Arguments]	${num}	${noop}	
	${size of cart}=	Size of cart		
And the total cost with	[Arguments]	${tax}	${noop}	${total}
	${calc total}=	total	${tax}	
	Should Be Equal	${calc total}	${total}	

5. Create a new file called `recipe40.py` to contain Python code that links the custom keywords to the `ShoppingCart` application.

```
from cart import *

class recipe40:
    def __init__(self):
        self.cart = None

    def create_empty_cart(self):
        self.cart = ShoppingCart()

    def lookup_item(self, index):
        try:
            return self.cart.item(int(index))
        except IndexError:
            return "ERROR"

    def lookup_price(self, index):
        try:
```

```python
            return format(self.cart.price(int(index)), ".2f")
        except IndexError:
            return "ERROR"
    def add_item(self, description, price):
        self.cart.add(description, float(price))
    def size_of_cart(self):
        return len(self.cart)
    def total(self, tax):
        return format(self.cart.total(float(tax)), ".2f")
```

> It is critical that this class is implemented *old-style*. If implemented *new-style* by extending `object`, Robot Framework will NOT link the keywords.

6. Add a third table to our `recipe40.html` file to import our Python module.

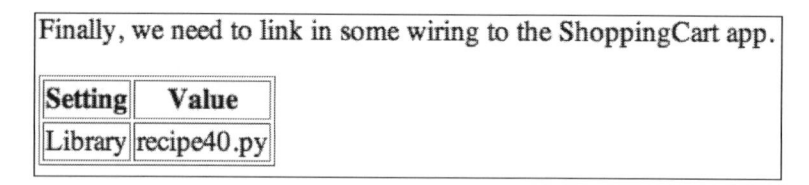

Finally, we need to link in some wiring to the ShoppingCart app.

Setting	Value
Library	recipe40.py

7. Run the story by typing `pybot recipe40.html`.

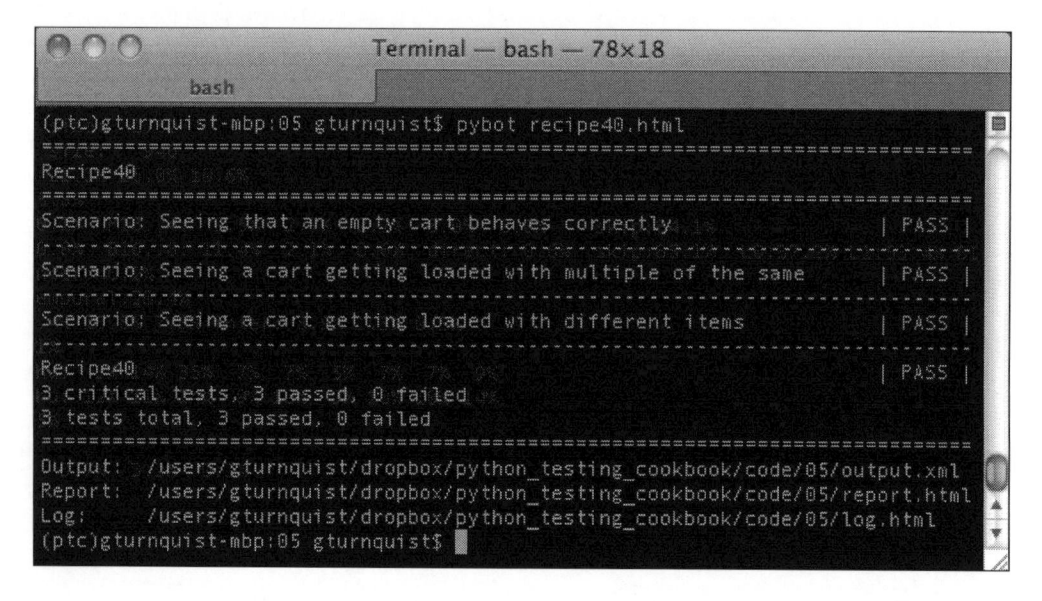

```
(ptc)gturnquist-mbp:05 gturnquist$ pybot recipe40.html
==============================================================================
Recipe40
==============================================================================
Scenario: Seeing that an empty cart behaves correctly            | PASS |
------------------------------------------------------------------------------
Scenario: Seeing a cart getting loaded with multiple of the same | PASS |
------------------------------------------------------------------------------
Scenario: Seeing a cart getting loaded with different items      | PASS |
------------------------------------------------------------------------------
Recipe40                                                         | PASS |
3 critical tests, 3 passed, 0 failed
3 tests total, 3 passed, 0 failed
==============================================================================
Output:  /users/gturnquist/dropbox/python_testing_cookbook/code/05/output.xml
Report:  /users/gturnquist/dropbox/python_testing_cookbook/code/05/report.html
Log:     /users/gturnquist/dropbox/python_testing_cookbook/code/05/log.html
(ptc)gturnquist-mbp:05 gturnquist$
```

How it works...

Robot Framework uses HTML tables to define test components. The header row of the table identifies what type of component the table defines.

The first table we created was a set of test cases. Robot Framework spots this by seeing `Test Case` in the first cell of the header row. The rest of the header cells aren't parsed, which leaves us free to put in descriptive text.

In this recipe, each of our test cases comprised several custom keywords using the Given-When-Then style familiar to BDD testers. Many of these keywords have one or more arguments.

The second table we wrote is used to define our custom Given-When-Then keywords. Robot Framework figures this out by seeing `Keyword` in the first cell of the header row.

The third table we made contains settings. This is identified by seeing `Setting` in the first cell of the header row. This table is used to import Python code that contains the final keywords by using the built-in keyword `Library`.

An important aspect of our custom keywords, in this recipe, is that we wrote them in a natural flowing language.

```
When I add a carton of milk for 2.50
```

This is broken up into four HTML cells in order to parameterize the inputs and make the keywords reusable for several test steps.

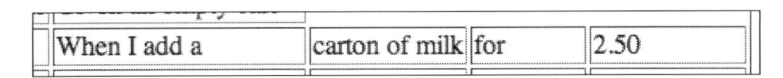

| When I add a | carton of milk | for | 2.50 |

Robot Framework sees this as a custom keyword, `When I add a`, with three arguments: `carton of milk`, `for`, and `2.50`.

Later on, we fill in the actual steps involved with this keyword. In doing so, we are really only concerned with using `carton of milk` and `2.50`. But we still have to treat `for` like an input variable. We do this by using a place holder variable, `${noop}`, which we will simply not use in any following keyword steps.

> In this recipe, we call the throwaway variable `${noop}`. We could have called it anything. We can also reuse it if we have more than one throwaway argument in the same keyword. This is because Robot Framework doesn't engage in strong type checks.

There's more...

This entire chunk of HTML that we had to write starts to feel a bit heavy. As mentioned in the earlier recipe *Creating a data-driven test suite with Robot*, `.rst` is a great alternative. Unfortunately, writing this recipe using `.rst` is too wide for the format of this book. Please see that recipe for more details about writing `.rst` and getting the tools to convert `.rst` to HTML.

Given-When-Then results in duplicate rules

It's true that we had to define both `Then item` and `Add item`, which are basically the same, in order to support two different test scenarios. In other BDD tools, these would have been automatically spotted as the same clause. Robot Framework doesn't directly provide a BDD domain specific language, so we had to fill this in for ourselves.

The most efficient way to handle this was to define `Then item` in detail with all the steps needed, and then code `And item` to just call `Then item`.

In contrast, `When I add a` and `And I add a` were implemented by both calling `add item`. Since this clause was a simpler pass-through to our Python module, it wasn't necessary to chain them together like the previous example.

Another option would be to investigate coding our own BDD plugin library to simplify all of this.

Do the try-except blocks violate the idea of keeping things light?

In the recipe *Creating a data-driven test suite with Robot*, we saw that the code that bridges the HTML tables with the `ShoppingCart` application should be kept as light as possible, and avoid transformations and other manipulations.

It is quite possible to view trapping of an expected exception and returning a string as crossing this line. In our case, the solution was to define a single clause that could handle errors and legitimate values. The clause takes whatever is returned and verifies it using the built-in keyword `Should Be Equal`.

If this wasn't the case, it may have been smoother to not have the try-expect block, and instead use the built-in keyword `Run Keyword And Expect Error` linked to another custom Python keyword. But in this situation, I think the goal of keeping things light was satisfied.

See also

- Installing the Robot Framework
- Creating a data-driven test suite with Robot

Tagging Robot tests and running a subset

Robot Framework provides a comprehensive way to capture test scenarios using table-driven structures. This includes the ability to add metadata in the form of tagging as well as documentation.

Tagging allows including or excluding tags for testing. Documentation appears on the command line and also in the outcome reports. This recipe will demonstrate both of these keen features.

Finally, HTML tables aren't the only way to define data tables with Robot Framework. In this recipe, we will explore using double-space-separated entries. While this isn't the only non-HTML way to write stories, it is the easiest non-HTML way to demonstrate that still fits within the font size limits of this book in printed form.

Getting ready

1. We first need to activate our `virtualenv` setup.
2. Create a new file called `cart41.py` to contain an alternate version of the shopping cart application.
3. Type in the following code that stores the cart to a database.

```python
class ShoppingCart(object):
    def __init__(self):
        self.items = []

    def add(self, item, price):
        for cart_item in self.items:
            # Since we found the item, we increment
            # instead of append
            if cart_item.item == item:
                cart_item.q += 1
                return self

        # If we didn't find, then we append
        self.items.append(Item(item, price))
        return self

    def item(self, index):
        return self.items[index-1].item

    def price(self, index):
        return self.items[index-1].price * self.items[index-1].q

    def total(self, sales_tax):
```

High Level Customer Scenarios with Acceptance Testing

```python
            sum_price = sum([item.price*item.q for item in self.
    items])
            return sum_price*(1.0 + sales_tax/100.0)
        def store(self):
            # This simulates a DB being created.
            f = open("cart.db", "w")
            f.close()
        def retrieve(self, id):
            # This simulates a DB being read.
            f = open("cart.db")
            f.close()
        def __len__(self):
            return sum([item.q for item in self.items])
    class Item(object):
        def __init__(self, item, price, q=1):
            self.item = item
            self.price = price
            self.q = q
```

> This version of the shopping cart has two extra methods: `store` and `retrieve`. They don't actually talk to a database, but instead create an empty file `cart.db`. Why? The purpose is to simulate interaction with a database. Later in the recipe, we will show how to tag test cases that involve this operation and easily exclude them from test runs.

4. Next, we need to install Robot Framework, as shown in the earlier sections of this chapter.

How to do it...

The following steps will show how to write scenarios in a format other than HTML tables, and also how to tag tests to allow picking and choosing which tests are run on the command line.

1. Create a new file called `recipe41.txt` using plain text and space separated entries that has a couple of test cases—one simple one and another more complex one with documentation and tags.

   ```
   ***Test Cases***
   Simple check of adding one item
       Given an empty cart
       When I add a  carton of milk  for  2.50
   ```

```
    Then the total with    0    % tax is   2.50
    And the total with    10   % tax is   2.75

More complex by storing cart to database
  [Documentation]   This test case has special tagging, so it can
be excluded. This is in case the developer doesn't have the right
database system installed to interact properly.cart.db
  [Tags]   database
  Given an empty cart
  When I add a    carton of milk    for   2.50
  And I add a     frozen pizza      for   3.50
  And I store the cart
  And I retrieve the cart
  Then there are    2    items
```

> It's important to note that two spaces are the minimum required to identify breaks between one cell and the next. The line with `When I add a carton of milk for 2.50` actually has four cells of information: | `When I add a` | `carton of milk` | `for` | `2.50` |. There is actually a fifth, empty cell that prefixes this row indicated by the two-space indentation. It is necessary to mark this row as a step in test case `Simple check of adding one item` rather than another test case.

2. Add a table for custom keyword definitions using plain text and space separated values.

```
***Keywords***
Given an empty cart
   create empty cart

When I add a
   [Arguments]    ${description}   ${noop}   ${price}
   add item    ${description}   ${price}

And I add a
   [Arguments]    ${description}   ${noop}   ${price}
   add item    ${description}   ${price}

Then the total with
   [Arguments]   ${tax}   ${noop}   ${total}
   ${calc total}=   total   ${tax}
   Should Be Equal    ${calc total}   ${total}

And the total with
   [Arguments]   ${tax}   ${noop}   ${total}
   Then the total with   ${tax}   ${noop}   ${total}
```

```
And I store the cart
    Set Test Variable    ${cart id}    store cart
```

```
And I retrieve the cart
    retrieve cart    ${cart id}
```

```
Then there are
    [Arguments]    ${size}    ${noop}
    ${calc size}=    Size of cart
    Should Be Equal As Numbers    ${calc size}    ${size}
```

3. Create a new file called recipe41.py that contains Python code that bridges some of the keywords with the shopping cart application.

```
from cart41 import *

class recipe41:
    def __init__(self):
        self.cart = None

    def create_empty_cart(self):
        self.cart = ShoppingCart()

    def lookup_item(self, index):
        try:
            return self.cart.item(int(index))
        except IndexError:
            return "ERROR"

    def lookup_price(self, index):
        try:
            return format(self.cart.price(int(index)), ".2f")
        except IndexError:
            return "ERROR"

    def add_item(self, description, price):
        self.cart.add(description, float(price))

    def size_of_cart(self):
        return len(self.cart)

    def total(self, tax):
        return format(self.cart.total(float(tax)), ".2f")

    def store_cart(self):
        return self.cart.store()

    def retrieve_cart(self, id):
        self.cart.retrieve(id)
```

```
        def size_of_cart(self):
            return len(self.cart)
```

4. Add a last table to `recipe41.txt` that imports our Python code as a library to provide the last set of needed keywords.

    `***Settings***`

    `Library   recipe41.py`

5. Run the test scenario as if we were on a machine that had database support by typing `pybot recipe41.txt`.

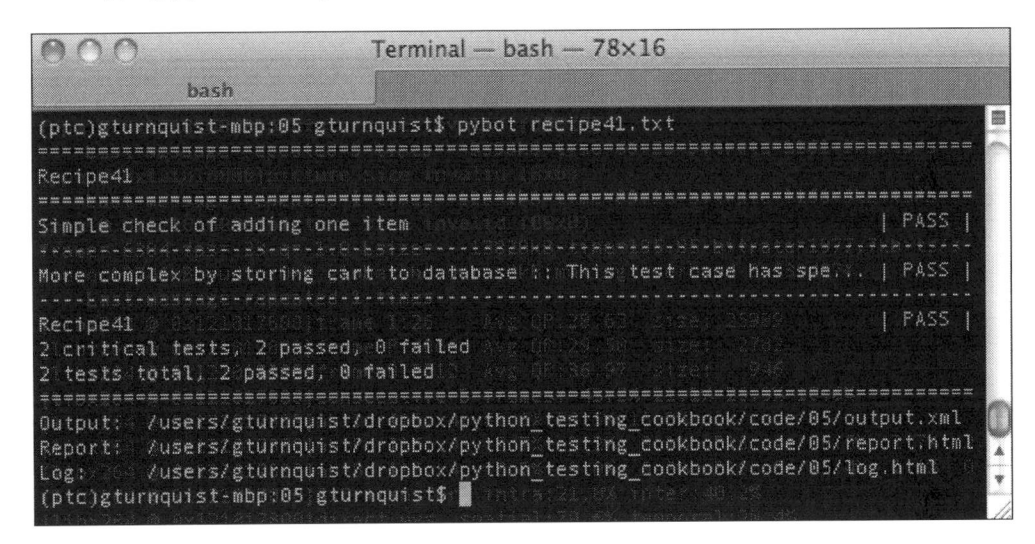

6. Run the test scenario, excluding tests that were tagged `database` by typing `pybot --exclude database recipe41.txt`.

High Level Customer Scenarios with Acceptance Testing

7. Run the test scenario, including tests that were tagged `database` by typing `pybot --include database recipe41.txt`.

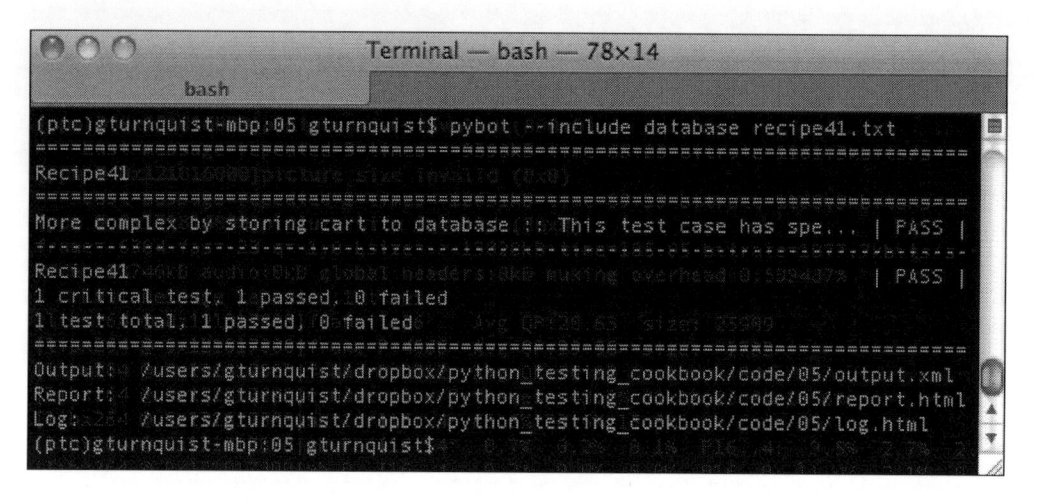

```
(ptc)gturnquist-mbp:05 gturnquist$ pybot --include database recipe41.txt
==============================================================================
Recipe41
==============================================================================
More complex by storing cart to database :: This test case has spe... | PASS |
------------------------------------------------------------------------------
Recipe41                                                              | PASS |
1 critical test, 1 passed, 0 failed
1 test total, 1 passed, 0 failed
==============================================================================
Output:  /users/gturnquist/dropbox/python_testing_cookbook/code/05/output.xml
Report:  /users/gturnquist/dropbox/python_testing_cookbook/code/05/report.html
Log:     /users/gturnquist/dropbox/python_testing_cookbook/code/05/log.html
(ptc)gturnquist-mbp:05 gturnquist$
```

8. Look at `report.html`, and observe where the extra `[Documentation]` text appears, as well as our `database` tag.

Test Details by Suite

Name	Documentation	Metadata / Tags
Recipe41		
More complex by storing cart to database	This test case has special tagging, so it can be excluded. This is in case the developer doesn't have the right database system installed to interact properly.cart.db	database

Test Details by Tag

Name	Documentation	Tags
database		N/A
Recipe41 . More complex by storing cart to database	This test case has special tagging, so it can be excluded. This is in case the developer doesn't have the right database system installed to interact properly.cart.db	database

How it works...

In this recipe, we added an extra section to the second test case, including both documentation and a tag.

```
More complex by storing cart to database
    [Documentation]   This test case has special tagging, so it can
be excluded. This is in case the developer doesn't have the right
database system installed to interact properly.cart.db
    [Tags]   database
    Given an empty cart
```

```
When I add a   carton of milk    for   2.50
And I add a    frozen pizza      for   3.50
And I store the cart
And I retrieve the cart
Then there are   2   items
```

Tags are usable on the command line, as shown in the previous example. They provide a useful way to organize test cases. Test cases can have as many tags as needed.

We showed earlier that this provides a convenient command-line option to include or exclude based on tags. Tags also provide useful documentation, and the previous screenshot of `report.html` shows that test results are also subtotaled by tag:

- Tags can be used to identify different layers of testing like smoke, integration, customer-facing, and so on
- Tags can also be used to mark subsystems like database, invoicing, customer service, billing, and so on

There's more...

This recipe demonstrates plain text formatting. Triple asterisks are used to surround header cells and two spaces are used to designate a break between two cells.

> It is debatable whether this is harder to read than HTML. It may not be as crisp as reading the HTML markup, but I personally preferred this to angle tax of reading HTML. It's possible to add more spaces, so the table's cells are clearer, but I didn't because the font sizes of this book don't work very well with it.

What about documentation?

We also added a little bit of documentation for demonstration purposes. A piece of the text appears when `pybot` runs, and it also appears in the resulting artifacts.

See also

- Installing the Robot Framework
- Creating a data-driven test suite with Robot
- Writing a testable story using Robot

Testing web basics with Robot

Web testing is a common style of acceptance testing, because the customer wants to know if the system is acceptable, and this is a perfect way to demonstrate it.

In previous recipes, we have explored writing tests against non-web applications. In this recipe, let's see how to use a third-party Robot Framework plugin to use Selenium to test a shopping cart web application.

Getting ready

1. We first need to activate our `virtualenv` setup.
2. For this recipe, we are using the `satchmo` shopping cart web application. To start it, switch to the `store` directory and type `python manage.py runserver`. You can explore it by visiting `http://localhost:8000`.
3. Next, install the Robot Framework and the third-party Selenium plugin, as shown in the recipe *Installing the Robot Framework*.

How to do it...

With the following steps, we will see how to get going with using some of the basic Robot commands for driving a web application.

1. Create a plain text story file called `recipe42.txt`, with an opening description of the story.

   ```
   As a store customer
   I want to put things into my cart
   So that I can verify the store's functionality.
   ```

2. Create a section for test cases, and add a scenario that verifies there is an empty shopping cart and captures a screenshot.

   ```
   ***Test Cases***
   Inspect empty cart in detail
       Click link    Cart
       Page Should Contain    Your cart is empty
       Page Should Contain    0 - $0.00
       Capture Page Screenshot    recipe42-scenario1-1.png
   ```

3. Add another scenario that picks a book, adds two copies of the cart, and confirms the total cart value.

   ```
   Load up a cart with 2 of the same
       Click link    Science Fiction    don't wait
   ```

```
        Capture Page Screenshot   recipe42-scenario2-1.png
        Click link   Robots Attack!
        Capture Page Screenshot   recipe42-scenario2-2.png
        Input text   quantity   2
        Capture Page Screenshot   recipe42-scenario2-3.png
        Click button   Add to cart
        Click link   Cart
        Capture Page Screenshot   recipe42-scenario2-4.png
        Textfield Value Should Be   quantity   2
        Page Should Contain   Robots Attack! (Hard cover)
        Html Should Contain   <td align="center">$7.99</td>
        Html Should Contain   <td align="center">$15.98</td>
        Html Should Contain   <td>$15.98</td>
```

4. Add a section of keywords and define a keyword for inspecting the raw HTML of the page.

```
***Keywords***
Html Should Contain
    [Arguments]      ${expected}
    ${html}=         Get Source
    Should Contain   ${html}   ${expected}

Startup
    Start Selenium Server
    Sleep   3s
```

> `Get Source` is a Selenium Library keyword that fetches the raw HTML of the entire page. `Start Selenium Server` is another keyword to launch the selenium server. A built-in `Sleep` call is included to avoid startup/shutdown timing issues, if this test happens before or after another selenium-based test suite.

5. Add a section that imports the Selenium Library, and also defines a setup and teardown process for launching and shutting down the browser for each test case.

```
***Settings***
Library           SeleniumLibrary
Test Setup        Open Browser   http://localhost:8000
Test Teardown     Close All Browsers

Suite Setup       Startup
Suite Teardown    Stop Selenium Server
```

High Level Customer Scenarios with Acceptance Testing

> `Test Setup` is a built-in keyword that defines steps executed before each test case. In this case, it uses the Selenium Library keyword `Open Browser` to launch a browser pointed at the `satchmo` application. `Test Teardown` is a built-in keyword that executes at the end of each test and closes the browsers launched by this test.
>
> `Suite Setup` is a built-in keyword that is only run before any tests are executed, and `Suite Teardown` is only run after all the tests in this suite. In this case, we use it to start and stop the Selenium library.

6. Run the test suite by typing `pybot recipe42.txt`.

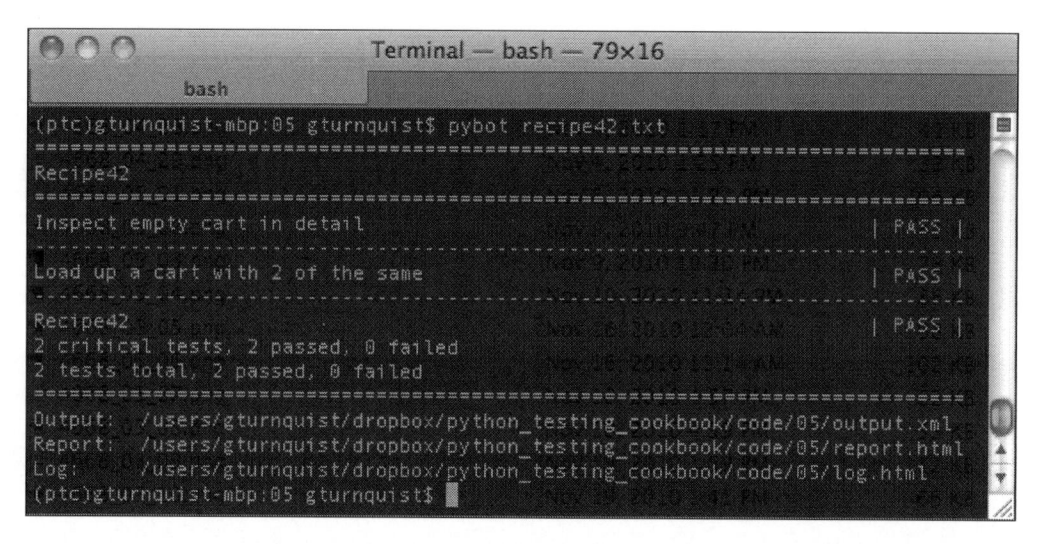

```
(ptc)gturnquist-mbp:05 gturnquist$ pybot recipe42.txt
==============================================================================
Recipe42
==============================================================================
Inspect empty cart in detail                                          | PASS |
------------------------------------------------------------------------------
Load up a cart with 2 of the same                                     | PASS |
------------------------------------------------------------------------------
Recipe42                                                              | PASS |
2 critical tests, 2 passed, 0 failed
2 tests total, 2 passed, 0 failed
==============================================================================
Output:  /users/gturnquist/dropbox/python_testing_cookbook/code/05/output.xml
Report:  /users/gturnquist/dropbox/python_testing_cookbook/code/05/report.html
Log:     /users/gturnquist/dropbox/python_testing_cookbook/code/05/log.html
(ptc)gturnquist-mbp:05 gturnquist$
```

7. Open `log.html`, and observe the details including the captured screenshots in each scenario. The following screenshot is just one of the many captured screenshots. Feel free to inspect the rest of the screenshots as well as the logs.

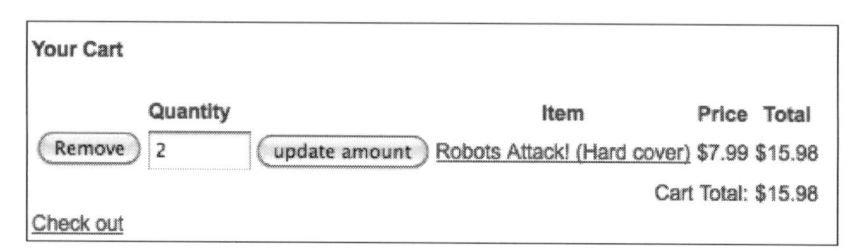

Your Cart				
	Quantity		**Item**	**Price Total**
Remove	2	update amount	Robots Attack! (Hard cover)	$7.99 $15.98
				Cart Total: $15.98
Check out				

How it works...

Robot Framework provides a powerful environment to define tests through keywords. The Selenium plugin interfaces with selenium and provides a whole set of keywords that are focused on manipulating web applications and reading and confirming their outputs.

An important part of web application testing is getting hold of an element to manipulate it or test values. The most common way of doing this is by checking key attributes of the element like `id`, `name`, or `href`. For example, in our scenario, there is a button we need to click to add the book to the cart. It can be identified by either the ID `addcart` or the displayed text `Add to cart`.

There's more...

While Robot Framework is free compared to other commercial front end test solutions, it is important to realize that the effort in writing automated tests isn't free and effortless. It takes effort to make this an active part of front end design.

Incorporating tools like Robot and SeleniumLibrary early in the process of screen design will encourage good practices like tagging frames and elements, so that they'll be testable early on. This is no different than attempting to write automated tests for a backend server system after it's already built. Both situations are much more costly if they are introduced later. Making automated testing a part of backend systems early on encourages similar coding to support testability.

In case we are looking at embracing acceptance testing late in our development cycle, or perhaps trying to test a system we inherited from another team, we need to include time to make changes to the web interface in order to add tags and identifiers to support writing the tests.

Learn about timing configurations—they may be important!

While the satchmo shopping cart application didn't have any significant delays in the tests we wrote, it doesn't mean other applications won't. If your web application has certain parts that are noticeably slower, it is valuable to read the online documentation (`http://robotframework-seleniumlibrary.googlecode.com/hg/doc/SeleniumLibrary.html?r=2.5`) about configuring how long Selenium should wait for a response from your application.

See also

- Installing the Robot Framework
- Creating a data-driven test suite with Robot
- Writing a testable story using Robot

High Level Customer Scenarios with Acceptance Testing

Using Robot to verify web app security

Web applications often have some sort of security in place. This is often in the form of a login page. A well written test case should start a new browser session at the beginning and close it at the end. This results in the user logging in repeatedly for every test case.

In this recipe, we will explore writing code to login in satchmo's admin page, as provided by Django. Then we will show how to capture this entire login procedure into a single keyword, allowing us to smoothly write a test that visits the product catalog without getting encumbered by logging in.

Getting ready

1. We first need to activate our `virtualenv` setup.
2. For this recipe, we are using the satchmo shopping cart web application. To start it, switch to the store directory and type `python manage.py runserver`. You can explore it by visiting `http://localhost:8000`.
3. Next, install the Robot Framework and the third-party Selenium plugin, as shown in the recipe *Installing the Robot Framework*.

How to do it...

The following steps will highlight how to capture login steps and then encapsulate them in a single custom keyword.

1. Create a new file called `recipe43.txt`, and write a test story for exercising Django's admin interface.

   ```
   As a system administrator
   I want to login to Django's admin page
   So that I can check the product catalog.
   ```

2. Add a section for test cases, and write a test case that exercises the login page.

   ```
   ***Test Cases***
   Logging in to the admin page
     Open Browser    http://localhost:8000/admin
     Input text   username   gturnquist
     Input text   password   password
     Submit form
     Page Should Contain Link   Products
     Close All Browsers
   ```

3. Add another test case that inspects the product catalog and verifies a particular row of the table.

   ```
   Check product catalog
       Given that I am logged in
       Click link    Products
       Capture Page Screenshot    recipe43-scenario2-1.png
       Table Should Contain    result_list    Robots Attack!
       Table Row Should Contain    result_list    4    Robots Attack!
       Table Row Should Contain    result_list    4    7.99
       Close All Browsers
   ```

4. Create a keyword section that captures the login procedure as a single keyword.

   ```
   ***Keywords***
   Given that I am logged in
       Open Browser    http://localhost:8000/admin/
       Input text    username    gturnquist
       Input text    password    password
       Submit form

   Startup
       Start Selenium Server
       Sleep    3s
   ```

   > For your own testing, put in the username and password you used when installing satchmo. `Start Selenium Server` is another keyword to launch the selenium server.

5. Finally, add a settings section that imports the SeleniumLibrary and also starts and stops the Selenium server at the beginning and end of the test suite.

   ```
   ***Settings***
   Library            SeleniumLibrary
   Suite Setup        Startup
   Suite Teardown     Stop Selenium Server
   ```

High Level Customer Scenarios with Acceptance Testing

6. Run the test suite by typing `pybot recipe43.txt`.

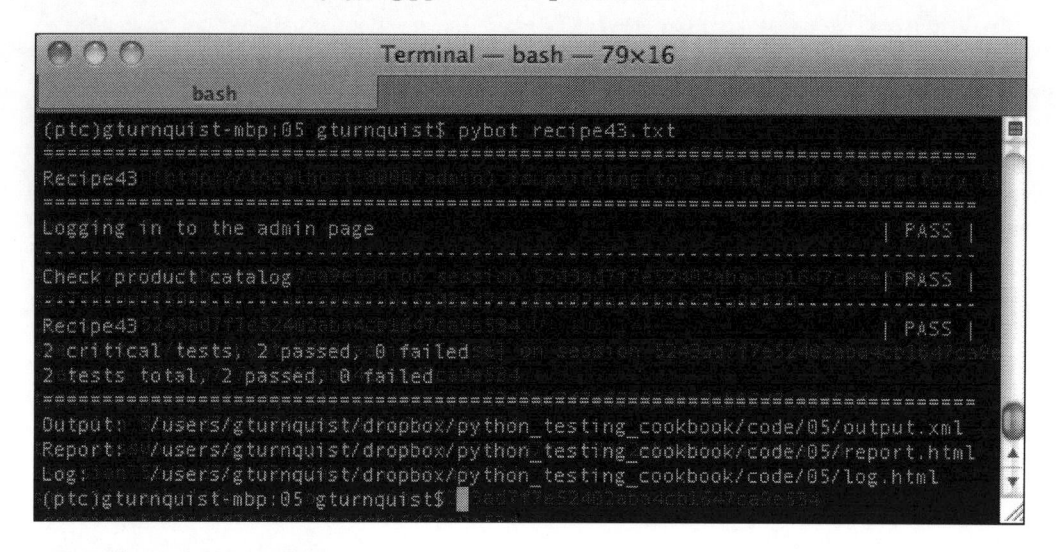

```
(ptc)gturnquist-mbp:05 gturnquist$ pybot recipe43.txt
==============================================================================
Recipe43
==============================================================================
Logging in to the admin page                                          | PASS |
------------------------------------------------------------------------------
Check product catalog                                                 | PASS |
------------------------------------------------------------------------------
Recipe43                                                              | PASS |
2 critical tests, 2 passed, 0 failed
2 tests total, 2 passed, 0 failed
==============================================================================
Output:  /users/gturnquist/dropbox/python_testing_cookbook/code/05/output.xml
Report:  /users/gturnquist/dropbox/python_testing_cookbook/code/05/report.html
Log:     /users/gturnquist/dropbox/python_testing_cookbook/code/05/log.html
(ptc)gturnquist-mbp:05 gturnquist$
```

How it works...

The first test case shows how we input username and password data and then submit the form. SeleniumLibrary allows us to pick a form by name, but in the event we don't identify it, it picks the first HTML form it finds. Since there is only one form on the login page, this works fine for us.

With the second test case, we want to navigate to the product catalog. Since it runs with a clean browser session, we are forced to deal with the login screen again. This means we need to include the same steps to login again. For more comprehensive testing, we would probably write lots of test cases. *Why should we avoid copying and pasting the same login steps for every test case?* Because it violates the DRY (Don't Repeat Yourself) principle. If the login page is modified, we might have to alter every instance.

Instead, we captured the login steps with keyword `Given that I am logged in`. This gives us a useful clause for many test cases, and lets us focus on the admin page.

There's more...

In this recipe, we are using some of SeleniumLibrary's table testing operations. We verified that a particular book exists both at the table level as well as the row level. We also verified the price of the book in that row.

Finally, we captured a screenshot of the product catalog. This screenshot gives us a quick, visual glance which we can use to either manually confirm the product catalog, or use to plan our next test step.

Why not use a 'remember me' option?

Lots of websites include a 'remember me' checkbox in order to save login credentials in a client-side cookie. The Django admin page doesn't have one, so *why is this relevant?* Because many websites do and we may be tempted to incorporate it into our tests to avoid logging in every time. Even if this option existed for the web app we want to test, it is not a good idea to use it. It creates a persistent state that can propagate from one test to the next. Different user accounts may have different roles, impacting what is visible. We may not know in what order test cases run, and therefore, have to add extra code to identify what user we are logged in as.

Instead, it is much easier and cleaner to *not* keep this information. Instead, explicitly logging in through a single keyword provides a clearer intent. This doesn't mean we shouldn't test and confirm the remember checkbox of our particular web application. On the contrary, we should actually test both good and bad accounts to make sure the login screen works as expected. But beyond that, it is best to not confuse future test cases with the stored results of the current test case.

Shouldn't we refactor the first test scenario to use the keyword?

To uphold the DRY principle, we should have the login procedure in only one place inside our test story. But for demonstration purposes, we coded it at the top, and then later copied the same code into a keyword. The best solution would be to encapsulate it into a single keyword that can be reused in either a test case or to define other custom keywords like `Given I am logged in`.

Would arguments make the login keyword more flexible?

Absolutely. In this test story, we hardcoded the username as well as the password. But good testing of the login page would involve a data-driven table with lots of combinations of good and bad accounts, along with valid and invalid passwords. This drives the need for some sort of login keyword that would accept username and password as arguments.

See also

- Installing the Robot Framework
- Using Pyccuracy to verify web app security
- Creating a data-driven test suite with Robot

Creating a project-level script to verify this chapter's acceptance tests

We have used `pyccuracy_console` and `pybot` to run various test recipes. But management of a Python project involves more than just running tests. Things like packaging, registering with the Python Project Index, and pushing to deployment sites are important procedures to manage.

Building a command-line script to encapsulate all of this is very convenient. With this recipe, we will run a script that runs ALL of the tests covered in this chapter.

Getting ready

1. We first need to activate our `virtualenv` setup.
2. For this recipe, we are using the satchmo shopping cart web application. To start it, switch to the store directory and type `python manage.py runserver`. You can explore it by visiting `http://localhost:8000`.
3. Next, install the Robot Framework and the third-party Selenium plugin, as shown in the earlier recipe *Installing the Robot Framework*.
4. This recipe assumes that all of the various recipes from this chapter have been coded.

How to do it...

With these steps, we will see how to programmatically run all the tests in this chapter.

1. Create a new file called `recipe44.py` to contain the code for this recipe.
2. Create a command-line script that defines several options.

   ```
   import getopt
   import logging
   import os
   import os.path
   import re
   import sys
   from glob import glob

   def usage():
       print
       print "Usage: python recipe44.py [command]"
       print
       print "\t--help"
   ```

```
            print "\t--test"
            print "\t--package"
            print "\t--publish"
            print "\t--register"
            print

        try:
            optlist, args = getopt.getopt(sys.argv[1:],
                "h",
                ["help", "test", "package", "publish", "register"])
        except getopt.GetoptError:
            # print help information and exit:
            print "Invalid command found in %s" % sys.argv
            usage()
            sys.exit(2)
```

3. Add a method that starts Selenium, runs the Pyccuracy-based tests, and then shuts down Selenium.

```
def test_with_pyccuracy():
    from SeleniumLibrary import start_selenium_server
    from SeleniumLibrary import shut_down_selenium_server
    from time import sleep

    f = open("recipe44_selenium_log.txt", "w")
    start_selenium_server(logfile=f)
    sleep(10)

    import subprocess
    subprocess.call(["pyccuracy_console"])

    shut_down_selenium_server()
    sleep(5)
    f.close()
```

4. Add a method that runs the Robot Framework tests.

```
def test_with_robot():
    from robot import run
    run(".")
```

5. Add a method to run both of these test methods.

```
def test():
    test_with_pyccuracy()
    test_with_robot()
```

6. Add some stubbed out methods for the other project functions.

   ```
   def package():
       print "This is where we can plug in code to run " + \
           "setup.py to generate a bundle."
   def publish():
       print "This is where we can plug in code to upload " + \
           "our tarball to S3 or some other download site."
   def register():
       print "setup.py has a built in function to " + \
           "'register' a release to PyPI. It's " + \
           "convenient to put a hook in here."
       # os.system("%s setup.py register" % sys.executable)
   ```

7. Add some code that parses the options.

   ```
   if len(optlist) == 0:
       usage()
       sys.exit(1)

   # Check for help requests, which cause all other
   # options to be ignored.
   for option in optlist:
       if option[0] in ("--help", "-h"):
           usage()
           sys.exit(1)

   # Parse the arguments, in order
   for option in optlist:
       if option[0] in ("--test"):
           test()

       if option[0] in ("--package"):
           package()

       if option[0] in ("--publish"):
           publish()

       if option[0] in ("--register"):
           register()
   ```

8. Run the script with the testing flag by typing `python recipe44 -test`. In the following screenshot, we can see that all the Pyccuracy tests passed:

```
================
Test Run Summary
================
Status: SUCCESSFUL

Test Data Stats
---------------
Successful Stories........3 of 3 (100.00%)
Successful Scenarios......5 of 5 (100.00%)

Failed Stories............0 of 3 (0.00%)
Failed Scenarios..........0 of 5 (0.00%)

Total timing: 19.43 secs
Scenarios/Minute: 15.44 scenarios per minute
```

In the next screenshot, we can see that the Robot Framework tests passed as well:

```
==========================================================
...                                                | PASS |
13 critical tests, 13 passed, 0 failed
13 tests total, 13 passed, 0 failed
==========================================================
```

How it works...

We use Python's `getopt` module to define command-line options.

```
optlist, args = getopt.getopt(sys.argv[1:],
        "h",
        ["help", "test", "package", "publish", "register"])
```

This maps:

- "h": `-h`
- "help": `--help`
- "test": `--test`
- "package": `--package`
- "publish": `--publish`
- "register": `--register`

We scan the list of received arguments and call the appropriate functions. For our test functions, we used Python's `subprocess` module to call `pyccuracy_console`. We could have done the same to call `pybot`, but Robot Framework provides a convenient API to call it directly.

```
from robot import run
run(".")
```

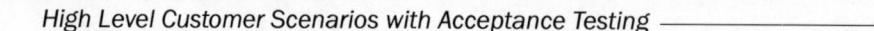

High Level Customer Scenarios with Acceptance Testing

This lets us use it inside our code.

There's more...

To run these tests, we need Selenium running. Our Robot Framework tests are built to run Selenium on their own. Pyccuracy doesn't have such a feature, so it needed another means. In those recipes, we used `java -jar selenium-server.jar`. We could try to manage this, but it is easier to use SeleniumLibrary's API to start and stop Selenium.

This is where writing code in pure Python gives us the most options. We are able to empower Pyccuracy with parts of another library that was never intended to work with it.

Can we only use getopt?

Python 2.7 introduces `argparse` as an alternative. Current documentation has no indication that `getopt` is deprecated, so it's safe to use it as we have just done. The `getopt` module is a nice, easy-to-use command-line parser.

What's wrong with using the various command-line tools?

There is nothing wrong with using tools like `pyccuracy_console`, `pybot`, `nosetests`, and many other tools that come with the Python libraries. The purpose of this recipe is to offer a convenient, alternative approach that brings all these tools into one central script. By investing a little bit of time in this script, we don't have to remember how to use all these features, but instead can develop our script to support the development workflow of our project.

6
Integrating Automated Tests with Continuous Integration

In this chapter, we will cover:

- Generating a continuous integration report for Jenkins with NoseXUnit
- Configuring Jenkins to run Python tests upon commit
- Configuring Jenkins to run Python tests when scheduled
- Generating a continuous integration report for TeamCity using teamcity-nose
- Configuring TeamCity to run Python tests upon commit
- Configuring TeamCity to run Python tests when scheduled

Introduction

The classic software development process known as the waterfall model involves the following stages:

1. Requirements are collected and defined.
2. Designs are drafted to satisfy the requirements.
3. An implementation strategy is written to meet the design.
4. Coding is done.

Integrating Automated Tests with Continuous Integration

5. The coded implementation is tested.
6. The system is integrated with other systems as well as future versions of this system.

In the waterfall model, these steps are often spread across several months of work. What this means is that the final step of integration with external systems is done after several months and often takes a lot of effort.

Continuous integration (CI) remedies the deficiencies of the waterfall model by introducing the concept of writing tests that exercise these points of integration and having them run automatically whenever the code is checked into the system. Teams that adopt continuous integration often adopt a corresponding policy of immediately fixing the baseline if the test suite fails.

This forces the team to continuously keep their code working and integrated, thus making this final step relatively cost free.

Teams that adopt a more agile approach work in much shorter cycles. Teams may work anywhere from weekly to monthly coding sprints. Again, by having integrating test suites run with every check in, the baseline is always kept functional; thus, ready for delivery at any time.

This prevents the system from being in a non-working state that is only brought into the working state at the end of a sprint or at the end of a waterfall cycle. It opens the door to more code demonstrations with either the customer or management, in which feedback can be garnered and more proactively fed into development.

This chapter is more focused on integrating automated tests with CI systems rather than writing the tests. For that reason, we will re-use the following Shopping Cart application. Create a new file called `cart.py` and enter the following code into it:

```python
class ShoppingCart(object):
    def __init__(self):
        self.items = []
    def add(self, item, price):
        for cart_item in self.items:
            # Since we found the item, we increment
            # instead of append
            if cart_item.item == item:
                cart_item.q += 1
                return self
        # If we didn't find, then we append
        self.items.append(Item(item, price))
        return self
    def item(self, index):
        return self.items[index-1].item
    def price(self, index):
```

```python
            return self.items[index-1].price * self.items[index-1].q
        def total(self, sales_tax):
            sum_price = sum([item.price*item.q for item in self.items])
            return sum_price*(1.0 + sales_tax/100.0)
        def __len__(self):
            return sum([item.q for item in self.items])
    class Item(object):
        def __init__(self, item, price, q=1):
            self.item = item
            self.price = price
            self.q = q
```

To exercise this simple application, the following set of unit tests will be used by various recipes in this chapter to demonstrate continuous integration. Create another file called `tests.py` and enter the following test code into it:

```python
    from cart import *
    import unittest
    class ShoppingCartTest(unittest.TestCase):
        def setUp(self):
            self.cart = ShoppingCart().add("tuna sandwich", 15.00)
        def test_length(self):
            self.assertEquals(1, len(self.cart))
        def test_item(self):
            self.assertEquals("tuna sandwich", self.cart.item(1))
        def test_price(self):
            self.assertEquals(15.00, self.cart.price(1))
        def test_total_with_sales_tax(self):
            self.assertAlmostEquals(16.39, \
                                    self.cart.total(9.25), 2)
```

This simple set of tests doesn't look very impressive, does it? In fact, it isn't really integration testing like we were talking about earlier, but instead it appears to be some basic unit tests, right?

Absolutely! This chapter isn't focusing on writing test code. So, if this book is about code recipes, why are we focusing on tools? Because there is more to making automated testing work with your team than writing tests. It's important to become aware of tools that take the concepts of automating tests and leveraging them into our development cycles.

Continuous integration products are a valuable tool, and we need to see how to link them with our test code, in turn allowing the whole team to come on board and make testing a first class citizen of our development process.

Integrating Automated Tests with Continuous Integration

This chapter explores two powerful CI products: Jenkins and TeamCity.

Jenkins (http://jenkins-ci.org/) is an open source product that was led by a developer originally from SUN Microsystems, who left after its acquisition by Oracle. It has a strong developer community with many people providing patches, plugins, and improvements. It was originally called Hudson, but the development community voted to rename it to avoid legal entanglements. There is more history to the entire Hudson/Jenkins naming that can be read online, but it's not relevant to the recipes in this book.

TeamCity (http://www.jetbrains.com/teamcity/) is a product created by Jet Brains, the same company that produces commercial products such as IntelliJ IDE, ReSharper, and PyCharm IDE. The Professional Edition is a free version that will be used in this chapter to show another CI system. It has an enterprise, commercial upgrade, which you can evaluate for yourself.

Generating a continuous integration report for Jenkins using NoseXUnit

JUnit (http://junit.org) is a software industry leader in automated testing. It provides the ability to generate XML report files that are consumed by many tools. This extends to continuous tools like Jenkins.

NoseXUnit (http://nosexunit.sourceforge.net/) is a Nose plugin that generates XML reports with Python test results in the same format. It works like JUnit with XML reporting but for unittest. Even though we aren't building Java code, there is no requirement that states our CI server can't be a Java-based system. As long as we can generate the right reports, those tools are candidates for usage. Considering that one of the most popular and well-supported CI systems is Jenkins, this type of plugin is very useful.

With this recipe, we will explore generating consumable reports from simple Python testing.

Getting ready

The following steps are needed to have all the components installed for this chapter.

1. Install Nose as shown in *Chapter 2*.
2. Install NoseXUnit (http://nosexunit.sourceforge.net/) by typing `pip install nosexunit`.

How to do it...

The following steps will show how to use the NoseXUnit plugin to generate an XML report in a Jenkins-compatible format:

1. Test the shopping cart application using nosetests and the NoseXUnit plugin by typing `nosetests tests.py --with-nosexunit`.

```
(ptc)gturnquist-mbp:06 gturnquist$ nosetests tests.py --with-nosexunit
....
----------------------------------------------------------------------
Ran 4 tests in 0.001s

OK
(ptc)gturnquist-mbp:06 gturnquist$
```

2. Open the report found in `target/NoseXUnit/core/TEST-tests.xml` using an XML or text editor. The following screenshot shows the report displayed in SpringSource Tool Suite (http://www.springsource.com/developer/sts), an Eclipse derivative. (This is by no means a recommendation. Many modern IDEs have built-in XML support as do other editors like emacs, textpad, and so on).

```xml
<?xml version="1.0" encoding="UTF-8"?>
<testsuite name="tests" tests="4" errors="0" failures="0" time="0.001">
    <testcase classname="tests.ShoppingCartTest" name="test_item" time="0.000"/>
    <testcase classname="tests.ShoppingCartTest" name="test_length" time="0.000"/>
    <testcase classname="tests.ShoppingCartTest" name="test_price" time="0.000"/>
    <testcase classname="tests.ShoppingCartTest" name="test_total_with_sales_tax" time="0.000"/>
    <system-out>
        <![CDATA[]]>
    </system-out>
    <system-err>
        <![CDATA[]]>
    </system-err>
</testsuite>
```

How it works...

NoseXUnit collects the outcome of each test and generates an XML report that has the same format as JUnit. The XML file isn't designed to be human consumable, but it's not too hard to discern the results. When we ran nosetests earlier, how many test cases passed? What were the test method names?

Integrating Automated Tests with Continuous Integration

In this XML file, we can see the names of the four test cases. In fact, if this file is opened inside certain tools like the SpringSource Tool Suite, it displays itself as a test outcome.

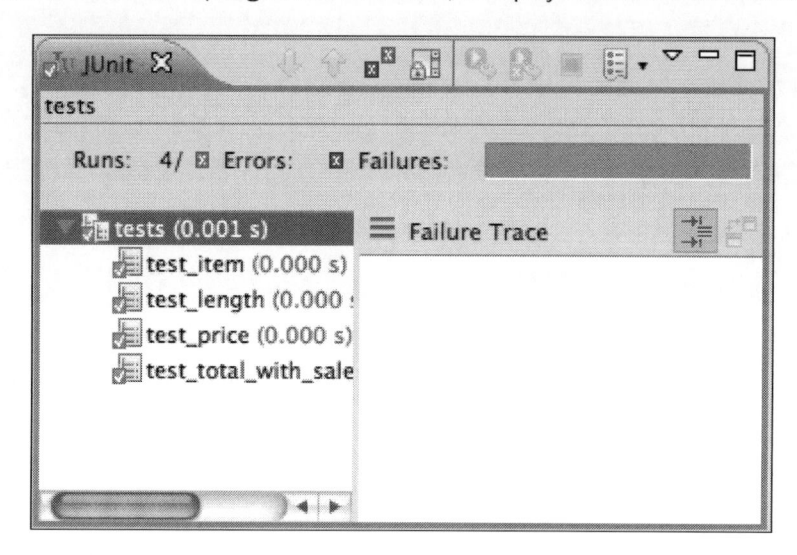

We don't have to use STS to do any of this. In fact, STS is a bit heavyweight for this simple task. Your favorite XML or text editor is fine to inspect the report. I just wanted to demonstrate how the output of this plugin neatly works with existing tools.

By typing **nosetests-help**, we can see all the options that nose has from all the installed plugins. This includes:

- `--core-target=CORE_TARGET`: Output folder for test reports (defaults to target/NoseXUnit/core)
- `--with-nosexunit`: Runs it through the plugin

Configuring Jenkins to run Python tests upon commit

Jenkins can be configured to invoke our test suite upon commit. This is very useful, because we can gear it to track our changes. Teams that use CI systems usually adopt an attitude of addressing CI failures immediately in order to keep the baseline functional.

Jenkins offers an almost unlimited number of features, such as retrieving the latest source from version control, packaging a release, running tests, and even analyzing source code. This recipe shows how to configure Jenkins to run our test suite against our shopping cart application.

Getting ready

1. Download Jenkins from `http://mirrors.jenkins-ci.org/war/latest/jenkins.war`.

```
(ptc)gturnquist-mbp:~ gturnquist$ wget http://mirrors.jenkins-ci.org/war/latest/jenkins.war
--2011-04-09 04:45:35--  http://mirrors.jenkins-ci.org/war/latest/jenkins.war
Resolving mirrors.jenkins-ci.org (mirrors.jenkins-ci.org)... 63.246.20.93
Connecting to mirrors.jenkins-ci.org (mirrors.jenkins-ci.org)|63.246.20.93|:80... connected.
HTTP request sent, awaiting response... 302 Found
Location: http://ftp-nyc.osuosl.org/pub/jenkins/war/1.405/jenkins.war [following]
--2011-04-09 04:45:35--  http://ftp-nyc.osuosl.org/pub/jenkins/war/1.405/jenkins.war
Resolving ftp-nyc.osuosl.org (ftp-nyc.osuosl.org)... 64.50.233.100
Connecting to ftp-nyc.osuosl.org (ftp-nyc.osuosl.org)|64.50.233.100|:80... connected.
HTTP request sent, awaiting response... 200 OK
Length: 38295284 (37M) [text/plain]
Saving to: "jenkins.war"
```

2. Start it up by running `java -jar jenkins.war`. It's important that no other applications are listening on port 8080.

```
(ptc)gturnquist-mbp:Downloads gturnquist$ java -jar jenkins.war
Running from: /Users/gturnquist/Downloads/jenkins.war
webroot: $user.home/.jenkins
[Winstone 2011/04/09 04:54:02] - Beginning extraction from war file
hudson home directory: /Users/gturnquist/.jenkins found at: $user.home
Apr 9, 2011 4:54:06 AM hudson.util.CharacterEncodingFilter init
INFO: CharacterEncodingFilter initialized. DISABLE_FILTER: false FOR
[Winstone 2011/04/09 04:54:06] - HTTP Listener started: port=8080
[Winstone 2011/04/09 04:54:06] - AJP13 Listener started: port=8009
Using one-time self-signed certificate
[Winstone 2011/04/09 04:54:06] - Winstone Servlet Engine v0.9.10 run
Apr 9, 2011 4:54:06 AM hudson.model.Hudson$5 onAttained
INFO: Started initialization
Apr 9, 2011 4:54:08 AM hudson.model.Hudson$5 onAttained
INFO: Listed all plugins
Apr 9, 2011 4:54:08 AM hudson.model.Hudson$5 onAttained
INFO: Prepared all plugins
Apr 9, 2011 4:54:08 AM hudson.model.Hudson$5 onAttained
INFO: Started all plugins
Apr 9, 2011 4:54:08 AM hudson.model.Hudson$5 onAttained
INFO: Augmented all extensions
Apr 9, 2011 4:54:08 AM hudson.model.Hudson$5 onAttained
INFO: Loaded all jobs
Apr 9, 2011 4:54:09 AM hudson.model.Hudson$5 onAttained
INFO: Completed initialization
Apr 9, 2011 4:54:09 AM hudson.TcpSlaveAgentListener <init>
INFO: JNLP slave agent listener started on TCP port 56937
```

3. Open the console to confirm Jenkins is working.

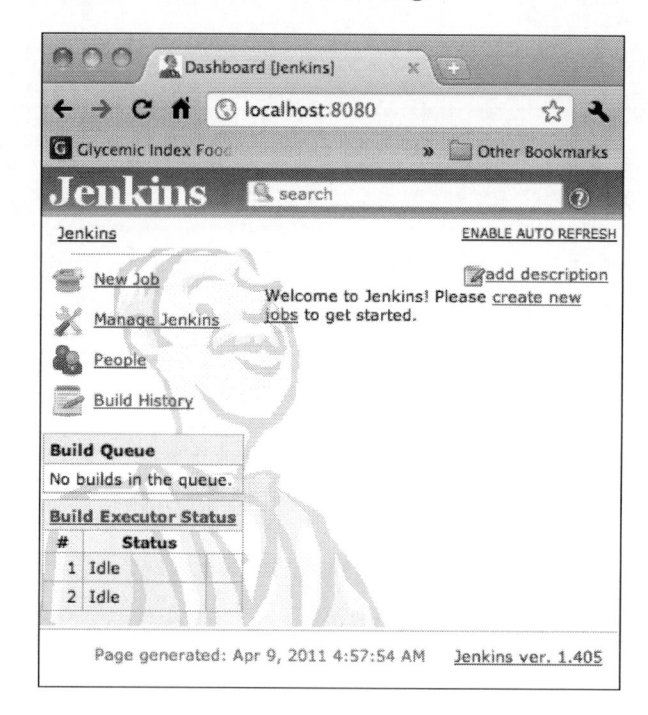

4. Click on **Manage Jenkins**.
5. Click on **Manage Plugins**.
6. Click on the **Available** tab.
7. Find the **Git Plugin** and click the checkbox next to it.
8. At the bottom of the page, click on the **Install** button. Verify that the plugin has successfully installed.
9. Navigate back to the dashboard screen.
10. Shutdown Jenkins and start it back up again.
11. Install git source code control on your machine. You can visit http://git-scm.com/ to find downloadable packages. It is also possible that your system may include package installation options like mac ports or homebrew for Macs, yum for Redhat-based Linux distributions, and apt-get for Debian/Ubuntu systems.
12. Create an empty folder for this recipe:

    `gturnquist$ mkdir /tmp/recipe46`

13. Initialize the folder for source code maintenance:

    `gturnquist$ git init /tmp/recipe46`

    `Initialized empty Git repository in /private/tmp/recipe46/.git/`

14. Copy the shopping cart application into the folder, add it, and commit the changes.

    ```
    gturnquist$ cp cart.py /tmp/recipe46/
    gturnquist$ cd /tmp/recipe46/
    gturnquist$ git add cart.py
    gturnquist$ git commit -m "Added shopping cart application to setup this recipe."
    [master (root-commit) 057d936] Added shopping cart application to setup this recipe.
     1 files changed, 35 insertions(+), 0 deletions(-)
     create mode 100644 cart.py
    ```

How to do it...

The following steps will show how to put our code under control and then run the test suite when we make any changes and commit them:

1. Open the Jenkins console.
2. Click on **New Job**.
3. Enter **recipe46** as the **Job name** and pick **build a free-style software project**.
4. Click on **a**.
5. In the **Source Code Management** section, pick **Git**. For **URL**, enter `/tmp/recipe46/`.
6. In the **Build Triggers** section, pick **Poll SCM** and enter * * * * * into the schedule box, to trigger a poll once every minute.
7. In the **Build** section, select **Execute shell** and enter the following adhoc script that loads the `virtualenv` and runs the test suite.

    ```
    . /Users/gturnquist/ptc/bin/activate
    nosetests tests.py –with-nosexunit
    ```

    You need to substitute the command to activate your own virtualenv, whether this is on Windows, Linux, or Mac, and then follow it with the command used to run the tests just like we did earlier in this chapter.

8. In the **Post-build Actions** section, pick **Publish JUnit test result report** and enter `target/NoseXUnit/core/*.xml`, so that the test results are collected by Jenkins.
9. Click on **Save** to store all the job settings.

Integrating Automated Tests with Continuous Integration

10. Click on **Enable Auto Refresh**. We should expect the first run to fail, because we haven't added any tests yet.

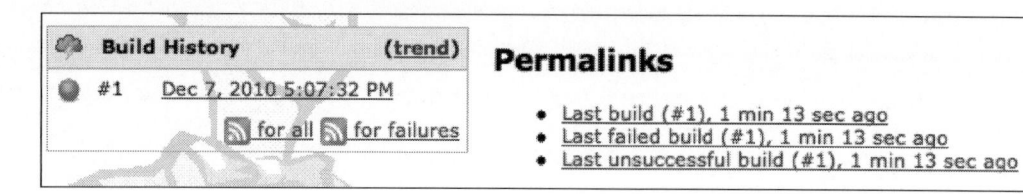

11. Copy the test suite into the controlled source folder, add it, and commit it.

    ```
    gturnquist$ cp tests.py /tmp/recipe46/
    gturnquist$ cd /tmp/recipe46/
    gturnquist$ git add tests.py
    gturnquist$ git commit -m "Added tests for the recipe."
    [master 0f6ef56] Added tests for the recipe.
     1 files changed, 20 insertions(+), 0 deletions(-)
     create mode 100644 tests.py
    ```

12. Watch to verify whether Jenkins launches a successful test run.

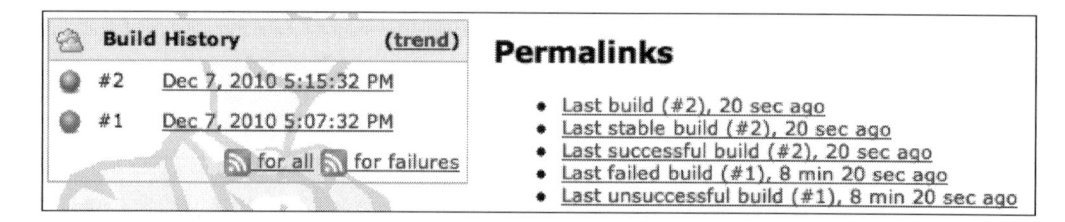

13. Navigate to the test results page, where we can see that four of our tests were run.

How it works...

Jenkins provides a powerful, flexible way to configure continuous integration jobs. In this recipe, we configured it to poll our software confirmation management system once a minute. When it detects a change, it pulls a fresh copy of the software and runs our test script.

By using the NoseXUnit plugin, we generated an artifact that was easy to harvest with Jenkins. With a handful of steps, we were able to configure a web page that monitors our source code.

There's more...

Jenkins has lots of options. If you examine the web interface, you can drill into output logs to see what actually happened. It also collects trends showing how long we have had success, when the last build failed, and more.

Do I have to use git for source code management?

The answer is No. We used it in this recipe to quickly show how to install a Jenkins plugin from inside the web interface. To apply the plugin, we had to restart Jenkins.

Subversion and CVS are supported out of the box. Jenkins also has plugins supporting every major source code control system out there, so it should be easy to meet your needs.

In fact, there is support for social coding sites like GitHub and BitKeeper. Instead of using the Git plugin, we could configure our Jenkins installation to watch a certain GitHub account for updates.

What is the format of polling?

We configured the polling with * * * * *, which means once a minute. This is based on the format used to configure crontab files. The columns from left to right are:

- **MINUTE**—Minutes within the hour (0-59)
- **HOUR**—The hour of the day (0-23)
- **DOM**—The day of the month (1-31)
- **MONTH**—The month (1-12)
- **DOW**—The day of the week (0-7) where 0 and 7 are Sunday

See also

- Generating a continuous integration report for Jenkins using NoseXUnit

Configuring Jenkins to run Python tests when scheduled

We just explored how to configure Jenkins to run our test suite when we commit the code changes. Jenkins can also be configured to invoke our test suite at scheduled intervals. This is very useful, because we can gear it to make scheduled releases. Daily or weekly releases can provide potential customers with a nice cadence of release.

Integrating Automated Tests with Continuous Integration

CI releases are usually understood to not necessarily be final, but instead provide bleeding edge support in case new features need to be investigated early and integrated by the customer.

Getting ready

The following steps are used to set up Jenkins as well as a copy of our tests, so we can poll it at a scheduled interval:

1. Set up Jenkins as shown in the earlier recipe *Configuring Jenkins to run Python tests upon commit*. This should include having setup the Git plugin.

2. Create an empty folder for this recipe.

   `gturnquist$ mkdir /tmp/recipe47`

3. Initialize the folder for source code maintenance.

   `gturnquist$ git init /tmp/recipe47`

   `Initialized empty Git repository in /private/tmp/recipe47/.git/`

4. Copy the shopping cart application into the folder, add it, and commit the changes.

   `gturnquist$ cp cart.py /tmp/recipe47/`

   `gturnquist$ cd /tmp/recipe47/`

   `gturnquist$ git add cart.py`

   `gturnquist$ git commit -m "Added shopping cart application to setup this recipe."`

   `[master (root-commit) 057d936] Added shopping cart application to setup this recipe.`

   `1 files changed, 35 insertions(+), 0 deletions(-)`

   `create mode 100644 cart.py`

How to do it...

The following steps will let us explore creating a Jenkins job to periodically run our automated test suite:

1. Open the Jenkins console.
2. Click on **New Job**.
3. Enter **recipe47** as the **Job name** and pick **Build a free-style software project**.
4. Click on **Ok**.
5. In the **Source Code Management** section, pick **Git**. For **URL**, enter `/tmp/recipe47/`.

6. In the **Build Triggers** section, pick **Build periodically** and enter some time in the future. While writing this recipe for the book, the job was created around 6:10 p.m., so entering `15 18 * * *` into the schedule box schedules the job five minutes into the future at 6:15 p.m.

7. In the **Build** section, select **Execute shell** and enter the following adhoc script that loads the `virtualenv` and runs the test suite.

   ```
   . /Users/gturnquist/ptc/bin/activate
   nosetests tests.py –with-nosexunit
   ```

   You need to replace this with the command used to activate your virtualenv followed by the step to run the tests.

8. In the **Post-build Actions** section, pick **Publish JUnit test result report** and enter `target/NoseXUnit/core/*.xml`, so that test results are collected by Jenkins.

9. Click on **Save** to store all the job settings.

10. Click on **Enable Auto Refresh**.

11. Copy the test suite into the controlled source folder, add it, and commit it.

    ```
    gturnquist$ cp tests.py /tmp/recipe47/
    gturnquist$ cd /tmp/recipe47/
    gturnquist$ git add tests.py
    gturnquist$ git commit -m "Added tests for the recipe."
    [master 0f6ef56] Added tests for the recipe.
     1 files changed, 20 insertions(+), 0 deletions(-)
     create mode 100644 tests.py
    ```

12. Watch to verify whether Jenkins launches a successful test run.

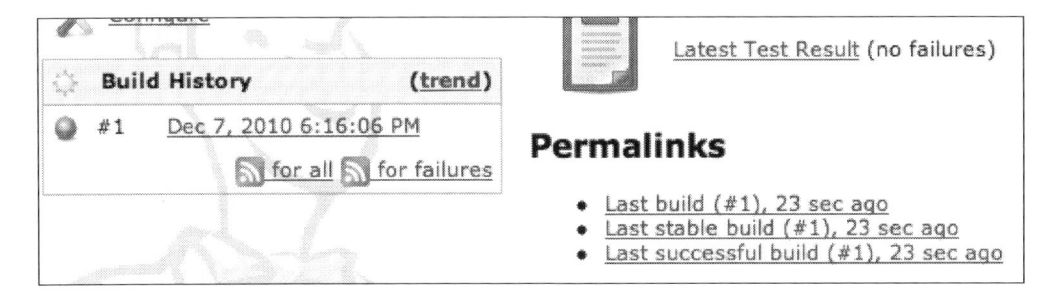

13. Navigate to test results, and we can see that four of our tests were run.

How it works...

This is very similar to the previous recipe, only this time we configured a polling interval for running our test suite instead of polling the version control system. It is useful to run a build once a day to make sure things are stable and working.

There's more...

Jenkins has lots of options. If you examine the web interface, you can drill into output logs to see what actually happened. It also collects trends showing how long we have had success, when the last build failed, and more.

To be honest, Jenkins has so many plugins and options that an entire book could be devoted to exploring its features. This half of the chapter is merely an introduction to using it with some common jobs that are test-oriented.

Jenkins versus TeamCity

So far, we have explored using Jenkins. Later in this chapter, we will visit TeamCity. What are the differences? Why should we pick one or the other?

Feature-wise, they both offer powerful choices. That is why they are both covered in this book. The key thing both provide is setting up jobs to run tests as well as other things like packaging.

A key difference is that Jenkins is an open source product and TeamCity is commercial. You or your company may prefer to have a paid company associated with the product (http://www.jetbrains.com/), which is what TeamCity offers. This doesn't make the decision crystal clear, because the principal developer of Jenkins currently works for CloudBees (http://www.cloudbees.com/), which invests effort in Jenkins as well as products surrounding it.

If commercial support isn't imperative, you may find the pace of development of Jenkins is faster and the number of plugins more diverse. The bottom line is that choosing the product that meets your CI needs requires a detailed analysis and simply can't be answered here.

See also

- Generating a continuous integration report for Jenkins using NoseXUnit

Generating a CI report for TeamCity using teamcity-nose

There is a Nose plugin that automatically detects when tests are being run from inside the TeamCity. This conveniently captures test results and communicates them with TeamCity. With this recipe, we will explore how to setup a CI job inside TeamCity that runs our tests and then manually invokes that job.

Getting ready

The following steps are needed to get us prepared to run a TeamCity CI job:

1. Install nosetests as shown in *Chapter 2*.
2. Install teamcity-nose by typing `pip install teamcity-nose`.
3. Download TeamCity using wget `http://download.jetbrains.com/teamcity/TeamCity-6.0.tar.gz`.
4. Unpack the download.
5. Switch to `TeamCity/bin` directory.
6. Start it up: `./runAll.sh start`.
7. Open a browser to `http://localhost:8111`.
8. If this is the first time you are starting TeamCity, accept the license agreement.
9. Create an administrator account by picking a username and password.
10. Install git source code control on your machine.
11. Create an empty folder for this recipe.

    ```
    gturnquist$ mkdir /tmp/recipe48
    ```

12. Initialize the folder for source code maintenance.

    ```
    gturnquist$ git init /tmp/recipe48
    Initialized empty Git repository in /private/tmp/recipe48/.git/
    ```

13. Copy the shopping cart application and tests into the folder, add it, and commit the changes.

    ```
    gturnquist$ cp cart.py /tmp/recipe48/
    gturnquist$ cp tests.py /tmp/recipe48/
    gturnquist$ cd /tmp/recipe48/
    gturnquist$ git add cart.py tests.py
    gturnquist$ git commit -m "Added shopping cart and tests to setup this recipe."
    ```

Integrating Automated Tests with Continuous Integration

```
[master (root-commit) ccc7155] Added shopping cart and tests to
setup this recipe.
 2 files changed, 55 insertions(+), 0 deletions(-)
 create mode 100644 cart.py
 create mode 100644 tests.py
```

How to do it...

The following steps will show us how to configure a CI job in TeamCity:

1. Login to TeamCity console.
2. Underneath **Projects** tab, click **Create project**.
3. Type in **recipe48**, and then click **Create**.
4. Click **Add a build configuration** for this project.
5. Enter **nose testing** for the name and then click **VCS settings**.
6. Click on **Create and attach new VCS root**.
7. Enter **recipe48** in **VCS root name**.
8. Select **Git** as the **Type of VCS**.
9. Enter `/tmp/recipe48` as the **Fetch URL**.
10. Click on **Test Connection** to confirm the settings and then click **Save**.
11. Click on **Add Build Step**.
12. Select **Command Line** for **Runner type**.
13. Select **Custom script** for **Run** type and enter the following script:

    ```
    . /Users/gturnquist/ptc/bin/activate
    nosetests tests.py
    ```

    You need to customize this with the command needed to activate your virtualenv.

14. Click on **Save**.
15. Go back to the project, and manually run it.

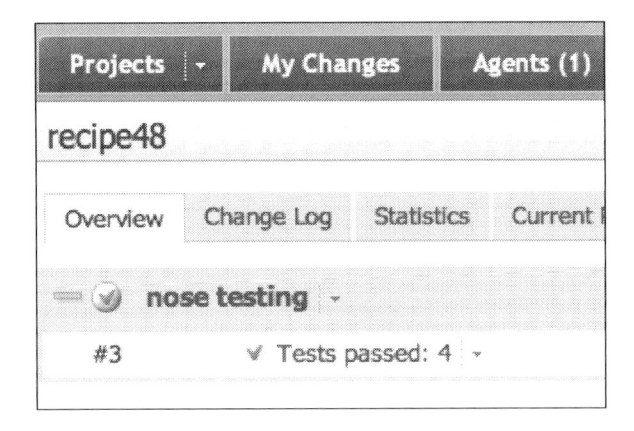

How it works...

This plugin is designed not to be used in the classic style of being invoked by a command-line argument. Instead, it is automatically run whenever nosetests is executed, and it checks if there is a TeamCity-specific environment variable set. If so, it kicks in by printing out viewable results as well as sending back useful information to TeamCity.

Otherwise, the plugin lets itself be bypassed and does nothing. If the plugin was NOT installed, the following screenshot would be the output:

In turn, drilling into the details shows the following output with little detail. There are four periods, one for each test method, but we don't know much more than that.

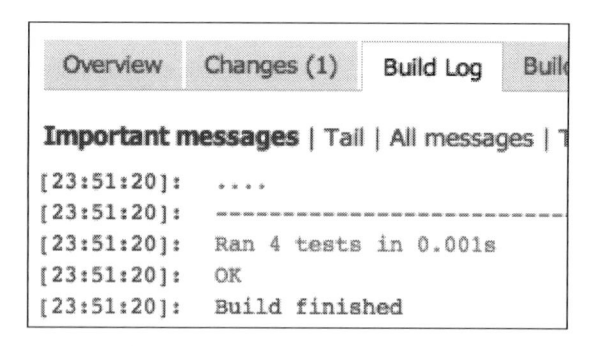

This means no extra arguments are needed to use the TeamCity plugin, but running it from the command line, outside of TeamCity, causes no changes.

Configuring TeamCity to run Python tests upon commit

TeamCity can be configured to invoke your test suite upon commit.

Getting ready

The following steps will help us prep are TeamCity to run our test suite when the code changes are committed:

1. Set up TeamCity like the previous recipe, and have it started up. You also need to have `git` installed, as mentioned earlier in this chapter.

2. Create an empty folder for this recipe.

   `gturnquist$ mkdir /tmp/recipe49`

3. Initialize the folder for source code maintenance.

   `gturnquist$ git init /tmp/recipe49`

   `Initialized empty Git repository in /private/tmp/recipe49/.git/`

4. Copy the shopping cart application into the folder, add it, and commit the changes.

   `gturnquist$ cp cart.py /tmp/recipe49/`

   `gturnquist$ cd /tmp/recipe49/`

   `gturnquist$ git add cart.py`

   `gturnquist$ git commit -m "Added shopping cart application to setup this recipe."`

   `[master (root-commit) 057d936] Added shopping cart application to setup this recipe.`

   `1 files changed, 35 insertions(+), 0 deletions(-)`

   `create mode 100644 cart.py`

How to do it...

These steps will show us how to create a TeamCity job that polls version control to detect a change and then run a test suite.

1. Login to TeamCity console.
2. Underneath **Projects** tab, click **Create project**.
3. Type in **recipe49**, and then click **Create**.
4. Click **Add a build configuration** for this project.
5. Enter **nose testing** for the name and then click **VCS settings**.
6. Click on **Create and attach new VCS root**.
7. Enter **recipe49** in **VCS root name**.
8. Select **Git** as the **Type of VCS**.
9. Enter `/tmp/recipe49` as the **Fetch URL**.
10. Click on **Test Connection** to confirm settings and then click **Save**.
11. Click on **Add Build Step**.
12. Select **Command Line** for **Runner type**.
13. Select **Custom script** for **Run** type and enter the following script:

    ```
    . /Users/gturnquist/ptc/bin/activate
    nosetests tests.py
    ```

Integrating Automated Tests with Continuous Integration

You must replace this with the command to activate your own virtualenv and invoke nosetests.

14. Click on **Save**.
15. Click on **Build Triggering**.
16. Click on **Add New Trigger**.
17. Pick **VCS Trigger** from **Trigger Type**.
18. At the top, it should display **VCS Trigger will add build to the queue if VCS check-in is detected**. Click **Save**.
19. Navigate back to **Projects**. There should be no jobs scheduled or results displayed.
20. Click on **Run**. It should fail, because we haven't added the tests to the repository.

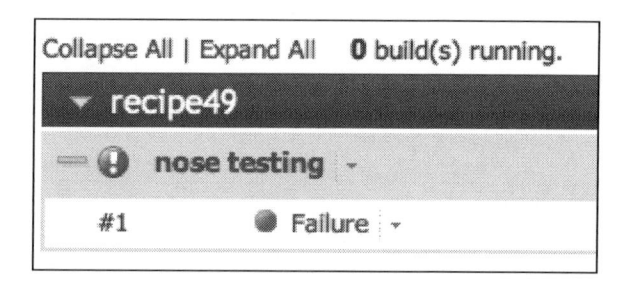

```
Collapse All | Expand All    0 build(s) running.
   ▼ recipe49
 — ⊘ nose testing ▾
       #1         ● Failure ▾
```

21. From the command line, copy the test file into the repository. Then add it and commit it.

    ```
    gturnquist$ cp tests.py /tmp/recipe49/
    gturnquist$ cd /tmp/recipe49/
    gturnquist$ git add tests.py
    gturnquist$ git commit -m "Adding tests."
    [master 4c3c418] Adding tests.
     1 files changed, 20 insertions(+), 0 deletions(-)
     create mode 100644 tests.py
    ```

22. Go back to the browser. It may take a minute for TeamCity to detect the change in the code and start another build job. It should automatically update the screen.

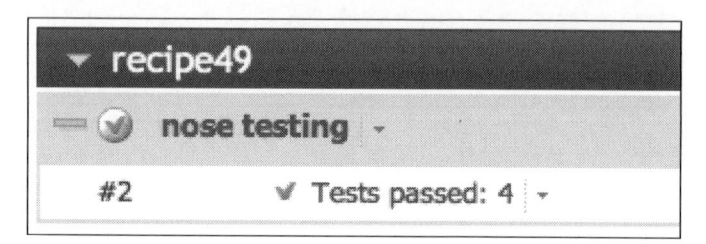

```
   ▼ recipe49
 — ✓ nose testing ▾
       #2         ✓ Tests passed: 4 ▾
```

236

How it works...

In this recipe, we configured TeamCity to do a job for us tied to a specific trigger. The trigger is: whenever a check in is done to the software baseline. We had to take several steps to configure this, but it demonstrates the flexible power TeamCity offers.

We also installed the teamcity-nose plugin, which gave us more details on the results.

There's more...

TeamCity calls our **nose testing** job a build job. That is because running tests isn't the only thing TeamCity is used for. Instead, it's geared to build packages, deploy to sites, and any other action we may want it to do anytime a commit happens. This is why CI servers are sometimes called **build servers**.

But if we start with simple jobs like testing the baseline, we are well on our way to discovering the other useful features TeamCity has to offer.

What did teamcity-nose give us?

This is a nose plugin that provided us with more detailed output. We didn't go into much detail in this recipe.

See also

- Generating a CI report for TeamCity using teamcity-nose
- Configuring Jenkins to run Python tests upon commit

Configuring TeamCity to run Python tests when scheduled

TeamCity can be configured to invoke our test suite and collect results in a scheduled interval.

Getting ready

These steps will prepare us for this recipe by starting up TeamCity and having some code ready for testing:

1. Set up TeamCity like we did earlier in this chapter, and have it up and running.
2. Create an empty folder for this recipe.
   ```
   gturnquist$ mkdir /tmp/recipe50
   ```

Integrating Automated Tests with Continuous Integration

3. Initialize the folder for source code maintenance.

   ```
   gturnquist$ git init /tmp/recipe50
   Initialized empty Git repository in /private/tmp/recipe50/.git/
   ```

4. Copy the shopping cart application into the folder, add it, and commit the changes.

   ```
   gturnquist$ cp cart.py /tmp/recipe50/
   gturnquist$ cp tests.py /tmp/recipe50/
   gturnquist$ cd /tmp/recipe50/
   gturnquist$ git add cart.py tests.py
   gturnquist$ git commit -m "Adding shopping cart and tests for this recipe."
   [master (root-commit) 01cd72a] Adding shopping cart and tests for this recipe.
    2 files changed, 55 insertions(+), 0 deletions(-)
    create mode 100644 cart.py
    create mode 100644 tests.py
   ```

How to do it...

These steps show the details of configuring TeamCity to run our test suite on a scheduled basis:

1. Login to TeamCity console.
2. Underneath **Projects** tab, click **Create project**.
3. Type in **recipe50**, and then click **Create**.
4. Click **Add a build configuration** for this project.
5. Enter **nose testing** for the name and then click **VCS settings**.
6. Click on **Create and attach new VCS root**.
7. Enter **recipe50** in **VCS root name**.
8. Select **Git** as the **Type of VCS**.
9. Enter `/tmp/recipe50` as the **Fetch URL**.
10. Click on **Test Connection** to confirm settings and then click **Save**.
11. Click on **Add Build Step**.
12. Select **Command Line** for **Runner type**.
13. Select **Custom script** for **Run** type and enter the following script:

    ```
    . /Users/gturnquist/ptc/bin/activate
    nosetests tests.py
    ```

Replace this with your own steps to activate your virtualenv and then run the tests using nosetests.

14. Click on **Save**.
15. Click on **Build Triggering**.
16. Click on **Add New Trigger**.
17. Select **Schedule Trigger** from **Trigger Type**.
18. Pick **daily** for frequency, and pick a time of about five minutes into the future.
19. Deselect the option to **Trigger build only if there are pending changes**.
20. Click **Save**.
21. Navigate back to **Projects**. There should be no jobs scheduled or results displayed.
22. Wait for the scheduled time to occur. The following screenshot shows the job when it is activated:

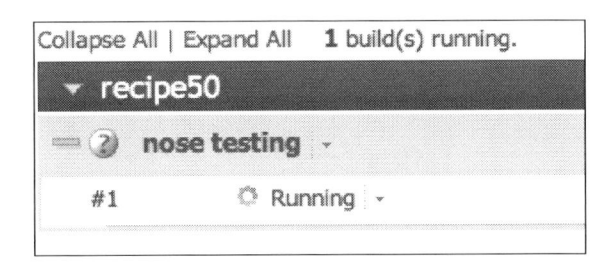

The following screenshot shows the results summarized with our tests having passed:

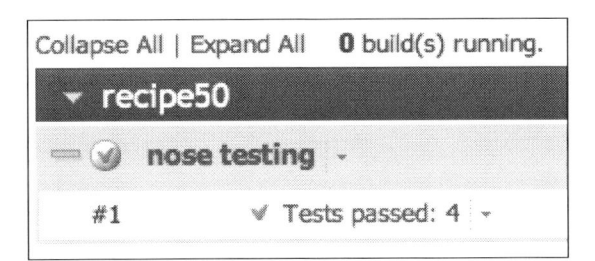

How it works...

Doesn't this look suspiciously similar to the previous recipe? Of course! We varied it a bit by creating a time-based trigger instead of a source-based trigger. The time trigger we picked is a daily, scheduled build at a set time. The point is showing a commonly used trigger rule. By seeing what is the same and what's different, we can start seeing how to bend TeamCity to serve our needs.

Integrating Automated Tests with Continuous Integration

TeamCity has other triggers that are very useful, like triggering one job when another one completes. This lets us build lots of small, simple jobs, and chain them together.

We also installed the teamcity-nose plugin, which gave us more details on the results.

See also

- Generating a CI report for TeamCity using teamcity-nose
- Configuring Jenkins to run Python tests when scheduled

7
Measuring your Success with Test Coverage

In this chapter, we will cover:

- Building a network management application
- Installing and running coverage on your test suite
- Generating an HTML report using coverage
- Generating an XML report using coverage
- Getting nosy with coverage
- Filtering out test noise from coverage
- Letting Jenkins get nosy with coverage
- Updating the project-level script to provide coverage reports

Introduction

Coverage analysis is measuring which lines in a program are run and which lines aren't. This is type of analysis is also known as **'code coverage'**, or more simply **'coverage'**.

A coverage analyzer can be used while running a system in production, but what are the pros and cons, if we used it this way? What about using a coverage analyzer when running test suites? What benefits would this approach provide compared to checking systems in production?

Measuring your Success with Test Coverage

Coverage helps us to see if we are adequately testing our system. But it must be performed with a certain amount of skepticism. This is because, even if we achieve 100 percent coverage, meaning every line of our system was exercised, in no way does this guarantee us having no bugs. A quick example involves a code we write and what it processes is the return value from a system call. What if there are three possible values, but we only handle two of them? We may write two test cases covering our handling of it, and this could certainly achieve 100 percent statement coverage. However, it doesn't mean we have handled the third possible return value; thus, leaving us with a potentially undiscovered bug. 100 percent code coverage can also be obtained by condition coverage but may not be achieved with statement coverage. The kind of coverage we are planning to target should be clear.

Another key point is that not all testing is aimed at bug fixing. Another key purpose is to make sure that the application meets our customer's needs. This means that, even if we have 100 percent code coverage, we can't guarantee that we are covering all the scenarios expected by our users. This is the difference between 'building it right' and 'building the right thing'.

In this chapter, we will explore various recipes to build a network management application, run coverage tools, and harvest the results. We will discuss how coverage can introduce noise, and show us more than we need to know, as well as introduce performance issues when it instruments our code. We will also see how to trim out information we don't need to get a concise, targeted view of things.

This chapter uses several third-party tools in many recipes.

> ▸ Spring Python (http://springpython.webfactional.com) contains many useful abstractions. The one used in this chapter is its DatabaseTemplate, which offers easy ways to write SQL queries and updates without having to deal with Python's verbose API. Install it by typing pip install springpython.

```
(ptc)gturnquist-mbp:python_testing_cookbook gturnquist$ pip install springpython
Downloading/unpacking springpython
  Downloading springpython-1.2.0.FINAL.tar.gz (104Kb): 104Kb downloaded
  Running setup.py egg_info for package springpython
Installing collected packages: springpython
  Running setup.py install for springpython
    changing mode of build/scripts-2.6/coily from 644 to 755
    changing mode of /Users/gturnquist/ptc/bin/coily to 755
Successfully installed springpython
```

> ▸ Install the coverage tool by typing pip install coverage. This may fail because other plugins may install an older version of coverage. If so, uninstall coverage by typing pip uninstall coverage, and then install it again with pip install coverage.
>
> ▸ Nose is a useful test runner covered in *Chapter 2, Running automated testsuites with Nose*. Refer to that chapter for steps to install Nose.

Building a network management application

For this chapter, we will build a very simple network management application, and then write different types of tests and check their coverage. This network management application is focused on digesting alarms, also referred to as **network events**. This is different from certain other network management tools that focus on gathering SNMP alarms from devices.

For reasons of simplicity, this correlation engine doesn't contain complex rules, but instead contains simple mapping of network events onto equipment and customer service inventory. We'll explore this in the next few paragraphs as we dig through the code.

How to do it...

With the following steps, we will build a simple network management application.

1. Create a file called `network.py` to store the network application.
2. Create a class definition to represent a network event.

   ```
   class Event(object):
       def __init__(self, hostname, condition, severity, event_time):
           self.hostname = hostname
           self.condition = condition
           self.severity = severity
           self.id = -1

       def __str__(self):
           return "(ID:%s) %s:%s - %s" % (self.id, self.hostname,
   self.condition, self.severity)
   ```

   - `hostname`: It is assumed that all network alarms originate from pieces of equipment that have a hostname.
   - `condition`: Indicates the type of alarm being generated. Two different alarming conditions can come from the same device.
   - `severity`: 1 indicates a clear, green status; and 5 indicates a faulty, red status.
   - `id`: The primary key value used when the event is stored in a database.

3. Create a new file called `network.sql` to contain the SQL code.
4. Create a SQL script that sets up the database and adds the definition for storing network events.

   ```
   CREATE TABLE EVENTS (
       ID INTEGER PRIMARY KEY,
       HOST_NAME TEXT,
       SEVERITY INTEGER,
   ```

Measuring your Success with Test Coverage

```
        EVENT_CONDITION TEXT
    );
```

5. Code a high-level algorithm where events are assessed for impact to equipment and customer services and add it to `network.py`.

```python
from springpython.database.core import*

class EventCorrelator(object):
    def __init__(self, factory):
        self.dt = DatabaseTemplate(factory)

    def __del__(self):
        del(self.dt)

    def process(self, event):
        stored_event, is_active = self.store_event(event)

        affected_services, affected_equip = self.impact(event)

        updated_services = [
            self.update_service(service, event)
            for service in affected_services]
        updated_equipment = [
            self.update_equipment(equip, event)
            for equip in affected_equip]

        return (stored_event, is_active, updated_services, updated_equipment)
```

> The `__init__` method contains some setup code to create a `DatabaseTemplate`. This is a Spring Python utility class used for database operations. See `http://static.springsource.org/spring-python/1.2.x/sphinx/html/dao.html` for more details. We are also using sqlite3 as our database engine, since it is a standard part of Python.

The `process` method contains some simple steps to process an incoming event.

- We first need to store the event in the EVENTS table. This includes evaluating whether or not it is an active event, meaning that it is actively impacting a piece of equipment.
- Then we determine what equipment and what services the event impacts.
- Next, we update the affected services by determining whether it causes any service outages or restorations.
- Then we update the affected equipment by determining whether it fails or clears a device.

- Finally, we return a tuple containing all the affected assets to support any screen interfaces that could be developed on top of this.

6. Implement the `store_event` algorithm.

```
def store_event(self, event):
    try:
        max_id = self.dt.query_for_int("""select max(ID)
                                            from EVENTS""")
    except DataAccessException, e:
        max_id = 0
    event.id = max_id+1
    self.dt.update("""insert into EVENTS
                (ID, HOST_NAME, SEVERITY,
                                EVENT_CONDITION)
                values
                (?,?,?,?)""",
                (event.id, event.hostname,
                event.severity, event.condition))
    is_active = \
            self.add_or_remove_from_active_events(event)
    return (event, is_active)
```

This method stores every event that is processed. This supports many things including data mining and post mortem analysis of outages. It is also the authoritative place where other event-related data can point back using a foreign key.

- The `store_event` method looks up the maximum primary key value from the `EVENTS` table.
- It increments it by one.
- It assigns it to `event.id`.
- It then inserts it into the `EVENTS` table.
- Next, it calls a method to evaluate whether or not the event should be added to the list of active events, or if it clears out existing active events. Active events are events that are actively causing a piece of equipment to be unclear.
- Finally, it returns a tuple containing the event and whether or not it was classified as an active event.

Measuring your Success with Test Coverage

> For a more sophisticated system, some sort of partitioning solution needs to be implemented. Querying against a table containing millions of rows is very inefficient. However, this is for demonstration purposes only, so we will skip scaling as well as performance and security.

7. Implement the method to evaluate whether to add or remove active events.

    ```
    def add_or_remove_from_active_events(self, event):
        """Active events are current ones that cause equipment
        and/or services to be down."""
        if event.severity == 1:
            self.dt.update("""delete from ACTIVE_EVENTS
                            where EVENT_FK in (
                              select ID
                              from   EVENTS
                              where  HOST_NAME = ?
                              and    EVENT_CONDITION = ?)""",
                          (event.hostname, event.condition))
            return False
        else:
            self.dt.execute("""insert into ACTIVE_EVENTS
                              (EVENT_FK) values (?)""",
                            (event.id,))
            return True
    ```

    When a device fails, it sends a `severity 5` event. This is an active event and in this method, a row is inserted into the `ACTIVE_EVENTS` table, with a foreign key pointing back to the `EVENTS` table. Then we return back `True`, indicating this is an active event.

8. Add the table definition for `ACTIVE_EVENTS` to the SQL script.

    ```
    CREATE TABLE ACTIVE_EVENTS (
        ID INTEGER PRIMARY KEY,
        EVENT_FK,
        FOREIGN KEY(EVENT_FK) REFERENCES EVENTS(ID)
    );
    ```

    This table makes it easy to query what events are currently causing equipment failures.

    Later, when the failing condition on the device clears, it sends a `severity 1` event. This means that `severity 1` events are never active, since they aren't contributing to a piece of equipment being down. In our previous method, we search for any active events that have the same hostname and condition, and delete them. Then we return `False`, indicating this is not an active event.

9. Write the method that evaluates the services and pieces of equipment that are affected by the network event.

```python
def impact(self, event):
    """Look up this event has impact on either equipment
        or services."""
    affected_equipment = self.dt.query(\
                """select * from EQUIPMENT
                    where HOST_NAME = ?""",
                (event.hostname,),
                rowhandler=DictionaryRowMapper())

    affected_services = self.dt.query(\
                """select SERVICE.*
                    from    SERVICE
                    join    SERVICE_MAPPING SM
                    on (SERVICE.ID = SM.SERVICE_FK)
                    join    EQUIPMENT
                    on (SM.EQUIPMENT_FK = EQUIPMENT.ID)
                    where   EQUIPMENT.HOST_NAME = ?""",
                (event.hostname,),
                rowhandler=DictionaryRowMapper())

    return (affected_services, affected_equipment)
```

- We first query the EQUIPMENT table to see if event.hostname matches anything.
- Next, we join the SERVICE table to the EQUIPMENT table through a many-to-many relationship tracked by the SERVICE_MAPPING table. Any service that is related to the equipment that the event was reported on is captured.
- Finally, we return a tuple containing both the list of equipment and list of services that are potentially impacted.

> Spring Python provides a convenient query operation that returns a list of objects mapped to every row of the query. It also provides an out-of-the-box DictionaryRowMapper that converts each row into a Python dictionary, with the keys matching the column names.

10. Add the table definitions to the SQL script for EQUIPMENT, SERVICE, and SERVICE_MAPPING.

```sql
CREATE TABLE EQUIPMENT (
    ID          INTEGER PRIMARY KEY,
    HOST_NAME   TEXT    UNIQUE,
    STATUS      INTEGER
);
```

Measuring your Success with Test Coverage

```
CREATE TABLE SERVICE (
    ID INTEGER PRIMARY KEY,
    NAME TEXT UNIQUE,
    STATUS TEXT
);
CREATE TABLE SERVICE_MAPPING (
    ID INTEGER PRIMARY KEY,
    SERVICE_FK,
    EQUIPMENT_FK,
    FOREIGN KEY(SERVICE_FK) REFERENCES SERVICE(ID),
    FOREIGN KEY(EQUIPMENT_FK) REFERENCES EQUIPMENT(ID)
);
```

11. Write the `update_service` method that stores or clears service-related events, and then updates the service's status based on the remaining active events.

```
def update_service(self, service, event):
    if event.severity == 1:
        self.dt.update("""delete from SERVICE_EVENTS
                        where EVENT_FK in (
                            select ID
                            from EVENTS
                            where HOST_NAME = ?
                            and EVENT_CONDITION = ?)""",
                    (event.hostname, event.condition))
    else:
        self.dt.execute("""insert into SERVICE_EVENTS
                        (EVENT_FK, SERVICE_FK)
                        values (?,?)""",
                    (event.id, service["ID"]))
    try:
        max = self.dt.query_for_int(\
                    """select max(EVENTS.SEVERITY)
                        from SERVICE_EVENTS SE
                        join EVENTS
                        on (EVENTS.ID = SE.EVENT_FK)
                        join SERVICE
                        on (SERVICE.ID = SE.SERVICE_FK)
                        where SERVICE.NAME = ?""",
                    (service["NAME"],))
    except DataAccessException, e:
        max = 1
    if max > 1 and service["STATUS"] == "Operational":
        service["STATUS"] = "Outage"
```

Chapter 7

```
            self.dt.update("""update SERVICE
                              set STATUS = ?
                              where ID = ?""",
                           (service["STATUS"], service["ID"]))
        if max == 1 and service["STATUS"] == "Outage":
            service["STATUS"] = "Operational"
            self.dt.update("""update SERVICE
                              set STATUS = ?
                              where ID = ?""",
                           (service["STATUS"], service["ID"]))
        if event.severity == 1:
            return {"service":service, "is_active":False}
        else:
            return {"service":service, "is_active":True}
```

Service-related events are active events related to a service. A single event can be related to many services. For example, what if we were monitoring a wireless router that provided Internet service to a lot of users, and it reported a critical error? This one event would be mapped as an impact to all the end users. When a new active event is processed, it is stored in SERVICE_EVENTS for each related service.

Then, when a clearing event is processed, the previous service event must be deleted from the SERVICE_EVENTS table.

12. Add the table definition for SERVICE_EVENTS to the SQL script.

```
CREATE TABLE SERVICE_EVENTS (
    ID INTEGER PRIMARY KEY,
    SERVICE_FK,
    EVENT_FK,
    FOREIGN KEY(SERVICE_FK) REFERENCES SERVICE(ID),
    FOREIGN KEY(EVENT_FK) REFERENCES EVENTS(ID)
);
```

> It is important to recognize that deleting an entry from SERVICE_EVENTS doesn't mean that we delete the original event from the EVENTS table. Instead, we are merely indicating that the original active event is no longer active and it does not impact the related service.

13. Prepend the entire SQL script with drop statements, making it possible to run the script for several recipes.

```
DROP TABLE IF EXISTS SERVICE_MAPPING;
DROP TABLE IF EXISTS SERVICE_EVENTS;
DROP TABLE IF EXISTS ACTIVE_EVENTS;
DROP TABLE IF EXISTS EQUIPMENT;
```

```
DROP TABLE IF EXISTS SERVICE;
DROP TABLE IF EXISTS EVENTS;
```

14. Append the SQL script used for database setup with inserts to preload some equipment and services.

    ```
    INSERT into EQUIPMENT (ID, HOST_NAME, STATUS) values (1,
    'pyhost1', 1);
    INSERT into EQUIPMENT (ID, HOST_NAME, STATUS) values (2,
    'pyhost2', 1);
    INSERT into EQUIPMENT (ID, HOST_NAME, STATUS) values (3,
    'pyhost3', 1);
    INSERT into SERVICE (ID, NAME, STATUS) values (1, 'service-abc',
    'Operational');
    INSERT into SERVICE (ID, NAME, STATUS) values (2, 'service-xyz',
    'Outage');
    INSERT into SERVICE_MAPPING (SERVICE_FK, EQUIPMENT_FK) values
    (1,1);
    INSERT into SERVICE_MAPPING (SERVICE_FK, EQUIPMENT_FK) values
    (1,2);
    INSERT into SERVICE_MAPPING (SERVICE_FK, EQUIPMENT_FK) values
    (2,1);
    INSERT into SERVICE_MAPPING (SERVICE_FK, EQUIPMENT_FK) values
    (2,3);
    ```

15. Finally, write the method that updates equipment status based on the current active events.

    ```python
    def update_equipment(self, equip, event):
        try:
            max = self.dt.query_for_int(\
                    """select max(EVENTS.SEVERITY)
                        from ACTIVE_EVENTS AE
                        join EVENTS
                        on (EVENTS.ID = AE.EVENT_FK)
                        where EVENTS.HOST_NAME = ?""",
                    (event.hostname,))
        except DataAccessException:
            max = 1

        if max != equip["STATUS"]:
            equip["STATUS"] = max
            self.dt.update("""update EQUIPMENT
                            set STATUS = ?""",
                            (equip["STATUS"],))

        return equip
    ```

Here, we need to find the maximum severity from the list of active events for a given host name. If there are no active events, then Spring Python raises a `DataAccessException` and we translate that to a severity of 1.

We check if this is different from the existing device's status. If so, we issue a SQL update. Finally, we return the record for the device, with its status updated appropriately.

How it works...

This application uses a database-backed mechanism to process incoming network events, and checks them against the inventory of equipment and services to evaluate failures and restorations. Our application doesn't handle specialized devices or unusual types of services. This real-world complexity has been traded in for a relatively simple application, which can be used to write various test recipes.

> Events typically map to a single piece of equipment and to zero or more services. A service can be thought of as a string of equipment used to provide a type of service to the customer. New failing events are considered active until a clearing event arrives. Active events, when aggregated against a piece of equipment, define its current status. Active events, when aggregated against a service, defines the service's current status.

Installing and running coverage on your test suite

Install the coverage tool and run it against your test suite. Then you can view a report showing what lines were covered by the test suite.

How to do it...

With the following steps, we will build some unit tests and then run them through the coverage tool.

1. Create a new file called `recipe52.py` to contain our test code for this recipe.
2. Write a simple unit test that injects a single, alarming event into the system.

   ```
   from network import *
   import unittest
   from springpython.database.factory import *
   from springpython.database.core import *

   class EventCorrelationTest(unittest.TestCase):
       def setUp(self):
   ```

```
            db_name = "recipe52.db"
            factory = Sqlite3ConnectionFactory(db_name)
            self.correlator = EventCorrelator(factory)

            dt = DatabaseTemplate(factory)
            sql = open("network.sql").read().split(";")
            for statement in sql:
                dt.execute(statement + ";")

        def test_process_events(self):
            evt1 = Event("pyhost1", "serverRestart", 5)

            stored_event, is_active, \
                updated_services, updated_equipment = \
                        self.correlator.process(evt1)

            print "Stored event: %s" % stored_event
            if is_active:
                print "This event was an active event."

            print "Updated services: %s" % updated_services
            print "Updated equipment: %s" % updated_equipment
            print "--------------------------------"

    if __name__ == "__main__":
        unittest.main()
```

3. Clear out any existing coverage report data using `coverage -e`.
4. Run the test suite using the coverage tool.

   ```
   gturnquist$ coverage -x recipe52.py
   Stored event: (ID:1) pyhost1:serverRestart - 5
   This event was an active event.
   Updated services: [{'is_active': True, 'service': {'STATUS':
   'Outage', 'ID': 1, 'NAME': u'service-abc'}}, {'is_active': True,
   'service': {'STATUS': u'Outage', 'ID': 2, 'NAME': u'service-
   xyz'}}]
   Updated equipment: [{'STATUS': 5, 'ID': 1, 'HOST_NAME':
   u'pyhost1'}]
   --------------------------------
   .
   --------------------------------------------------------------
   ----
   Ran 1 test in 0.211s
   OK
   ```

Chapter 7

5. Print out the report captured by the previous command by typing `coverage -r`. If the report shows several other modules listed from Python's standard libraries, it's a hint that you have an older version of the coverage tool installed. If so, uninstall the old version by typing `pip uninstall coverage` followed by reinstalling with `pip install coverage`.

```
(ptc)gturnquist-mbp:07 gturnquist$ coverage -r
Name                                                                    Stmts   Miss  Cover
---------------------------------------------------------------------------------------------
/Users/gturnquist/ptc/lib/python2.6/site-packages/springpython/__init__      0      0   100%
/Users/gturnquist/ptc/lib/python2.6/site-packages/springpython/database/__init__   13      5    62%
/Users/gturnquist/ptc/lib/python2.6/site-packages/springpython/database/core    123     34    72%
/Users/gturnquist/ptc/lib/python2.6/site-packages/springpython/database/factory   99     48    52%
network                                                                    65     10    85%
recipe52                                                                   23      0   100%
---------------------------------------------------------------------------------------------
TOTAL                                                                     323     97    70%
```

6. Create another file called `recipe52b.py` to contain a different test suite.
7. Write another test suite that generates two faults and then clears them out.

```
from network import *
import unittest
from springpython.database.factory import *
from springpython.database.core import *

class EventCorrelationTest(unittest.TestCase):
    def setUp(self):
        db_name = "recipe52b.db"
        factory = Sqlite3ConnectionFactory(db=db_name)
        self.correlator = EventCorrelator(factory)

        dt = DatabaseTemplate(factory)
        sql = open("network.sql").read().split(";")
        for statement in sql:
            dt.execute(statement + ";")

    def test_process_events(self):
        evt1 = Event("pyhost1", "serverRestart", 5)
        evt2 = Event("pyhost2", "lineStatus", 5)
        evt3 = Event("pyhost2", "lineStatus", 1)
        evt4 = Event("pyhost1", "serverRestart", 1)

        for event in [evt1, evt2, evt3, evt4]:
            stored_event, is_active, \
                updated_services, updated_equipment = \
                    self.correlator.process(event)
            print "Stored event: %s" % stored_event
            if is_active:
                print "This event was an active event."
```

253

Measuring your Success with Test Coverage

```
            print "Updated services: %s" % updated_services
            print "Updated equipment: %s" % updated_equipment
            print "-------------------------------"

if __name__ == "__main__":
    unittest.main()
```

8. Run this test suite through the coverage tool using `coverage -x recipe52b.py`.
9. Print out the report by typing `coverage -r`.

```
(ptc)gturnquist-mbp:07 gturnquist$ coverage -r
Name                                                                    Stmts    Miss  Cover
-----------------------------------------------------------------------------------------------
/Users/gturnquist/ptc/lib/python2.6/site-packages/springpython/__init__      0       0   100%
/Users/gturnquist/ptc/lib/python2.6/site-packages/springpython/database/__init__   13       5    62%
/Users/gturnquist/ptc/lib/python2.6/site-packages/springpython/database/core      123      34    72%
/Users/gturnquist/ptc/lib/python2.6/site-packages/springpython/database/factory    99      48    52%
network                                                                    65       0   100%
recipe52                                                                   23       0   100%
recipe52b                                                                  27       0   100%
-----------------------------------------------------------------------------------------------
TOTAL                                                                     350      87    75%
```

The first test suite only injects a single alarm. We expect it to cause a service outage as well as taking its related piece of equipment down. Since this would *not* exercise any of the event clearing logic, we certainly don't expect 100 percent code coverage.

In the report, we can see it scoring `network.py` as having 65 statements, and having executed 55 of them, resulting in 85 percent coverage. We also see that `recipe52.py` had 23 statements and executed all of them. This means all of our test code ran.

At this point, we realize that we are only testing the alarming part of the event correlator. To make this more effective, we should inject another alarm followed by a couple of clears to make sure that everything clears out and the services return to operational status. This should result in 100 percent coverage in our simple application.

The second screenshot indeed shows that we have reached full coverage of `network.py`.

There's more...

We also see Spring Python reported as well. If we had used any other third-party libraries, then they would also appear. Is this right? It depends. The previous comments seem to indicate that we don't really care about coverage of Spring Python but, in other situations, we may be very interested. And how can the coverage tool know where to draw the line?

In later recipes, we will look into how to be more selective of what to measure so we can filter out noise.

Why are there no asserts in the unit test?

It is true that the unit test isn't adequate with regard to testing the outcome. To draw up this recipe, I visually inspected the output to see whether the network management application was performing as expected. But this is incomplete. A real production grade unit test needs to finish this with a set of assertions so that visual scanning is not needed.

So why didn't we code any? Because the focus of this recipe was on how to generate a coverage report and then use that information to enhance the testing. We covered both of those. By thinking about what was and wasn't tested, we wrote a comprehensive test that shows services going into outage and back to operational status. We just didn't put the finishing touch of confirming this automatically.

Generating an HTML report using coverage

Using the coverage tool, generate an HTML visual coverage report. This is useful because we can drill into the source code and see what lines were not exercised in the test procedures.

Reading a coverage report without reading the source code is not very useful. It may be tempting to compare two different projects based on the coverage percentages. But unless the actual code is analyzed, this type of comparison can lead to faulty conclusions about the quality of software.

How to do it...

With these steps, we will explore creating a nicely viewable HTML coverage report.

1. Generate coverage metrics by following the steps in *Installing and running coverage on your test suite* recipe and only running the first test suite (which has resulted in less than 100 percent coverage).
2. Generate an HTML report by typing: `coverage.html`.

Measuring your Success with Test Coverage

3. Open `htmlcov/index.html` using your favorite browser and inspect the overall report.

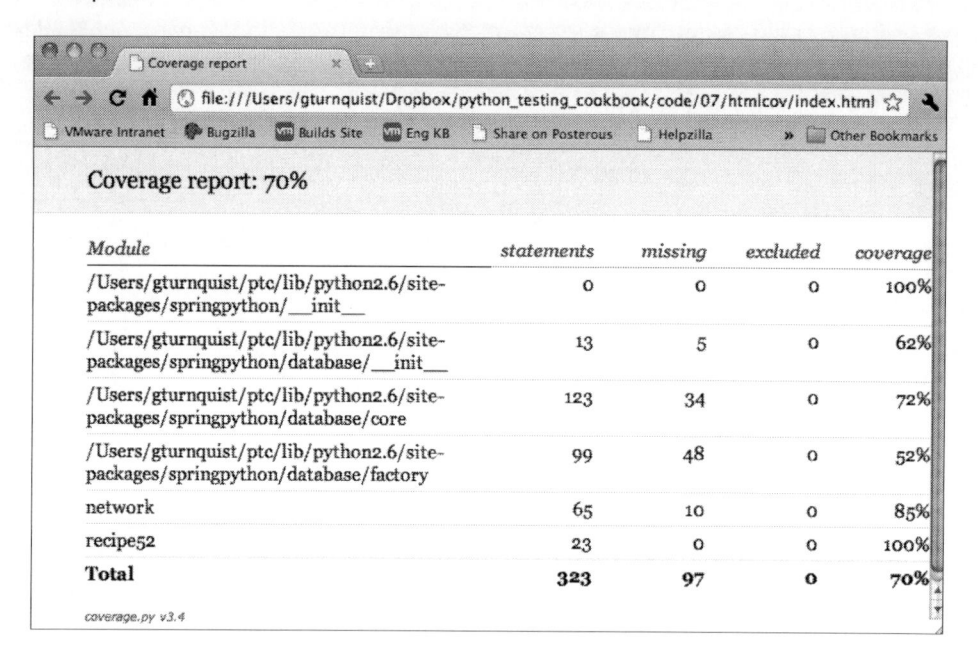

Coverage report: 70%

Module	statements	missing	excluded	coverage
/Users/gturnquist/ptc/lib/python2.6/site-packages/springpython/__init__	0	0	0	100%
/Users/gturnquist/ptc/lib/python2.6/site-packages/springpython/database/__init__	13	5	0	62%
/Users/gturnquist/ptc/lib/python2.6/site-packages/springpython/database/core	123	34	0	72%
/Users/gturnquist/ptc/lib/python2.6/site-packages/springpython/database/factory	99	48	0	52%
network	65	10	0	85%
recipe52	23	0	0	100%
Total	**323**	**97**	**0**	**70%**

coverage.py v3.4

4. Click on **network**, and scroll down to see where the event clearing logic wasn't exercised due to no clearing events being processed.

```
54    def add_or_remove_from_active_events(self, event):
55        """Active events are current ones that cause equipment
56           and/or services to be down."""
57
58        if event.severity == 1:
59            self.dt.update("""delete from ACTIVE_EVENTS
60                              where EVENT_FK = (
61                                  select ID
62                                  from    EVENTS
63                                  where  HOST_NAME = ?
64                                  and    CONDITION = ?)""",
65                           (event.hostname,event.condition))
66            return False
67        else:
68            self.dt.execute("""insert into ACTIVE_EVENTS
69                               (EVENT_FK) values (?)""",
70                            (event.id,))
71            return True
```

How it works...

The coverage tool has a built-in feature to generate an HTML report. This provides a powerful way to visually inspect the source code and see what lines were not executed.

By looking at this report, we can clearly see that the lines not executed involve the lack of clearing network events that are being processed. This can tip us off about another test case which involves clearing events that need to be drafted.

Generating an XML report using coverage

The coverage tool can generate an XML coverage report in Cobertura format (http://cobertura.sourceforge.net/). This is useful if we want to process the coverage information in another tool. In this recipe, we will see how to use the coverage command-line tool, and then view the XML report by hand.

It's important to understand that reading a coverage report without reading the source code is not very useful. It may be tempting to compare two different projects based on the coverage percentages. But unless the actual code is analyzed, this type of comparison can lead to faulty conclusions about the quality of the software.

For example, a project with 85 percent coverage may appear, on the surface, to be better tested than one with 60 percent. However, if the 60 percent application has much more thoroughly exhaustive scenarios – as they are only covering the core parts of the system that are in heavy use – then it may be much more stable than the 85 percent application.

> Coverage analysis serves a useful purpose when comparing test results between iterations, and using it to decide which scenarios need to be added to our testing repertoire.

How to do it...

With these steps, we will discover how to create an XML report using the coverage tool, consumable by other tools:

1. Generate coverage metrics by following the steps in *Installing and running coverage on your test suite* recipe (mentioned in *Chapter 1, Using Unittest to Develop Basic Tests*) and only running the first test suite (which has resulted in less than 100 percent coverage).
2. Generate an XML report by typing: `coverage xml`.

3. Open `coverage.xml` using your favorite text or XML editor. The format of the XML is the same as Cobertura—a Java code coverage analyzer. This means that many tools, like Jenkins, can parse the results.

```xml
<?xml version="1.0" ?>
<!DOCTYPE coverage
    SYSTEM 'http://cobertura.sourceforge.net/xml/coverage-03.dtd'>
<coverage branch-rate="0" line-rate="0.6997" timestamp="1293777896667" version="3.4">
    <!-- Generated by coverage.py: http://nedbatchelder.com/code/coverage -->
    <packages>
        <package branch-rate="0" complexity="0" line-rate="0.8864" name=".">
            <classes>
                <class branch-rate="0" complexity="0" filename="network.py" line-rate="0.8462" name="network">
                    <methods/>
                    <lines>
                </class>
                <class branch-rate="0" complexity="0" filename="recipe52.py" line-rate="1" name="recipe52">
                    <methods/>
                    <lines>
                </class>
            </classes>
        </package>
```

How it works...

The coverage tool has a built-in feature to generate an XML report. This provides a powerful way to parse the output using some type of external tool.

> In the previous screenshot, I opened it using SpringSource Tool Suite (you can download it from `http://www.springsource.com/developer/sts`), partly because I happen to use STS every day, but you can use any text or XML editor you like.

What use is an XML report?

XML is not the best way to communicate coverage information to users. *Generating an HTML report with coverage* is a more practical recipe when it comes to human users.

What if we want to capture a coverage report and publish it inside a continuous integration system like Jenkins? All we need to do is install the Cobertura plugin (refer `https://wiki.jenkins-ci.org/display/JENKINS/Cobertura+Plugin`), and this report becomes traceable. Jenkins can nicely monitor trends in coverage and give us more feedback as we develop our system.

See also

- Letting Jenkins get nosy with coverage
- Generating an HTML report with coverage

Getting nosy with coverage

Install the coverage nose plugin, and run your test suite using nose. This provides a quick and convenient report using the ubiquitous nosetests tool. This recipe assumes you have already created the network management application as described in the *Building a network management application* section.

How to do it...

With these steps, we will see how to combine the coverage tool with nose.

1. Create a new file called `recipe55.py` to store our test code.
2. Create a test case that injects a faulting alarm.

```python
from network import *
import unittest
from springpython.database.factory import *
from springpython.database.core import *

class EventCorrelationTest(unittest.TestCase):
    def setUp(self):
        db_name = "recipe55.db"
        factory = Sqlite3ConnectionFactory(db=db_name)
        self.correlator = EventCorrelator(factory)

        dt = DatabaseTemplate(factory)
        sql = open("network.sql").read().split(";")
        for statement in sql:
            dt.execute(statement + ";")

    def test_process_events(self):
        evt1 = Event("pyhost1", "serverRestart", 5)
        stored_event, is_active, \
            updated_services, updated_equipment = \
                self.correlator.process(evt1)

        print "Stored event: %s" % stored_event
        if is_active:
            print "This event was an active event."
        print "Updated services: %s" % updated_services
```

Measuring your Success with Test Coverage

```
            print "Updated equipment: %s" % updated_equipment
            print "---------------------------------"
```

3. Run the test module using the coverage plugin by typing `nosetests recipe55 --with-coverage`.

```
[ptc]gturnquist-mbp:07 gturnquist$ nosetests recipe55 --with-coverage
Name                          Stmts   Miss  Cover   Missing
-----------------------------------------------------------
network                          65     10    85%   59-66, 98, 121-122, 132-133, 139, 152-153
recipe55                         21      0   100%
springpython                      0      0   100%
springpython.database            13      5    62%   24-25, 29-31
springpython.database.core      123     34    72%   31-32, 36-38, 70-72, 76-77, 80, 92, 106,
122-124, 128-129, 132, 145, 155, 160, 163, 172-173, 190, 203, 211, 214-220
springpython.database.factory    99     48    52%   29, 37-38, 41-42, 45, 48, 54, 58-62, 66-6
7, 70, 73, 77-81, 85-86, 89, 92, 106-109, 112, 115, 123, 127-131, 135-136, 140-141, 145-147, 15
0, 153, 157
sqlite3                           1      1     0%   24
sqlite3.dbapi2                   41     41     0%   24-88
-----------------------------------------------------------
TOTAL                           363    139    62%
-----------------------------------------------------------
Ran 1 test in 0.186s

OK
```

How it works...

The nose plugin for coverage invokes the coverage tool and provides a formatted report. For each module, it displays:

- Total number of statements
- Number of missed statements
- Percentage of covered statements
- Line numbers for the missed statements

There's more...

A common behavior of nose is to alter `stdout`, disabling the print statements embedded in the test case.

Why use the nose plugin instead of the coverage tool directly?

The coverage tool works fine by itself, as was demonstrated in other recipes in this chapter, however, nose is a ubiquitous testing tool used by many developers. Providing a plugin makes it easy to support this vast community by empowering them to run the exact set of test plugins they want, with coverage being part of that test complement.

Why are sqlite3 and springpython included?

Sqlite3 is a relational database library that is included with Python. It is file based which means that no separate processes are required to create and use a database. Details about Spring Python can be found in the earlier sections of this chapter.

The purpose of this recipe was to measure coverage of our network management application and the corresponding test case. So why are these third-party libraries included? The coverage tool has no way of automatically knowing what we want and the things we don't want to see from a coverage perspective. To delve into this, refer to the next section *Filtering out test noise from coverage*.

Filtering out test noise from coverage

Using command-line options, you can filter out counted lines. This recipe assumes you have already created the network management application as described in the *Building a network management application* section.

How to do it...

With these steps, we will see how to filter out certain modules from being counted in our coverage report.

1. Create a test suite that exercises all the code functionality.

    ```
    from network import *
    import unittest
    from springpython.database.factory import *
    from springpython.database.core import *
    class EventCorrelationTest(unittest.TestCase):
        def setUp(self):
            db_name = "recipe56.db"
            factory = Sqlite3ConnectionFactory(db=db_name)
            self.correlator = EventCorrelator(factory)

            dt = DatabaseTemplate(factory)
            sql = open("network.sql").read().split(";")
            for statement in sql:
                dt.execute(statement + ";")
        def test_process_events(self):
            evt1 = Event("pyhost1", "serverRestart", 5)
            evt2 = Event("pyhost2", "lineStatus", 5)
            evt3 = Event("pyhost2", "lineStatus", 1)
            evt4 = Event("pyhost1", "serverRestart", 1)

            for event in [evt1, evt2, evt3, evt4]:
    ```

Measuring your Success with Test Coverage

```
                stored_event, is_active, \
                updated_services, updated_equipment = \
                        self.correlator.process(event)
            print "Stored event: %s" % stored_event
            if is_active:
                print "This event was an active event."
            print "Updated services: %s" % updated_services
            print "Updated equipment: %s" % updated_equipment
            print "-------------------------------"
if __name__ == "__main__":
    unittest.main()
```

2. Clear out any previous coverage data by running `coverage -e`.
3. Run it using `coverage -x recipe56.py`.
4. Generate a console report using `coverage -r`. In the following screenshot, observe how Spring Python is included in the report and reduces the total metric to 73 percent.

```
(ptc)gturnquist-mpro:07 gturnquist$ coverage -r
Name                                                                          Stmts   Miss  Cover
--------------------------------------------------------------------------------------------------
/Users/gturnquist/ptc/lib/python2.6/site-packages/springpython/__init__          0      0   100%
/Users/gturnquist/ptc/lib/python2.6/site-packages/springpython/database/__init__ 13      5    62%
/Users/gturnquist/ptc/lib/python2.6/site-packages/springpython/database/core    123     34    72%
/Users/gturnquist/ptc/lib/python2.6/site-packages/springpython/database/factory  99     48    52%
network                                                                         65      0   100%
recipe56                                                                        27      0   100%
--------------------------------------------------------------------------------------------------
TOTAL                                                                          327     87    73%
```

5. Clean out coverage data by running `coverage -e`.
6. Run the test again using `coverage run --source network.py,recipe56.py recipe56.py`.
7. Generate another console report using `coverage -r`. Notice in the next screenshot, how Spring Python is no longer listed, bringing our total coverage back up to 100 percent.

```
(ptc)gturnquist-mpro:07 gturnquist$ coverage -r
Name         Stmts   Miss  Cover
---------------------------------
network         65      0   100%
recipe56        27      0   100%
---------------------------------
TOTAL           92      0   100%
```

8. Clean out coverage data by running `coverage -e`.

9. Run the test using `coverage -x recipe56.py`.
10. Generate a console report using `coverage -r recipe56.py network.py`.

```
(ptc)gturnquist-mpro:07 gturnquist$ coverage -r recipe56.py network.py
Name          Stmts    Miss  Cover
-----------------------------------
network         65       0    100%
recipe56        27       0    100%
-----------------------------------
TOTAL           92       0    100%
```

How it works...

Coverage provides the ability to decide what files will be analyzed and what files will be reported. The steps in the previous section gather metrics several times, either running it with a restricted set of source files (in order to filter out Spring Python), or by requesting an explicit set of modules in the report.

One question which arises from all this is *what's the best choice?* For our test scenario, the two choices were equivalent. With approximately the same amount of typing, we filtered out Spring Python and got a report showing `network.py` and `recipe56.py` with 100 percent coverage either way. However, a real project with a lot of modules and possibly different teams working in different areas would probably do better by gathering all the metric data available and filtering at the report level.

This way, different reports on subsystems can be run as needed without having to keep recapturing metric data, and an overall report can still be run for whole system coverage, all from the same gathered data.

There's more...

The options used in the previous section were inclusive. We picked what was to be included. The coverage tool also comes with an `-omit` option. The challenge is that it's a file-based option, not module based. It doesn't work to `-omit springpython`. Instead, every file must be specified, and in this case, that would have required four complete files to exclude it all.

To further complicate this, the full path of the Spring Python files needs to be included. This results in a very lengthy command, not providing much benefit over the ways we demonstrated.

In other situations, if the file to be excluded is local to where coverage is being run, then it might be more practical.

The coverage tool has other options not covered in this chapter, such as measuring branch coverage instead of statement coverage, excluding lines, and the ability to run in parallel to manage collecting metrics from multiple processes.

Measuring your Success with Test Coverage

As mentioned previously, the coverage tool has the ability to filter out individual lines. In my opinion, this sounds very much like trying to get the coverage report to meet some mandated percentage. The coverage tool is best used to work towards writing more comprehensive tests, fixing bugs, and improving development, and not towards building a better report.

See also

Building a network management application recipe mentioned in the earlier sections of the chapter

Letting Jenkins get nosy with coverage

Configure Jenkins to run a test suite using nose, generating a coverage report. This recipe assumes you have already created the network management application as described in the *Building a network management application* section.

Getting ready

1. If you have already downloaded Jenkins and used it for previous recipes, look for a .jenkins folder in your home directory and delete it, to avoid unexpected variances caused by this recipe.

2. Install Jenkins as explained in *Chapter 6*: *Configuring Jenkins to run Python tests upon commit*.

3. Open the console to confirm that Jenkins is working.

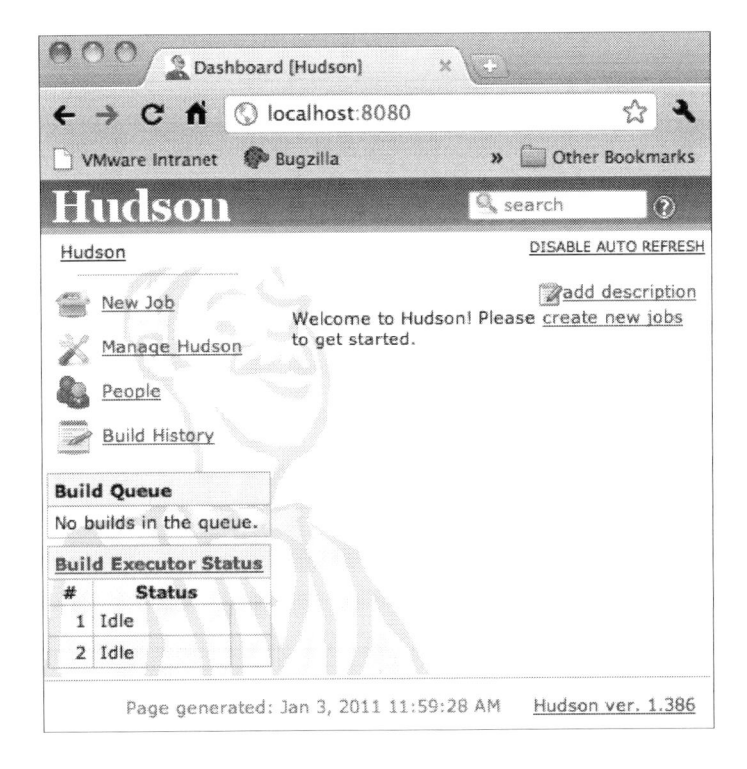

4. Click on **Manage Jenkins**.
5. Click on **Manage Plugins**.
6. Click on the **Available** tab.
7. Find the `Cobertura Plugin` and click the checkbox next to it.
8. Find the `Git Plugin` and click the checkbox next to it.
9. At the bottom of the page, click on the **Install** button.
10. Navigate back to the dashboard screen.
11. Shutdown Jenkins and start it again.
12. Install git source code control on your machine. Refer to *Chapter 6, Configuring Jenkins to run Python tests upon commit* for links on installing git.
13. Create an empty folder for this recipe.

    `gturnquist$ mkdir /tmp/recipe57`

14. Initialize the folder for source code maintenance.

    `gturnquist$ git init /tmp/recipe57`

Measuring your Success with Test Coverage

15. Copy the network application and SQL script into the folder, add it, and commit the changes.

```
gturnquist$ cp network.py /tmp/recipe57/
gturnquist$ cp network.sql /tmp/recipe57/
gturnquist$ cd /tmp/recipe57/
gturnquist$ git add network.py network.sql
gturnquist$ git commit -m "Add network app"
[master (root-commit) 7f78d46] Add network app
 2 files changed, 221 insertions(+), 0 deletions(-)
 create mode 100644 network.py
 create mode 100644 network.sql
```

How to do it...

With these steps, we will explore how to configure Jenkins to build a coverage report and serve it through Jenkins' interface.

1. Create a new file called `recipe57.py` to contain our test code for this recipe.
2. Write a test case that partially exercises the network management application.

```python
from network import *
import unittest
from springpython.database.factory import *
from springpython.database.core import *
class EventCorrelationTest(unittest.TestCase):
    def setUp(self):
        db_name = "recipe57.db"
        factory = Sqlite3ConnectionFactory(db=db_name)
        self.correlator = EventCorrelator(factory)

        dt = DatabaseTemplate(factory)
        sql = open("network.sql").read().split(";")
        for statement in sql:
            dt.execute(statement + ";")
    def test_process_events(self):
        evt1 = Event("pyhost1", "serverRestart", 5)
        stored_event, is_active, \
            updated_services, updated_equipment = \
                    self.correlator.process(evt1)
        print "Stored event: %s" % stored_event
        if is_active:
```

```
            print "This event was an active event."
        print "Updated services: %s" % updated_services
        print "Updated equipment: %s" % updated_equipment
        print "--------------------------------"
```

3. Copy it into the source code repository. Add it and commit the changes.

   ```
   gturnquist$ cp recipe57.py /tmp/recipe57/
   gturnquist$ cd /tmp/recipe57/
   gturnquist$ git add recipe57.py
   gturnquist$ git commit -m "Added tests."
   [master 0bf1761] Added tests.
    1 files changed, 37 insertions(+), 0 deletions(-)
    create mode 100644 recipe57.py
   ```

4. Open the Jenkins console.
5. Click on **New Job**.
6. Enter **recipe57** as the **Job Name** and pick **Build a free-style software project**.
7. Click on **Ok**.
8. In the **Source Code Management** section, pick **Git**. For **URL** enter `/tmp/recipe57/`.
9. In the **Build Triggers** section, pick **Poll SCM** and enter * * * * * into the schedule box, to trigger a poll once a minute.
10. In the **Build** section, select **Execute Shell** and enter the following adhoc script that loads virtualenv and runs the test suite.

    ```
    . /Users/gturnquist/ptc/bin/activate
    coverage -e
    coverage run /Users/gturnquist/ptc/bin/nosetests recipe57.py
    coverage xml --include=network.py,recipe57.py
    ```

> You need to include the step to activate your virtualenv and then run the coverage tool as shown in the following steps.

11. In the **Post-build Actions** section, pick **Publish Cobertura Coverage Report**.
12. Enter `coverage.xml` for **Cobertura xml report pattern**.
13. Click on **Save** to store all job settings.
14. Navigate back to the dashboard.
15. Click on **Enable Auto Refresh**.

Measuring your Success with Test Coverage

16. Wait about a minute for the build job to run.

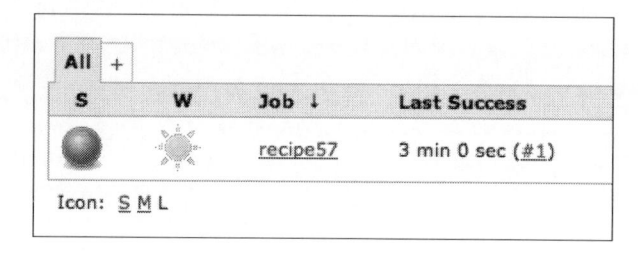

S	W	Job ↓	Last Success
●	☼	recipe57	3 min 0 sec (#1)

Icon: S M L

17. Click on results (**#1** in the previous screenshot).
18. Click on **Coverage Report**. Observe the next screenshot where it reports 89 percent coverage.

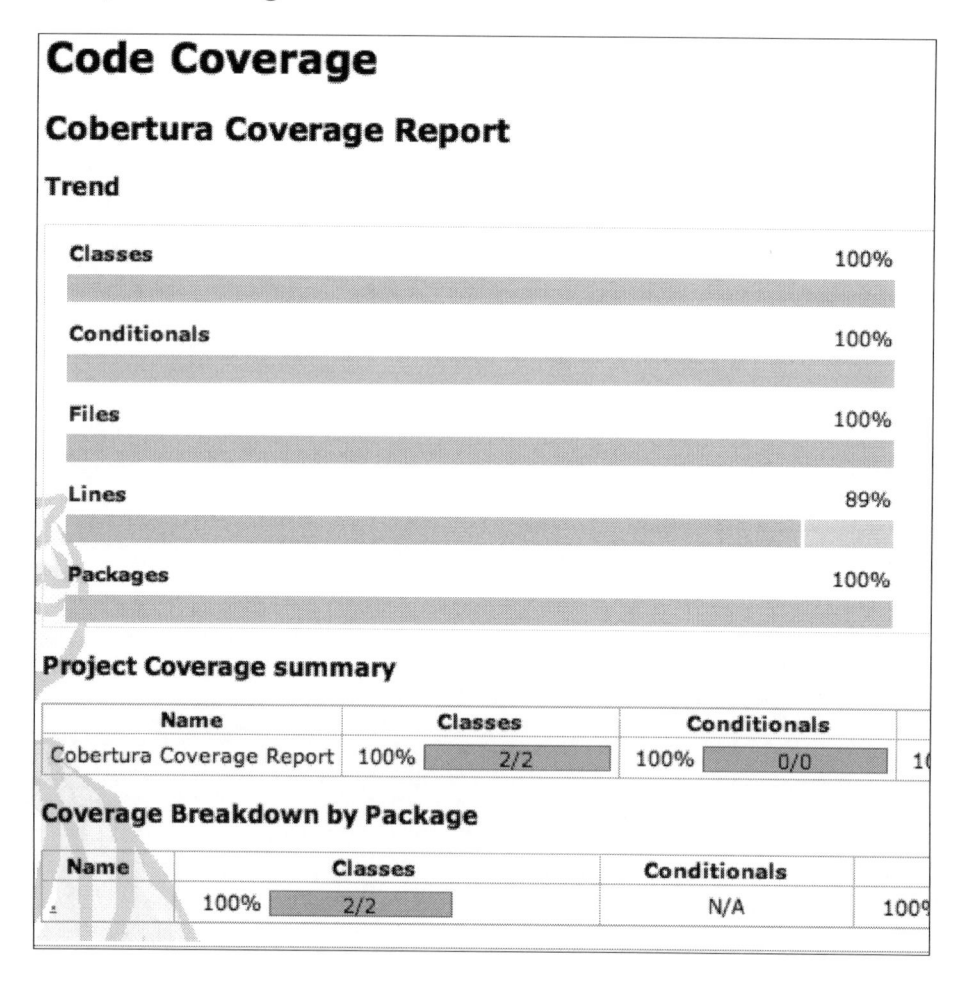

Code Coverage

Cobertura Coverage Report

Trend

Classes — 100%

Conditionals — 100%

Files — 100%

Lines — 89%

Packages — 100%

Project Coverage summary

Name	Classes		Conditionals	
Cobertura Coverage Report	100%	2/2	100%	0/0

Coverage Breakdown by Package

Name	Classes		Conditionals	
	100%	2/2	N/A		100%

19. Click on module . (dot) to see `network.py` and `recipe57.py`.
20. Click on `recipe57.py` to see which lines were covered and which ones were missed.

How it works...

The coverage tool generates a useful XML file that the Jenkins Cobertura plugin can harvest. It's possible to just generate the HTML report and serve it up through Jenkins, but the XML file allows Jenkins to nicely chart the trend of coverage. It also provides the means to drill down and view the source code along with lines covered and missed.

We also integrated it with source control so that, as changes are committed to the repository, new jobs will be run.

There's more...

It's important not to get too wrapped up in the coverage report. The coverage tool is useful to track testing, but working purely to increase coverage doesn't guarantee building better code. It should be used as a tool to illuminate what test scenarios are missing instead of thinking about testing the missing line of code.

Nose doesn't directly support coverage's XML option

The nose plugin for the coverage tool doesn't include the ability to generate XML files. This is because the coverage plugin is part of nose and NOT part of the coverage project. It is not up-to-date with the latest features including the XML report.

> I asked Ned Batchelder, the creator of the coverage project, about this lack of XML support from nose. He gave me the tip to run `nosetests` inside `coverage`, as shown previously in the Jenkins job. It generates the same `.coverage` trace data file. It is easy to then execute `coverage xml` with needed arguments to get our desired report. In fact, we can use any reporting feature of coverage at this stage. Unfortunately, the coverage tool needs the explicit path to `nosetests`, and running inside Jenkins requires the path to be spelled out.

Updating the project-level script to provide coverage reports

Update the project-level script to generate HTML, XML, and console coverage reports as runnable options.

Measuring your Success with Test Coverage

Getting ready

- Install coverage by typing `pip install coverage`.
- Create the network management application as described in the *Building a network management application* section.

How to do it...

With these steps, we will explore how to use coverage programmatically in a project management script.

1. Create a new file called `recipe58.py` to store this command-line script.
2. Create a script that uses `getopt` to parse command-line arguments.

   ```
   import getopt
   import logging
   import nose
   import os
   import os.path
   import re
   import sys
   from glob import glob

   def usage():
       print
       print "Usage: python recipe58.py [command]"
       print
       print "\t--help"
       print "\t--test"
       print "\t--package"
       print "\t--publish"
       print "\t--register"
       print

   try:
       optlist, args = getopt.getopt(sys.argv[1:],
           "h",
           ["help", "test", "package", "publish", "register"])
   except getopt.GetoptError:
       # print help information and exit:
       print "Invalid command found in %s" % sys.argv
       usage()
       sys.exit(2)
   ```

3. Add a test function that uses coverage's API to gather metrics and then generate a console report, an HTML report, and an XML report while also using nose's API to run the tests.

```python
def test():
    from coverage import coverage

    cov = coverage()
    cov.start()

    suite = ["recipe52", "recipe52b", "recipe55", "recipe56", "recipe57"]
    print("Running suite %s" % suite)
    args = [""]
    args.extend(suite)
    nose.run(argv=args)

    cov.stop()

    modules_to_report = [module + ".py" for module in suite]
    modules_to_report.append("network.py")

    cov.report(morfs=modules_to_report)
    cov.html_report(morfs=modules_to_report, \
                    directory="recipe58")
    cov.xml_report(morfs=modules_to_report, \
                   outfile="recipe58.xml")
```

4. Add some other stubbed out functions to simulate packaging, publishing, and registering this project.

```python
def package():
    print "This is where we can plug in code to run " + \
          "setup.py to generate a bundle."

def publish():
    print "This is where we can plug in code to upload " + \
          "our tarball to S3 or some other download site."

def register():
    print "setup.py has a built in function to " + \
          "'register' a release to PyPI. It's " + \
          "convenient to put a hook in here."
    # os.system("%s setup.py register" % sys.executable)
```

5. Add code that processes the command-line arguments and calls the functions defined earlier.

```python
if len(optlist) == 0:
    usage()
    sys.exit(1)

# Check for help requests, which cause all other
```

```
        # options to be ignored.
        for option in optlist:
            if option[0] in ("--help", "-h"):
                usage()
                sys.exit(1)

        # Parse the arguments, in order
        for option in optlist:
            if option[0] in ("--test"):
                test()

            if option[0] in ("--package"):
                package()

            if option[0] in ("--publish"):
                publish()

            if option[0] in ("--register"):
                register()
```

6. Run the script using the `--test` option.

```
(ptc)gturnquist-mbp:07 gturnquist$ python recipe58.py --test
Running suite ['recipe52', 'recipe52b', 'recipe55', 'recipe56', 'recipe57']
.....
Ran 5 tests in 0.743s

OK
Name       Stmts   Miss  Cover   Missing
-----------------------------------------
network       65      0   100%
recipe52      24      1    96%   33
recipe52b     28      1    96%   37
recipe55      22      0   100%
recipe56      28      1    96%   37
recipe57      24      1    96%   33
-----------------------------------------
TOTAL        191      4    98%
```

7. Open the HTML report using your favorite browser.

Chapter 7

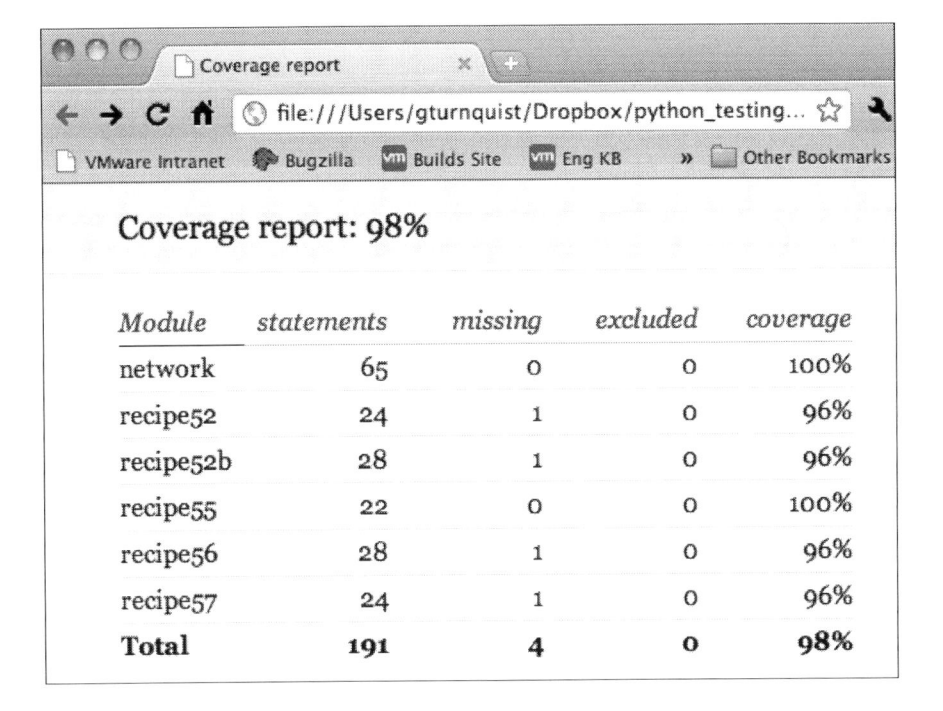

Coverage report: 98%

Module	statements	missing	excluded	coverage
network	65	0	0	100%
recipe52	24	1	0	96%
recipe52b	28	1	0	96%
recipe55	22	0	0	100%
recipe56	28	1	0	96%
recipe57	24	1	0	96%
Total	**191**	**4**	**0**	**98%**

8. Inspect `recipe58.xml`.

How it works...

The coverage API is easy to use as shown in the following steps:

1. In the test method, we create a `coverage()` instance.

   ```
   from coverage import coverage
   
   cov = coverage()
   ```

2. We need to call the `start` method to begin tracing.

   ```
   cov.start()
   ```

3. Next, we need to exercise the main code. In this case, we are using the nose API. We will use it to run the various recipes coded in this chapter.

   ```
   suite = ["recipe52", "recipe52b", "recipe55", "recipe56", "recipe57"]
   print("Running suite %s" % suite)
   args = [""]
   args.extend(suite)
   nose.run(argv=args)
   ```

273

Measuring your Success with Test Coverage

4. Then we need to stop coverage from tracing.
   ```
   cov.stop()
   ```

5. Now that we have gathered metrics, we can generate a console report, an HTML report, and an XML report.
   ```
   modules_to_report = [module + ".py" for module in suite]
   modules_to_report.append("network.py")
   
   cov.report(morfs=modules_to_report)
   cov.html_report(morfs=modules_to_report, \
                   directory="recipe58")
   cov.xml_report(morfs=modules_to_report, \
                  outfile="recipe58.xml")
   ```

The first report is a console report. The second report is an HTML report written into the subdirectory `recipe58`. The third report is an XML report in Cobertura format written to `recipe58.xml`.

There's more...

There are many more options to fine tune the gathering as well as reporting. Just visit the online documentation at `http://nedbatchelder.com/code/coverage/api.html` for more details.

Can we only use getopt?

Python 2.7 introduces `argparse` as an alternative. Current documentation gives no indication that `getopt` is deprecated, so it's safe to use as we have just done. The `getopt` module is a nice, easy-to-use command-line parser.

What's wrong with using the various command-line tools?

There is nothing wrong with using tools like `nosetests`, the coverage tool, `setup.py`, and the many other tools that come with the Python libraries. The purpose of this recipe is to offer a convenient, alternative approach that brings all these tools into one central script. By investing a little bit of time in this script, we don't have to remember how to use all these features, but instead can develop our script to support the development workflow of our project.

8
Smoke/Load Testing—Testing Major Parts

In this chapter, we will cover:

- Defining a subset of test cases using import statements
- Leaving out integration tests
- Targeting end-to-end scenarios
- Targeting the test server
- Coding a data simulator
- Recording and playing back live data in real time
- Recording and playing back live data as fast as possible
- Automating your management demo

Introduction

Smoke testing is something less commonly embraced by teams that write automated tests. Writing tests to verify things are working, or to expose bugs, is a commonly adopted practice, and many teams pick up the idea of acceptance testing to verify whether their applications are meeting customer demands.

But smoke testing is a little different. One of the key ideas with smoke testing is to see if the system has a pulse. What does this mean? It's similar to when a doctor first sees a patient. The first thing they do is check the patient's pulse along with other vital signs. No pulse; critical issue! So what exactly, in software, constitutes a pulse? That is what we'll explore in the recipes in this chapter.

Smoke/Load Testing—Testing Major Parts

Instead of thinking about comprehensive test suites that make sure every corner of the system has been checked, smoke testing takes a much broader perspective. A set of smoke tests is meant to make sure the system is up and alive. It's almost like a ping check. Compare it with sanity tests. Sanity tests are used to prove a small set of situations actually work. Smoke testing, which is similar in the sense that it is quick and shallow, is meant to see if the system is in an adequate state to proceed with more extensive testing.

If you imagine an application built to ingest invoices, a set of smoke tests could include:

- Verify the test file has been consumed
- Verify the number of lines parsed
- Verify the grand total of the bill

Does this sound like a small set of tests? Is it incomplete? Yes it is. And that's the idea. Instead of verifying our software parsed everything correctly, we are verifying just a few key areas that MUST be working. If it fails to read one file, then there is a major issue that needs to be addressed. If the grand total of the bill is incorrect, again, something big must be taken care of.

> A key side effect of smoke testing is that these tests should be quick to run. What if we altered the function that handles files? If our test suite involves parsing lots of different file types, it could take a long time to verify we didn't break anything. Instead of spending 30 minutes to run a comprehensive test suite, wouldn't it be better to run a one minute quick test and then spend the other 29 minutes working on the software?

Smoke tests are also good to use when preparing for a customer demo. With the tension turned up, it's good to run tests more often to make sure we haven't broken anything. Before launching a demo, one last pulse check to know the system is alive may be needed.

This chapter also dives into load testing. Load testing is crucial to verify whether our applications can handle the strain of real-world situations. This often involves collecting real-world data and playing it back through our software for a reproducible environment. While we need to know our system can handle today's load, how likely is it that tomorrow's load will be the same? Not much.

It is very useful to seek out the next bottleneck in our application. That way, we can work towards eliminating it before we hit that load in production. One way to stress the system is to play back real-world data as fast as possible.

Chapter 8

In this chapter, we will look at some recipes involving both smoke testing and load testing the network management application we developed in the previous chapter with the recipe from *Chapter 7, Building a network management application*. The types of loads we will be placing on the application could also be described as soak testing and stress testing. Soak testing is described as putting a significant load on the system over a significant period of time. Stress testing is described as loading down a system until it breaks.

> In my opinion, soak testing and stress testing are different sides of the same coin of load testing. That is why this chapter simply uses the term load testing when the various recipes can easily extend to these types of testing.

The code in this chapter also uses several utilities provided by Spring Python (`http://springpython.webfactional.com`). You can read more details about its use and functionality, as well as how to install it, in *Chapter 7*.

Many of the recipes in this chapter interact with a MySQL database. Install the Python MySQLdb library by typing: `pip install mysql-python`.

Several of the recipes in this chapter use Python Remote Objects or Pyro (`http://www.xs4all.nl/~irmen/pyro3/`). It is a **Remote Procedure Call** (**RPC**) library that supports communicating between threads and processes. Install Pyro by typing: `pip install pyro`.

Defining a subset of test cases using import statements

Create a Python module that selectively imports what test cases to run.

How to do it...

With these steps, we will explore selectively picking a smaller set of tests to facilitate a faster test run.

1. Create a test module called `recipe59_test.py` for writing some tests against our network application.

   ```
   import logging
   from network import *
   import unittest
   from springpython.database.factory import *
   from springpython.database.core import *
   ```

Smoke/Load Testing—Testing Major Parts

2. Create a test case that removes the database connection and stubs out the data access functions.

```python
class EventCorrelatorUnitTests(unittest.TestCase):
    def setUp(self):
        db_name = "recipe59.db"
        factory = Sqlite3ConnectionFactory(db=db_name)
        self.correlator = EventCorrelator(factory)

        # We "unplug" the DatabaseTemplate so that
        # we don't talk to a real database.
        self.correlator.dt = None

        # Instead, we create a dictionary of
        # canned data to return back
        self.return_values = {}

        # For each sub-function of the network app,
        # we replace them with stubs which return our
        # canned data.
        def stub_store_event(event):
            event.id = self.return_values["id"]
            return event, self.return_values["active"]
        self.correlator.store_event = stub_store_event

        def stub_impact(event):
            return (self.return_values["services"],
                    self.return_values["equipment"])
        self.correlator.impact = stub_impact

        def stub_update_service(service, event):
            return service + " updated"
        self.correlator.update_service = stub_update_service

        def stub_update_equip(equip, event):
            return equip + " updated"
        self.correlator.update_equipment = stub_update_equip
```

3. Create a test method that creates a set of canned data values, invokes the application's process method, and then verifies the values.

```python
    def test_process_events(self):
        # For this test case, we can preload the canned data,
        # and verify that our process function is working
        # as expected without touching the database.
        self.return_values["id"] = 4668
        self.return_values["active"] = True
        self.return_values["services"] = ["service1",
                                          "service2"]
```

```
            self.return_values["equipment"] = ["device1"]
            evt1 = Event("pyhost1", "serverRestart", 5)
            stored_event, is_active, \
               updated_services, updated_equipment = \
                        self.correlator.process(evt1)
            self.assertEquals(4668, stored_event.id)
            self.assertTrue(is_active)
            self.assertEquals(2, len(updated_services))
            self.assertEquals(1, len(updated_equipment))
```

4. Create another test case that preloads the database using a SQL script (see *Chapter 7, Building a network management application* for details about the SQL script).

```
   class EventCorrelatorIntegrationTests(unittest.TestCase):
      def setUp(self):
         db_name = "recipe59.db"
         factory = Sqlite3ConnectionFactory(db=db_name)
         self.correlator = EventCorrelator(factory)
         dt = DatabaseTemplate(factory)
         sql = open("network.sql").read().split(";")
         for statement in sql:
            dt.execute(statement + ";")
```

5. Write a test method that calls the network application's process method, and then prints out the results.

```
      def test_process_events(self):
         evt1 = Event("pyhost1", "serverRestart", 5)
         stored_event, is_active, \
            updated_services, updated_equipment = \
                     self.correlator.process(evt1)
         print "Stored event: %s" % stored_event
         if is_active:
            print "This event was an active event."
         print "Updated services: %s" % updated_services
         print "Updated equipment: %s" % updated_equipment
         print "---------------------------------"
```

6. Create a new file called `recipe59.py` that only imports the SQL-based test case.

```
   from recipe59_test import EventCorrelatorIntegrationTests
   if __name__ == "__main__":
      import unittest
      unittest.main()
```

Smoke/Load Testing—Testing Major Parts

7. Run the test module.

```
(ptc)gturnquist-mbp:08 gturnquist$ python recipe59.py
Stored event: (ID:1) pyhost1:serverRestart - 5
This event was an active event.
Updated services: [{'is_active': True, 'service': {'STATUS': 'Outage',
'ID': 1, 'NAME': u'service-abc'}}, {'is_active': True, 'service': {'STA
TUS': u'Outage', 'ID': 2, 'NAME': u'service-xyz'}}]
Updated equipment: [{'STATUS': 5, 'ID': 1, 'HOST_NAME': u'pyhost1'}]
----------------------------------------------------------------------
Ran 1 test in 0.474s

OK
```

How it works...

We need to write various test cases to cover the different levels of testing we need. By separating the test runner from the test case, we were able to decide to only run the test that integrated with the database.

Why would we do this? In our situation, we only have one unit test and it runs pretty quickly. Do you think that a real-world application with months or years of development and a corresponding test suite will run as quickly? Of course not!

Some of the tests may be complex. They may involve talking to real systems, parsing huge sample data files, and other time consuming tasks. This could realistically take minutes or hours to run.

When we are about to make a presentation to a customer, we don't need a long running test suite. Instead, we need to be able to run a quick subset of these tests that gives us the confidence that things are working. Using Python's import statements makes this easy to define.

Some suites we may want to think about include:

- `pulse.py`: Import a set of test cases that provide broad, yet shallow testing of the application, to verify the system "has a pulse"
- `checkin.py`: Import a set of test cases that are currently functioning and provide enough confidence that code is ready to be committed
- `integration.py`: Import a set of test cases that startup, interact, and then shutdown external systems like LDAP, databases, or other subsystems
- `security.py`: Import a set of test cases that are focused on various security scenarios, confirming both good and bad credential handling
- `all.py`: Import all test cases to make sure everything is working

This is just a sample of the types of test modules we could define. It's possible to define a module for each subsystem we handle. But since we are talking about smoke testing, we may want to think more broadly, and instead pick some key tests from each subsystem and tie them together to give us a sense that the application is working.

Security, checking, and integration aren't smoke tests!

That is absolutely right. The previous list shows that using Python import statements isn't confined to defining smoke test suites. It can be used to bundle together test cases that serve differing needs. So why bring this up since we are talking about smoke tests? I wanted to convey how useful this mechanism is to organizing tests and that it extends beyond smoke testing.

What provides good flexibility?

In order to have good flexibility in being able to pick test classes, we should avoid making the test classes too big. But putting each test method inside a different class is probably too much.

See also

- Chapter 7, Building a network management application
- Leaving out integration tests

Leaving out integration tests

A fast test suite avoids connecting to remote systems, like databases, LDAP, etc. Just verifying the core units and avoiding external systems can result in a faster running test suite with more coverage. This can lead to a useful smoke test that provides developers with confidence in the system without running all the tests.

How to do it...

With these steps, we will see how to cut out test cases that interact with external systems.

1. Create a test module called `recipe60_test.py` for writing some tests against our network application.

   ```
   import logging
   from network import *
   import unittest
   from springpython.database.factory import *
   from springpython.database.core import *
   ```

Smoke/Load Testing—Testing Major Parts

2. Create a test case that removes the database connection and stubs out the data access functions.

   ```python
   class EventCorrelatorUnitTests(unittest.TestCase):
       def setUp(self):
           db_name = "recipe60.db"
           factory = Sqlite3ConnectionFactory(db=db_name)
           self.correlator = EventCorrelator(factory)

           # We "unplug" the DatabaseTemplate so that
           # we don't talk to a real database.
           self.correlator.dt = None

           # Instead, we create a dictionary of
           # canned data to return back
           self.return_values = {}

           # For each sub-function of the network app,
           # we replace them with stubs which return our
           # canned data.
           def stub_store_event(event):
               event.id = self.return_values["id"]
               return event, self.return_values["active"]
           self.correlator.store_event = stub_store_event

           def stub_impact(event):
               return (self.return_values["services"],
                       self.return_values["equipment"])
           self.correlator.impact = stub_impact

           def stub_update_service(service, event):
               return service + " updated"
           self.correlator.update_service = stub_update_service

           def stub_update_equip(equip, event):
               return equip + " updated"
           self.correlator.update_equipment = stub_update_equip
   ```

3. Create a test method that creates a set of canned data values, invokes the applications process method, and then verifies the values.

   ```python
   def test_process_events(self):
       # For this test case, we can preload the canned data,
       # and verify that our process function is working
       # as expected without touching the database.
       self.return_values["id"] = 4668
       self.return_values["active"] = True
       self.return_values["services"] = ["service1",
                                         "service2"]
   ```

```
        self.return_values["equipment"] = ["device1"]
        evt1 = Event("pyhost1", "serverRestart", 5)
        stored_event, is_active, \
            updated_services, updated_equipment = \
                    self.correlator.process(evt1)
        self.assertEquals(4668, stored_event.id)
        self.assertTrue(is_active)
        self.assertEquals(2, len(updated_services))
        self.assertEquals(1, len(updated_equipment))
```

4. Create another test case that preloads the database using a SQL script (see *Chapter 7, Building a network management application* for details about the SQL script).

```
class EventCorrelatorIntegrationTests(unittest.TestCase):
    def setUp(self):
        db_name = "recipe60.db"
        factory = Sqlite3ConnectionFactory(db=db_name)
        self.correlator = EventCorrelator(factory)
        dt = DatabaseTemplate(factory)
        sql = open("network.sql").read().split(";")
        for statement in sql:
            dt.execute(statement + ";")
```

5. Write a test method that calls the network application's process method, and then prints out the results.

```
    def test_process_events(self):
        evt1 = Event("pyhost1", "serverRestart", 5)
        stored_event, is_active, \
            updated_services, updated_equipment = \
                    self.correlator.process(evt1)
        print "Stored event: %s" % stored_event
        if is_active:
            print "This event was an active event."
        print "Updated services: %s" % updated_services
        print "Updated equipment: %s" % updated_equipment
        print "-------------------------------"
```

6. Create a module called `recipe60.py` that only imports the unit test that avoids making SQL calls.

```
from recipe60_test import EventCorrelatorUnitTests
if __name__ == "__main__":
```

```
            import unittest
            unittest.main()
```

7. Run the test module.

```
(ptc)gturnquist-mbp:08 gturnquist$ python recipe60.py
.
----------------------------------------------------------------------
Ran 1 test in 0.000s

OK
```

How it works...

This test suite exercises the unit tests and avoids running the test case that integrates with a live database. It uses Python import statements to decide what test cases to include.

In our contrived scenario, there is little gained performance. But with a real project, there are probably a lot more computer cycles spent on integration testing due to the extra costs of talking to external systems.

The idea is to create a subset of tests that verify to some degree that our application works by covering a big chunk of it in a smaller amount of time.

The trick with smoke testing is deciding what is a good enough test. Automated testing cannot completely confirm that our application has no bugs. We are foiled by the fact that either a particular bug doesn't exist, or we haven't written a test case that exposes such a bug. To engage in smoke testing, we are deciding to use a subset of these tests for a quick pulse read. Again, deciding what subset gives us a good enough pulse may be more art than science.

This recipe focuses on the idea that unit tests will probably run quicker, and that cutting out the integration tests will remove the slower test cases. If all the unit tests pass, then there is some confidence that our application is in good shape.

There's more...

I must point out that test cases don't just easily fall into the category of **unit test** or **integration test**. It is more of a continuum. In this recipe's sample code, we wrote one unit test and one integration test, and picked the unit test for our smoke test suite.

Does this appear arbitrary and perhaps contrived? Sure it does. That is why smoke testing isn't cut and dry, but instead requires some analysis and judgment about what to pick. And as development proceeds, there is room for fine tuning.

> I once developed a system that ingested invoices from different suppliers. I wrote unit tests that setup empty database tables, ingested files of many formats, and then examined the contents of the database to verify processing. The test suite took over 45 minutes to run. This pressured me to not run the test suite as often as desired. I crafted a smoke test suite that involved only running the unit tests that did NOT talk to the database (since they were quick) combined with ingesting one supplier invoice. It ran in less than five minutes, and provided a quicker means to assure myself that fundamental changes to the code did not break the entire system. I could run this many times during the day, and only run the comprehensive suite about once a day.

Should a smoke test include integration or unit tests?

Does this code appear very similar to that shown in the recipe *Defining a subset of test cases using import statements*? Yes it does. So why include it in this recipe? Because what is picked for the smoke test suite is just as critical as the tactics used to make it happen. The other recipe decided to pick up an integration test while cutting out the unit tests to create a smaller, faster running test suite.

This recipe shows that another possibility is to cut out the lengthier integration tests and instead run as many unit tests as possible, considering they are probably faster.

As stated earlier, smoke testing isn't cut and dry. It involves picking the best representation of tests without taking up too much time in running them. It is quite possible that all the tests written up to this point don't precisely target the idea of capturing the pulse of the system. A good smoke test suite may involve mixing together a subset of unit and integration tests.

See also

- Chapter 7, Building a network management application
- Defining a subset of test cases using import statements

Targeting end-to-end scenarios

Pick a complement of tests that exercises enough parts to define a thread of execution. This is sometimes referred to as thread testing. Not because we are using software threading, but instead, because we are focusing on a story thread. Often, our threads either come from customer scenarios or are at least inspired by them. Other threads can involve other groups of operations.

For example, a network management system may push out customer-affecting alarms, but the internal operations team that has to solve the network problems may have a totally different perspective. Both of these situations demonstrate valid end-to-end threads that are good places to invest in automated testing.

Smoke/Load Testing—Testing Major Parts

> If the different teams are viewed as different types of customers, then the concepts of acceptance testing certainly apply. And it's also possible to overlap this with the concepts of BDD.

Getting ready

1. Copy the SQL script from *Chapter 7, Creating a network management application* into a new file called `recipe61_network.sql` and replace the insert statements at the bottom with the following:

   ```
   INSERT into EQUIPMENT (ID, HOST_NAME, STATUS) values (1,
   'pyhost1', 1);
   INSERT into EQUIPMENT (ID, HOST_NAME, STATUS) values (2,
   'pyhost2', 1);
   INSERT into EQUIPMENT (ID, HOST_NAME, STATUS) values (3,
   'pyhost3', 1);
   INSERT into SERVICE (ID, NAME, STATUS) values (1, 'service-abc',
   'Operational');
   INSERT into SERVICE_MAPPING (SERVICE_FK, EQUIPMENT_FK) values
   (1,1);
   INSERT into SERVICE_MAPPING (SERVICE_FK, EQUIPMENT_FK) values
   (1,2);
   ```

   In this set of test data, `pyhost1` and `pyhost2` map into `service-abc`. However, `pyhost3` doesn't map into any service.

How to do it...

With these steps, we will build up an end-to-end test scenario.

1. Create a test module called `recipe61_test.py`.
2. Create a test case where each test method captures a different thread of execution.

   ```python
   import logging
   from network import *
   import unittest
   from springpython.database.factory import *
   from springpython.database.core import *

   class EventCorrelatorEquipmentThreadTests(unittest.TestCase):
       def setUp(self):
           db_name = "recipe61.db"
           factory = Sqlite3ConnectionFactory(db=db_name)
           self.correlator = EventCorrelator(factory)
   ```

```
            dt = DatabaseTemplate(factory)
            sql = open("recipe61_network.sql").read().split(";")
            for statement in sql:
                dt.execute(statement + ";")
        def tearDown(self):
            self.correlator = None
```

3. Create a test method that captures the thread of failing and recovering a piece of equipment.

    ```
        def test_equipment_failing(self):
            # This alarm maps to a device
            # but doesn't map to any service.
    ```

4. Have the test method inject a single, faulting alarm and then confirm that a related piece of equipment has failed.

    ```
            evt1 = Event("pyhost3", "serverRestart", 5)
            stored_event, is_active, \
                updated_services, updated_equipment = \
                    self.correlator.process(evt1)
            self.assertTrue(is_active)
            self.assertEquals(len(updated_services), 0)
            self.assertEquals(len(updated_equipment), 1)
            self.assertEquals(updated_equipment[0]["HOST_NAME"],
                                                    "pyhost3")
            # 5 is the value for a failed piece of equipment
            self.assertEquals(updated_equipment[0]["STATUS"], 5)
    ```

5. In the same test method, add code that injects a single, clearing alarm and confirms that the equipment has recovered.

    ```
            evt2 = Event("pyhost3", "serverRestart", 1)
            stored_event, is_active, \
                updated_services, updated_equipment = \
                    self.correlator.process(evt2)
            self.assertFalse(is_active)
            self.assertEquals(len(updated_services), 0)
            self.assertEquals(len(updated_equipment), 1)
            self.assertEquals(updated_equipment[0]["HOST_NAME"],
                                                    "pyhost3")
            # 1 is the value for a clear piece of equipment
            self.assertEquals(updated_equipment[0]["STATUS"], 1)
    ```

6. Create another test method that captures the thread of failing and clearing a service.

   ```
   def test_service_failing(self):
       # This alarm maps to a service.
   ```

7. Write a test method that injects a single, faulting alarm and confirms that both a piece of equipment and a related service fails.

   ```
   evt1 = Event("pyhost1", "serverRestart", 5)
   stored_event, is_active, \
       updated_services, updated_equipment = \
           self.correlator.process(evt1)
   self.assertEquals(len(updated_services), 1)
   self.assertEquals("service-abc",
           updated_services[0]["service"]["NAME"])
   self.assertEquals("Outage",
           updated_services[0]["service"]["STATUS"])
   ```

8. In the same test method, add code that injects a single, clearing alarm and confirms that both the equipment and the service have recovered.

   ```
   evt2 = Event("pyhost1", "serverRestart", 1)
   stored_event, is_active, \
       updated_services, updated_equipment = \
           self.correlator.process(evt2)
   self.assertEquals(len(updated_services), 1)
   self.assertEquals("service-abc",
           updated_services[0]["service"]["NAME"])
   self.assertEquals("Operational",
           updated_services[0]["service"]["STATUS"])
   ```

9. Create a test runner called `recipe61.py` that imports both of these thread tests.

   ```
   from recipe61_test import *

   if __name__ == "__main__":
       import unittest
       unittest.main()
   ```

10. Run the test suite.

How it works...

In this recipe we coded two end-to-end test scenarios:

- The first scenario tested how our application processes a fault followed by a clear that only impacts a piece of equipment
- The second scenario tested how our application processes a fault followed by a clear that impacts a service

We injected a fault and then checked the results to confirm the proper piece of inventory failed. Then we injected a clear and again confirmed that the proper piece of inventory recovered.

Both of these scenarios show how our application processes different types of events from the beginning to the end.

There's more...

In a more complex, realistic version of this application, what other systems do you think would be involved in an end-to-end thread? What about security? Transactions? Publishing results to an external interface?

This is where we need to define where the ends are. Imagine that our application was grown to the point where incoming events are received by a web request and equipment and service updates are pushed out as JSON data to be received by a web page.

A good end-to-end test would include these parts as well. For the JSON output, we can use Python's JSON library to decode the output and then confirm the results. For the incoming web request, we can use many different techniques including acceptance testing tools like the Robot Framework.

How does this define smoke tests?

If the time to run all the end-to-end tests is too long, we should pick a subset of them that cover some key parts. For example, we could skip the equipment-based thread but keep the service-based one.

See also

- Chapter 5, Testing web basics with the Robot Framework
- Chapter 5, Using Robot to verify web application security

Smoke/Load Testing—Testing Major Parts

Targeting the test server

Does your test server have all the parts? If not, then define an alternative set of tests.

This recipe assumes that the production server is installed with an enterprise grade MySQL database system while the developer's workstation is not. We will explore writing some tests that use the MySQL database. But when we need to run them in the development lab, we will make adjustments so they run on SQLite, which comes bundled with Python.

> Are you wondering why MySQL isn't on the developer's workstation? It is true that MySQL is easy to install and not a huge performance load. But this scenario applies just the same if the production server was Oracle and management deemed it too costly for our developers to be granted an individual license. Due to the cost of setting up a commercial database, this recipe is demonstrated using MySQL and SQLite rather than Oracle and SQLite.

Getting ready

1. Make sure the MySQL production database server is up and running.

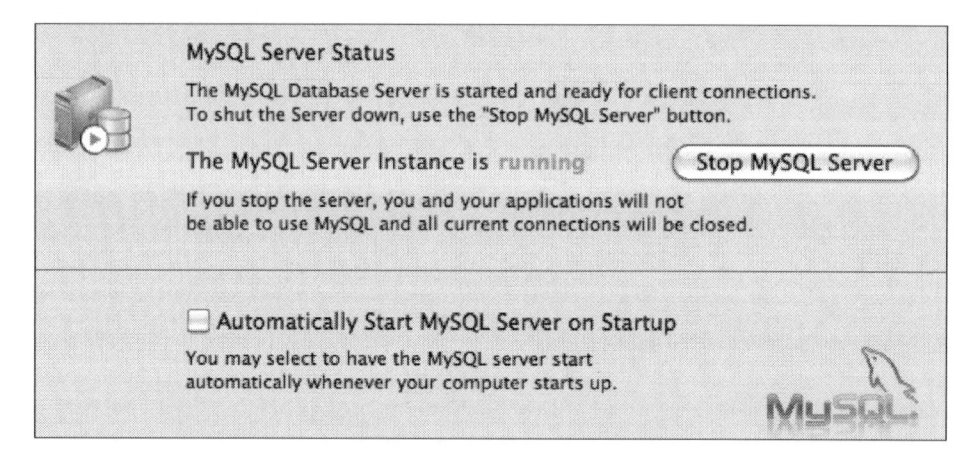

   MySQL Server Status
   The MySQL Database Server is started and ready for client connections.
   To shut the Server down, use the "Stop MySQL Server" button.

   The MySQL Server Instance is running   [Stop MySQL Server]

   If you stop the server, you and your applications will not be able to use MySQL and all current connections will be closed.

   ☐ Automatically Start MySQL Server on Startup
   You may select to have the MySQL server start automatically whenever your computer starts up.

2. Open a command line MySQL client shell as the root user.
3. Create a database for this recipe called `recipe62` as well as a user with permission to access it.
4. Exit the shell. Contrary to what is shown in the following screenshot, never, ever, EVER create a live production database with passwords stored in the clear. This database is for demonstration purposes only.

```
(ptc)gturnquist-mbp:08 gturnquist$ mysql -u root -p
Enter password:
Welcome to the MySQL monitor.  Commands end with ; or \g.
Your MySQL connection id is 17
Server version: 5.1.44 MySQL Community Server (GPL)

Type 'help;' or '\h' for help. Type '\c' to clear the current input statement.

mysql> create database recipe62;
Query OK, 1 row affected (0.00 sec)

mysql> grant all on recipe62.* to 'user'@'localhost' identified by 'password';
Query OK, 0 rows affected (0.00 sec)

mysql> quit;
Bye
```

How to do it...

In these steps, we will see how to build tests that are aimed at different servers.

1. Create an alternate version of the SQL script called `recipe62_network.mysql` used in earlier recipes that use MySQL conventions.

    ```
    DROP TABLE IF EXISTS SERVICE_MAPPING;
    DROP TABLE IF EXISTS SERVICE_EVENTS;
    DROP TABLE IF EXISTS ACTIVE_EVENTS;
    DROP TABLE IF EXISTS EQUIPMENT;
    DROP TABLE IF EXISTS SERVICE;
    DROP TABLE IF EXISTS EVENTS;

    CREATE TABLE EQUIPMENT (
         ID          SMALLINT PRIMARY KEY AUTO_INCREMENT,
         HOST_NAME TEXT,
         STATUS    SMALLINT
         );
    CREATE TABLE SERVICE (
         ID SMALLINT PRIMARY KEY AUTO_INCREMENT,
         NAME TEXT,
         STATUS TEXT
         );
    CREATE TABLE SERVICE_MAPPING (
         ID SMALLINT PRIMARY KEY AUTO_INCREMENT,
         SERVICE_FK SMALLINT,
         EQUIPMENT_FK SMALLINT
         );
    CREATE TABLE EVENTS (
    ```

```
            ID SMALLINT PRIMARY KEY AUTO_INCREMENT,
            HOST_NAME TEXT,
            SEVERITY SMALLINT,
            EVENT_CONDITION TEXT
            );
    CREATE TABLE SERVICE_EVENTS (
            ID SMALLINT PRIMARY KEY AUTO_INCREMENT,
            SERVICE_FK SMALLINT,
            EVENT_FK SMALLINT
            );
    CREATE TABLE ACTIVE_EVENTS (
            ID SMALLINT PRIMARY KEY AUTO_INCREMENT,
            EVENT_FK SMALLINT
            );
    INSERT into EQUIPMENT (ID, HOST_NAME, STATUS) values (1,
    'pyhost1', 1);
    INSERT into EQUIPMENT (ID, HOST_NAME, STATUS) values (2,
    'pyhost2', 1);
    INSERT into EQUIPMENT (ID, HOST_NAME, STATUS) values (3,
    'pyhost3', 1);
    INSERT into SERVICE (ID, NAME, STATUS) values (1, 'service-abc',
    'Operational');
    INSERT into SERVICE_MAPPING (SERVICE_FK, EQUIPMENT_FK) values
    (1,1);
    INSERT into SERVICE_MAPPING (SERVICE_FK, EQUIPMENT_FK) values
    (1,2)
```

> You might not have noticed, but this schema definition has no foreign key constraints. In a real world SQL script, those should definitely be included. They were left out in this case to reduce complexity.

2. Create a new module called `recipe62_test.py` to store our test code.
3. Create an abstract test case that has one test method verifying event-to-service correlation.

```
import logging
from network import *
import unittest
from springpython.database.factory import *
from springpython.database.core import *

class AbstractEventCorrelatorTests(unittest.TestCase):
    def tearDown(self):
```

```
            self.correlator = None

    def test_service_failing(self):
        # This alarm maps to a service.
        evt1 = Event("pyhost1", "serverRestart", 5)
        stored_event, is_active, \
           updated_services, updated_equipment = \
                    self.correlator.process(evt1)
        self.assertEquals(len(updated_services), 1)
        self.assertEquals("service-abc",
             updated_services[0]["service"]["NAME"])
        self.assertEquals("Outage",
             updated_services[0]["service"]["STATUS"])
        evt2 = Event("pyhost1", "serverRestart", 1)
        stored_event, is_active, \
           updated_services, updated_equipment = \
                self.correlator.process(evt2)
        self.assertEquals(len(updated_services), 1)
        self.assertEquals("service-abc",
             updated_services[0]["service"]["NAME"])
        self.assertEquals("Operational",
             updated_services[0]["service"]["STATUS"])
```

4. Create a concrete subclass that connects to the MySQL database and uses the MySQL script.

```
class MySQLEventCorrelatorTests(AbstractEventCorrelatorTests):
    def setUp(self):
        factory = MySQLConnectionFactory("user", "password",
                                        "localhost", "recipe62")
        self.correlator = EventCorrelator(factory)
        dt = DatabaseTemplate(factory)
        sql = open("recipe62_network.mysql").read().split(";")
        for statement in sql:
            dt.execute(statement + ";")
```

5. Create a corresponding production test runner called `recipe62_production.py`.

```
from recipe62_test import MySQLEventCorrelatorTests

if __name__ == "__main__":
    import unittest
    unittest.main()
```

Smoke/Load Testing—Testing Major Parts

Run it and verify if it connects with the production database.

```
(ptc)gturnquist-mbp:08 gturnquist$ python recipe62_production.py
.
----------------------------------------------------------------------
Ran 1 test in 0.782s

OK
```

6. Now create a SQLite version of the SQL script called `recipe62_network.sql`.

```sql
DROP TABLE IF EXISTS SERVICE_MAPPING;
DROP TABLE IF EXISTS SERVICE_EVENTS;
DROP TABLE IF EXISTS ACTIVE_EVENTS;
DROP TABLE IF EXISTS EQUIPMENT;
DROP TABLE IF EXISTS SERVICE;
DROP TABLE IF EXISTS EVENTS;
CREATE TABLE EQUIPMENT (
    ID          INTEGER PRIMARY KEY,
    HOST_NAME   TEXT    UNIQUE,
    STATUS      INTEGER
    );

CREATE TABLE SERVICE (
    ID INTEGER PRIMARY KEY,
    NAME TEXT UNIQUE,
    STATUS TEXT
    );

CREATE TABLE SERVICE_MAPPING (
    ID INTEGER PRIMARY KEY,
    SERVICE_FK,
    EQUIPMENT_FK,
    FOREIGN KEY(SERVICE_FK) REFERENCES SERVICE(ID),
    FOREIGN KEY(EQUIPMENT_FK) REFERENCES EQUIPMENT(ID)
    );

CREATE TABLE EVENTS (
    ID INTEGER PRIMARY KEY,
    HOST_NAME TEXT,
    SEVERITY INTEGER,
    EVENT_CONDITION TEXT
    );

CREATE TABLE SERVICE_EVENTS (
    ID INTEGER PRIMARY KEY,
    SERVICE_FK,
    EVENT_FK,
```

```
            FOREIGN KEY(SERVICE_FK) REFERENCES SERVICE(ID),
            FOREIGN KEY(EVENT_FK) REFERENCES EVENTS(ID)
            );
    CREATE TABLE ACTIVE_EVENTS (
            ID INTEGER PRIMARY KEY,
            EVENT_FK,
            FOREIGN KEY(EVENT_FK) REFERENCES EVENTS(ID)
            );
    INSERT into EQUIPMENT (ID, HOST_NAME, STATUS) values (1,
    'pyhost1', 1);
    INSERT into EQUIPMENT (ID, HOST_NAME, STATUS) values (2,
    'pyhost2', 1);
    INSERT into EQUIPMENT (ID, HOST_NAME, STATUS) values (3,
    'pyhost3', 1);
    INSERT into SERVICE (ID, NAME, STATUS) values (1, 'service-abc',
    'Operational');
    INSERT into SERVICE_MAPPING (SERVICE_FK, EQUIPMENT_FK) values
    (1,1);
    INSERT into SERVICE_MAPPING (SERVICE_FK, EQUIPMENT_FK) values
    (1,2);
```

7. Create another concrete subclass of the abstract test case, only have it connect as SQLite using the SQLite script and add it to `recipe62_test.py`.

    ```
    class Sqlite3EventCorrelatorTests(AbstractEventCorrelatorTests):
        def setUp(self):
            factory = Sqlite3ConnectionFactory("recipe62.db")
            self.correlator = EventCorrelator(factory)

            dt = DatabaseTemplate(factory)
            sql = open("recipe62_network.sql").read().split(";")
            for statement in sql:
                dt.execute(statement + ";")
    ```

8. Create a corresponding development workstation test runner called `recipe62_dev.py`.

    ```
    from recipe62_test import Sqlite3EventCorrelatorTests

    if __name__ == "__main__":
        import unittest
        unittest.main()
    ```

Smoke/Load Testing—Testing Major Parts

9. Run it and verify if it connects with the development database.

```
(ptc)gturnquist-mbp:08 gturnquist$ python recipe62_dev.py
.
----------------------------------------------------------------------
Ran 1 test in 0.156s

OK
```

How it works...

It is not uncommon to have a production environment with full-fledged servers and software installed while at the same time having a smaller development environment. Some shops even have a test bed that is somewhere in between these configurations.

Our network application handles this situation by allowing database connection information to get injected into it. In each test case, we used the exact same application, but with different database systems.

We wrote a test case that used the production MySQL database, and we wrote a test case that used the development SQLite database. Of course MySQL, even though used in many production environments, doesn't sound like something which is unavailable to developers. But it provides an easy-to-see example of having to switch database systems.

There's more...

In this recipe, we showed the need to switch database systems. This isn't the only type of external system that may require alternate configurations for test purposes. Other things like LDAP servers, third-party web services, and separate subsystems may have totally different configurations.

> I have worked on several contracts and often seen management cut development lab resources to save costs. They seem to conclude that the cost of maintaining multiple configurations and handling non-reproducible bugs is less than the cost of having the exact same complement of equipment and software. I feel this conclusion is faulty, because at some time in the future, they end up buying more hardware and upgrade things due to increasing issues involving platform variance.

This means we can't always write tests that target the production environment. Writing our software so that it has maximum flexibility, like injecting database configuration as we did earlier, is a minimum.

It's important that we write as many tests as possible that work on the developer's platform. When developers have to start sharing server-side resources, then we run into resource collisions. For example, two developers sharing a single database server will have to do one of these:

- Have separate schemas so they can empty and load test data
- Coordinate times when they each have access to the same schema
- Have different servers set up for each developer

The third option is highly unlikely given that we are talking about a development lab with a smaller footprint than the production one.

A positive note is that developers are getting faster and more powerful machines. Compared to 10 years ago, a commonly seen workstation far exceeds old server machines. But even though we may each be able to run the entire software stack on our machine, it doesn't mean management will pay for all the necessary licensing.

Unfortunately, this limitation may never change. Hence, we have to be ready to write tests for alternate configurations and manage the discrepancies with the production environment.

How likely is it that a dev versus production environment would use two different database systems?

Admittedly, it is unlikely to have something as big as switching between SQLite and MySQL. That alone required slightly different dialects of SQL in order to define the schema. Some would immediately consider this too difficult to manage. But there are smaller differences in environments that can still yield the same need for reduced testing.

> I worked on a system for many years where the production system used Oracle 9i RAC while the development lab just had Oracle 9i. RAC required extra hardware and we were never allocated the resources for it. To top it off, Oracle 9i was too big to install on the relatively lightweight PCs we developed with. While everything spoke Oracle's dialect of SQL, the uptime differences between RAC and non-RAC generated a fair number of bugs that we couldn't reproduce in the dev lab. It really did qualify as two different database systems. Given that we couldn't work in the production environment, we tested as much as we could in the dev lab and then scheduled time in the test lab where an RAC instance existed. Since many people needed access to that lab, we confined our usage to RAC-specific issues to avoid schedule delays.

This isn't just confined to database systems

As stated earlier, this isn't just about database systems. We have discussed MySQL, SQLite, and Oracle, but this also involves any sort of system we work with or depend on that varies between production and development environments.

Smoke/Load Testing—Testing Major Parts

Being able to code subsets of tests to achieve confidence can help cut down on the actual issues we will inevitably have to deal with.

Coding a data simulator

Coding a simulator that spits out data at a defined rate can help simulate real load.

This recipe assumes that the reader's machine is installed with MySQL.

Getting ready

1. Make sure the MySQL production database server is up and running.
2. Open a command line MySQL client shell as the root user.
3. Create a database for this recipe called `recipe63` as well as a user with permission to access it.
4. Exit the shell.

```
(ptc)gturnquist-mbp:08 gturnquist$ mysql -u root -p
Enter password:
Welcome to the MySQL monitor.  Commands end with ; or \g.
Your MySQL connection id is 3
Server version: 5.1.44 MySQL Community Server (GPL)

Type 'help;' or '\h' for help. Type '\c' to clear the current input statement.

mysql> create database recipe63;
Query OK, 1 row affected (0.00 sec)

mysql> grant all on recipe63.* to 'user'@'localhost' identified by 'password';
Query OK, 0 rows affected (0.02 sec)

mysql> quit;
Bye
```

How to do it...

With these steps, we will explore coding a test simulator:

1. Create a test generator script called `recipe63.py` that uses various Python libraries.

   ```
   import getopt
   import random
   import sys
   import time
   from network import *
   from springpython.remoting.pyro import *
   ```

2. Create a usage method that prints out command-line options.

   ```python
   def usage():
       print "Usage"
       print "====="
       print "-h, --help          read this help"
       print "-r, --rate [arg]    number of events per second"
       print "-d, --demo          demo by printing events"
   ```

3. Use Python's `getopt` library to parse command-line arguments.

   ```python
   try:
       opts, args = getopt.getopt(sys.argv[1:], "hr:d", ["help",
   "rate=", "demo"])
   except getopt.GetoptError, err:
       print str(err)
       usage()
       sys.exit(1)

   rate = 10
   demo_mode = False

   for o, a in opts:
       if o in ("-h", "--help"):
           usage()
           sys.exit(1)
       elif o in ("-r", "--rate"):
           rate = a
       elif o in ("-d", "--demo"):
           demo_mode = True
   ```

4. Add a switch so when NOT in demo mode, it uses Spring Python's `PyroProxyFactory` to connect to a server instance of the network management application defined in *Chapter 7, Building a network management application*.

   ```python
   if not demo_mode:
       print "Sending events to live network app. Ctrl+C to exit..."
       proxy = PyroProxyFactory()
       proxy.service_url = "PYROLOC://127.0.0.1:7766/network"
   ```

5. Code an infinite loop that creates a random event.

   ```python
   while True:
       hostname = random.choice(["pyhost1","pyhost2","pyhost3"])
       condition = random.choice(["serverRestart", "lineStatus"])
       severity = random.choice([1,5])

       evt = Event(hostname, condition, severity)
   ```

Smoke/Load Testing—Testing Major Parts

6. If in demo mode, print out the event.

   ```
   if demo_mode:
       now = time.strftime("%a, %d %b %Y %H:%M:%S +0000",
                                               time.localtime())
       print "%s: Sending out %s" % (now, evt)
   ```

7. If not in demo mode, make a remote call through the proxy to the network app's process method.

   ```
   else:
       stored_event, is_active, updated_services, \
             updated_equipment = proxy.process(evt)
       print "Stored event: %s" % stored_event
       print "Active? %s" % is_active
       print "Services updated: %s" % updated_services
       print "Equipment updated; %s" % updated_equipment
       print "================"
   ```

8. Sleep a certain amount of time before repeating the loop.

   ```
   time.sleep(1.0/float(rate))
   ```

9. Run the generator script. In the following screenshot, notice there is an error because we haven't started the server process yet. This can also happen if the client and server have mismatched URLs.

   ```
   (ptc)gturnquist-mbp:08 gturnquist$ python recipe63.py
   Sending events to live network app. Ctrl+C to exit.
   Traceback (most recent call last):
     File "recipe63.py", line 76, in <module>
       proxy.process(evt)
     File "/Users/gturnquist/ptc/lib/python2.6/site-packages/Pyro/c
       return self.__send(self.__name, args, kwargs)
     File "/Users/gturnquist/ptc/lib/python2.6/site-packages/Pyro/c
       self.adapter.bindToURI(self.URI)
     File "/Users/gturnquist/ptc/lib/python2.6/site-packages/Pyro/p
       raise ProtocolError('connection failed')
   Pyro.errors.ProtocolError: connection failed
   ```

10. Create a server script called `recipe63_server.py` that will run our network management app connected to MySQL using SQL script `recipe62_network.sql` from **Targeting the test server**.

    ```
    from springpython.database.factory import *
    from springpython.database.core import *
    from springpython.remoting.pyro import *

    from network import *

    import logging
    ```

```python
logger = logging.getLogger("springpython")
loggingLevel = logging.DEBUG
logger.setLevel(loggingLevel)
ch = logging.StreamHandler()
ch.setLevel(loggingLevel)
formatter = logging.Formatter("%(asctime)s - %(name)s - %(levelname)s - %(message)s")
ch.setFormatter(formatter)
logger.addHandler(ch)
# Initialize the database
factory = MySQLConnectionFactory("user",      "password",
                                  "localhost", "recipe63")
dt = DatabaseTemplate(factory)
sql = open("recipe62_network.mysql").read().split(";")
for statement in sql:
    dt.execute(statement + ";")
```

11. Add code to expose the app using Pyro.

    ```python
    # Create an instance of the network management app
    target_service = EventCorrelator(factory)

    # Expose the network app as a Pyro service
    exporter = PyroServiceExporter()
    exporter.service_name = "network"
    exporter.service = target_service
    exporter.after_properties_set()
    ```

12. Run the server script in a different shell.

```
(ptc)gturnquist-mbp:08 gturnquist$ python recipe63_server.py
2011-01-20 22:20:30,969 - springpython.remoting.pyro.PyroServiceExporter - DEBUG - Exporting network as a
2011-01-20 22:20:31,114 - springpython.remoting.pyro.PyroDaemonHolder - DEBUG - Registering network at loc
2011-01-20 22:20:31,116 - springpython.remoting.pyro.PyroDaemonHolder - DEBUG - Pyro thread needs to be st
2011-01-20 22:20:31,120 - springpython.remoting.pyro.PyroDaemonHolder._PyroThread - DEBUG - Starting up Py
```

Smoke/Load Testing—Testing Major Parts

13. The default rate is 10 events/second. Run the generator script with a rate of one event/second. In the following screenshot, notice how the script generated a clear, fault, and then another fault. The service started at Operational, moved to Outage, and stayed there.

```
(ptc)gturnquist-mbp:08 gturnquist$ python recipe63.py -r 1
Sending events to live network app. Ctrl+C to exit...
Stored event: (ID:1) pyhost1:serverRestart - 1
Active? False
Services updated: [{'is_active': False, 'service': {'STATUS': 'Operational', 'ID': 1, 'NAM
Equipment updated: [{'STATUS': 1, 'ID': 1, 'HOST_NAME': 'pyhost1'}]
================
Stored event: (ID:2) pyhost2:serverRestart - 5
Active? True
Services updated: [{'is_active': True, 'service': {'STATUS': 'Outage', 'ID': 1, 'NAME': 's
Equipment updated: [{'STATUS': 5, 'ID': 2, 'HOST_NAME': 'pyhost2'}]
================
Stored event: (ID:3) pyhost2:lineStatus - 1
Active? False
Services updated: [{'is_active': False, 'service': {'STATUS': 'Outage', 'ID': 1, 'NAME': '
Equipment updated: [{'STATUS': 5, 'ID': 2, 'HOST_NAME': 'pyhost2'}]
================
```

How it works...

Python's `random.choice` method makes it easy to create a range of random events. By using the `time.sleep` method, we can control the rate at which the events are created.

We used Pyro to connect the test generator to the network management application. This isn't the only way to connect things together. We could have exposed the application through other means, such as REST, JSON, or perhaps by communicating through a database table. That's not important. What is important is that we built an independent tool that fed data into our application as if it came from a live network.

There's more...

We built a test generator. It's easy to run multiple copies of it in different shells, at different rates. We have an easy way to simulate different subnets producing different volumes of traffic.

We could also add more command-line options to fine tune the events. For example, we could make the event condition a parameter, and emulate different rates for different types of events.

Why does the server script initialize the database?

A production version of the server wouldn't do this. For demonstration purposes of this recipe, it is convenient to put it there. Every time we stop and start the server script, it relaunches the database.

Why MySQL instead of SQLite?

SQLite has some limitations when it comes to multithreading. Pyro uses multithreading and SQLite can't pass objects across threads. SQLite is also relatively lightweight and probably not well suited for a real network management application.

See also

- Targeting the test server
- Chapter 7, Building a network management application

Recording and playing back live data in real time

Nothing beats live production data. With this recipe, we will write some code to record the live data. Then we will play it back with delays added to simulate playing back the live data stream.

Getting ready

1. Make sure the MySQL production database server is up and running.
2. Open a command-line MySQL client shell as the root user.
3. Create a database for this recipe called `recipe64` as well as a user with permission to access it.
4. Exit the shell.

```
(ptc)gturnquist-mbp:08 gturnquist$ mysql -u root -p
Enter password:
Welcome to the MySQL monitor.  Commands end with ; or \g.
Your MySQL connection id is 92
Server version: 5.1.44 MySQL Community Server (GPL)

Type 'help;' or '\h' for help. Type '\c' to clear the current input statement.

mysql> create database recipe64;
Query OK, 1 row affected (0.06 sec)

mysql> grant all on recipe64.* to 'user'@'localhost' identified by 'password';
Query OK, 0 rows affected (0.10 sec)

mysql> quit;
Bye
(ptc)gturnquist-mbp:08 gturnquist$
```

How to do it...

With these steps, we will see how to record and play back data at a real-time pace.

1. Write a script called `recipe64_livedata.py` that simulates live data being sent every one to ten seconds.

   ```python
   import random
   import sys
   import time
   from network import *
   from springpython.remoting.pyro import *

   print "Sending events to live network app. Ctrl+C to exit..."
   proxy = PyroProxyFactory()
   proxy.service_url = "PYROLOC://127.0.0.1:7766/network_advised"

   while True:
       hostname = random.choice(["pyhost1","pyhost2","pyhost3"])
       condition = random.choice(["serverRestart", "lineStatus"])
       severity = random.choice([1,5])

       evt = Event(hostname, condition, severity)

       stored_event, is_active, updated_services, \
           updated_equipment = proxy.process(evt)
       print "Stored event: %s" % stored_event
       print "Active? %s" % is_active
       print "Services updated: %s" % updated_services
       print "Equipment updated; %s" % updated_equipment
       print "================"

       time.sleep(random.choice(range(1,10)))
   ```

2. Write a server script called `recipe64_server.py` that initializes the database using the SQL script `recipe62_network.mysql` from **Targeting the test server**.

   ```python
   from springpython.database.factory import *
   from springpython.database.core import *
   from springpython.remoting.pyro import *
   from springpython.aop import *

   from network import *
   from datetime import datetime
   import os
   import os.path
   import pickle

   import logging
   logger = logging.getLogger("springpython.remoting")
   loggingLevel = logging.DEBUG
   ```

```
logger.setLevel(loggingLevel)
ch = logging.StreamHandler()
ch.setLevel(loggingLevel)
formatter = logging.Formatter("%(asctime)s - %(name)s -
%(levelname)s - %(message)s")
ch.setFormatter(formatter)
logger.addHandler(ch)

# Initialize the database
factory = MySQLConnectionFactory("user", "password",
                                "localhost", "recipe64")
dt = DatabaseTemplate(factory)
sql = open("recipe62_network.mysql").read().split(";")
for statement in sql:
    dt.execute(statement + ";")
```

3. Add some code that creates an instance of the network management application and advertises it using Pyro and Spring Python.

```
# Create an instance of the network management app
target_service = EventCorrelator(factory)

# Expose the original network app as a Pyro service
unadvised_service = PyroServiceExporter()
unadvised_service.service_name = "network"
unadvised_service.service = target_service
unadvised_service.after_properties_set()
```

4. Add some more code that defines an interceptor that captures incoming event data along with a time stamp to disk.

```
class Recorder(MethodInterceptor):
    """
    An interceptor that catches each event,
    write it to disk, then proceeds to the
    network management app.
    """
    def __init__(self):
        self.filename = "recipe64_data.txt"
        self.special_char = "&&&"
        if os.path.exists(self.filename):
            os.remove(self.filename)

    def invoke(self, invocation):
        # Write data to disk
        with open(self.filename, "a") as f:
            evt = invocation.args[0]
            now = datetime.now()
```

```
            output = (evt, now)
            print "Recording %s" % evt
            f.write(pickle.dumps(output).replace(
                            "\n", "&&&") + "\n")
        # Now call the advised service
        return invocation.proceed()
```

5. Add some code that wraps the network management application with the interceptor and advertises it using Pyro.

```
# Wrap the network app with an interceptor
advisor = ProxyFactoryObject()
advisor.target = target_service
advisor.interceptors = [Recorder()]

# Expose the advised network app as a Pyro service
advised_service = PyroServiceExporter()
advised_service.service_name = "network_advised"
advised_service.service = advisor
advised_service.after_properties_set()
```

6. Start up the server app by typing `python recipe64_server.py`. Notice in the following screenshot that there is both a `network` service and a `network_advised` service registered with Pyro.

7. Run the live data simulator by typing `python recipe64_livedata.py` until it generates a few events, and then hit *Ctrl+C* to break out of it.

```
(ptc)gturnquist-mbp:08 gturnquist$ python recipe64_livedata.py
Sending events to live network app. Ctrl+C to exit.
Stored event: (ID:1) pyhost3:lineStatus - 1
Active? False
Services updated: []
Equipment updated: [{'STATUS': 1, 'ID': 3, 'HOST_NAME': 'pyhost3'}]
================
Stored event: (ID:2) pyhost1:serverRestart - 5
Active? True
Services updated: [{'is_active': True, 'service': {'STATUS': 'Outage', 'ID
Equipment updated: [{'STATUS': 5, 'ID': 1, 'HOST_NAME': 'pyhost1'}]
================
Stored event: (ID:3) pyhost1:lineStatus - 5
Active? True
Services updated: [{'is_active': True, 'service': {'STATUS': 'Outage', 'ID
Equipment updated: [{'STATUS': 5, 'ID': 1, 'HOST_NAME': 'pyhost1'}]
================
Stored event: (ID:4) pyhost3:lineStatus - 5
Active? True
Services updated: []
Equipment updated: [{'STATUS': 5, 'ID': 3, 'HOST_NAME': 'pyhost3'}]
================
^CTraceback (most recent call last):
  File "recipe64_livedata.py", line 26, in <module>
    time.sleep(random.choice(range(1,10)))
KeyboardInterrupt
(ptc)gturnquist-mbp:08 gturnquist$
```

8. Look at the server-side of things, and notice how it recorded several events.

```
Recording (ID:-1) pyhost3:lineStatus - 1
Recording (ID:-1) pyhost1:serverRestart - 5
Recording (ID:-1) pyhost1:lineStatus - 5
Recording (ID:-1) pyhost3:lineStatus - 5
```

9. Inspect the `recipe64_data.txt` data file, noting how each line represents a separate event and time stamp. While it's hard to decipher the data stored in a pickled format, it's possible to spot bits and pieces.

10. Create a script called `recipe64_playback.py` that de-pickles each line of the data file.

```
from springpython.remoting.pyro import *
from datetime import datetime
import pickle
import time

with open("recipe64_data.txt") as f:
    lines = f.readlines()
events = [pickle.loads(line.replace("&&&", "\n"))
                                    for line in lines]
```

Smoke/Load Testing—Testing Major Parts

11. Add a function that finds the time interval between the current event and the previous one.

    ```
    def calc_offset(evt, time_it_happened, previous_time):
        if previous_time is None:
            return time_it_happened - time_it_happened
        else:
            return time_it_happened - previous_time
    ```

12. Define a client proxy to connect to the unadvised interface of our network management application.

    ```
    print "Sending events to live network app. Ctrl+C to exit..."
    proxy = PyroProxyFactory()
    proxy.service_url = "PYROLOC://127.0.0.1:7766/network"
    ```

13. Add code that iterates over each event, calculating the difference, and then delaying the next event by that many seconds.

    ```
    previous_time = None
    for (e, time_it_happened) in events:
        diff = calc_offset(e, time_it_happened, previous_time)

        print "Original: %s Now: %s" % (time_it_happened, datetime.now())

        stored_event, is_active, updated_services, \
            updated_equipment = proxy.process(e)

        print "Stored event: %s" % stored_event
        print "Active? %s" % is_active
        print "Services updated: %s" % updated_services
        print "Equipment updated; %s" % updated_equipment
        print "Next event in %s seconds" % diff.seconds
        print "================"

        time.sleep(diff.seconds)

        previous_time = time_it_happened
    ```

14. Run the playback script by typing `python recipe64_playback.py` and observe how it has the same delays as the original live data simulator.

Chapter 8

```
(ptc)gturnquist-mbp:08 gturnquist$ python recipe64_playback.py
Sending events to live network app. Ctrl+C to exit...
Original: 2011-01-30 15:03:50.899632 Now: 2011-01-30 15:38:33.884653
Stored event: (ID:5) pyhost3:lineStatus - 1
Active? False
Services updated: []
Equipment updated: [{'STATUS': 1, 'ID': 3, 'HOST_NAME': 'pyhost3'}]
Next event in 0 seconds
================
Original: 2011-01-30 15:03:51.920052 Now: 2011-01-30 15:38:33.891618
Stored event: (ID:6) pyhost1:serverRestart - 5
Active? True
Services updated: [{'is_active': True, 'service': {'STATUS': 'Outage',
Equipment updated: [{'STATUS': 5, 'ID': 1, 'HOST_NAME': 'pyhost1'}]
Next event in 1 seconds
================
Original: 2011-01-30 15:04:00.934825 Now: 2011-01-30 15:38:34.900973
Stored event: (ID:7) pyhost1:lineStatus - 5
Active? True
Services updated: [{'is_active': True, 'service': {'STATUS': 'Outage',
Equipment updated: [{'STATUS': 5, 'ID': 1, 'HOST_NAME': 'pyhost1'}]
Next event in 9 seconds
================
Original: 2011-01-30 15:04:06.928285 Now: 2011-01-30 15:38:43.907574
Stored event: (ID:8) pyhost3:lineStatus - 5
Active? True
Services updated: []
Equipment updated: [{'STATUS': 5, 'ID': 3, 'HOST_NAME': 'pyhost3'}]
Next event in 6 seconds
================
(ptc)gturnquist-mbp:08 gturnquist$
```

How it works...

Normally, we would be recording data coming in from the live network. In this situation, we need a simulator that generates random data. The simulator we coded in this recipe is very similar to the one shown in the *Coding a data simulator* recipe.

To capture the data, we coded an interceptor that is embedded between Pyro and the network management application. Every event published to the `network_advised` Pyro service name seamlessly passes through this interceptor:

- Each event that comes in is appended to the data file that was initialized when the interceptor was first created
- The event is also stored with a copy of `datetime.now()` in order to capture a time stamp
- The event and time stamp are combined into a tuple, and pickled, making it easy to write and later read back from disk
- The data is pickled to make it easy to transfer to and from disk

Smoke/Load Testing—Testing Major Parts

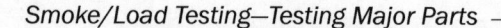

- After writing it to disk, the interceptor calls the target service and passes the results back to the original caller

Finally, we have a playback script that reads in the data file, one event per line. It de-pickles each line into the tuple format it was originally stored in, and builds a list of events.

The list of events is then scanned, one at a time. By comparing the current event's time stamp with the previous one, a difference in seconds is calculated in order to use Python's `time.sleep()` method to play the events back at the same rate they were recorded.

The playback script uses Pyro to send the events into the network management application. But it talks to a different exposure point. This is to avoid re-recording the same event.

There's more...

The code in this recipe uses Pyro as the mechanism connecting clients and servers communicate in a publish/subscribe paradigm. This isn't the only way to build such a service. Python has XML-RPC built in as well. It just isn't as flexible as Pyro. A more thorough analysis of real traffic is needed to determine if this interface is good enough. Alternatives include pushing events through a database EVENT table, where the client inserts rows, and the server polls the table for new rows, and then removes them as they are consumed.

This recipe also makes heavy use of Spring Python for its **Aspect Oriented Programming** features to insert the data recording code (`http://static.springsource.org/spring-python/1.1.x/reference/html/aop.html`). This provides a clean way to add the extra layer of functionality we need to sniff and record network traffic without having to touch the already built network management code.

I thought this recipe was about live data!

Well, the recipe is more about **recording** the live data and controlling the speed of playback. To capture this concept in a reusable recipe requires that we simulate the live system. But the fundamental concept of inserting a tap point in front of the network management processor, as we have done, is just as valid.

Is opening and closing a file for every event a good idea?

The recipe was coded to ensure that stopping the recording would have minimal risk of losing captured data not yet written to disk. Analysis of production data is required to determine the most efficient way of storing data. For example, it may take less I/O intensity to write data in batches of 10, or perhaps 100 events. But the risk is that data can be lost in similar bundles.

If the volume of traffic is low enough, writing each event one-by-one, as shown in this recipe, may not be a problem at all.

What about offloading the storage of data?

It is not uncommon to have the actual logic of opening the file, appending the data, and then closing the file contained in a separate class. This utility could then be injected into the interceptor we built. This may become important if some more elaborate means to storing or piping the data is needed. For example, another Pyro service may exist in another location that wants a copy of the live data feed.

Injecting the data consumer into the aspect we coded would give us more flexibility. In this recipe, we don't have such requirements, but it's not hard to imagine making such adjustments as new requirements arrive.

See also

- Writing a data simulator
- Chapter 7, Building a network management application
- Recording and playing back live data as fast as possible

Recording and playing back live data as fast as possible

Replaying production data as fast as possible (instead of in real time) can give you insight into where your bottlenecks are.

Getting ready

1. Make sure the MySQL production database server is up and running.
2. Open a command-line MySQL client shell as the root user.
3. Create a database for this recipe called `recipe65` as well as a user with permission to access it.

Smoke/Load Testing—Testing Major Parts

4. Exit the shell.

```
(ptc)gturnquist-mbp:08 gturnquist$ mysql -u root -p
Enter password:
Welcome to the MySQL monitor.  Commands end with ; or \g.
Your MySQL connection id is 98
Server version: 5.1.44 MySQL Community Server (GPL)

Type 'help;' or '\h' for help. Type '\c' to clear the current input statement.

mysql> create database recipe65;
Query OK, 1 row affected (0.00 sec)

mysql> grant all on recipe65.* to 'user'@'localhost' identified by 'password';
Query OK, 0 rows affected (0.00 sec)

mysql> quit;
Bye
```

How to do it...

In these steps, we will write some code that lets us put a big load on our system.

1. Write a script called `recipe65_livedata.py` that simulates live data being sent every one to ten seconds.

   ```python
   import random
   import sys
   import time
   from network import *
   from springpython.remoting.pyro import *

   print "Sending events to live network app. Ctrl+C to exit..."
   proxy = PyroProxyFactory()
   proxy.service_url = "PYROLOC://127.0.0.1:7766/network_advised"
   while True:
       hostname = random.choice(["pyhost1","pyhost2","pyhost3"])
       condition = random.choice(["serverRestart", "lineStatus"])
       severity = random.choice([1,5])

       evt = Event(hostname, condition, severity)

       stored_event, is_active, updated_services, \
               updated_equipment = proxy.process(evt)
       print "Stored event: %s" % stored_event
       print "Active? %s" % is_active
       print "Services updated: %s" % updated_services
       print "Equipment updated; %s" % updated_equipment
       print "================"

       time.sleep(random.choice(range(1,10)))
   ```

2. Write a server script called `recipe65_server.py` that initializes the database using the SQL script `recipe62_network.mysql` from **Targeting the test server**.

   ```
   from springpython.database.factory import *
   from springpython.database.core import *
   from springpython.remoting.pyro import *
   from springpython.aop import *

   from network import *
   from datetime import datetime
   import os
   import os.path
   import pickle

   import logging
   logger = logging.getLogger("springpython.remoting")
   loggingLevel = logging.DEBUG
   logger.setLevel(loggingLevel)
   ch = logging.StreamHandler()
   ch.setLevel(loggingLevel)
   formatter = logging.Formatter("%(asctime)s - %(name)s - 
   %(levelname)s - %(message)s")
   ch.setFormatter(formatter)
   logger.addHandler(ch)

   # Initialize the database
   factory = MySQLConnectionFactory("user", "password",
                                    "localhost", "recipe65")
   dt = DatabaseTemplate(factory)
   sql = open("recipe62_network.mysql").read().split(";")
   for statement in sql:
       dt.execute(statement + ";")
   ```

3. Add some code that creates an instance of the network management application and advertises it using Pyro and Spring Python.

   ```
   # Create an instance of the network management app
   target_service = EventCorrelator(factory)

   # Expose the original network app as a Pyro service
   unadvised_service = PyroServiceExporter()
   unadvised_service.service_name = "network"
   unadvised_service.service = target_service
   unadvised_service.after_properties_set()
   ```

4. Add some more code that defines an interceptor that captures incoming event data along with a time stamp to disk.

   ```
   class Recorder(MethodInterceptor):
       """
   ```

```
            An interceptor that catches each event,
            write it to disk, then proceeds to the
            network management app.
            """
            def __init__(self):
                self.filename = "recipe65_data.txt"
                self.special_char = "&&&"
                if os.path.exists(self.filename):
                    os.remove(self.filename)

            def invoke(self, invocation):
                # Write data to disk
                with open(self.filename, "a") as f:
                    evt = invocation.args[0]
                    now = datetime.now()
                    output = (evt, now)
                    print "Recording %s" % evt
                    f.write(pickle.dumps(output).replace(
                                    "\n", "&&&") + "\n")

                # Now call the advised service
                return invocation.proceed()
```

5. Add some code that wraps the network management application with the interceptor and advertises it using Pyro.

```
# Wrap the network app with an interceptor
advisor = ProxyFactoryObject()
advisor.target = target_service
advisor.interceptors = [Recorder()]

# Expose the advised network app as a Pyro service
advised_service = PyroServiceExporter()
advised_service.service_name = "network_advised"
advised_service.service = advisor
advised_service.after_properties_set()
```

6. Start up the server app by typing `python recipe65_server.py`. In the following screenshot, notice that there is both a `network` service and a `network_advised` service registered with Pyro:

7. Run the live data simulator by typing `python recipe65_livedata.py` and watch it run until it generates a few events, and then hit **Ctrl+C** to break out of it.

```
(ptc)gturnquist-mbp:08 gturnquist$ python recipe65_livedata.py
Sending events to live network app. Ctrl+C to exit...
Stored event: (ID:1) pyhost3:lineStatus - 5
Active? True
Services updated: []
Equipment updated: [{'STATUS': 5, 'ID': 3, 'HOST_NAME': 'pyhost3'}]
================
Stored event: (ID:2) pyhost3:serverRestart - 1
Active? False
Services updated: []
Equipment updated: [{'STATUS': 5, 'ID': 3, 'HOST_NAME': 'pyhost3'}]
================
Stored event: (ID:3) pyhost1:lineStatus - 5
Active? True
Services updated: [{'is_active': True, 'service': {'STATUS': 'Outage',
Equipment updated: [{'STATUS': 5, 'ID': 1, 'HOST_NAME': 'pyhost1'}]
================
Stored event: (ID:4) pyhost3:serverRestart - 5
Active? True
Services updated: []
Equipment updated: [{'STATUS': 5, 'ID': 3, 'HOST_NAME': 'pyhost3'}]
================
^CTraceback (most recent call last):
  File "recipe65_livedata.py", line 26, in <module>
    time.sleep(random.choice(range(1,10)))
KeyboardInterrupt
```

8. Look at the server side of things, and notice how it recorded several events.

```
Recording (ID:-1) pyhost3:lineStatus - 5
Recording (ID:-1) pyhost3:serverRestart - 1
Recording (ID:-1) pyhost1:lineStatus - 5
Recording (ID:-1) pyhost3:serverRestart - 5
```

9. Inspect the `recipe65_data.txt` data file, noting how each line represents a separate event and time stamp. While it's hard to decipher the data stored in a pickled format, it's possible to spot bits and pieces.

10. Create a playback script called `recipe65_playback.py` that de-pickles each line of the data file.

    ```
    from springpython.remoting.pyro import *
    from datetime import datetime
    import pickle
    import time
    with open("recipe65_data.txt") as f:
        lines = f.readlines()
    events = [pickle.loads(line.replace("&&&", "\n"))
                                        for line in lines]
    ```

Smoke/Load Testing—Testing Major Parts

11. Define a client proxy to connect to the unadvised interface of our network management application.

    ```
    print "Sending events to live network app. Ctrl+C to exit..."
    proxy = PyroProxyFactory()

    proxy.service_url = "PYROLOC://127.0.0.1:7766/network"
    ```

12. Add code that iterates over each event, playing back the events as fast as possible.

    ```
    for (e, time_it_happened) in events:
        stored_event, is_active, updated_services, \
            updated_equipment = proxy.process(e))
        print "Stored event: %s" % stored_event
        print "Active? %s" % is_active
        print "Services updated: %s" % updated_services
        print "Equipment updated; %s" % updated_equipment
        print "================="
    ```

13. Run the playback script by typing `python recipe65_playback.py`, observing how it doesn't delay events but instead plays them back as fast as possible.

    ```
    (ptc)gturnquist-mbp:08 gturnquist$ python recipe65_playback.py
    Sending events to live network app. Ctrl+C to exit...
    Stored event: (ID:9) pyhost3:lineStatus - 5
    Active? True
    Services updated: []
    Equipment updated; [{'STATUS': 5, 'ID': 3, 'HOST_NAME': 'pyhost3'}]
    =================
    Stored event: (ID:10) pyhost3:serverRestart - 1
    Active? False
    Services updated: []
    Equipment updated; [{'STATUS': 5, 'ID': 3, 'HOST_NAME': 'pyhost3'}]
    =================
    Stored event: (ID:11) pyhost1:lineStatus - 5
    Active? True
    Services updated: [{'is_active': True, 'service': {'STATUS': 'Outage'
    Equipment updated; [{'STATUS': 5, 'ID': 1, 'HOST_NAME': 'pyhost1'}]
    =================
    Stored event: (ID:12) pyhost3:serverRestart - 5
    Active? True
    Services updated: []
    Equipment updated; [{'STATUS': 5, 'ID': 3, 'HOST_NAME': 'pyhost3'}]
    =================
    ```

Chapter 8

How it works...

Normally, we would be recording data coming in from the live network. In this situation, we need a simulator that generates random data. The simulator we coded in this recipe is very similar to the one shown in the *Coding a data simulator* recipe.

To capture the data, we coded an interceptor that is embedded between Pyro and the network management application. Every event published to the `network_advised` Pyro service name seamlessly passes through this interceptor:

- Each event that comes in is appended to the data file that was initialized when the interceptor was first created
- The event is also stored with a copy of `datetime.now()` in order to capture a time stamp
- The event and time stamp are combined into a tuple, and pickled, making it easy to write and later read back from disk
- The data is pickled to make it easy to transfer to and from disk
- After writing it to disk, the interceptor calls the target service and passes the results back to the original caller

Finally, we have a playback script that reads in the data file, one event per line. It de-pickles each line into the tuple format it was originally stored in, and builds a list of events.

The list of events is then scanned, one at a time. Instead of evaluating the time stamps to figure out how long to delay playing back the events, they are injected immediately into the network management application.

The playback script uses Pyro to send the events in to the network management application, but it talks to a different exposure point. This is to avoid re-recording the same event.

There's more...

The code in this recipe uses Pyro as the mechanism connecting clients and servers and communicates in a publish/subscribe paradigm. This isn't the only way to build such a service. Python has XML-RPC built in as well. It just isn't as flexible as Pyro. A more thorough analysis of real traffic is needed to determine if this interface is good enough. Alternatives include pushing events through a database EVENT table, where the client inserts rows, and the server polls the table for new rows, and then removes them as they are consumed.

This recipe also makes heavy use of Spring Python for its **Aspect Oriented Programming** features to insert the data recording code (http://static.springsource.org/spring-python/1.1.x/reference/html/aop.html). This provides a clean way to add the extra layer of functionality we need to sniff and record network traffic without having to touch the already built network management code.

What is the difference between this and playing back in real time?

Real time playback is useful to see how the system handles production load. But this doesn't answer the question of where the system is expected to break. Traffic flow is never steady. Instead, it often has bursts that are not expected. That is when playing back live data at an accelerated rate will help expose the system's next break points.

Preemptively addressing some of these concerns will make our system more resilient.

Where are the breaking points of this application?

Admittedly, this recipe didn't break when we played back four events as fast as possible. Would this be the same result in production? Things break in different ways. We may not get a real exception or error message, but instead discover that certain parts of the system become backlogged.

That is where this recipe reaches its limit. While we have demonstrated how to overload the system with a large volume of traffic, we are NOT showing how to monitor where the bottlenecks are.

If the application under load uses database tables to queue up work, then we would need to write the code that monitors them all and report back which one is:

- the longest
- getting longer and showing no sign of catching up
- earliest in the pipeline of activity

In systems with stages of processing, there is often one bottleneck that makes itself known. When that bottleneck is fixed, it is rarely the only bottleneck. It was simply either the most critical one or the first one in a chain.

Also, this recipe cannot solve your bottleneck. The purpose of this recipe is to find it.

> I once built a network load tester very much like this one. The code could handle processing lots of traffic in parallel, but events from the same device had to be processed in order. Replaying a day's worth of events all at once exposed the fact that too many events from the same device caused the entire queue system to become overloaded and starve out handling other devices. After improving the service update algorithm, we were able to replay the same load test and verify it could keep up. This helped avoid non-reproducible outages that happened after hours or on weekends.

What amount of live data should be collected?

It is useful to capture things like a 24-hour block of traffic to allow playing back an entire day of events. Another possibility is an entire week. Live systems may be apt to have different loads on weekends rather than weekdays and a week of data will allow better investigation.

The problem with this much data is that it is hard to pick out a window to investigate. This is why 24 hours of data from the weekend and 24 hours of data during the week may be more practical.

If there is some sort of network instability where huge outages are occurring and causing a huge flow of traffic, it may be useful to turn on the collector and wait for another similar outage to occur. After such an outage occurs, it may be useful to shift through the data file and trim it down to where the uptick in traffic occurred.

These types of captured scenarios are invaluable in load testing new releases, because it confirms that new patches either improve performance as expected, or at least don't reduce performance when fixing non-performance issues.

See also

- Writing a data simulator
- Chapter 7, Building a network management application
- Recording and playing back live data in real time

Automating your management demo

Got a demo coming? Write automated tests that simulate the steps you'll be taking. Then print out your test suite, and use it like a script.

How to do it...

With these steps, we will see how to write our management demo script in a runnable fashion.

1. Create a new file called `recipe66.py` to store the test code for our management demo.
2. Create a `unittest` test scenario to capture your demo.
3. Write a series of operations as if you were driving the application from this automated test.
4. Include asserts at every point where you will vocally point out something during the demo.

   ```
   import unittest
   from network import *
   ```

```python
from springpython.database.factory import *

class ManagementDemo(unittest.TestCase):
    def setUp(self):
        factory = MySQLConnectionFactory("user", "password",
                                         "localhost", "recipe62")
        self.correlator = EventCorrelator(factory)

        dt = DatabaseTemplate(factory)
        sql = open("recipe62_network.mysql").read().split(";")
        for statement in sql:
            dt.execute(statement + ";")

    def test_processing_a_service_affecting_event(self):
        # Define a service-affecting event
        evt1 = Event("pyhost1", "serverRestart", 5)

        # Inject it into the system
        stored_event, is_active, \
            updated_services, updated_equipment = \
                self.correlator.process(evt1)

        # These are the values I plan to call
        # attention to during my demo
        self.assertEquals(len(updated_services), 1)
        self.assertEquals("service-abc",
                updated_services[0]["service"]["NAME"])
        self.assertEquals("Outage",
                updated_services[0]["service"]["STATUS"])

if __name__ == "__main__":
    unittest.main()
```

5. Run the test suite by typing `python recipe66.py`.

```
(ptc)gturnquist-mbp:08 gturnquist$ python recipe66.py

Ran 1 test in 0.906s

OK
```

How it works...

This recipe is more philosophical and less code based. While the concept of this recipe is valuable, it is hard to capture in a single nugget of reusable code.

In this test case, I inject an event, process it, and then confirm what it impacts. This test case is headless, but our demo probably won't be. So far in this chapter, we haven't built any user screens. As we develop user screens, we need to ensure they call the same APIs as this automated test.

Given this, we are setup to use the screens to define the same event shown in the test. After the event is digested, another screen will probably exist that shows current service status. We would expect it to reflect the update to Outage.

During our management demo, we will then point out/zoom in to this part of the screen and show how **service-abc** switched from **Operational** to **Outage**.

If the screens are built to delegate to this underlying logic, then the screen logic is little more than components put together to display information. The core logic being tested maintains its headless and easy-to-test nature.

Our code sample isn't complete, and wouldn't amount to more than a one minute demo. But the concept is sound. By capturing the steps we plan to execute in our demo in a runnable form, our management demo should go off without a hitch.

> Did I say without a hitch? Well, demos rarely work that well. Doesn't something about management appearances cause things to break? At one time, I began prepping for a senior management demo a month in advance using this recipe. I uncovered and subsequently fixed several bugs, such that my demo worked flawlessly. Management was impressed. No promises, but sincerely making your demo 100 percent runnable will greatly increase your odds.

There's more...

What is the secret to this recipe? It seems to be a bit short on code. While it's important to make the demo 100 percent runnable, the key is then printing out the test and **using it like a script**. That way, the only steps you are taking have already been **proven to work**.

What if my manager likes to take detours?

If your manager likes to ask lots of what-if questions that pulls you off script, then you are sailing into uncharted territory. Your odds for a successful demo may drop quickly.

You can politely dodge this by capturing their what-ifs for a future demo and try to keep the current one on track. If you take the plunge to try other things out, realize the risk you are taking.

Smoke/Load Testing—Testing Major Parts

> Don't be afraid to promise a future demo where you will travel down the path requested instead of risking it in this demo. Managers are actually pretty open to accepting a response like: "I haven't tested that yet. How about another demo next month where we cover that?". Failed demos leave a bad taste with management and put your reputation in jeopardy. Successful ones have an equally positive effect to your reputation as a developer. Management tends to have a more optimistic view of seeing 70 percent of the system succeed 100 percent rather than viewing 100 percent of the system succeed 70 percent.

This is where the line between engineer and manager needs to be observed. While managers want to see what's available, it is our job to show them what is currently working and give an accurate status on what is and isn't available. Asking to see something we haven't tested yet definitely warrants pushing back and telling them such a demo isn't ready yet.

9
Good Test Habits for New and Legacy Systems

In this chapter, we will cover:

- Something is better than nothing
- Coverage isn't everything
- Be willing to invest in test fixtures
- If you aren't convinced on the value of testing, your team won't be either
- Harvesting metrics
- Capturing a bug in an automated test
- Separating algorithms from concurrency
- Pause to refactor when test suite takes too long to run
- Cash in on your confidence
- Be willing to throw away an entire day of changes
- Instead of shooting for 100 percent coverage, try to have a steady growth
- Randomly breaking your app can lead to better code

Good Test Habits for New and Legacy Systems

Introduction

I hope you have enjoyed the previous chapters of this book. Up to this point, we have explored a lot of areas of automated testing:

- Unit testing
- Nose testing
- Doctest testing
- Behavior Driven Development
- Acceptance testing
- Continuous integration
- Smoke and Load testing

In this chapter, we will do something different. Instead of providing lots of code samples for various tips and tricks, I want to share some ideas I have picked up in my career as a software engineer.

All of the previous recipes in this book had very detailed steps on how to write the code, run it, and review its results. Hopefully, you have been able to take those ideas, expand, and improvise, and ultimately apply them to your own problems.

In this chapter, let's explore some of the bigger ideas behind testing and how they can empower our development of quality systems.

Something is better than nothing

Don't get caught up in the purity of total isolation or worry about obscure test methods. First thing, start testing.

How to do it...

You have just been handed an application that was developed by others no longer with your company. Been there before? We all have. Probably on several occasions. Can we predict some of the common symptoms?

- Few (if any) automated tests
- Little documentation
- Chunks of code that are commented out
- Either no comments in the code, or comments that were written ages ago and are no longer correct

And here is the fun part: we don't know all of these issues up front. We are basically told where to check out the source tree, and to get cracking. For example, it's only when we run into an issue and seek out documentation that we discover what does (or does not) exist.

Maybe I didn't catch everything you have encountered in that list, but I bet I hit a fair number. I don't want to sound like an embittered software developer, because I'm not. Not every project is like this. But I'm sure we have all had to deal with this at one time or another. So what do we do? We start testing.

But the devil is in the details. Do we write a unit test? What about a thread test or an integration test? You know what? It doesn't matter what type of test we write. In fact, it doesn't matter if we use the right name.

When it's just you and the code sitting in a cubicle, terminology doesn't matter. Writing a test is what matters. If you can pick out one small unit of code and write a test, then go for it! But what if you picked up a jumbled piece of spaghetti code that doesn't come with nicely isolated units?

Consider a system where the smallest unit you can get hold of is a module that parses an electronic file and then stores the parsed results in a database. The parsed results aren't handed back through the API. They just silently, mysteriously end up in the database. How do we automate that?

1. Write a test that starts by emptying all the tables relevant to the application.
2. Find one of your users who has one of these files and get a copy of it.
3. Add code to the test that invokes the top-level API to ingest the file.
4. Add some more code that pulls data out of the database and checks the results. (You may have to grab that user to make sure it is working correctly.)

Congratulations, you just wrote an automated test! It probably didn't qualify as a unit test. In fact, it may look kind of ugly to you. But so what? Maybe it took five minutes to run, but isn't that better than no test at all?

How it works...

Since the database is the place where we can assert results, we need to have a cleaned out version before every run of our test. This is definitely going to require coordination if other developers are using some of the same tables. We may need our own schema allocated to us, so that we can empty tables at will.

The modules probably suffer from a lack of cohesion and too much tight coupling. While we can try to identify why the code is bad, it doesn't advance our cause of building automated tests.

Instead, we must recognize that if we try to jump immediately into unit level testing, we would have to refactor the modules to support us. With little or no safety net, the risk is incredibly high, and we can feel it! If we try to stick to textbook unit testing, then we will probably give up and deem automated testing as an impossibility.

So we have to take the first step and write the expensive, end-to-end automated test to build the first link in a chain. That test may take a long time to run and not be very comprehensive in what we can assert. But it's a start. And that is what's important. Hopefully, after steady progress in writing more tests like this, we will build up enough of a safety net to go back and refactor this code.

That can't be everything!

Does "just write the test" sound a little too simple? Well the concept is simple. The work is going to be hard. Very hard.

You will be forced to crawl through lots of APIs and find out exactly how they work. And guess what? You probably won't be handed lots of intermediate results to assert. Understanding the API is just so that you can track down where the data travels to.

When I described the data of our situation as "mysteriously ending up in the database", I was referring to the likelihood that the APIs you have probably weren't designed with lots of return values aimed at testability.

Just don't let anyone tell you that you are wasting your time building a long-running test case. An automated test suite that takes an hour to run and is exercised at least once a day probably instills more confidence than clicking through the screens manually. Something is better than nothing.

See also

- Cash in on your confidence

Coverage isn't everything

You've figured out how to run coverage reports. But don't assume that more coverage is automatically better. Sacrificing test quality in the name of coverage is a recipe for failure.

How to do it...

Coverage reports provide good feedback. They tell us what is getting exercised and what is not. But just because a line of code is exercised doesn't mean it is doing everything it is meant to do.

Are you ever tempted to brag about coverage percentage scores in the break room? Taking pride in good coverage isn't unwarranted, but when it leads to comparing different projects using these statistics, we are wandering into risky territory.

How it works...

Coverage reports are meant to be read in the context of the code they were run against. The reports show us what was covered and what was not, but this isn't where things stop. Instead, it's where they begin. We need to look at what was covered, and analyze how well the tests exercised the system.

It's obvious that 0 percent coverage of a module indicates we have work to do. But what does it mean when we have 70 percent coverage? Do we need to code tests that go after the other 30 percent? Sure we do! But there are two different schools of thought on how to approach this. One is right and one is wrong:

- The first approach is to write the new tests specifically targeting the uncovered parts while trying to avoid overlapping the original 70 percent. Redundantly, testing code already covered in another test is an inefficient use of resources.
- The second approach is to write the new tests so they target scenarios the code is expected to handle, but which we haven't tackled yet. What was not covered should give us a hint about what scenarios haven't been tested yet.

The right approach is the second one. Okay, I admit I wrote that in a leading fashion. But the point is that it's very easy to look at what wasn't hit, and write a test that shoots to close the gap as fast as possible.

There's more...

Python gives us incredible power to monkey patch, inject alternate methods, and do other tricks to exercise the uncovered code. But doesn't this sound a little suspicious? Here are some of the risks we are setting ourselves up for:

- The new tests may be more brittle when they aren't based on sound scenarios.
- A major change to our algorithms may require us to totally rewrite these tests.
- Ever written mock-based tests? It's possible to mock the target system out of existence and end up just testing the mocks.

> Even though some (or even most) of our tests may have good quality, the low quality ones will cast our entire test suite as low quality.

The coverage tool may not let us "get away" with some of these tactics if we do things that interfere with the line counting mechanisms. But whether or not the coverage tool counts the code should not be the gauge by which we determine the quality of tests.

Instead, we need to look at our tests and see if they are trying to exercise real use cases we should be handling. When we are merely looking for ways to get more coverage percentage, we stop thinking about how our code is meant to operate, and that is not good.

Are we not supposed to increase coverage?

We are supposed to increase coverage by improving our tests, covering more scenarios, and by removing code no longer supported. These things all lead us towards overall better quality.

Increasing coverage for the sake of coverage doesn't lend itself to improving the quality of our system.

But I want to brag about the coverage of my system!

I think it's alright to celebrate good coverage. Sharing a coverage report with your manager is alright. But don't let it consume you.

If you start to post weekly coverage reports, double check your motives. Same goes if your manager requests postings as well.

If you find yourself comparing the coverage of your system against another system, then watch out! Unless you are familiar with the code of both systems and really know more than the bottom line of the reports, you are probably wandering into risky territory. You may be headed into faulty competition that could drive your team to write brittle tests.

Be willing to invest in test fixtures

Spend time working on some test fixtures. You may not get a lot of tests written at first, but this investment will pay off.

How to do it...

When we start building a new green field project, it's a lot easier to write test-oriented modules. But when dealing with legacy systems, it may take more time to build a working test fixture. This may be tough to go through, but it's a valuable investment.

As an example, in *Something is better than nothing*, we talked about a system that scanned electronic files and put the parsed results in database tables. What steps would our test fixture require?

- Setup steps to clean out the appropriate tables
- Quite possibly, we may need to use code or a script to create a new database schema to avoid collisions with other developers
- It may be necessary to stage the file in a certain location so the parser can find it

These are all steps that take time in order to build a working test case. More complex legacy systems may require even more steps to gear up for a test run.

How it works...

All of this can become intimidating, and may push us to drop automated testing and just continue with clicking through the screens to verify things. But taking the time to invest in coding this fixture will begin to pay off as we write more test cases that use our fixture.

Have you ever built a test fixture and had to alter it for certain scenarios? After having developed enough test cases using our fixture, we will probably encounter another use case we need to test that exceeds the limits of our fixture. Since we are now familiar with it, it is probably easier to create another fixture.

> This is another way that coding the first fixture pays off. Future fixtures have a good chance of being easier to code. This isn't a cut-and-dried guarantee of improvement. Often, the first variation of our test fixture is a simple one.

There's more...

We will probably run into the situation where we need another test fixture that is totally different from what we've built. At this point, investing in the first test fixture doesn't have the same payoff. But by this time, we will have become more seasoned test writers and have a better handle on what works and what doesn't when it comes to testing the system.

All the work done up to this point will have sharpened our skill set and that, in and of itself, is a great payoff for investing in the test fixture.

Is this just about setting up a database?

Not at all. If our system interacts extensively with an LDAP server, we may need to code a fixture that cleans out the directory structure and loads it up with test data.

If the legacy system is flexible enough, we can put this whole test structure into some subnode in the hierarchy. But it's just as likely that it expects the data to exist at a certain location. In that situation, we may have to develop a script that spins up a separate, empty LDAP server, and then shuts it down after the test is complete.

Setting up and tearing down an LDAP server may not be the fastest, nor the most efficient test fixture. But if we invest the time to build this fixture to empower ourselves to write automated tests, we will eventually be able to refactor the original system to decouple it from a live LDAP server. And this whole process will sharpen our skill set. That is why creating the original test fixture truly is an investment.

If you aren't convinced on the value of testing, your team won't be either

Test bitten developers exhibit zeal. They are excited to run their test suite, and see things complete with 100 percent success. This sort of emotion and pride tends to rub off on fellow developers.

But the reverse is also true. If you aren't excited by all this and don't spread the word, none of your team mates will realize it either. The idea of adding automated tests to your system will die a sad death.

This isn't just confined to my own personal experience. At the devLink conference in 2010, I attended an open space discussion about testing, and saw this sort of reaction among a dozen other developers I don't work with (`pythontestingcookbook.posterous.com/greetings-programs`). The testers showed a certain type of excitement as they relayed their experiences with testing. The ones that were on the fence about embracing automated testing were listening with glee in their eyes, drinking it in. Those not interested simply weren't there for the discussion.

If you are reading this book (which of course you are), there is a fair chance you are the only person on your team seriously interested in automated testing. Your team mates may have heard of it, but aren't as bitten by the idea as you. To add it to your system will require a lot of investment by you. But don't confine yourself to just sharing the code:

- Demonstrate the excitement you feel as you make progress and tackle thorny issues
- Share your test results by posting them on your walls where others can see
- Talk about your accomplishments while chatting with co-workers in the break room

Testing isn't a cold, mechanical process. It's an exciting, fiery area of development. Test bitten developers can't wait to share it with others. If you look for ways to spread the fire of automated testing, eventually others will warm up to it and you will find yourself talking about new testing techniques together.

Harvesting metrics

Start a spreadsheet that shows lines code, number of tests, total test execution time, and number of bugs, and track this with every release. The numbers will defend your investment.

How to do it...

These high level steps show how to capture metrics over time:

1. Create a spreadsheet to track number of test cases, time to run test suite, date of test run, bugs, and average time per test.
2. Check the spreadsheet into your code base as another controlled artifact.
3. Add some graphs to show the curve of test time versus test quantity.
4. Add a new row of data at least every time you do a release. If you can capture data more often, like once/week or even once/day, that is better.

How it works...

As you write more tests, the test suite will take longer to run. But you will also find that the number of bugs tend to decrease. The more testing you do, and the more often you do it leads to overall code quality. Capturing the metrics of your testing can act as hard evidence that the time spent writing and running tests is a well-placed investment.

There's more...

Why do I need this document? Don't I already know that testing works? Think of it as a backup for your assertion of quality. Months down the road, you may be challenged by the management to speed things up. Maybe they need something faster, and they think you are simply spending too much time on this "testing stuff".

If you can pull out your spreadsheet and show how bugs decreased with testing effort, they will have little to argue with. But if you don't have this, and simply argue that "testing makes things better", you may lose the argument.

Metrics aren't just for defending yourself to management

I personally enjoyed seeing the tests grow and the bugs decline. It was a personal way to track myself and keep a handle on how much progress was made. And to be honest, my last manager gave me full support for automated testing. He had his own metrics of success, so I never had to pull out mine.

Capturing a bug in an automated test

Before you fix that one line bug you spotted, write an automated test instead, and make sure it's repeatable. This helps to build up insulation from our system regressing back into failures we fixed in the past.

How to do it...

These high level steps capture the workflow of capturing bugs in automated tests before we fix them:

1. When a new bug is discovered, write a test case that recreates it. It doesn't matter if the test case is long running, complex, or integrates with lots of components. The critical thing is to reproduce the bug.
2. Add it to your suite of tests.
3. Fix the bug.
4. Verify the test suite passes before checking in your changes.

How it works...

The simplest way to introduce automated testing to an application that never had it before is to test one bug at a time. This method ensures that newly discovered bugs won't sneak back into the system later on.

The tests may have a loose knit feel instead of a comprehensive one, but that doesn't matter. What does matter is that over time, you will slowly develop a solid safety net of test cases that verify the system performs as expected.

There's more...

I didn't say this would be easy. Writing an automated test for software that wasn't built with testability in mind is hard work. As mentioned in the recipe *Something is better than nothing*, the first test case is probably the hardest. But over time, as you develop more tests, you will gain the confidence to go back and refactor things. You will definitely feel empowered by knowing that you can't break things without knowing it.

When the time comes to add a completely new module, you will be ready for it

This approach of capturing a bug with a test case is useful, but slow. But that's okay, because slowly adding testing will give you time to grow your testing skills at a comfortable pace.

Where does this pay off? Well, eventually, you will need to add some new module to your system. Doesn't this always happen? By that time, your investment in testing and test fixtures should already be paying you dividends in improvement of the quality of existing code. But you will also have a head start on testing the new module:

- You will not just know, but really understand the meaning of "test-oriented code".
- You will be able to write both the code and its tests at the same time in a very effective way.
- The new module will have a head start of higher quality and not require as much effort to "catch up" as did the legacy parts of your system.

Don't give in to the temptation to skip testing

As I stated earlier, the first test case will be very hard to write. And the next few after that won't be much easier. This makes it very tempting to throw up your hands and skip automated testing. But if you stick with it and write something that works, then you can continue building off that successful bit of effort.

This may sound like a cliché, but if you stick with it for about a month, you will start to see some results of your work. This is also a great time to start **Harvesting metrics**. Capturing your progress and being able to reflect on it can provide positive encouragement.

Separating algorithms from concurrency

Concurrency is very hard to test, but most algorithms are not, when decoupled.

How to do it...

Herb Sutter wrote an article in 2005 entitled *The Free Lunch Is Over*, where he points out how microprocessors are approaching a physical limitation in serial processing that will be forcing developers to turn towards concurrent solutions (http://www.gotw.ca/publications/concurrency-ddj.htm).

Newer processors come with multiple cores. To build scalable applications, we can no longer just wait for a faster chip. Instead, we must use alternate, concurrent techniques. This issue is being played out in a whole host of languages. Erlang was one of the first languages on the scene that allowed a telecommunications system to be built with nine 9's of availability, which means about 1 second of downtime every 30 years.

One of its key features is the use of immutable data sent between actors. This provides a nice isolation and allows multiple units to run across the CPU cores. Python has libraries that provide a similar style of decoupled, asynchronous message passing. The two most common ones are Twisted and Kamaelia.

But before you dive into using either of these frameworks, there is something important to keep in mind: it's very hard to test concurrency while also testing algorithms. To use these libraries, you will register code that issues messages and also register handlers to process messages.

How it works...

It's important to decouple the algorithms from the machinery of whatever concurrency library you pick. This will make it much easier to test the algorithms. It doesn't mean that you shouldn't conduct load tests or try to overload your system with live data playback scenarios.

What it means is that starting with large volume test scenarios is the wrong priority. Your system needs to correctly handle one event in an automated test case before it can handle a thousand events.

Research test options provided by your concurrency frameworks

A good concurrency library should provide sound testing options. Seek them out and try to use them to their fullest. But don't forget to verify that your custom algorithms work in a simple, serial fashion as well. Testing both sides will give you great confidence that the system is performing as expected under light and heavy loads.

Pause to refactor when test suite takes too long to run

As you start to build a test suite, you may notice the runtime getting quite long. If it's so long that you aren't willing to run it at least once a day, you need to stop coding and focus on speeding up the tests, whether it involves the tests themselves or the code under test.

How to do it...

This assumes you have started to build a test suite using some of the following practices:

- Something is better than nothing
- Be willing to invest in test fixtures
- Capturing a bug in an automated test

These are slow starting steps to start adding tests to a system that was originally built without any automated testing. One of the trade offs to get moving on automated testing involves writing relatively expensive tests. For instance, if one of your key algorithms is not adequately decoupled from the database, you will be forced to write a test case that involves setting up some tables, processing the input data, and then making queries against the state of the database afterwards.

As you write more tests, the time to run the test suite will certainly grow. At some point, you feel less inclined to spend the time waiting for your test suite to run. Since a test suite is only good when used, you must pause development and pursue refactoring either the code or the test cases themselves in order to speed things up.

This is a problem I ran into. My test suite initially took about 15 minutes to run. It eventually grew to take one-and-a-half hours to run all the tests. I reached a point where I would only run it once a day and even skipped some days. One day I tried to do a massive code edit. When most of the test cases failed, I realized that I had not run the test suite often enough to detect which step broke things. I was forced to throw away all the code edits and start over. Before proceeding further, I spent a few days refactoring the code as well as the tests, bringing the run time of the test suite back down to a tolerable 30 minutes.

How it works...

That is the key measurement: when you feel hesitant to run the test suite more than **once a day**, this may be a sign that things need to be cleaned up. Test suites are meant to be run multiple times a day.

This is because we have competing interests: **writing code** and **running tests**. It's important to recognize this:

- To run the tests, we must suspend our coding efforts
- To write more code, we must suspend testing efforts

When testing takes a big chunk of our daily schedule, we must start choosing which is more important. We tend to migrate towards writing more code, and this is probably the key reason people abandon automated testing and consider it unsuitable for their situation.

It's tough, but if we can resist taking the easy way out, and instead do some refactoring of either the code or our tests, we will be encouraged to run the tests more often.

There's more...

It's less science and more voodoo exactly what to refactor. It's important to seek out opportunities that give us a good yield. It's important to understand this can be either our test code, or production code, or some combination of both that needs to be refactored:

- Performance analysis can show us where the hotspots are. Refactoring or rewriting these chunks can improve the tests.
- Tight coupling often forces us to pull in more parts of the system than we want, such as database usage. If we can look for ways to decouple the code from the database and replace it with mocks or stubs, that sets us up to update the relevant tests to come up with a faster running test suite.

Coverage obtained from tests can help. All of these approaches have positive consequences for our code's quality. More efficient algorithms lead to better performance and looser coupling helps to keep our long-term maintenance costs down.

See also

- Be willing to throw away an entire day of changes

Cash in on your confidence

After building up enough tests, you will feel a new confidence to rewrite some big chunk of code, or conduct shotgun surgery that touches almost every file. Go for it!

How to do it...

As you build more tests and run them several times a day, you will start to get a feel for what you know and don't know about the system. Even more so, when you've written enough expensive, long running tests about a particular part of the system, you will feel a strong desire to rewrite that module.

What are you waiting for? This is the point of building a runnable safety net of tests. Understanding the ins and outs of a module gives you the knowledge to attack it. You might rewrite it, better decouple its parts, or whatever else is needed to make it work better as well as better support tests.

How it works...

While you may feel a strong desire to attack the code, there may be an equal and opposing feeling to resist making such changes. This is risk aversion, and we all have to deal with it. We want to avoid diving in head first to a situation that could have drastic consequences.

Assuming we have built an adequate safety net, it's time to engage the code and start cleaning it up. If we run the test suite frequently while making these changes, we can safely move through the changes we need to make. This will improve the quality of the code and possibly speed up the run time of the test suite.

> **While making changes, we don't have to go "all in"**
>
> Cashing in on our confidence means we move in and make changes to the code base, but it doesn't mean we go into areas of code where the tests are shallow and inadequate. There may be several areas we want to clean up, but we should only go after the parts we are most confident about. There will be future opportunities to get the other parts as we add more tests in the future.

Be willing to throw away an entire day of changes

Work for a whole day making changes and now half the tests fail because you forgot the test suite more often? Be ready to throw away the changes. This is what automated testing lets us do…back up to when everything ran perfectly. It will hurt, but next time you will remember to run the test suite more often.

How to do it...

This recipe assumes you are using version control and are making regular commits. This idea is no good if you haven't made a commit for two weeks.

If you run your test suite at least once a day, and when it passes, you commit the changes you have made, then it becomes easy to back up to some previous point, such as the beginning of the day.

I have done this many times. The first time was the hardest. It was a new idea to me, but I realized the real value of software was now resting on my automated test suite. In the middle of the afternoon, I ran the test suite for the first time that day after having edited half the system. Over half of the tests failed.

I tried to dig in and fix the issue. The trouble was, I couldn't figure out where the issue stemmed from. I spent a couple of hours trying to track it down. It began to dawn on me that I wasn't going to figure it out without wasting loads of time.

But I remembered that everything had passed with flying colors the previous day. I finally decided to throw away my changes, run the test suite verifying everything passed, and then grudgingly go home for the day.

The next day, I attacked the problem again. Only this time I ran the tests more often. I was able to get it coded successfully. Looking back at the situation, I realized that this issue only cost me one lost day. If I had tried to ride it out, I could have spent a week and STILL probably ended up throwing things away.

How it works...

Depending on how your organization manages source control, you may have to:

- Simply do it yourself by deleting a branch or canceling your checkouts
- Contact your CM team to delete the branch or the commits you made for the day

This isn't really a technical issue. The source control system makes it easy to do this regardless of who is in charge of branch management. The hard part is making the decision to throw away the changes. We often feel the desire to fix what is broken. The more our efforts cause it to break further, the more we want to fix it. At some point, we must realize that it is more costly to move forward rather than to back up and start again.

There is an axis of agility that stretches from classic waterfall software production to heavily agile processes. Agile teams tend to work in smaller sprints and commit in smaller chunks. This makes it more palatable to throw away a day of work. The bigger the task and longer the release cycle, the greater the odds are that your changes haven't been checked in since you started a task two weeks ago.

Believe me; throwing away two weeks of work is totally different than throwing away one day. I would never advocate throwing out two weeks of work.

The core idea is to NOT go home without your test suite passing. If that means you have to throw away things to make it happen, then that is what you must do. It really drives the point home of code a little/test a little until a new feature is ready for release.

There's more...

We also need to reflect on why didn't we run the test suite often enough. It may be because the test suite is taking too long to run, and you are hesitating to use up that time. It may be time to **Pause to refactor when test suite takes too long to run**. The time I really learned this lesson was when my test suite took one-and-a-half hours to run. After I got through this whole issue, I realized that I needed to speed things up and spent probably a week or two cutting it down to a tolerable 30 minutes.

How does this mesh with "Something is better than nothing"

Earlier in this chapter, we talked about writing a test case that may be quite expensive to run in order to get some automated testing in action. What if our testing becomes too expensive that it is time prohibitive? After all, couldn't what we just said lead to the situation we are dealing with?

Code a little/test a little may seem to be a very slow way to proceed. This is probably the reason many legacy systems never embrace automated testing. The hill we must climb is steep. But if we can hang in there, start building the tests, make sure they run at the end of the day, and then eventually pause to refactor our code and tests, we can eventually reach a happy balance of better code quality and system confidence.

See also

- Something is better than nothing
- Pause to refactor when test suite takes too long

Instead of shooting for 100 percent coverage, try to have a steady growth

You won't know how you're doing without coverage analysis. However, don't aim too high. Instead, focus on a gradual increase. You will find your code gets better over time, maybe even drops in volume, while quality and coverage steadily improve.

How to do it...

If you start with a system that has no tests, don't get focused on a ridiculously high number. I worked on a system that had 16 percent coverage when I picked it up. A year later, I had worked it up to 65 percent. This was nowhere near 100 percent, but the quality of the system had grown by leaps and bounds due to **Capturing a bug in an automated test** and **Harvesting metrics**.

At one time I was discussing the quality of my code with my manager, and he showed me a report he had developed on his own. He had run a code counting tool on every release of every application he was overseeing. He said my code counts had a unique shape. All the other tools had a constant increase in lines of code. Mine had grown, peaked, and then started to decrease and was still on the decline.

This happened despite the fact that my software did more than ever. It's because I started throwing away unused features, bad code, and clearing out cruft during refactorings.

How it works...

By slowly building an automated test suite, you will gradually cover more of your code. By keeping a focus on building quality code with corresponding tests, the coverage will grow naturally. When we shift to focusing on the coverage reports, we may grow the numbers quicker, but it will tend to be more artificial.

From time to time, as you **Cash in on your confidence** and rewrite chunks, you should feel empowered to throw away old junk. This will also grow your coverage metrics in a healthy way.

All of these factors will lead to increased quality and efficiency. While your code may eventually peak and then decrease, it isn't unrealistic for it to eventually grow again due to new features. By that time, the coverage will probably be much higher, because now you are building completely new features, hand in hand with tests, instead of just maintaining legacy parts.

Randomly breaking your app can lead to better code

The best way to avoid failure is to fail constantly.—Netflix (http://techblog.netflix.com/2010/12/5-lessons-weve-learned-using-aws.html).

How to do it...

Netflix has built a tool they call a **Chaos Monkey**. Its job is to randomly kill instances and services. This forces the developers to make sure their system can fail smoothly and safely.

To build our own version of this, some of the things we would need it to do include:

- Randomly kill processes
- Inject faulty data at interface points
- Shutdown network interfaces between distributed systems
- Issue shutdown commands to subsystems
- Create denial-of-service attacks by overloading interface points with too much data

This is a starting point. The idea is to inject errors wherever you can imagine them happening. This may require writing scripts, cron jobs, or any means necessary to cause these errors to happen.

How it works...

Given there is a chance for a remote system to be unavailable in production, we should introduce ways for this to happen in our development environment. This will encourage us to code higher fault tolerance into our system.

Before we introduce a random running "Chaos Monkey" like Netflix has, we need to see that our system can handle these situations manually. For example, if our system includes communication between two servers, a fair test is unplugging the network cable to one box, simulating network failure. When we verify our system can continue working with acceptable means, then we can add scripts to do this automatically and eventually, randomly.

Audit logs are valuable tools to verify our system is handling these random events. If we can read a log entry showing a forced network shutdown and then see log entries of similar time stamps, we can easily evaluate whether or not the system handled the situation.

After building that in, we can work on the next error to randomly introduce into the system. By following this cycle, we can build up the robustness of our system.

There's more...

This doesn't exactly fit into the realm of automated testing. This is also very high level. It's hard to go into much more detail because the type of faulty data to inject requires an intimate understanding of the actual system.

How does this compare to fuzz testing?

Fuzz testing is a style of testing where invalid, unexpected, and random data is injected into input points of our software (http://en.wikipedia.org/wiki/Fuzz_testing). If the application fails, this is considered a failure. If it doesn't, then it has passed. This type of testing goes in a similar direction, but the blog article written by Netflix appears to go much farther than simply injecting different data. They speak about killing instances and interrupting distributed communications. Basically, anything you can think of that would happen in production, we should try to replicate in a test bed.

Fusil (https://bitbucket.org/haypo/fusil) is a Python tool that aims to provide fuzz testing. You may want to investigate if it is useful for your project needs.

Are there any tools to help with this?

Jester (for Java), Pester (for Python), and Nester (for C#) are used to conduct mutation testing (http://jester.sourceforge.net/). These tools find out what code is not covered by test cases, alters the source code, and re-runs the test suites. Finally, it gives a report on what was changed, and what passed, and didn't pass. It can illuminate what is and is not covered by our test suites in ways coverage tools can't.

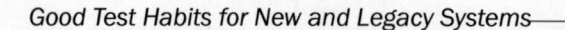

This isn't a complete "Chaos Monkey", but it provides one area of assistance in trying to "break the system" and force us to improve our test regime. To really build a full blown system probably wouldn't fit inside some test project, because it requires writing custom scripts based on the environment it's meant to run in.

Index

Symbols

__init__ method 244
#when comment 136

A

acceptance testing 170
Agiledox
  about 118
  URL 118
algorithms
  separating, from concurrency 333, 334
assertEquals
  about 43
  selecting 9
AssertionError 28
assertions
  assertEquals 9
  assertFalse 9
  assertRaises 9
  assertTrue 9
audit logs 341
automated test
  changes, discarding 337, 338
  steady growth 339
  working 325
  writing 324, 325
automated testing 5
automated tests
  writing, unittest used 7
automated unittest test
  basic concepts 7

B

basics, Pyccuracy test
  exploring 176-178
BDD
  about 117, 118
  doctest documents, testing 126-129
  project-level script, updating 163-168
  testable novel, writing with doctest 136-140
  testable story, writing with doctest 130-135
  testable story, writing with Lettuce 150-155
  testable story, writing with Lettuce and Should DSL 158-162
  testable story, writing with mockito and nose 147-150
  testable story, writing with Voidspace Mock and noise 142, 143
  test, making easy-to-read 120-125
BddDocTestRunner 136
Behavior Driven Development. *See* **BDD**
BitKeeper 227
bug
  about 28
  capturing, in automated test 332, 333
build servers 237

C

CartWithTwoItems 125
Chaos Monkey 340
checkout_edge function 43
CI report, for Jenkins
  generating, NoseXUnit used 220, 221
CI report, for TeamCity
  generating, teamcity-nose used 231-234
class under test 7

CloudBees
  about 230
  URL 230
Cobertura format
  URL 257
code coverage 241
cohesiveness 179
combo_test1 test method 28
command-line nosetests tool
  using 48
concurrency 333
continuous integration (CI)
  about 218, 219
  Jenkins 220
  TeamCity 220
convert_to_roman function 43
corner cases
  testing 35-38
  testing, by iteration 39-42, 104-106
coupling 179
coverage 241
coverage analysis 241
coverage analyzer 241
coverage nose plugin
  features 260
  installing 259
  sqlite3 261
  working 260
coverage tool
  installing 242, 251, 253
  running 254
  working 254
cron jobs 340
Cucumber 150

D

DataAccess class 143
DatabaseTemplate 244
data-driven test suite
  creating, with Robot 186-188
data simulator, smoke tests
  coding 298-302
datetime.now() 317
docstrings
  about 77
  using 78-81

doctest.DocTestRunner 132
doctest documents
  testing 126-129
doctest module 81, 82
doctest runner 130
DocTestRunner 136
doctests
  running, from command line 85-87
doctest.testmod() statements 85
documentation
  printing 96-100
docutils
  URL 190

E

easy_install 52
edges
  testing 101-103
end-to-end scenarios, smoke tests
  targeting 285-289
Erlang
  building 333
e-store web application
  creating 170

F

fail method 10
figleaf
  installing 148
FunctionTestCase 27-29
Fusil
  about 341
  URL 341
fuzz testing
  about 341
  URL 341

G

getopt 75, 274
getopt() function 72, 115
getopt library
  about 72, 110
  create_pydocs function 73
  key function 73
  publish function 73

register function 73
URL 73
Get Source 205
GitHub 227

H

HTML coverage report
generating 255, 256
HTML report
generating, coverage tool used 255, 257

I

integration tests
excluding, from smoke tests 281-284
IntelliJ IDE 220

J

Jenkins
about 220
configuring, for building coverage report 264-269
configuring, to run Python tests upon commit 222-226
configuring, to run Python tests when scheduled 227-230
downloading 223
polling format 227
running 223
URL 220
versus, TeamCity 230
working 226
Jenkins Cobertura plugin 269
Jester 341
JUnit
about 5, 220
URL 5, 220

K

Kamaelia 333
keyword approach 183
keywords 186

L

Lettuce
about 150
installing 151, 158
URL 150, 158
working 156, 157
live data
playing, as fast as possible 311-317
playing, in real time 303-310
recording 303-317
load testing 276
loadTestsFromTestCase method 20, 48

M

management demo, smoke tests
automating 319, 320
mercurial 170
metrics
capturing 331
mockito
installing 148
URL 147
mutation testing 341
MySQL database system 290

N

Nester 341
Netflix 340
network events 243
network management application
building 242-251
store_event algorithm, implementing 245
working 251
non-web shopping cart application
creating 171, 172
nose
about 45
embeddable, feature 49
embedding, in Python 49-52
extensible, feature 49
features 45, 49
installing 46
reference link 46
run() method 50
running, with doctest 107-110

test cases, finding automatically 46-48
test cases, running 46-48
nose extension
  writing, for generating CSV report 59-65
  writing, for selecting test methods 52-58
nose.run() 51
nose testing 237
nosetests 109
NoseXUnit
  about 220
  installing 220
  URL 220
  working 221

O

obscure tests
  breaking down, into simple tests 29, 31
  bugs 34
  working 33
optparse module 24, 75

P

performance analysis 335
Pester 341
Pinocchio project 142
Plugin.options 57
project-level script
  creating, to run acceptance tests 212-216
  updating, to provide coverage reports
       269-274
  updating, to run BDD tests 163-168
  updating, to run doctest 110-115
  writing 66-74
Pyccuracy
  about 172
  basics, exploring 176, 177
  installing 172, 174
  selenium-server.jar, downloading 172
  shopping cart application, driving 176
  used, for verifying web app security 179-182
  working 175, 178
PyCharm IDE 220
Pyro
  about 277
  installing 277
  URL 277

Python
  basics, documenting 78-81
  corner cases, testing by iteration 104-106
  docstrings 77
  doctests, running from command line 85-87
  documentation, printing 96-100
  edges, testing 101-103
  getopt library 73, 110
  nose, embedding 49-52
  nose extension, writing for generating CSV
       report 59-65
  nose extension, writing for selecting test methods 52-58
  nose, running with doctest 107-109
  project-level script, updating 110-115
  project-level script, writing 66-74
  reports, printing 96-100
  stack traces, capturing 82-84
  test harness, coding for doctest 88-91
  test noise, filtering out 92-95
Python import statements
  all.py 280
  checkin.py 280
  integration.py 280
  pulse.py 280
  security.py 280
Python MySQLdb library
  installing 277
PyUnit 6

R

real time playback 318
recipe1.py 7
recipe26_plugin.py 121
Remote Procedure Call (RPC) library 277
report_failure function 132
reports
  printing 96-100
report_start function 132
ReSharper 220
reStructuredText
  URL 190
Robot Framework
  about 183
  code, writing 190
  HTML tables, writing 190

installing 183-185
keywords, mapping 190
testable story, writing 191-195
unicode strings, using 191
used, for creating data-driven test suite 186-188
used, for verifying web app security 208-210
web testing 204-207
working 189
Robot tests
subset, running 197-203
tagging 197-203
run() method, nose 50

S

scalable applications
building 333
SeleniumLibrary 209
Selenium plugin 207
self.fail([msg]) 10
setUp method 11, 22, 91
severity 5 event 246
ShoppingCart class 89
Should DSL
alternatives 162
installing 158
URL 158
smoke testing 275
smoke tests
about 276
data simulator, coding 298-302
end-to-end scenarios, targeting 285-289
integration tests, excluding 281-284
management demo, automating 319, 320
subset of test cases, defining 277-280
test server, targeting 290-296
spec nose plugin 142
Spring Python
about 242
Aspect Oriented Programming features 310
Spring Python
URL 242
SpringSource Tool Suite
URL 221, 258
SQLite
about 290

limitations 303
sqlite3
about 261
stack traces
capturing 82-84
store_cart function 150
store_event method 245
stress testing 277
subset, of test cases
defining, import statements used 277-281
subset, Robot tests
running 197-203
subsets of tests
running 16-18
succinct assertions
writing, Should DSL used 158, 160

T

tagging 197
TDD 117
TeamCity
about 220
configuring, to run Python tests upon commit 234-237
configuring, to run Python tests when scheduled 237-239
URL 220
teamcity-nose
installing 231
teamcity-nose plugin
installing 237
tearDown method 11
testable novel
writing, with doctest 136-140
testable story
writing, with doctest 130-136
writing, with Lettuce 150-155
writing, with Lettuce and Should DSL 158-162
writing, with mockito and nose 147-150
writing, with Robot 191-195
writing, with Voidspace Mock and nose 142-146
test cases
about 16
chaining, into TestSuite 18-20

running, from command line 14, 16
test code
  bugs 28
  retooling 25, 27
  working 28
Test Driven Development. *See* **TDD**
test fixtures
  working on 328, 329
test harness
  coding, for doctest 88-91
  setting up 11-13
  tearing down 11-13
test iterator 43
TestLoader().loadTestsFromTestCase 16
test module
  test suites, defining 21, 23
test noise
  filtering out 92-95
  filtering out, from coverage 261-263
tests
  analyzing 326-328
  refactoring 334-335
test selection 58
test server, smoke tests
  targeting 290-297
Test Setup 206
TestSuite 18
TestSuite class 20
test suites
  about 16
  defining, in test module 21-23
  methods 24
  optparse, replacing by argparse 25
  working 24
TextTestRunner 16, 20
third-party tools
  Spring Python 242
tight coupling 335
time.sleep() method 310
tuple 245
Twisted 333

U

unittest
  about 6
  corner cases, testing by iteration 39-42

obscure tests, breaking down into simple tests 29-32
recommendations, on selecting options 9, 10
self.fail([msg]) 10
subset of tests, running 16-18
test cases, chaining into TestSuite 18, 20
test cases, running 14-16
test code, retooling 25, 27
test harness, setting up 11-13
test harness, tearing down 11-13
testing corner cases 35, 36
test suites, defining 21
versus, integration tests 35
unittest.main() 48, 51
unittest module 20
unittest.TestCase 8
update_service method 248

V

virtualenv
  installing 6
Voidspace Mock
  about 142
  installing 143
  URL 142
Voidspace Mock library 145

W

wantMethod 58
waterfall model
  stages 217
web app security
  verifying, Pyccuracy used 179-182
  verifying, Robot used 208-210
web basics
  testing, with Robot 204-206
web testing 204

X

XML coverage report
  generating 257, 258
XML report
  generating, coverage tool used 257, 258
  using 258

Thank you for buying Python Testing Cookbook

About Packt Publishing

Packt, pronounced 'packed', published its first book "*Mastering phpMyAdmin for Effective MySQL Management*" in April 2004 and subsequently continued to specialize in publishing highly focused books on specific technologies and solutions.

Our books and publications share the experiences of your fellow IT professionals in adapting and customizing today's systems, applications, and frameworks. Our solution based books give you the knowledge and power to customize the software and technologies you're using to get the job done. Packt books are more specific and less general than the IT books you have seen in the past. Our unique business model allows us to bring you more focused information, giving you more of what you need to know, and less of what you don't.

Packt is a modern, yet unique publishing company, which focuses on producing quality, cutting-edge books for communities of developers, administrators, and newbies alike. For more information, please visit our website: `www.packtpub.com`.

About Packt Open Source

In 2010, Packt launched two new brands, Packt Open Source and Packt Enterprise, in order to continue its focus on specialization. This book is part of the Packt Open Source brand, home to books published on software built around Open Source licences, and offering information to anybody from advanced developers to budding web designers. The Open Source brand also runs Packt's Open Source Royalty Scheme, by which Packt gives a royalty to each Open Source project about whose software a book is sold.

Writing for Packt

We welcome all inquiries from people who are interested in authoring. Book proposals should be sent to author@packtpub.com. If your book idea is still at an early stage and you would like to discuss it first before writing a formal book proposal, contact us; one of our commissioning editors will get in touch with you.

We're not just looking for published authors; if you have strong technical skills but no writing experience, our experienced editors can help you develop a writing career, or simply get some additional reward for your expertise.

Python Testing: Beginner's Guide

ISBN: 978-1-847198-84-6   Paperback: 276 pages

An easy and convenient approach to testing your powerful Python projects

1. Covers everything you need to test your code in Python
2. Easiest and enjoyable approach to learn Python testing
3. Write, execute, and understand the result of tests in the unit test framework
4. Packed with step-by-step examples and clear explanations

Python Geospatial Development

ISBN: 978-1-84951-154-4   Paperback: 508 pages

Build a complete and sophisticated mapping application from scratch using Python tools for GIS development

1. Build applications for GIS development using Python
2. Analyze and visualize Geo-Spatial data
3. Comprehensive coverage of key GIS concepts
4. Recommended best practices for storing spatial data in a database

Please check www.PacktPub.com for information on our titles

Python 3 Object Oriented Programming

ISBN: 978-1-849511-26-1 Paperback: 404 pages

Harness the power of Python 3 objects

1. Learn how to do Object Oriented Programming in Python using this step-by-step tutorial
2. Design public interfaces using abstraction, encapsulation, and information hiding
3. Turn your designs into working software by studying the Python syntax
4. Raise, handle, define, and manipulate exceptions using special error objects

Linux Shell Scripting Cookbook

ISBN: 978-1-84951-376-0 Paperback: 360 pages

Solve real-world shell scripting problems with over 110 simple but incredibly effective recipes

1. Master the art of crafting one-liner command sequence to perform tasks such as text processing, digging data from files, and lot more
2. Practical problem solving techniques adherent to the latest Linux platform
3. Packed with easy-to-follow examples to exercise all the features of the Linux shell scripting language

Please check **www.PacktPub.com** for information on our titles

Printed in Great Britain
by Amazon.co.uk, Ltd.,
Marston Gate.